WITHDRAWN
UTSA L

International Law

D0396363

International Law and Organization

Closing the Compliance Gap

EDITED BY EDWARD C. LUCK AND
MICHAEL W. DOYLE

ROWMAN & LITTLEFIELD PUBLISHERS, INC.
Lanham • Boulder • New York • Toronto • Oxford

ROWMAN & LITTLEFIELD PUBLISHERS, INC.

Published in the United States of America
by Rowman & Littlefield Publishers, Inc.
A wholly owned subsidiary of The Rowman & Littlefield Publishing Group, Inc.
4501 Forbes Boulevard, Suite 200, Lanham, MD 20706
www.rowmanlittlefield.com

P.O. Box 317, Oxford OX2 9RU, UK

British Library Cataloguing in Publication Information Available

Library of Congress Cataloging-in-Publication Data

International law and organization: closing the compliance gap / edited by Michael W.
Doyle and Edward C. Luck.
    p. cm.
Includes bibliographical references and index.
ISBN 0-7425-2991-6 (cloth : alk. paper) — ISBN 0-7425-2992-4 (pbk. : alk. paper)
1. International law. 2. International organization. 3. Compliance. I. Doyle, Michael
W., 1948– II. Luck, Edward C.

KZ3410.I578 2004
341—dc22
                                                   2004012966
Printed in the United States of America

Contents

Preface

This volume, more than most, is the result of a broad-based collaborative effort. It represents the culmination of a multiyear project of dialogue, study, and policy assessment that involved a wide circle of scholars, diplomats, NGO leaders, and policymakers. More than a hundred individuals from a range of continents, disciplines, and sectors participated in the roundtables and workshops convened by the Project on International Law and Organization: Closing the Compliance Gap. Each, to some extent, had a hand in crafting the information, ideas, and conclusions presented here. Though presumably few would endorse the results in their entirety, the coeditors trust that they would detect at least a pale reflection of the global dialogue to which they contributed so much time and thought.

Our first debt of gratitude, therefore, goes to those who attended the initial two-day research workshop at Princeton University in February 2000 and the series of roundtable discussions with the authors of the case studies at New York University in 2001. We also are most grateful to the faculty, administrators, and staff of Princeton's Woodrow Wilson School of Public and International Affairs and of the New York University School of Law for their support and encouragement of this, and other, endeavors. In particular, we benefited enormously from the foresight and agility of then-Deans Michael Rothschild and John Sexton, respectively, who oversaw the establishment of their schools' joint Center for the Study of International Organization, which sponsored the project.

The work of assembling and editing this volume was completed at Columbia University, where both editors now serve on the faculty of the School of International and Public Affairs (SIPA). Under Dean Lisa Anderson's guidance, SIPA has proven a most congenial place to complete this project and to launch several more under the recently created Center on International Organization. At every stage of the project, and in all its dimensions, we have depended heavily on the ample skills, enormous experience, and ceaseless energy of Marilyn Messer, administrative director of the new as well as the old center. Her efforts ensured that both the events and paperwork flowed with maximal efficiency and minimal surprises throughout the project.

Michael Doyle particularly wants to thank his coeditor Ed Luck, who took up the reins of the project when Michael joined the United Nations as special adviser to Secretary-General Kofi Annan in 2001. Michael was a partner in the conceptualization of the project and the editing of the first drafts, while Ed took on the entire task of editing the final drafts.

Organizing and implementing a multiyear research effort involving authors from five continents is an expensive and time-consuming enterprise. We were fortunate in having the support of a foundation whose officers understood the value of engaging scholars and practitioners not only from different parts of the world, but also from distinct policy sectors, in the consideration of the compliance challenges facing international law and organization in these dynamic times. Without the generous support of the John D. and Catherine T. MacArthur Foundation, neither the project nor this book would have been possible. Without the substantive input of Kennette Benedict and Mary Page in the planning stages, it would have been a less productive exercise.

Edward C. Luck
Michael W. Doyle
New York City

Introduction

Katharina P. Coleman and Michael W. Doyle

The 1990s were both heady and troubling days for proponents of international law. On the one hand, there was exceptional dynamism in the development of international norms and laws. Rarely had there been such a bull market in terms of simultaneous multilateral efforts to create and expand international law on such a wide array of issues. Areas as diverse as arms control, war crimes and human rights violations, environmental protection, sustainable development, and international trade were affected. In field after field, transnational citizens groups joined like-minded countries to develop and codify new standards for performance by governments and nonstate actors.

On the other hand, however, the very success of these norm-creating efforts raised important concerns. After the exuberance of norm creation came the more sobering question of compliance. States do not always live up to the standards they set themselves. Yet in many cases the explosion of international norms has not been accompanied by a complementary development of international institutions to monitor states' efforts to implement these norms, and to facilitate or to compel such compliance. Institution building, on the whole, has faced an uneven, at times even bearish, market. States that see themselves as losers under the new norms have no interest in developing compliance-promoting institutions. Meanwhile, many key complying nations find it easier to sign high-minded accords than to accept the political and material costs of establishing effective systems of inducements and penalties to encourage broad international compliance.

An important and related question is which, or whose, norms are implemented? To illustrate the striking ways in which norms, enforcement, and national interests inseparably interact in world politics, one only needs to contrast the recent U.S. rejection of the International Criminal Court and the Kyoto Protocol with the extraordinary commitment made by the Bush administration to the enforcement of Security Council resolutions mandating the nuclear, chemical, and biological disarmament of Iraq. Prior to the horrendous attacks of September 11, 2001, the Security Council members were discussing ways to ease the sanctions on Iraq, limiting them to a weapons material embargo enforced at the frontier. Following those attacks, the Taliban were toppled in Afghanistan in the winter of 2001-2002, and the Bush administration decided to bring down Saddam Hussein's regime in Iraq. President Bush, speaking to the General Assembly on September 12, 2002, challenged the United Nations community to enforce its resolutions:

> The conduct of the Iraqi regime is a threat to the authority of the United Nations, and a threat to peace. Iraq has answered a decade of U.N. demands with a decade of defiance. All the world now faces a test, and the United Nations a difficult and defining moment. Are Security Council resolutions to be honored and enforced, or cast aside without consequence? Will the United Nations serve the purpose of its founding, or will it be irrelevant?[1]

It would be difficult to match anywhere in the statements before the United Nations the stark language of enforcement the president uttered. But as subsequent events revealed, the Iraq crisis and the decision of the United States and its allies to invade without renewed Security Council endorsement both raised new expectations and highlighted previous concerns.

The heady dynamics of regime growth, therefore, are balanced by more challenging questions about which (or whose) norms are implemented, how extensively they are applied, why compliance gaps persist in some sectors and areas, and how effective the institutional mechanisms to limit defection can be. These are the issues this book seeks to address. It is inspired by the current expansion of international regimes but it is not about this expansion. Instead, it investigates the impact and consequences of regime growth on actual state behavior. In short, this is a book about compliance.

Defining the Project

It has become traditional in international relations theory to define *regimes*, following Stephen Krasner, as sets of "principles, norms, rules, and decision making procedures around which actors' expectations converge in a given issue area."[2] However, for our purposes John Ruggie's simpler definition of regimes as consisting simply of norms (the values which the regime is meant to enshrine) and rules (procedures by which states should implement these norms) will be sufficient.[3] Rules, in this sense, can be understood as operationalized norms: they represent a translation (though not necessarily the only one possible) from theoretical values to practical behavioral prescriptions. Regime growth requires a development in both aspects of regimes. It occurs when existing norms are expanded or more fully articulated, or when new norms are established, with a concomitant elaboration of the regime rules indicating how states should put these new norms into practice.

Such regime growth can occur either formally or informally. As Haggard and Simmons note, the easiest kind of regime to observe is a regime anchored in multilateral agreements among states.[4] These agreements generally spell out both the fundamental norms of the regime and the kinds of behavior expected from states to implement them, and regime growth is relatively easily discernable by comparing the content of successive agreements reached within the same issue area. Haggard and Simmons also recognize, however, that the price of conceptual clarity may be an excessive formalism that obscures subtler but equally important kinds of regimes and regime change. Not all international norms are codified, nor is every evolution in these norms charted by a new international agreement. Scholars of international law distinguish between "hard" treaty law and the "soft" law generated by general (uncodified) practice among states as sources of international law.[5] Regime growth can occur through an expansion of soft law, an evolution in accepted practices among states, as well as through formal multilateral agreements.

The past decade has seen a spectacular burst of regime growth, both in terms of formal agreements and informal evolution of norms. The academic literature on regimes has expanded commensurately. Traditionally, this literature has paid more attention to the political and diplomatic process of producing international regimes than to empirically tracing their effects on state behavior. As Downs and Trento note in chapter 2, the debate about why regimes matter has been overwhelmingly theoretical. It is possible to derive several hypotheses about regime effectiveness from the existing literature—what is missing is an understanding of which dynamics are or could be at work in which cases, and why.

Some hypotheses suggested by the contemporary literature focus on the nature of regimes and the manner in which they are established. If, as Susan Strange maintained, regimes are simply an expression of state power, regime effectiveness would depend entirely on the strength of its lead state.[6] However, such a "realist" emphasis on power as the foundation of international regimes need not dismiss regimes as entirely ineffectual. As Krasner pointed out, regimes can act as "intervening variables" between raw state power and international behavior.[7] A hegemon may seek to institutionalize its rule within an international regime to avoid the costs of overtly coercing compliance.[8] However, the success of this strategy (and thus the effectiveness of the regime) depends on the degree to which other states accept their new obligations. Neo-institutionalists, headed by Keohane, argue that states may comply because the regime facilitates mutually beneficial cooperation among its members.[9] Alternatively, Ikenberry suggests that secondary states may comply because they view the regime as a legitimate compromise in which the lead state addressed their concerns about domination and abandonment.[10] Meanwhile, influential legal theorists argue that the emphasis on power as a foundation of international law is fundamentally misplaced, and that more attention should be paid to the legitimacy of the laws themselves and the process by which they were negotiated. Franck argues that compliance depends on states viewing rules as legitimate, that is, as fairly negotiated.[11] The Chayeses stress that the bargaining process about an emerging regime itself socializes negotiating states and predisposes them to compliance.[12]

Regime effectiveness may not entirely depend on the nature of the regime itself, however. A second strand of international relations theory stresses domestic sources of state behavior. Risse-Kappen, for example, argues that in liberal democracies policy on international regimes depends on domestic structures (political and societal structures as well as policy networks) and the coalition-building processes among elites.[13] In this interpretation, a regime will be effective if it resonates with the principal domestic actors shaping foreign policy in the liberal democracies within the regime. Especially in newly established democracies, however, influence over state behavior can be transitory. Moravcsik thus points out that currently dominant elites may join and develop international regimes (e.g., human rights regimes) in order to ensure that their country is "locked in" to certain norms and policy commitments regardless of the preferences of their successors.[14]

Finally, the third set of hypotheses offered by international relations theory about factors ensuring the effectiveness of a regime concerns nonstate actors. Keck and Sikkink draw attention to the role of transnational advocacy networks headed by domestic and international nongovernmental organizations (NGOs) in both developing international regimes and promoting compliance with them through "naming and shaming" of violating states.[15] Sikkink has applied this analysis specifically to compliance with the human rights regime in Latin America,[16] but the impact of NGO activism can also be discerned in the cases of the International Campaign to Ban Landmines and the Jubilee 2000 movement on debt relief. Peter Haas also notes the potential influence of transnational actors on regime effectiveness, but focuses on "epistemic communities" of experts that rise to prominence during state negotiations about a regime and later promote compliance insofar as they are integrated into national bureaucracies charged with implementing the resultant accords.[17]

Finally, functionalists, led by Ernst Haas, hold that formal international organizations can develop autonomous influence over the development of regimes by addressing unanticipated systemic consequences of the regime as these emerge.[18] While Haas focused on the International Labour Organization (ILO), Burley and Mattli have proposed a similar "neo-functionalist" model of how functional and political spillover effects coupled with a continual effort to upgrade definitions of the common interest has helped the European Court of Justice (ECJ) expand its influence.[19] Functionalists acknowledge, however, that international organizations' influence depends on whether they can persuade states to accept their increasingly activist role. The ILO has learned that where states grant international organizations the autonomy to shape the international agenda they rarely grant them the strength to enforce compliance, whereas stronger organizations like the International Monetary Fund (IMF) or the World Bank are granted considerable enforcement powers but little autonomy in developing the agenda.[20]

It is remarkable how little this plethora of competing hypotheses has been put to an empirical test. There is a budding literature on international compliance, advanced by major studies by Abram Chayes and Antonia Handler Chayes and by Edith Brown Weiss and Harold K. Jacobson. However, it has provoked more theoretical debate about defining compliance than empirical investigation of compliance levels in different kinds of regimes.[21] Meanwhile, regime theorists still tend to privilege explaining the emergence of regimes over investigating their implications for state behavior. The 2000 special issue of *International Organization* on legalization of world politics, for example, seeks primarily to explain the development of binding, precise, and independently supervised rules of state behavior in some areas of international relations rather than others.[22] Contributors' attention to and consensus on the effect of legalization on compliance is less pronounced. The volume's case studies do link compliance to the presence of domestic "compliance constituencies" within regimes based on the rule of law,[23] but ultimately the editors concede that "a systematic evaluation of the net effects of legalization on cooperation is beyond the reach of this special issue."[24]

By contrast, this book is self-consciously not about regime growth per se. Its contributors do not primarily aim to chart or explain the dynamism in contemporary rule and norm creation. Instead, they take regime growth as a point of departure and concentrate on investigating its impact on international behavior. In other words, they focus explicitly on compliance as a practical measure of whether, to what degree, and why regimes are, in fact, working.

By *compliance*, we mean, first, conformity to the rules, laws, and norms of a particular regime and, second, because these rules are often ambiguous or actors are for unanticipated reasons unable or unwilling to comply, acquiescence in the procedures that resolve disputes about the practical meaning of the rules, laws, or norms in question.[25]

The authors, therefore, assess whether actors are actually obeying the rules set out by international regimes, or, to put the same question in traditional regime-theoretical terms, whether and to what extent a convergence of actors' expectations is, in fact, warranted by the development of international principles, norms, rules, and decision making procedures.

To effect this analysis, it is important to disaggregate both international law and compliance. Already in 1961, Stanley Hoffmann distinguished between three kinds of international law: First, the "law of political framework" identifies international actors and provides the basic rules of their interaction. Second, Hoffmann identified the "law of reciprocity," which defines the rules of interstate relations in areas that affect less vitally state power and in which states have a mutual and lasting interest in cooperation. And finally, for Hoffmann, the "law of community . . . deals with problems which can best be handled . . . on the basis of a community of action independent from politics: problems of technical or scientific nature in which borders are irrelevant."[26] Hoffmann believed that levels of contestation (and by implication compliance) would differ across these three types of law in any given international system and that international systems—whether "moderate" or "revolutionary"—would differ in the overall levels of compliance. He thought that the law of political framework, which closely reflects and depends on the distribution of power in the system, would be most highly contested. By contrast, the law of reciprocity should elicit significant compliance because it recognizes mutual interests among states. Hoffmann predicted, however, that the strongest sense of obligation emanated from the law of community, "because it rests on a common positive purpose" shared by all states.

With the end of the "revolutionary" cold war in which almost all legal norms became subject to contestation, it might be expected that compliance in general would increase, but, as Edward Luck notes in his conclusion to this volume, the case studies included here offer a more complicated account of how much compliance is to be expected and which kinds of international law elicit most compliance. What continues to remain relevant is Hoffmann's core insight that compliance reflects the politics of the international system and different issue areas are governed by different types of political dynamics. Some sectors of international law correspond to realist expectations, others to the neo-institutionalist model, and others again to managerial ideas.

Cutting across all three sectors, however, is the notion of a *compliance gap*, the difference between states' obligations under prevailing international regimes and their actual behavior. It is important to realize that this is a relative measure. The extent of the compliance gap in a particular regime is a function both of the level of demands that a regime places on behavior and of the activities in fact undertaken by international actors. Thus the presence of a compliance gap is not necessarily an indication either of an ineffective regime or of state recalcitrance, while, conversely, a narrow gap need not indicate regime effectiveness or states' commitment to high moral standards. If a regime places very onerous obligations on a state, a compliance gap may exist despite strenuous compliance efforts by that state—efforts which under a less stringent regime might result in perfect compliance. Indeed, it may be that a certain level of noncompliance is the hallmark of a healthy, effective regime.

Thus from a policy point of view, the optimal size of the gap between the norm and behavior becomes an important issue. If the norm tracks usual behavior, valuable sources of normative encouragement for progress could be lost. If the norm greatly exceeds behavior, frustration and cynicism may erode what otherwise could have been valuable encouragement for marginal improvements. Whether to plan for a compliance gap and what the optimum size of that gap would be will vary by the case. No one will plan for an optimum murder rate, though the resources invested in police and prisons give a sense of how much—or how little—society is prepared to spend to enforce the norm against murder. By contrast, the optimum gap logic is clearly relevant in many regimes, ranging from global environmental protection (e.g., green house gas emissions) to local and interstate traffic speed limits. A variety of factors come into play, including the willingness to invest in compliance, the cost of defections and the social benefits of compliance, whether defection is a matter of will or capacity (and whether capacity can be developed or is static), and whether the regime is designed for homogeneous agents or covers leaders and laggards.

While compliance gaps cannot, therefore, be used as unambiguous measures of regime effectiveness, they do provide a critical vantage point from which to inquire into the dynamics and evolution of particular international regimes and international relations more generally. Focusing on the concept of a compliance gap allows a myriad of highly significant questions to emerge, which can be grouped into four main clusters:

First, to what extent do compliance gaps currently exist and what does this imply about the evolution of international relations and the shaping of public policy? Are the norms that have recently emerged being obeyed by states? Have recent developments broadened compliance gaps by creating substantial new norms that states resist or struggle to comply with? That is, has the end of Cold War deadlock produced an overload of newly negotiable regimes, with the newer regimes demonstrating less effectiveness than their predecessors? Or is the apparent proliferation of new norms, in fact, little more than a series of shallow international agreements that impose relatively few costs on states parties and thus generate few compliance gaps? Are there patterns revealing differential rates of compliance across different sectors of state activity, with some kinds of regimes less or more resistant to noncompliance? All this amounts to asking whether the new regimes have been effective in promoting the norms that underlie them. Thinking of this issue in terms of compliance gaps emphasizes that there may be two distinct possible reasons for regime ineffectiveness: the behavior of affected actors, or flaws in the regime itself which make it either ineffectual or inappropriate for addressing a particular problem.

Second, where compliance gaps do exist, what explains when and why they arise? Who are the actors at the root of noncompliance? In some fields, states may not be the only, or even the most important, actors whose behavior needs to be brought into line to ensure full implementation. With regard to the nonproliferation of weapons of mass destruction, for example, some of the most likely potential violators remain outside the circle of parties to the key conventions. Once key actors have been identified, the question becomes why these actors are not complying with prevailing norms. Are the norms themselves legitimate, enjoying wide support? The norms codified in the Nuclear Non-Proliferation Treaty (NPT), for example, suffer because many states question whether the nuclear states have lived up to their part of the bargain, which is to pursue arms control and make peaceful forms of nuclear energy available. On the other hand, if the norms are widely viewed as legitimate, perhaps individual violators are genuine "rogues?" What core factors explain compliance or noncompliance? Are states and/or nonstate actors simply unwilling to live up to international standards or are they unable to do so? In other words, is noncompliance a result of institutional incapacity or of the incentive structure faced by the various actors?

Third, what measures can help reduce existing compliance gaps in the different sectors? In part, this is a question about institutionalization. Although institution building has generally lagged behind the creation of new international norms, some structures have been erected to promote compliance. What solutions to noncompliance have been tried, and how successful have they been? Might other mechanisms prove more effective? In what circumstances? More generally, however, there is the broader issue of whether and to what extent lack of institutionalization has really been the source of compliance gaps. How much can further institutionalization improve compliance? To what extent are other factors, such as the nature of accepted norms or the incentives facing international actors, to blame for compliance gaps? How could these issues be addressed?

And, fourth, do we find systematic biases in the kinds of norms—that is, whose norms—that are enforced and those that are neglected? Establishing a regime generally requires leadership. But if leadership becomes hegemony, serving the interests overwhelmingly of one state, other states will lose interest in enforcement and resistance will follow.[27] Charges of this sort are frequently heard today. Are they warranted?

These are the kinds of questions that the contributors to this volume are seeking to address. Put very briefly, they aim to identify, assess, explain, and suggest how to help narrow the compliance gaps that have arisen in the context of today's rapidly expanding international regimes.

Methodology

This volume is comparative in nature and practice oriented in its objectives. It unites eight substantive case studies of compliance behavior across four crucial areas of international cooperation and seeks to draw both issue-specific and more general policy conclusions on ways to enhance compliance with international regimes. Because this policy advice is tendered on politically sensitive issues, care was taken to include contributions from a range of countries and cultures. In brief, this study is international, cross-sectoral, and policy oriented.

The study is also designed to be multidisciplinary. So far, much of the work on compliance has been done by legal scholars or political scientists. While neither of these disciplines can provide the full picture, each can offer essential pieces of a well-rounded analysis. To this end, the proposed project includes not only distinguished scholars of law and politics, but also those with expertise in related economic, technological, and institutional matters.

Cross-Sectoral Case Studies for Nuanced Policy Advice

In chapter 2 of this book, Downs and Trento argue convincingly for disaggregating compliance as an international phenomenon in order to generate a nuanced investigation of compliance issues. They maintain that compliance gaps are concentrated in particular regimes and that noncompliance occurs predominantly among a specific kind of state (mostly war-torn, poor, and nondemocratic countries). Moreover, the reasons for noncompliance vary, depending on the issue at hand, the costs of compliance, and the capacities and intentions of affected states. Therefore, appropriate strategies for promoting compliance must be adapted to the specific circumstances of the case as well as to the incentive structures facing the states that must bear the costs of implementing these strategies.

Regrettably, as Downs and Trento also argue, much of the recent literature on compliance treats international law and compliance in overly general terms, without specifying the parameters and assumptions that underlie its models and thus determine their applicability to specific situations. It therefore provides little practical guidance for resolving compliance gaps. At best, Downs and Trento point out, it offers a list of potential strategies among which policymakers must choose on a case-by-case basis.

The methodology of this book reflects Downs' and Trento's call for a nuanced, case-sensitive approach to the compliance issue. At its core are eight case studies, each of which focuses on compliance questions in one of the following four issue areas: international trade and monetary policy, international environmental protection, human rights and humanitarian norms, and arms control and disarmament. These studies describe in some detail the evolution of the prevailing regime in their respective issue areas, assess compliance levels, describe compliance-promoting structures and institutions, and judge their effectiveness. They also offer specific policy recommendations for dealing with the compliance gaps they have identified. What emerges is a series of "snapshots" of the nature and extent of current compliance gaps in specific issue areas as well as predictions of future compliance trends and practical policy advice for addressing compliance problems.

However, detailed and issue-specific analysis also has its pitfalls. It can provide invaluable data and insights, but its usefulness is often limited by selectivity problems. It is not possible to fully understand international compliance issues or to arrive at a balanced assessment of the effectiveness of compliance-promoting mechanisms by focusing on a single sector of international activity. There is no reason to assume that compliance behavior and the results of particular strategies to enhance compliance would be uniform across diverse fields of international cooperation. Therefore, while the individual contributions to this book are area specific, the volume as a whole adopts a broad cross-sectoral and comparative approach. The eight case studies in this book provide the basis for a revealing comparison of compliance behavior and the effectiveness of institutional strategies to promote compliance across four very different areas of international cooperation governed by an extremely diverse set of regimes. This broad selection of issue areas does not make this volume comprehensive, since other international regimes (e.g., rules on labor standards) are neglected. Neither is it exhaustive: the case studies in this volume necessarily focus only on particular aspects of the regimes in question. However, juxtaposing these case studies offers the opportunity to begin comparing compliance behavior and institutional strategies to promote compliance across four of the most crucial areas of international activity.

In his conclusion to this volume, Edward Luck draws out some general lessons about international compliance that have emerged, both from the juxtaposition of these diverse case studies and from the discussions that took place during the elaboration of this volume, as contributors exchanged information across lines of sectoral specialization. Among the most critical insights is that international law—and, therefore, international compliance—is multidimensional. The relevant question to ask of the various hypotheses proposed by international relations theory is not *whether* they are true but *when* they are true. As Luck put it, "Each of the schools . . . has its place in the overall scheme. Each describes some piece of the whole; but none comes close to capturing the breadth and diversity of the compliance challenge."

International Contributions on Global Issues

The methodology of this volume also reflects our awareness of the supreme importance of giving unbiased policy advice, especially in politically highly contentious areas. We have sought not only to understand international compliance issues more thoroughly, but also to provide the United Nations, the United States and other national governments, and key nonstate actors with specific policy recommendations for enhancing compliance with international regimes. However, international regimes create winners and losers, and not all states may wish to see particular regimes more thoroughly implemented. Especially among those states that have had little say in the establishment of prevailing regimes, the escalating debate about increasing compliance, and more particularly about international enforcement actions, has raised significant concerns. Within the United Nations, the debate about appropriate strategies for bolstering the authority and credibility of international regimes has thus often been conducted along geographic, economic, and political lines of division.

Methodologically, this meant that each issue area should, as far as possible, be covered by at least two authors representing distinct perspectives who would prepare separate case studies, rather than coauthored chapters, to allow the presentation of a range of views on the issue areas under examination.

The Case Studies

The case studies begin with trade and finance, an issue area in which compliance is substantial and widespread. Kathleen McNamara charts the evolution of both the highly institutionalized and legally formalized world trade regime and the more weakly institutionalized, soft law-based international monetary regime. She finds high compliance levels in both regimes, despite the differences between them. However, she also notes future challenges. Within the trade regime, the recent process of judicialization leading from the General Agreement on Tariffs and Trade (GATT) to the World Trade Organization (WTO) framework may yet prove counterproductive. Whereas the GATT dealt with relatively simple tariff-reduction requirements, the WTO is increasingly being called upon to adjudicate contentious distributional issues raised by expanding trade law. Since the institution lacks the resources and the mandate to settle these matters, this trend threatens both the WTO's legitimacy and that of the international trade regime as a whole. The IMF faces similar pressures, albeit in a more attenuated form. Recurring global financial crises raise questions about reforming the "international financial architecture," including by greater international oversight of domestic financial regulation, an option hotly resisted in debtor states, and a global version of chapter 11, which has been equally contested by money center banks. Moreover, even in the generally high-compliance economic domain, problems associated with the dominance of particular states have arisen. Indeed, increasingly controversial norms attributed to a small set of dominant actors may be the most significant limitation on the further evolution of international economic regimes.

McNamara argues that the central problem is that within the world's economic regimes, the removal of market barriers ("negative integration") has not been matched with "positive integration," that is, the proactive management and regulation of those markets. She argues that rather than continuously seeking to expand the scope of these regimes the international economic system should be allowed to reach—and remain within—its political limits.

The alternative, McNamara points out, would be to extend the current institutional framework to provide greater and more intrusive international governance. To elicit compliance, however, this expansion would have to be balanced by increasing the accountability and transparency of international institutions and by initiating a more inclusive dialogue on the nature of international economic good governance. There may, however, be very real limits to the extent to which even the most ambitious institutional engineering can narrow compliance gaps. This is the conclusion that Chung-in Moon arrives at in his study of South Korea's recent transitions toward greater compliance with the prevailing trade and financial regimes.

Moon finds compelling evidence that institutional design does have an impact on compliance behavior. He argues that South Korea's selective noncompliance with the WTO regime regarding rice and intellectual property rights is partly due to the weakness of the WTO's decentralized enforcement mechanism. By contrast, he believes that the IMF's more centralized enforcement capacity, credible incentive structures, and intense monitoring and consultation procedures help explain South Korea's sweeping reforms to bring its financial and corporate sectors into compliance with international norms after the 1997 economic crisis.

However, according to Moon domestic factors are even more important determinants of states' compliance behavior with respect to international economic regimes. South Korea's protectionism of its rice markets and lax enforcement of intellectual property laws reflect profound cultural values, namely, the special symbolic status of rice in South Korean society and Korea's intellectual tradition of freely shared knowledge. Similarly, South Korea's revolutionary reforms in 1997 were only made possible by capable domestic leadership and a sense of acute crisis among Koreans. Once this sense of crisis abated, further reform efforts stalled.

Thus Moon suggests that while appropriate institutional design can certainly facilitate greater compliance with international norms, it is not possible to deduce compliance levels from institutional structures alone. This echoes McNamara's observation that despite their very different institutional designs, both the world trade and the international monetary regimes currently elicit high compliance levels. It is also a conclusion that appears to hold across sectors of international activity, since Philippe Sands and Jan Linehan reach the same insight in their study of compliance with multilateral environmental agreements (MEAs).

Sands and Linehan examine in some detail the range of instruments available for fostering compliance with MEAs. Traditional mechanisms include both diplomatic means (such as interstate negotiation and third party mediation) and legal instruments like arbitration or court settlements. Contemporary arrangements vary considerably, but most rely on a combination of these mechanisms, as well as on more recently emerged institutions routinizing international scrutiny, dialogue, and transparency. Thus the proposed enforcement structures for the Kyoto Protocol, for example, include not only reporting and monitoring procedures but also a compliance committee with both a facilitative and an enforcement branch. The authors argue that this trend is a sensible one, since all these settlement mechanisms play important complementary roles in promoting compliance.

However, Sands and Linehan warn against deducing compliance levels simply from institutional structure. They stress that compliance also depends on the subject matter of the MEA in question, the nature of obligations it imposes, and the identity of the parties concerned. In particular, since access to compliance mechanisms is currently restricted largely to states, their effectiveness depends critically on states' willingness to invoke them. Compliance could thus be further improved by opening these mechanisms to nonstate actors. Even then, however, institutional design can only be part of the compliance picture and hence only part of the remedy for compliance gaps.

Of the four issue areas under investigation, compliance gaps are most immediately evident in the domain of human rights and humanitarian norms. Compliance gaps with regard to these norms are not restricted to any particular area of the world. Violations of these international norms can be observed in most regions—but nowhere does the contrast between these norms and actual behavior seem to be as strikingly and cruelly apparent as in Africa. In several African countries, intrastate conflicts have led to an almost total disregard for human rights or the laws of war as civilians, primarily women and children, are targeted by all warring factions. The result has been horrendous loss of life and massive flows of displaced people and refugees. Three complementary contributions to this volume help explain this tragic compliance gap.

Focusing on Africa's Great Lakes Region, James Katalikawe, Henry Onoria, and Baker Wairama of Makerere University explain that noncompliance with existing humanitarian and human rights norms results from both states' policies and their incapacities. On the one hand, many weak states have responded to their own insecurity and the fragmentation of their societies with repression. Governments choose to violate human rights standards in their quest to remain in power. On the other hand, weak states may also find themselves unable to uphold humanitarian laws within their territories. The region's intractable conflicts involve numerous rebel groups that are often as guilty of violating humanitarian norms as the states themselves. The prevailing culture of impunity for violators of humanitarian law aggravates this situation: armed groups on all sides habitually target civilian populations with no fear of ever being held accountable. And, finally, the international community also bears responsibility for this broadening compliance gap because it has shirked its obligation to help maintain international peace and security in the region.

Katalikawe, Onoria, and Wairama thus recommend three policies for improving compliance in this region. First, states should democratize. Second, non-state actors should be recognized as subjects of humanitarian law and participants in peace negotiations. These two changes should produce a greater commitment to humanitarian norms among all warring parties. Third, the international community must make greater efforts to elicit compliance from the actors involved. The role of international organizations should be strengthened, and they should work with local actors to challenge the culture of impunity for violators of humanitarian norms.

This solution is comprehensive—but to what extent is it feasible? Luc Côté and Jeffrey Herbst focus, respectively, on obstacles to ending impunity and engaging nonstate actors. Côté investigates one of the most commonly proposed solutions to impunity: the creation of an international criminal court. As a former member of the Office of the Prosecutor of the International Criminal Tribunal for Rwanda (ICTR) and currently chief of prosecutions for the Special Court for Sierra Leone, he is well qualified to assess the effectiveness of this measure. Unfortunately, his analysis of the political and legal impact of the ICTR and the International Criminal Tribunal for the former Yugoslavia (ICTY) on compliance with international laws of war yields mixed results. Côté argues that the tribunals' short-term political impact has been modest. The tribunals have helped challenge the culture of impunity and succeeded in neutralizing some agitators. They have also produced a formal record of atrocities, protecting against future historical revisionism. However, both tribunals have been hampered by credibility problems and, even more damagingly, by their inability to try more than a handful of individuals. They are, therefore, only modest deterrents for continuing violations of humanitarian norms.

For Côté, the most important aspect of the tribunals' work has been their longer-term normative contribution to international humanitarian law, through both the interpretation of existing laws and the creation of new legal norms. Crucially, the tribunals have extended the laws of war to internal conflicts and recognized the legal rights of combatants on all sides of civil wars. According to Côté, therefore, the establishment of tribunals is more appropriate as a tool for the long-term development of international law than as a measure for enhancing short-term compliance.

Jeffrey Herbst, however, questions the value of further developing existing norms without making the hard choices that could actually increase compliance. Focusing on the stark contrast between international legal protection for children in war and the degree to which children have been embroiled in Africa's civil wars, Herbst finds this compliance gap to be a consequence of the weakness of the law itself, which reflects the biases of legislating states. States seek control over international norms by reserving the right to adjudicate their applicability to a given situation. They insist on holding rebel groups to higher standards than states. And, finally, they adamantly oppose international legal recognition for rebel groups, which eliminates the possibility of moral suasion: international law is not allowed to offer rebel groups recognition as an incentive to comply with its norms.

Herbst concludes that international law must be significantly amended before compliance gaps can be narrowed. First, despite the resistance of some states, the international community should develop (and occasionally use) legal mechanisms to recognize rebel groups. It may, however, decide that a particular rebel organization is simply too odious to recognize. In this case, it should also be willing to encourage (and perhaps assist) states to actually defeat these rebels. Both solutions are unpalatable: one infringes state sovereignty and the other authorizes an escalation of violence. For Herbst, however, the only other alternative is to keep reiterating accepted norms without improving compliance.

Herbst's contribution highlights the crucial connection between the origins of international regimes and the rates of compliance they can elicit. In the case Herbst investigates, the problem is the bias that results from the dominance of states over nonstate actors in norm formulation. Turning to the international regime on arms control and disarmament, the contributions of Zia Mian and of Harold Feiveson and Jacqueline Shire emphasize the detrimental effects of the dominance of large states over smaller ones.

Feiveson and Shire offer a survey of compliance issues within the domain of arms control, but find that the most interesting compliance dynamics occur at the levels of multilateral conventions regarding weapons of mass destruction (WMD) and of international norms not codified in formal treaties. They find that noncompliance with the provisions of multilateral WMD treaties is usually limited to medium or small states. Larger countries have a panoply of strategies for addressing such infractions, though their reactions vary according to their relationship with the offending state and include measures of questionable efficiency, such as sanctions. In the United States, the compliance debate centers on improving this kind of enforcement, if necessary by stronger unilateral measures.

Feiveson and Shire argue, however, that defining compliance simply in terms of adherence to existing treaty obligations obscures more profound compliance issues. First, it disregards the powerful international norms that underlie these treaties. Thus while it would be technically legal to withdraw from the Non-Proliferation Treaty, for example, it would be internationally unacceptable to do so. The international community must begin to consider how to address this more intricate compliance challenge. Second, focusing on compliance with existing treaties obscures the compliance dilemma posed by powerful states that can tailor treaties to suit their own purposes—and thus never need to violate treaty obligations—but that offend against such international norms as the nonpossession of nuclear weapons stockpiles. For Feiveson and Shire, the flouting of global norms of disarmament by the most powerful states in the system undermines the legitimacy of WMD regimes and, therefore, weakens them. Instead of focusing on unilateral retaliation against noncomplying smaller states, large nations should strengthen prevailing regimes by improving their own behavior.

Recent actions by the United States have further reinforced the trends Feiveson and Shire documented. Although compliance with numerous treaties still holds and powerful norms, such as those against nuclear testing, continue to constrain behavior outside established treaty frameworks, the invasion of Iraq (and reactions to it by Iran and North Korea) and the United States' withdrawal from the 1972 Anti-Ballistic Missile (ABM) Treaty highlight the exceptionalism that has come to characterize arms control. The authors warn that when the United States and others combine exceptionalism with a shift toward an enforcement doctrine based on anticipatory prevention, the international community will suffer not merely increased international tension but also an erosion of the normative strength that underlies the arms control regime.

Mian agrees with Feiveson and Shire that in the area of nuclear arms control and nonproliferation, the focus of attention should be on noncompliance by major powers ("emperors") rather than by smaller states ("pirates"). He argues specifically that U.S. behavior since the end of the Cold War has thrown the arms control process into a possibly terminal crisis. Focusing on the Anti-Ballistic Missile Treaty, the Comprehensive Test Ban Treaty (CTBT), and the Nuclear Non-Proliferation Treaty, Mian argues that the United States has consistently subverted these regimes to further its own interests while refusing to proceed with its own nuclear disarmament. Mian believes that U.S. noncompliance with the spirit, if not the letter, of these regimes weakens them and raises larger questions about international justice and the legitimacy of international rules. The solution, in his opinion, must be a reform of U.S. domestic political institutions that would allow civil society movements favoring arms control and non-proliferation to impose compliance from within. For Mian, "this may be the only hope to achieve compliance by the most powerful."

Conclusion

International law—and, therefore, international compliance—is not only complex but also multidimensional. In his conclusion to this volume, Luck distinguishes three clusters of international law based on the kinds of interest they seek to address: human interests (e.g., human rights, humanitarian concerns, etc.), transnational interests (e.g., environment, global health, or crime issues) and core national interests (physical security, economic prosperity). Where core national interests are affected, powerful states tend toward unilateralism. They sometimes comply with international norms and when they enforce those norms on weaker states they are engaging in bilateral coercion rather than relying on multilateral mechanisms. International compliance mechanisms are most developed in the middle cluster of transnational interests, because states have a common interest in resolving transnational problems. States generally are less committed to eliciting compliance on human interest issues that do not directly affect their national interests.

Policy recommendations for improving compliance must take into account both the varying degrees of state commitment to ensuring compliance and the kinds of domestic constituencies that can be mobilized within or around states to promote compliance. Compliance with laws on human interest, which elicit low state commitment and broad but thin public support supplemented by committed advocacy NGOs, is best promoted by monitoring, public diplomacy, the provision of compliance incentives, and civil society involvement. Laws addressing core national interests will tend to be promoted by unilateral national actions stressing reciprocity and relying on deterrence. It is in the middle category of transnational interest law that such multilateral mechanisms as arbitration, capacity building, monitoring, and reporting have the greatest applicability.

Notes

1. "President's Remarks at the United Nations General Assembly, New York, New York, September 12, 2002," www.whitehouse.gov/news/releases/2002/09/print/20020912-1.html, 5.

2. Stephen D. Krasner, "Structural Causes and Regime Consequences: Regimes as Intervening Variables," in Stephen Krasner, *International Regimes* (Ithaca, NY: Cornell University Press, 1983).

3. John G. Ruggie, "International Regimes, Transactions, and Change: Embedded Liberalism in the Postwar Economic Order," *International Organization* 36, no. 2 (Spring 1982). Krasner himself suggests the validity of this regrouping of his four elements into

two main categories by arguing that changes in principles and norms constitute a regime change, while changes in rules and decision making procedures point merely to change within a regime.

4. Stephan Haggard and Beth A. Simmons, "Theories of International Regimes," *International Organization* 41, no. 3 (Summer 1987).

5. Article 38 of the Statute of the International Court of Justice identifies both multilateral treaties and international practice as valid sources of international law.

6. Susan Strange, "Cave! Hic Dragones: A Critique of Regime Analysis," in Krasner, *International Regimes*.

7. Krasner, "Structural Causes and Regime Consequences."

8. Robert Gilpin, *War and Change in World Politics* (New York: Cambridge University Press, 1981).

9. Robert O. Keohane, *After Hegemony: Cooperation and Discord in the World Political Economy* (Princeton, NJ: Princeton University Press, 1984).

10. G. John Ikenberry, *After Victory: Institutions, Strategic Constraint, and the Rebuilding of Order after Major Wars* (Princeton, NJ: Princeton University Press, 2001).

11. Thomas M. Franck, *The Power of Legitimacy among Nations* (New York: Oxford University Press, 1990).

12. Abram Chayes and Antonia Chayes, "On Compliance," *International Organization* 47, no. 2 (Spring 1993).

13. Thomas Risse-Kappen, "Public Opinion, Domestic Structure, and Foreign Policy in Liberal Democracies," *World Politics* 43, no. 4 (July 1991).

14. Andrew Moravcsik, "The Origins of Human Rights Regimes: Democratic Delegation in Postwar Europe," *International Organization* 54, no. 2 (Spring 2000).

15. Margaret E. Keck and Kathryn Sikkink, "Transnational Advocacy Networks in International and Regional Politics," *International Social Science Journal* 159 (March 1999).

16. Kathryn Sikkink, "Human Rights, Principled Issue Networks, and Sovereignty in Latin America," *International Organization* 47, no. 3 (Summer 1993).

17. Peter Haas, "Do Regimes Matter? Epistemic Communities and Mediterranean Pollution Control," *International Organization* 4, no. 3 (Summer 1989).

18. Ernst B. Haas, *Beyond the Nation-State—Functionalism and International Organization* (Stanford, CA: Stanford University Press, 1964).

19. Anne-Marie Burley [Slaughter] and Walter Mattli, "Europe Before the Court: A Political Theory of Legal Integration," *International Organization* 47, no. 1 (Winter 1993).

20. The ECJ may have partly escaped this dilemma only because it is part of a much larger set of European institutions that member states value enough to tolerate a limited reduction in their sovereignty.

21. See Abram Chayes and Antonia Handler Chayes, *The New Sovereignty: Compliance with Treaties in International Regulatory Regimes* (Cambridge, MA: Harvard University Press, 1995) and Edith Brown Weiss and Harold K. Jacobson, eds., *Engaging Countries: Strengthening Compliance with International Environmental Accords* (Cambridge, MA: The MIT Press, 1998). For a trenchant challenge to this literature, see George Downs, David M. Rocke, and Peter Barsoon, "Is Good News about Compliance Good News about Cooperation?" *International Organization* 50, no. 3 (Summer 1996).

22. The volume's contributors conclude that where it occurs, legalization can be explained in terms of its functional value, the preferences and incentives of domestic actors, and its embodiment of particular international norms: Judith Goldstein, Miles Kahler,

Robert O. Keohane, and Anne-Marie Slaughter, "Introduction: Legalization and World Politics," *International Organization* 54, no. 3 (Summer 2000). Where the contracting, sovereignty, and uncertainty costs of legalization outweigh its benefits, however, or when compromise between diverse interests is imperative, states may eschew legalization or elect a "soft law" approach with lower levels of rule precision, obligation, and delegation to a third party: Kenneth W. Abbott and Duncan Snidal, "Hard Law and Soft Law in International Governance," *International Organization* 54, no. 3 (Summer 2000).

23. Miles Kahler, "Conclusion: The Causes and Consequences of Legalization," *International Organization* 54, no. 3 (Summer 2000).

24. Judith Goldstein, Miles Kahler, Robert O. Keohane, and Anne-Marie Slaughter, "Introduction: Legalization and World Politics," 398.

25. See the discussion in Chayes and Chayes, *The New Sovereignty.*

26. Stanley Hoffmann, "International Systems and International Law," *World Politics* 14, no. 1 (October 1961): 210-211.

27. On hegemony, among others see Charles Kindleberger, *The World in Depression* (Berkeley, University of California, 1973); Stephen Krasner, "State Power and the Structure of Foreign Trade," *World Politics* 28 (1976): 317-47; and Gilpin, *War and Change in World Politics*; on hegemonic leadership, Fred Hirsch and Michael Doyle, "Politicization in the World Economy," in Hirsch, Doyle, and Edward Morse, *Alternatives to Monetary Disorder* (New York: McGraw Hill, 1977), 9-64; Keohane, *After Hegemony*; and Ikenberry, *After Victory.*

1

Conceptual Issues Surrounding
the Compliance Gap

George W. Downs and Andrea W. Trento

The Compliance Gap: Some Conceptual Issues

This chapter explores some of the conceptual issues that are connected with research on the "compliance gap" or the difference between the norms established by international agreements and the actual behavior of the signatory states. While there are any number of such issues in an area that is only beginning to be theoretically and empirically developed, the focus here will be on five broad topics that are particularly central for policy researchers: (1) the nature of the compliance gap; (2) the significance of the compliance gap for the future of multilateralism and the reputation of states that exhibit compliance problems; (3) compliance theory as a source for solutions to compliance problems; (4) the evaluation of strategies for reducing noncompliance; and (5) incentive compatibility or the problem of designing a compliance strategy that members of a multilateral regime will be willing to implement.

Although the goal of what follows is the modest one of identifying some of the major research and interpretive issues connected with each topic area, a picture does begin to emerge as to how far the field has come in understanding the nature of the compliance problems that currently exist in different areas and some of their policy implications. That picture is decidedly mixed. On the positive side, while modest and sometimes severe compliance problems exist in connection with some of the most ambitious agreements in the areas such as

19

environmental regulation and human rights, there appears to be little reason at the present time to believe that this noncompliance jeopardizes the future of multilateralism as a movement or cooperation in areas such as trade and financial regulation. On the negative side, the international systems' capacity to reduce noncompliance in areas where it has proved to be a problem has not been impressive.

The Nature of Compliance Gaps

Although the quality of compliance information in the international system is generally poor (a noteworthy fact in itself), it is clear that compliance rates vary considerably. They are highest in connection with the dozens of coordination agreements which make up a significant percentage of all multilateral agreements and typically establish conventions that make business easier to conduct (e.g., agreements that establish international banking practices or the allotment of overseas airline routes) and make technology and transportation safer and more reliable (e.g., agreements that establish procedures for radiological or aircraft emergencies or that regulate commercial air and sea lanes). States gain nothing from defecting from these agreements and if they accidentally do so, they usually incur a cost that can be substantial.

Compliance is also high in connection with those mixed-motive agreements where an incentive to defect exists but where it is so small that it can be offset by the weakest of punishments or even by the transaction costs that would be associated with planning and carrying out a defection. Some arms control treaties such as the Outer Space Treaty and the Seabed Arms Control Treaty fall into this category because (at least to date) the cost of developing an effective weapon is greater than the advantage it would provide. Other agreements fall into this category because their requirements are not appreciably different from what states had intended to do in the absence of a treaty. It has been argued that the Strategic Arms Limitation Talks (SALT) agreements fall into this category because the limitations they called for differed very little from the levels previously projected by both the United States and the Soviet Union.[1] States also appear to have little to gain from defecting from the vast majority of environmental agreements, where agreements frequently contain variable speed provisions that limit state responsibility.[2] A prominent example is the Montreal Protocol, which required virtually nothing of developing states for the first ten years that it was in effect. As a result, the level of compliance associated with such agreements, while not necessarily perfect, is higher than their level of substantive effectiveness, a topic that we will revisit in what follows.

In situations where the regulatory standards embodied in multilateral agreements are more ambitious and compliance is either economically or politically costly, compliance problems and compliance gaps are far more common. Yet even in these cases the size and growth rate of the resultant compliance gap varies a great deal. In the area of economic cooperation, the compliance gap is fairly stable. Problems with the World Trade Organization (WTO) (e.g., recently in the case of bananas and beef hormones) do not appear to be significantly more numerous than they were with the General Agreement on Tariffs and Trade (GATT), its less ambitious predecessor, and most of the regional agreements such as the European Union (EU) to the Association of Southeast Asian Nations (ASEAN) appear to be living up to expectations.

In the area of environmental cooperation, however, there have been and continue to be serious problems in connection with a subset of the more ambitious agreements. Those agreements in which the greatest burden falls on developed states such as the Antarctic Agreements and the Montreal Protocol have experienced relatively few compliance problems. But those agreements that place the bulk of compliance responsibility on developing states, such as the Convention on International Trade in Endangered Species of Wild Fauna and Flora (CITES) and the International Timber Agreement, have experienced serious and persistent problems.

Multilateral as opposed to bilateral arms control agreements such as the Treaty on the Nonproliferation of Nuclear Weapons (NPT) have also experienced significant compliance problems, but it is not clear that the rate of that fraying is substantially greater than it has been for quite some time. The ambitious new landmine agreement appears to have achieved considerable success, but there are still major noncompliance problems in states such as Chechnya, Kosovo, Myanmar, and Angola.[3] Similarly isolated but significant compliance problems exist in connection with the conventions on both biological and chemical weapons.

The situation in the human rights area is probably the bleakest and least encouraging. Many of these problems have accompanied the dramatic increase in intrastate conflict that has taken place in the wake of the end of the cold war in locations such as East Timor, Ethiopia, Sierra Leone, Angola, Congo, and Kosovo, and the trend shows no signs of abating. In addition to these, intermittent but serious human rights violations continue to exist during peacetime as well in any number of states. There is an undeniable compliance gap here.

Yet even in the area of human rights the picture is more complicated than it might first appear and there are even some bright spots. The European Convention on Human Rights, which has forty-one signatories, including every state in the EU, shows every evidence of being a well-functioning treaty that has extended the rights the citizens of member states and their powers of redress.[4] During much of the same period that human rights abuses were growing in Africa and elsewhere, Lutz and Sikkink have shown that there has been a marked decline in the rate of human rights abuses that have taken place in Latin America over the past twenty years.[5] Rates of torture, disappearance, and nondemocracy have all fallen, although the rate of decline varies across area and across states.

In every regulatory area, compliance problems are greatest in states at war or experiencing internal conflict, nondemocratic states, and in less economically developed states. Civil war operates both to divert the administrative and financial resources needed to meet the costs of regulation and oversee compliance and to raise the benefits attached to opportunistic violations of human rights and arms agreements. Autocrats face fewer internal pressures to follow through with agreements, they possess an incentive to restrict human rights as a mechanism by which to control the population and preserve power, and they frequently rely on the short-term exploitation of natural resources in order to maintain their grip on power. And the status of developing state reduces, at the very least, the amount of administrative and financial resources that are available to ensure compliance while at the same time increasing the likelihood that the state will be engaged in civil war or be nondemocratic. Together, these three statuses place many developing states in a kind of triple jeopardy that frequently leads to non-compliance.

A very useful portrait of the compliance gap that exists in the environmental area is contained in Weiss and Jacobson, who carefully analyzes the compliance record of nine states in connection with six prominent multilateral agreements. [6] Although what Weiss and Jacobson call weak compliance the exception rather than the rule, when there are problems developing states are invariably involved and several are persistent noncompliers. Cameroon, for example, was found to be in weak compliance with the World Heritage Agreement, CITES, and the Tropical Timber Agreement. Brazil and China were in weak compliance with both CITES and the Tropical Timber Agreement.[7] Other studies tend to reinforce these findings and suggest that there are cases where the noncompliance of developing states is so persistent and so severe that it has contributed to what is clearly a worsening of conditions. Although the International Tropical Timber Agreement created in 1983 employs a conservationist rhetoric in emphasizing the sustainable utilization and conservation of tropical timber forests, producer states—all of them developing countries—have paid little more than lip service to the agreement's sustainability aims and have consistently blocked developed-country efforts to enforce them. In 1992—nine years after the agreement's entry-into-force—only 1 percent of all tropical timber was harvested sustainably.[8]

The pattern is much the same in the area of human rights. Of the thirty-one reports that Human Rights Watch generated in the last six months of 1999, twenty-five, or about 80 percent, deal with problems in developing states. The list of problems is a long one: a lack of freedom of the press and assembly in Croatia; forced emigration from East Timor; high rates of domestic violence and the routine torture of children in Pakistani detention facilities; political repression in Uganda; attacks on Christians in India; ethnic cleansing in Yugoslavia; the displacement of 10 percent of the population in Angola as the result of the breakdown of the Lusaka peace process; and widespread murder, mutilation, and rape in connection with Sierra Leone's civil war.

The Significance of Compliance Gaps

Compliance statistics like these are provocative, but it is important to be extremely cautious when interpreting them. Inferences about relative effectiveness are especially treacherous because it is a mistake to assume that a high level of compliance means that an agreement is effective. It is easy to see why: full compliance with an environmental agreement that requires states to do nothing more than report the amount of fish that their boats catch each month will do little by itself to accomplish the goal of replenishing a rapidly depleting stock of fish. The existence of a compliance gap or a low compliance rate is usually more meaningful in the sense that it more reliably reflects the existence of an effectiveness shortfall, but even here differences in the noncompliance rates across agreements or across regulatory areas are subject to the same interpretation problems because the levels of cooperative ambition—roughly the difference between the present status quo and what the treaty requires—vary across regulatory areas and across treaties within a given area. For example, the compliance rates associated with human rights agreements are far worse than they are in any other area, but, because these agreements also tend to be the most consistently demanding, an agreement with a compliance rate of 80 percent may more effective than a less ambitious environmental or arms agreement with a compliance rate of 95 percent.

Even in connection with a given treaty regime, trends in compliance rates can be misleading because agreements sometimes evolve, generally in the direction of more cooperation. For example, because the WTO is more demanding than GATT in the range of products it covers, a slightly lower level of compliance with it would still represent an increase in liberalization and more total cooperation. The Montreal Protocol to the Vienna Convention for Substances that Deplete the Ozone Layer is likely to provide one contemporary example of this paradox. As noted above, the protocol did not require that many developing-state signatories impose regulatory controls until 1997, ten years after it had originally entered into force. As a result, the level of developing state compliance for these ten years was outstanding.[9] Now that these states are being pulled under the regulatory umbrella of the regime for the first time, their overall compliance rates can only go down, even as their contribution to the regulatory regime grows larger.[10]

The potential impact of noncompliance extends beyond its impact on agreement effectiveness. Another set of concerns about the political effects of noncompliance involves its impact on reputation: on the reputation of individual states, and on the reputation of multilateralism as a movement. For example, many theorists believe that when a state exhibits a pattern of noncompliance in connection with a given agreement, it damages its overall reputation for reliability as a treaty partner and that this reduces the likelihood that other states will invite it to participate in future agreements. If this were, in fact, the case it would represent a huge cost to any state but particularly to a developing state whose economic future is often directly dependent on its relations with developed states.

There are doubts, however, that this is the way that reputation operates. One source of doubt comes directly from the rate at which different categories of states are joining and continuing to participate in international regimes. If the cost of a general reputation for noncompliance was as high as the general theory suggests, then one would expect that states with poor compliance records would be excluded from new multilateral agreements. Yet no one has yet produced evidence that such exclusion is taking place.

Another source of doubt about the traditional view of reputation follows from the variation in compliance across regulatory arenas. The fact that the overall compliance rate in areas such as trade is significantly higher than in human rights suggests that state reliabilities vary from area to area. Given that this is the case, it would seem to make little sense to adopt a "unitary" view of reputation that implicitly assumes that a state's reliability rate is similar across areas. This would require other states to punish a state that fails to comply with a human rights agreement by lowering their estimate of its reliability in connection with other areas, such as trade and arms control, *despite* the available historical evidence, which suggests that compliance rates in these areas are only weakly if at all connected to compliance in human rights. Such a unitary reputational assignment strategy, which involves ignoring a large amount of relevant information, would be extremely inefficient if it were followed over the long term.

We suspect that it is more likely that states assign each other different reputations in different areas, reflecting historical variations in compliance rates. The noncompliance of a state with a human rights agreement will have an impact for other states' estimates of its reliability in connection with other human rights agreements, but very little impact for treaties in other areas. A state's failure to live up to the provisions of the International Covenant on Civil and Political Rights does not lead other states to believe that it will fail to live up to WTO obligations or will deny its treaty partners access to its jointly operated bases in time of war. More significantly, it means that an incident of noncompliance in a specific area will *not* jeopardize a state's future participation in multilateral agreements generally.

Moreover, there is even some doubt that a unitary reputation strategy is efficient within a single regulatory arena. Imagine the following scenario. The United States makes a defensive alliance with a small state in Southeast Asia, which is soon attacked by a neighboring state. In response, the United States offers to provide some token military aid and offers to mediate the conflict but refuses to take a more active role claiming that it believes that both sides played a provocative role in initiating the conflict. To what extent can one expect that this lack of action will damage the reputation of the United States with its other allies?

Those who hold to the view that states possess a unitary reputation would argue that this act should lead every other state to reduce its estimate of the United States' reliability as an ally in connection with every security agreement.

However, an alternative view argues that whatever it is that leads states to have a different level of reliability in connection with different kinds of agreements can also lead to different levels of reliability (and different reputations) within a given area. For example, one of the factors that is almost certainly associated with reliability is the value that a state attaches to a given agreement. The more a state values an agreement the less likely it is to defect from it. If this is true, states that believe that the United States values their alliance about the same or less than it does with the Southeast Asian state should be worried, but the North Atlantic Treaty Organization (NATO) members should not, because they have plenty of evidence that suggests that the United States values NATO more. Experience and billions of dollars of direct and indirect military aid have already taught them better.

The evidence that states assign each other different reputations to reflect their different rates of compliance with different kinds of agreements has at least two important implications for the international system and the compliance gap. The first implication is that it is probably a mistake to depend too heavily on the ability of reputational concerns to promote compliance. While reputation does matter, the likelihood that states possess different reputations in different areas and perhaps even within a given area means that it is unlikely to matter nearly as much as some theorists have hoped. Reputational concerns are unlikely to replace more traditional within-treaty penalties and reciprocity-based punishments, and they are unlikely to turn out to be the magic bullet that will dramatically improve compliance with human rights agreements.

The second implication is that developing states do not have to worry that their compliance records in one area will result in their being systematically excluded from membership in new multilaterals. This is good news, especially for African states that all too frequently have a history of loan defaults that by the standard view of reputation risks isolating them from participation in the international system for the foreseeable future.

A last aspect of reputation that we have not yet discussed involves the reputation of multilateralism itself. To what extent does the compliance gap jeopardize the future of multilateralism as a movement? Generally speaking, the answer appears to be "very little if at all." While at the time of this writing there are plenty of discussions in the media about the Bush administration's predilection for unilateralism and its growing indifference to established multilateral organizations and processes, there is less discussion in the media of a broad crisis in multilateral institutions and many of these institutions, such as the International Monetary Fund (IMF), WTO, and the World Bank, appear to be doing quite well. Perhaps even more significantly, there appears to be no deterioration in the rate at which new multilateral agreements and organizations are being created or established ones are being reformed. In fact, in both cases these rates may be increasing. One possible reason for this relative health of the multilateral system even in the face of significant compliance problems in some areas is that policymakers are not as inclined as academics to think in terms of multilateral cooperation as an undifferentiated category. In the policy world, where each policy arena tends to function as a decomposable system, there is less of a tendency to generalize about the health of multilateralism generally and more of a tendency to worry about particular areas. As a consequence, while people are aware of the compliance gap in human rights and in connection with certain environmental agreements in a general sort of way, the reputational consequences of these problems appear to have been contained.

If noncompliance is not a threat to the reputation of multilateralism generally, is it nonetheless a threat to multilateralism and multilateral progress within some areas of cooperation? The answer is still far from clear. Consider human rights, where the most serious category-wide compliance problem lies. One view holds that the persistently large compliance gap in the human rights area is leading policymakers and the public to view human rights agreements as largely symbolic exercises that they do not have to take seriously. A more sophisticated version of the same argument might even contend that it is this very reputation for noncompliance without consequence that has led to the current proliferation of agreements as states increasingly reason that, since there are no real penalties for noncompliance, there is no cost and some symbolic benefit attached to signing such agreements by the dozen. This might help explain the paradox of why human rights agreements are characteristically deeper and more ambitious (in the sense that they embody a larger departure from the current status quo) than is usually the case in areas (e.g., trade and arms control) where the compliance record is considerably better. Because no one expects to have to enforce them, there is no reason not to match ambitions with accomplishments.

A less pessimistic perspective argues that these agreements are not designed so much to produce changes in states' human rights policies in the short run as to establish a set of universally accepted human rights standards that will gradually be incorporated into state constitutions and diffuse into the agendas of political parties within states. Those who promote this strategy see little alternative. Reciprocal punishments in which other member states threaten to suspend human rights in their states in response to an abuse in another state are obviously out of the question, and advocates worry that the strategy of expelling noncomplying states from human rights agreements will be counterproductive. Linkage punishments in which noncomplying states would be threatened with trade penalties seem more likely to be effective. However, at least to date, other states have been reluctant to take this step except in isolated cases involving relatively small states, such as South Africa, where the cost of the sanctions is relatively modest.

Compliance Theory as a Source of Solutions to the Compliance Gap

Historically, most theorizing about state compliance with international obligations has been done by international lawyers. Their goal was to account for why the compliance rate was so high (or seemed to be so high, given that the quality of the compliance data associated with most agreements is very poor) when there was no underlying enforcement agent. Relatively little attention was devoted to how the compliance rate could be improved, because it was simply not thought to be a problem. This view has undergone some change in recent years, but it remains the case that anyone interested in designing a strategy to improve compliance has to get the bulk of her/his theoretical inspiration indirectly from one of the many theories about why states comply. One of the most helpful descriptions of these theories can be found in Koh.[11] In what follows, we will alter Koh's list of the five major perspectives slightly and characterize seven relatively distinct schools that, implicitly at least, suggest different ways to approach the problem of noncompliance.

The *realist* school generally views international law and the institutions that promulgate it as an epiphenomenon of international politics—an arena for acting out power relationships between self-interested state actors bent on maintaining (and increasing) their own relative power in the system. Law has little normative impact: states will comply with institutional rules only as long as they believe that these represent their interests or they are coerced into doing so by more powerful states. Because coercion is important, the power structure of the international system plays a critical role in determining whether compliance takes place or not and hegemons often play a critical role in creating and sustaining institutional rules.[12]

This theory suggests that, if powerful states believe the noncompliance of less powerful states is problematic, they will exert some kind of pressure on them to improve their compliance rate. This pressure might come in any of a number of forms: economic sanctions, withholding military or financial assistance, charging higher interest rates for loans, discouraging their companies from investing or encouraging them to buy products elsewhere, and so forth. If a powerful state falls into noncompliance, the problem is not so easily solved and the stability of the regime itself is likely to be threatened.

The *Kantian liberal school* is represented by international lawyers, such as Thomas Franck, and argues that a state's decision to comply with an international law is determined by its perception of a law's procedural and substantive "fairness."[13] Laws that are legitimate, or procedurally fair, that have been constructed democratically and inclusive of all affected parties, will exhibit a "compliance pull" that is independent of other factors or interests—a reiteration of the age-old Kantian ideal that states will obey international laws out of a sense of moral obligation.[14] This pull is tempered, however, by the reluctance of states to obey even a legitimate law if it is perceived to be substantively unfair, or unjust.[15]

A Kantian liberal might argue that part of the explanation for the noncompliance that exists is that all but the largest or most developed states are relegated to playing a very small role in the formulation of some multilateral regulatory standards and that, as a result, these standards are both far from their "ideal point" and are insensitive to the problems that they face in trying to comply. It follows that, if you want developing states to have a compliance rate that is as high as developed states, then you give them the same voice as the developed states (and especially the major powers) in designing agreements.

The *democratic process school* of political economy possesses some of the same preoccupations with legitimacy as the Kantian liberals, but its emphasis is on the character of the government and politics within states rather than on the fairness of the international institution charged with formulating and implementing the multilateral agreement. Political scientists such as Andrew Moravcsik[16] and legal theorists like Anne-Marie Slaughter-Burley[17] argue that liberal or democratic states regularly comply more willingly with international law because the rule of law is ingrained in them and the transparency of their governmental structure operates to ensure that they will implement the provisions of any treaty that have been ratified by domestic due process. Significantly, democratic states also expect that other democracies will do the same, and this reduces their fear that they will be exploited by the free riding of other parties. Compliance for liberals, then, is an issue related to the domestic identity of the state: the more liberal the state, the more likely it is to comply with international law.

The democratic process school is not oriented toward addressing isolated instances of noncompliance, but implicitly it suggests that anything that is done to promote democracy and democratic institutions within member states, such as the establishment of a free press and an independent judiciary, will operate to increase a state's compliance rate.

The *strategic school* of political economy focuses on the structure of the incentives represented by an agreement and the role of strategic interaction among treaty parties.[18] It retains many of the fundamental assumptions of realists—for example that states are egoistic interest maximizers—but here it is the benefits of cooperation rather than the power of coercion that sustains multilateral institutions. Because these benefits are often substantial, political economists predict that states will cooperate far more often and the institutional rules that they create will be far more robust across different distributions of power than does realism.

Members of the strategic school emphasize that the rules and institutions of the international system are the equilibria that emerge from the strategic games that states play with each other in different issue areas. Institutions affect each other's behavior by changing the incentives and disincentives attached to the different options that states have for acting. Over time, institutions can even alter the distribution of underlying preferences in a state through the operation of complex feedback mechanisms that alter the balance of power of different constituencies.[19] There are numerous institutional strategies through which institutions can alter incentives, ranging from reducing the cost of information and increasing transparency to the use of the direct manipulation of payoffs through subsidies and technological transfers. Political economists in the strategic school also emphasize the influence of factors that are only partly under the control of decision makers, such as the relative price changes that result from technological changes, alterations in income redistribution, and economic growth.

A member of the strategic school would argue that the best way to address the compliance gap in the short run is to increase the benefits that states can obtain by complying or increase the costs that they face for defecting. The first might be done through the use of subsidies, technological transfers or some other kind of aid linked to compliance. The second might be accomplished by increasing the punishment that states face when they fail to comply. This punishment could also take on any number of forms, ranging from fines that are specified in the agreement to things that might not be specified, such as the imposition of harsher terms for loans or trade sanctions. Whatever the punishment strategy, it is important to recognize that it should be scaled to the level of benefits that states derive from being in the treaty. If the punishment level is too high, then states will simply withdraw from the treaty. Members of the strategic school would also be open to the idea that it might be in the interest of all parties to tolerate a small amount of noncompliance that seemed to result from uncontrollable shocks to the developing state's economy or from an inefficient administrative system.[20]

In the long run, members of the strategic school anticipate that the compliance problems associated with a given agreement will lessen as states' level of development rises. This is because, as per capita income goes up, the tastes of citizenries will typically change in the direction of wanting more consumer goods and placing a higher value on the quality of the environment. Because an increase in per capita income increases a state's tax base and government revenue, the efficiency and effectiveness with which their bureaucracies will be able to carry out the necessary regulatory activities will usually rise as well.

The *managerial school*, which Koh refers to as one of the two strands of the International Legal Process School (ILPS), is most elaborately worked out in the books and articles of the international legal scholars Abram and Antonia Chayes.[21] This approach treats a state's desire to comply as given in the sense that treaty signatories are not believed to be interested in free riding. Instead, noncompliance is attributed to complicating external factors such as treaty ambiguity, the administrative and/or financial incapacity of states to implement the agreements they sign, and the time lag between a law's entry into force and its impact.[22]

More than members of most other schools, the managerialists have been quite explicit in describing how noncompliance problems should be addressed. They denounce the use of coercive instruments on the grounds of impracticality, arguing that "sanctioning authority is rarely granted by treaty, rarely used when granted, and likely to be ineffective when used."[23] It is far more sensible, they believe, to treat instances of apparent noncompliance as problems that need to be solved, rather than as wrongs to be punished. The only remnant of coercion lies in "the various manifestations of disapproval [of a state's noncompliant behavior]: exposure, shaming, and diffuse impacts on the reputation and international relationships of a resisting party."[24]

As an alternative to punishing noncompliance, the Chayeses advocate the use of the same kind of positive incentives that the strategic school of political economy favors, such as subsidies and technology transfers. When shrinking budgets make the use of these relatively costly instruments problematic, managerialists suggest that progress in obtaining compliance can often be made through negotiation by a process of give and take ("jawboning") and trading off present noncompliance for greater assurance of future compliance.[25] The Chayeses also believe that in the long run, compliance is also served by the creation of better-funded and more politically responsive international bureaucracies.[26]

The *transformationalist* school—the theoretical home of many constructivists—hearkens back to Grotian notions of communitarian values, and the constructivist properties of "international society" in shaping not only a state's interest, but even its identity. According to Grotius, states obey international rules—even the most inconvenient ones—because of an underlying, long-term interest in preserving a law-based international community.[27] For contemporary transformationalists, the institutions and laws operate over time to dynamically transform the interests of the state, so that it comes to value the preservation of the international society over other interests.

In the long run, transformationalists believe noncompliance will gradually diminish as problematic states become resocialized to more progressive internationalist values. This often takes place through a reflectivist process that operates in two ways. First, problematic states treated as cooperative by more progressive states will gradually adopt the progressive states' implied characterization as a self-image and become more cooperative. Second, as they gradually act more cooperatively, they will increasingly see themselves in a new, more cooperative light.[28]

Transformationalists do not usually focus on short-term compliance problems. When they do, they recommend avoiding enforcement-based compliance mechanisms—that is, those mechanisms which emphasize material (dis)incentives to comply, such as treaty, trade, and military sanctions—in favor of the managerial approach. Transformationalists, however, take the Chayeses one step further and argue against the use of what they believe are stigmatizing terms, such as noncompliance, on the grounds that they can precipitate an unraveling of the consensus-building process.

The last school is referred to as *transnationalism* and is largely the product of Koh himself.[29] Transnationalism argues that the key to understanding compliance lies in the process by which norms established at the international level are internalized at the domestic level and become indistinguishable from domestic norms. This norm-internalization occurs by a process Koh calls "vertical domestication," whereby international legal norms 'trickle down' and become incorporated into domestic legal systems that are the proximate source of compliance.[30] This process frequently unfolds outside the boundaries of formal negotiation, with as many as six different kinds of "agents" exerting their influence in numerous fora. These include (1) transnational norm entrepreneurs; (2) governmental norm sponsors; (3) transnational issue networks; (4) interpretive communities and legal-declaring fora; (5) bureaucratic compliance procedures; and

(6) issue linkages. Koh, like the transformationalists, does not focus on short-term solutions to compliance problems. In the longer run, any of the agents listed above can potentially play a key role.

Evaluating the Effectiveness of Different Compliance Strategies

The brief descriptions of the six schools presented above make it clear that there is considerable overlap in the strategies that they recommend for closing the compliance gap. For example, the strategic interactionists and managerialists overlap in their recommendation of positive incentives, and the managerialists and the transformationalists overlap with respect to their condemnation of punishments or negative sanctions for noncompliance. At other points, schools stress mechanisms that are consistent with the perspectives of other schools but which are not discussed by them. For example, while the transnationalists are the only school that focuses on the process by which international norms are translated into domestic law, none of the other schools with the exception of realism would argue that this process is never present or that its effect is trivial. It is just that their emphasis lies elsewhere, often because of the trajectory of academic debate at the time they were developed.

Yet for all the overlap that exists among the schools, there are still real differences among them regarding the importance of enforcement and the relative importance of short-term socialization that have real policy implications. How is one to go about deciding what to do when noncompliance is a problem?

One way to answer this question would be to try to determine what kind of strategy is most consistently associated with a high compliance rate in a sample of regulatory agreements. Unfortunately, however reasonable this approach may seem on the surface, it implicitly assumes that the underlying cases in which different strategies are being used do not differ in any systematic way that affects success, and this is simply not the case. The problem of "selection" always arises when different strategies are used in different contexts, instead of being employed randomly as in an experimental design. Recall the argument that the agreements with the highest developing state compliance rates are often those that demand the least. No state has ever failed to comply with either the Convention Concerning the Protection of the World Cultural and National Heritage or the Convention on Wetlands of International Importance since they require nothing more than the optional registration of cultural sites and wetlands at the discretion of the state. Nor have the vast majority of the thirty-nine states that are signatories to the International Convention for the Regulation of Whaling, but which have never done any whaling, failed to comply with that agreement. Given that many agreements have few if any compliance provisions, as well as no compliance problems, a simple comparative study may well lead us to conclude that the best compliance strategy is no compliance strategy at all: in such cases there obviously is no need for incentives or for enforcement.

This problem might seem to be easily solved by simply eliminating such agreements from the analysis and only including those that require states to alter their behavior in a significant way. Even then, however, the problem of confounding the impact of the multilateral accord's requirements with the impact of the compliance strategy will persist unless we can figure out how to control for the relative temptation that states have to defect from the agreement, something that is usually correlated with the "depth" of the agreement or the magnitude of the change in behavior that an agreement requires. If we don't do this, then a large proportion of a given strategy's effectiveness will still be attributable to the fact that it is being used in easier or more difficult contexts.

Inference is likely to be further complicated by the fact that different strategies are more useful in connection with some categories of agreements than others. For example, technology transfers and subsidies might be highly effective in connection with point source industrial pollution, but may have little relevance to environmental agreements dealing with fur seal preservation or desertification, much less nuclear proliferation and human rights. Similarly, standard enforcement strategies, such as fines and compensation, are likely to be most effective in connection with trade agreements, where the threat of excluding the state from the benefits of belonging to the agreement looms in the background to ensure that the fines will be paid. In the areas of human rights and environmental treaties, where the threat of exclusion carries less weight, a state might simply refuse to pay the fine that is levied on it.

Even this sort of analysis, which attempts to control for both the cost of compliance and the policy area, can be misleading because it is blind to the precise nature of the reasons why a state is not complying. This is what Jacobson and Weiss, in their study of compliance with environmental agreements, call motivation.[31] They stress the importance of motivation as a conditioning variable and advocate tailoring the compliance promoting strategy to the combination of intention and capacity that determine motivation in a given case. They argue that when both the intention to comply and the capacity are strong, the only compliance strategy that should be needed is some modest sanction for noncompliance or some incentive tied to compliance to stave off the temptation of reaping the benefits of being a free rider. When states have an intention to comply with an agreement's regulatory provisions but lack the capacity, positive incentives like subsidies, low interest loans, and technological transfers are important. When states do not intend to comply or have only a weak intention to do so but nonetheless possess a high capacity to comply if they desired, Jacobson and Weiss argue that the situation is often better suited to the use of some form of coercion by other members of the multilateral regime. This could consist of some kind of sanctions to persuade the state that it is in its best interest to comply or the careful use of a reputational strategy if there are likely to be a substantial number of related agreements in the future.

For countries that lack both the intention and the capacity to comply or are weak in both—the category in which many developing states can be found—Jacobson and Weiss argue that multiple strategies must often be employed simultaneously. Positive incentive strategies are needed to help build capacity. Transparency strategies that involve publicizing states' progress or lack of progress toward meeting their obligations may help foster a culture of compliance and prevent backsliding, especially if there is the threat of sanctions in the background. Sanctions also play a valuable role in providing some assurance to the states providing incentives that they will not be exploited.

Jacobson and Weiss also make the point (reminiscent of the strategic school and its interest in the impact of changing relative prices) that another complication lies in the fact that the intention and capacity of states to comply may change over time.

> A country weak in capacity and intention could become stronger in both, as in Cameroon's compliance with procedural obligations under the Montreal Protocol. Or a country that was strong in capacity and intention could find that either or both were diminished, as in the weakening of the Russian Federation's capacity to comply with CITES after the dissolution of the Soviet Union.[32]

Situations such as these call for a flexible compliance strategy that can be periodically altered as conditions change. This requires a fairly sophisticated institutional apparatus that can monitor the evolution of an agreement and respond appropriately. If this is not present—and it is often not—the necessary changes will obviously not be forthcoming and compliance will either be lower than it might otherwise have been or more inefficiently obtained.

War is a source of instability that Jacobson and Weiss don't focus on, but it deserves to be singled out for special attention because its effects are so great and because its role in fostering noncompliance in a significant number of the most underdeveloped states, especially in Africa, is so large. Nothing has a greater impact on a state's intention and capacity to comply with multilateral agreements in the areas of human rights and the environment and nothing renders so many of the compliance-building efforts of outside parties more ineffective.

There is no systematic study of state compliance rates during wartime, except in connection with such conflict-related activities as the treatment of prisoners and the recruitment of underage soldiers.[33] However, the existence of war is relevant to the present discussion because, unless its effects are controlled for, any compliance failures will be incorrectly attributed to the ineffectiveness of the compliance strategy that is being used rather than to the real cause, which is the conflict. It is difficult to imagine any compliance strategy succeeding under the conditions that currently exist in the Congo, Sierra Leone, or Liberia.

Incentive Compatibility: Designing a Compliance Strategy that States Will Agree to Implement

If it is important to follow Jacobson and Weiss's advice of trying to understand the motivation of states that are not complying, it is no less important to understand what other states will be willing to do about it. A policy recommendation that will not be adopted because it ignores critical political and resource constraints is of limited practical value. It is like telling a friend with a modest budget that she should seriously consider buying a Ferrari rather than a Fiat because evidence suggests that it is a far better car. No one has much difficulty thinking of an expensive incentive package or a powerful linkage penalty that would, if implemented, dramatically reduce the compliance gap in almost any area, but the very fact that it is so easy to think of means that it has probably already been considered and rejected or dismissed out of hand.

This suggests that policy analysts and academics interested in reducing compliance problems, particularly those of developing states, would be wise to study the conditions under which states have been willing to employ different compliance enhancing strategies in different policy areas so that policy prescriptions that are made are "incentive compatible," which in this context simply means consistent with the incentives of the states that will have to agree to implement them. Oddly, there is no general treatment of the topic of incentive compatibility in the literature and, with the possible exception of peacekeeping, there is relatively little material on the topic to be found in specific policy areas.

For example, in the environmental area even Jacobson and Weiss, who, as we have seen, are very attuned to the importance of motivation in designing an effective compliance strategy, spend very little time discussing (1) the determinants of state motivation in dealing with compliance problems, (2) the kinds of strategies that states prefer to use in different environmental areas, (3) how and why compliance strategies have changed over time and (4) what, if anything, nongovernmental organizations (NGOs) and other actors of various kinds can do to help prompt multilateral institutions to alter their current strategy in cases where it is clearly failing. This last is especially challenging and, at present, more of an art than a science.

Keohane and Levy represent one of the few attempts to grapple with aspects of incentive compatibility in conjunction with the attempts of developed states to increase the compliance rate of developing states in the area of environmental regulation.[34] The essay by Connolly emphasizes the extent to which environmental aid from developed states is inspired by the self-interest of strong political forces that are invested in the mitigation of the subset of transboundary environmental problems that affect wealthy countries the most (e.g., ozone depletion, biodiversity) or interested in the export of goods and services made possible by aid programs.[35] Predictably, this produces a strong bias toward "rich country" environmental problems rather than toward those that are considered to be a priority by developing states.

Connolly also points out that the very low levels of aid that are characteristic of so many of these programs suggest that donors are often more interested in symbolically reassuring concerned publics at home than they are in improving the environment. While she notes the cynicism that this strategy seems to suggest, it is not clear whether this is simply the consequence of the fact that environmental goals are frequently dominated by other political priorities in donor countries or the consequence of development experiences that have led them to believe that aid accomplishes relatively little because many developing states place a low priority on the environmental goals and tend to have very inefficient bureaucratic infrastructures.[36]

Developed states, both directly and more frequently indirectly through the World Bank and the International Monetary Fund, also appear to be attracted to the use of conditional loans of the type used for promoting structural adjustment as a tool for promoting developing state compliance with environmental agreements. Fairman and Ross describe two types of conditional loans.[37] One type, called policy-based lending, requires recipients to pledge to implement an accepted set of policy changes as a condition for the receipt of the loan. These have generally fared poorly. Monitoring by lenders is unreliable and governments that receive the loans often renege on fulfilling their conditions if they are not really committed to goals of the project. In some cases, this reneging is accomplished by "taking advantage of the limited enforcement capacity of the lender." At other times it is accomplished by engaging in "false compliance: by fulfilling the letter of their obligations but nullifying their impact with countervailing measures."[38] Given this experience, Fairman and Ross believe that such loans are likely to be employed less frequently in the future and only in cases where the lender is convinced that the developing state really wants to change its policies and only requires an infusion of resources to do so.

The other type of conditional loan, based on the principal of allocative efficiency, requires that funders distribute aid to countries based on their current adherence to various regulatory standards. There are not enough data to estimate the ultimate fate of this strategy, but Fairman and Ross suggest that it too is likely to run into trouble because bilateral funders simply do not have the capacity to carefully gauge the performance progress of the recipients and will be reluctant to alter the direction of their foreign aid programs, which usually have deep political roots tied to interests outside the environmental area.

Two other more complex quasi-linkage strategies are also chronicled in the Keohane and Levy volume. One such strategy is the debt-for-nature swap. In its first incarnation, this involved NGOs purchasing the foreign debt title of a developing state in the secondary market at a steep discount. The debt title was then given back to the developing state on the condition that the domestic currency equivalent or some agreed-upon fraction of it would be used to finance environmental projects.[39] These debt-for-nature swaps worked less well than expected and gradually became irrelevant as developing states began working toward the larger goal of debt forgiveness. The other linkage strategy involved a payment of funds by the Japanese government, the Asian Development Bank, and the World Bank to the Philippine Central Bank to ease a balance of payment crisis in exchange for a series of forest policy reforms.[40] This strategy worked relatively well in this one instance, but it is not clear how often or under what conditions it will be used in the future.

The characterization of what developed states are willing to do to address compliance problems in developing states found in the Keohane and Levy book is fairly consistent with what can be found in the scattered historical studies of individual agreements such as Benedick's[41] and Nangle's[42] studies of the Montreal Protocol. When the problem addressed by the agreement is salient among the domestic constituencies in developed states, they have generally displayed a willingness to create modest positive incentives for developing states to comply in the form of conditional loans, outright grants, or technical assistance. Only in very rare cases, however, where the developing state is considered to be the lynchpin of a particular regulatory regime (e.g., the Philippines and the timber agreement), has this aid really been substantial. Still more rarely, and only in connection with problems that they consider to be very high priority (e.g., The Montreal Protocol, the environmental aspects of the North American Free Trade Agreement [NAFTA]), have developed states employed linkage strategies and sanctions to coerce developing states into compliance. Even in those isolated cases where such strategies have been used, developed states usually ensure that more powerful developing states, such as India, are provided with some exemption in order to avoid a politically difficult confrontation.

Clearly, we need to better understand the reluctance of states to employ incentives and disincentives that are sufficiently strong to bring about compliance and think more deeply about what, if anything, can motivate states to invest more resources in this project. Will effective incentive-compatible solutions only be implemented when the cost of the problem rises to some critical level? Can increased political activities on the part of domestic constituencies and NGOs also make a difference? These questions and ones like them need to be asked in every area where there is a compliance problem.

Conclusion

The preceding discussion of the conceptual issues associated with five compliance gap-related research topics has a number of implications. One implication is that, while a high level of noncompliance is associated with some agreements, the inability or reluctance of states to engage in agreements that commit them to doing very much may be a far greater threat to the future of international cooperation than is noncompliance. Most states continue to comply with most multilateral agreements most of the time, if only because a high percentage of multilateral agreements are either coordination agreements from which states have little incentive to defect or very modest regulatory agreements that require relatively few departures from what states are currently doing.

Despite the general pattern of good compliance, there are some marked exceptions, most of which arise in connection with the few ambitious agreements that require substantial departures in behavior from what has been past practice. The most serious problems are in the area of human rights, where agreements are frequently the most ambitious and where many of the most commonly employed compliance strategies (e.g., reciprocity) are ruled out by the structure of the game. Serious compliance problems also exist in connection with a subset of the most ambitious environmental and arms agreements. In the majority of these cases, the most persistent violators are usually a subset of developing states that are relatively poor, undemocratic, and plagued by internal conflict.

The question of what to do about the noncompliance that currently exists has no easy answer. Although one might think that the literature on why states comply with international agreements would provide plenty of practical policy guidance about how to reduce noncompliance, it turns out to be less useful than one might hope. One reason for this is that the primary goal of the authors who have contributed to this literature is to characterize the motivation(s) for compliance as generally as possible, rather than to offer specific policy advice. The level of generalization is problematic because any number of quite different policy recommendations are consistent with most of the theories and authors rarely, if ever, say very much about the conditions under which each is most appropriate. Several of the theories are so general that it is not clear how they could be operationalized at all.

Another limiting aspect of the theoretical compliance literature is that evidence other than illustrative examples is rare and systematic comparisons of theories are rarer still. Given that there are a number of theories and that several of these theories contain contradictory prescriptions (e.g., enforce vs. don't enforce), anyone interested in reducing the compliance gap in connection with a specific agreement has good reason to be frustrated. At best, the current theories provide a list of potential solutions that need to be fitted to a specific implementation context, but they offer few guidelines for how to go about doing this.

Finally, in addition to a lack of specificity and rigorous collaborating evidence, there is the more subtle problem that theories rarely offer any help in identifying the subset of compliance strategies that states will collectively be willing to implement. This is a potentially crippling limitation that those studying compliance gaps should do everything in their power to remedy.

Notes

1. See George W. Downs, David M. Rocke, and Peter N. Barsoom, "Is the Good News about Compliance Good News about Cooperation?" *International Organization* 50, no. 3 (Autumn 1996): 390.

2. See Kal Raustiala and David G. Victor, "Biodiversity since Rio: The Future of the Convention on Biodiversity," *Environment* 38, no. 31 (1996); and James C. Murdoch and Thomas Sandler, "The Voluntary Provision of a Pure Public Good: The Case of Reduced

CFC Emissions and the Montreal Protocol," *Journal of Public Economics* 63 (1996): 331-49.

3. "Early Success Is Reported for Global Treaty Banning Landmines," *New York Times*, September 7, 2000.

4. "Europe: Draft-Dodging," *Economist* 356, no. 8184 (August 19, 2000): 45.

5. Ellen Lutz and Kathryn Sikkink, "International Human Rights Law and Practice in Latin America," *International Organization* 54, no. 3 (Summer 2000): 633-60.

6. Edith Brown Weiss and Harold K. Jacobson, *Engaging Countries: Strengthening Compliance with International Accords* (Cambridge, MA: MIT Press, 1998).

7. Weiss and Jacobson, *Engaging Countries*, 519.

8. This is not to imply that the records of some developing states are not better than those of some developed states. Brazil, for example, has a higher compliance rate in connection with both the London Convention and Montreal Protocol than does Russia. India has a better compliance record in connection with CITES and the Tropical Timber agreement than does Japan. This last is particularly surprising since skepticism in India about the justice of international environmental regimes in a world in which economic resources are so unequally distributed is rampant. This is especially true in connection with first world advocacy of environmentally conscious restrictions on unsustainable environmental practices—the very practices that allowed the developed world to achieve the industrialization that it did years ago—which will inevitably make "industrialization slower and more costly in comparative historical terms." See Weiss and Jacobson, *Engaging Countries*, 425; and Marcus Colchester, "The International Tropical Timber Organization: Kill or Cure for the Rainforests?" *Transnational Associations* 43, no. 4 (1991): 226-35.

9. Richard Benedick, *Ozone Diplomacy: New Dimensions in Safeguarding the Planet*, 2d ed. (Cambridge, MA: Harvard University Press, 1998).

10. The data are not yet available: Compliance data for Article 5 developing countries for 1998—the year at which they were to have frozen consumption of certain ozone-depleting chlorofluorocarbons at their 1995-97 average levels—will be published at the convention's 12th Meeting of Parties in December 2000.

11. Harold H. Koh, "Review Essay: Why Do Nations Obey International Law?" *Yale Law Journal* 106, no. 8 (June 1997): 2599-2660.

12. Peter M. Haas, "Why Comply? Or Some Hypotheses in Search of an Analyst," in Edith Brown Weiss, ed., *International Compliance with Nonbinding Accords*, ASIL Studies in Transnational Legal Policy, no. 29 (Washington, D.C.: American Society of International Law, 1997), 63, 69.

13. Thomas M. Franck, *Fairness in International Law and Institutions* (New York: Oxford University Press, 1995), 5.

14. Thomas M. Franck, *The Power of Legitimacy among Nations* (New York: Oxford University Press, 1990), 25.

15. For Franck, an important implication of the tension between "legitimacy" and "justice" is that the former tends to support the stability of the status quo, while the latter tends to undermine it. Franck, *Fairness in International Law*, chapter 2.

16. Andrew Moravcsik, *Liberalism and International Relations Theory*, Working Paper no. 92-6 (Center for International Affairs, Harvard University: 1992).

17. Anne-Marie Slaughter Burley, "Law among Liberal States: Liberal Internationalism and the Act of State Doctrine," *Columbia Law Review* 92, no. 8 (December 1992): 1907, 1920-1; and Anne-Marie Slaughter Burley, "International Law and International Relations Theory: A Dual Agenda," *American Journal of International Law* 87, no. 2

(April 1993): 205-39.

18. See, for example, Downs, Rocke, Barsoom, "Is the Good News about Compliance," 379; George W. Downs, "Enforcement and the Evolution of Cooperation," *Michigan Journal of International Law* 19: 319; Kenneth W. Abbott, "Modern International Relations Theory: A Prospectus for International Lawyers," *Yale Journal of International Law* 14, no. 2 (Summer 1989): 335, 411; John K. Setear, "An Iterative Perspective on Treaties: A Synthesis of International Relations Theory and International Law," *Harvard International Law Journal* 37 (Winter 1996): 139, 142-7; Duncan Snidal, "The Game Theory of International Politics," *World Politics* 38 (1985): 226; Robert O. Keohane, Jr., *After Hegemony: Cooperation and Discord in the World Political Economy* (Princeton, NJ: Princeton University Press, 1984); Robert O. Keohane, Jr., *International Institutions and State Power: Essays in International Relations Theory* (Boulder, CO: Westview Press, 1989); Lisa Martin, *Coercive Cooperation: Explaining Multilateral Economic Sanctions* (Princeton, NJ: Princeton University Press, 1992); James D. Morrow, *Game Theory for Political Scientists* (Princeton, NJ: Princeton University Press, 1994); and Todd Sandler, *Collective Action: Theory and Applications* (Ann Arbor, MI: University of Michigan Press, 1992).

19. For example, the preferences of states become increasingly free trade oriented as trade organizations, such as GATT/WTO, reduce the number and power of protectionist groups as inefficient import competing businesses gradually go out of business. See Michael J. Gilligan, *Empowering Exporters: Reciprocity, Delegation, and Collective Action in American Trade Policy* (Ann Arbor, University of Michigan Press, 1997).

20. George W. Downs and David M. Rocke, *Optimal Imperfection?: Domestic Uncertainty and Institutions in International Relations* (Princeton, NJ: Princeton University Press, 1995), chapter 4.

21. See Abram Chayes, Thomas Ehrlich, and Andreas Lowenfeld, *International Legal Process : Materials for an Introductory Course*, 2 vols. (Boston: Little Brown, 1968); Abram Chayes and Antonia Handler Chayes. *The New Sovereignty: Compliance with International Regulatory Agreements* (Cambridge, MA: Harvard University Press 1995); Abram Chayes, *The Cuban Missile Crisis: International Crises and the Role of Law* (New York: Oxford University Press, 1974).

22. Chayes and Chayes, *The New Sovereignty*, 10.

23. Chayes and Chayes, *The New Sovereignty*, 32-33.

24. Chayes and Chayes, *The New Sovereignty*, 109.

25. Chayes and Chayes, *The New Sovereignty*, 276-77.

26. Chayes and Chayes, *The New Sovereignty*, 282-85.

27. See characterization of Grotius in Hedley Bull, "The Emergence of a Universal International Society," in Hedley Bull and Adam Watson, eds., *The Expansion of International Society* (New York: Oxford University Press, 1984).

28. Alexander Wendt, *Social Theory of International Politics* (New York: Cambridge University Press, 1999).

29. See, for example, Harold H. Koh, "The 1998 Frankel Lecture: Bringing International Law Home," *Houston Law Review* 35 (1998): 623; Koh, "The 1994 Roscoe Pound Lecture: Transnational Legal Process," *Nebraska Law Review* 75 (1996): 181; Koh, "Why Do Nations Obey International Law," 2599; Koh, "Transnational Public Law Litigation," *Yale Law Journal* 100 (1991): 2347; Koh, "Refugees, the Courts, and the New World Order," *Utah Law Review* (1994): 999; and Koh, "The 'Haiti Paradigm' in United States Human Rights Policy," *Yale Law Journal* 103 (1994): 2391.

30. Koh, "Bringing International Law Home," 627.

31. Weiss and Jacobson, *Engaging Countries*, 548-51.

32. Weiss and Jacobson, *Engaging Countries*, 550.

33. See chapter 7 by Jeffrey Herbst in this volume.

34. Robert O. Koehane, Jr. and Marc A. Levy, eds., *Institutions for Environmental Aid: Pitfalls and Promise* (Cambridge, MA: MIT Press, 1996).

35. Barbara Connolly, "Increments for the Earth: The Politics of Environmental Aid," in Koehane and Levy, *Institutions for Environmental Aid*, 330.

36. As officials in developing states understand all too well, their states are not the only parties that contain inefficient institutions. David Fairman and Michael Ross observe that the costs of uncoordinated aid programs by developed states frequently outweigh their benefits. See Fairman and Ross, "Old Fads, New Lessons: Learning from Economic Development Assistance," in Koehane and Levy, *Institutions for Environmental Aid*, 45.

37. Fairman and Ross, "Old Fads."

38. Fairman and Ross, "Old Fads," 32.

39. Cord Jakobeit, "Nonstate Actors Leading the Way: Debt-for-Nature Swaps," in Koehane and Levy, *Institutions for Environmental Aid*, 133.

40. Michael Ross, "Conditionality and Logging Reform in the Tropics," in Koehane and Levy, *Institutions for Environmental Aid*, 167-98.

41. Benedick, *Ozone Diplomacy*.

42. Orval E. Nangle, "Stratospheric Ozone: United Sates Regulation of Chlorofluorocarbons," *Boston College Environmental Law Review* 16 (1989): 531-80.

2

The Institutional Dilemmas of Market Integration: Compliance and International Regimes for Trade and Finance

Kathleen R. McNamara

International economic interactions, a key component of globalization, have reached historic proportions. This level of globalization is not entirely new. Today's trade and capital flows match those of the last period of global capitalism, the end of the nineteenth century, despite some qualitative differences in the nature of these flows.[1] Yet the international institutional terrain within which this market integration is occurring is very different from any historical precedent. Building on the foundations provided by the Bretton Woods institutions established in the aftermath of World War II, today's international organizations and regimes attempt to govern the terms of globalization in ways that far exceed any such efforts at the turn of the previous century. At the same time, however, these governance efforts fall far short of a comprehensive global legal framework for economic integration. The goal of this chapter is to provide an overview (a) of the evolution of governance regimes regulating economic relations among states, and (b) of the nature of the compliance challenges faced in managing the terms of globalization. In particular, the chapter emphasizes the institutional dilemmas created by the deepening of international integration and the increasingly contentious nature of the issues being subjected to monetary and trade regimes. The interaction of domestic and international politics suggests that there may be self-limiting dynamics inherent in the expansion of governance: these dynamics will need to be overcome for globalization to continue.

The chapter proceeds as follows. First, it sets out a typology of regime types and asserts that trade and finance evidence very different modes of international regulation, from the highly institutionalized and legal formality of the trade regime to the weakly institutionalized, soft law of the international monetary regime. Then, taking these differences into account, the chapter evaluates compliance in these two realms. In doing so, it emphasizes the considerable challenges these developments present to the international system. The conclusion briefly outlines two alternative policy paths for addressing the institutional dilemmas of governing the global economy.

The Nature of the Institutional Dilemma

Before assessing the status of international regimes for trade and finance, it is necessary to lay out more fully the nature of the institutional dilemma posed by this era of globalization. Simply put, the thrust of international rulemaking efforts over the postwar period has been to encourage the dismantling of barriers to economic activity in order to promote the widening and deepening of markets. However, this "negative integration" may not ultimately succeed without concomitant efforts to negotiate, construct, and enforce positive rules, standards of behavior, and institutions capable of governing international markets, or "positive integration." As in the domestic setting, international markets are not sustainable without highly developed political and social frameworks for regulating economic interactions. However, except in the case of the European Union (EU), states have not moved very far in promoting such positive supranational integration.

Therefore, in the international arena, this disjuncture between positive and negative integration creates a vexing dilemma. It is unclear whether the international political community will fully engage with, much less be able to solve, the politically and socially divisive issues arising from the deepening penetration of trade and financial policy issues into the domestic realm, be it on national food safety standards or capital mobility. In the meantime, these developments have triggered clashes between competing institutions and values within nations. The most visible effect has been a vocal backlash against globalization, evidenced by protests against the World Trade Organization (WTO) and the Bretton Woods institutions in Seattle and elsewhere. In response, the international economic policy community has encouraged the institutions to remain true to their mandates: so the WTO stresses the goal of free trade, while the International Monetary Fund (IMF) pursues market reform. As the EU has found in pursuing its own internal market integration program, however, these efforts may not be enough as market integration deepens.

In sum, as will be shown, the international political system has developed a variety of ways to manage the terms of globalization, and compliance is quite high in certain areas, but, under the current arrangement, there remain certain critical tensions that polities and their leaders need to address. The international political economy thus is in an awkward and possibly untenable halfway house: it is neither fully integrated with a supranational institution to adjudicate across nations and competing values, nor is it still so closed that national policies can independently address the distributional issues that arise from the workings of national and international markets. The tensions inherent in this situation present a major challenge to policymakers seeking to find a better way forward.

Types of Regimes

The key question of this volume—to what degree is there a compliance gap in international law and organization?—can only be understood in the area of trade and finance within a broad context of mechanisms for managing international economic interactions. While some areas of international economic interaction are governed by international treaties and explicit legal mechanisms, an equal amount rely on much less legalized forms of governance to regulate activity. At the broadest level, then, a term like *international regimes* captures the elements that direct and coordinate contemporary international economic behavior. *Regimes*, broadly defined, can be understood as "principles, norms, rules, and decision-making procedures around which actor expectations converge in a given issue area."[2]

These international regimes vary greatly along three continua: (1) institutional formality; (2) normative precision; and (3) the nature of their enforcement mechanisms.[3] First, the institutional form can range from formal to informal. That is, the regime may take on a concrete organizational presence, with a secretariat, bureaucracy, and significant resources, such as the WTO. Or it may exist only as an informal institution based on discrete, although perhaps regular, interactions, and supported by national-level resources and personnel, such as the Group of Seven (G-7) summit process. Interactions may be bilateral or between states and international organizations, such as the IMF, pursued in a relatively informal way, not bound by treaty rules but rather by power or organizational dynamics. In its most informal guise, a regime may be a purely ideational, or social, institution that exists as shared ideas and expectations about causal relationships and normative values, such as the norm of free trade or a commitment to a balanced budget.

Second, a regime can formally specify standards of conduct with a great degree of precision, or it can rest on a more informal, but perhaps no less powerful, set of shared expectations or norms about the rules of behavior in the international realm. For example, the EU's Maastricht Treaty gave legal status to precise numerical targets for the national budget deficits of each member state, while in contrast, less precise rules concerning the importance of transparency and information have marked the discussions of the global financial architecture to date.

Finally, the nature of enforcement mechanisms differs importantly across issue areas in terms of how disputes are mediated and standards enforced. Enforcement in international regimes can range from formalized, third-party dispute arrangements with sanctions for noncompliance, to collective or bilateral compliance mechanisms consisting of material rewards or sanctions, to more informal mechanisms, such as persuasion efforts by political actors, sometimes reinforced by market mechanisms for compliance with certain international standards.

These elements—institutional formality, rule precision, and enforcement mechanisms—do not necessarily move together, appearing in a variety of different combinations. These elements also do not appear to readily map onto specific outcomes of compliance or noncompliance, that is, institutional formality does not always correspond to a high likelihood of compliance and so on. The case study discussion below will demonstrate the diversity that exists across these categories in the global trade and finance setting.

The Institutional Landscape

Today's international trade and monetary regimes share a strong commonality: they were both formed in the aftermath of World War II as the Cold War was just beginning. The commitment by the great powers, particularly the United States, to maintaining open international markets as a bulwark against war and communism drove the initial establishment and continued support for the international economic institutions (e.g., the General Agreement on Tariffs and Trade [GATT], the IMF, and the World Bank). This geopolitically and ideologically driven national commitment, forged in the aftermath of war, paralleled that in the political-security realm. Geopolitics and great power determination may have provided the foundation for the international organization of economic policy, but further legalization and policy coordination has been encouraged as well by the interests of private actors, which have benefited from further liberalization and stabilization of global markets.[4] As discussed below, however, while regimes and rules have been constructed to meet the demands of globalized business, it has proven harder to provide for the politically important task of dealing with the concerns of those less well placed to profit from the global economy.

Despite their shared policy roots, trade and finance inhabit two different worlds in terms of their international regime characteristics. Drawing on the typology outlined above, the trade area can be characterized as being underpinned by a highly formalized international institution, the WTO, which has a strong basis in treaty law. International rules, directed toward the goal of free trade, are specified very precisely in the body of law built up over decades in the GATT, the WTO's precursor. Enforcement of the trade rules is also highly routinized and legalized in the WTO's third-party dispute mechanism. In the sovereignty-conscious finance area, however, the character of governance is very different. Institutionally, it is not a highly legalized or formalized regime, and its legitimacy and causal force rest on a very different basis from the trade regime. In international finance, rules take the form of normative standards or policy recommendations, not legal treaties. These norms are promoted by international organizations such as the IMF and, to a lesser extent, the Bank for International Settlements (BIS) and the Organization for Economic Cooperation and Development (OECD). The precision of these rules varies, from the general neoliberal norms of "good financial housekeeping" to the more detailed policy reform packages of IMF loan conditionality programs. Rules may thus be more informal, in the sense of not being embodied in international treaties, but perhaps very precise, in the sense of IMF codes. In the finance area, we have also seen the development of ad hoc, private actor collaboration on standards, such as in the case of the Basle Accords of the 1980s on banking standards.[5] Finally, the nature of the enforcement mechanism is quite distinct in the finance realm. Instead of a legalized, third-party dispute mechanism, enforcement of the norms of the international financial regime tend to be enforced through socialization among transnational epistemic communities or expert groups, through loan conditionality programs designed by the IMF to promote these norms, or through the pressures of market actors who pass judgment on the policies pursued by nation-states by investing or divesting of national assets.

Having provided this brief overview of the trade and finance regimes, the chapter next examines each area in more detail.

International Trade and Compliance

Whereas the GATT required states to act to meet international treaty agreements to decrease tariffs and nontariff barriers to trade, the WTO requires a deeper level of compliance to international regimes by asking states to act on authoritative decisions on the part of third-party legal adjudicators. The GATT established rules of engagement in the world economy in which compliance was achieved relatively simply by the act of tariff reduction, while the WTO sets up a court to adjudicate among the conflicting claims of nation-states as to how those rules should be applied. As the rules governing trade have become more complex over time to deal with nontariff barriers and thus have penetrated more deeply into the national regulatory environments, such a decision making mechanism is both more necessary and more problematic. As such, it demonstrates some of the promises and pitfalls of attempting to increase institutionalization and compliance more generally in the international system.

The evolution of the international trading system since World War II clearly has been toward increasing openness, in line with the original intentions of the GATT founders in 1947. While the establishment of the Havana Charter's proposed International Trade Organization (ITO), a highly institutionalized supranational institution, was thwarted by opposition in the U.S. Senate in the late 1940s, the less ambitious GATT succeeded in rapidly reducing the high tariffs of the immediate postwar period.

As the GATT progressed through subsequent rounds of negotiations, tariffs were cut or removed altogether on a wide (and widening) range of products, a process which helped to stimulate a huge increase in the quantity of international trade. The first five rounds achieved a total reduction in tariffs of 73 percent, and the high point for tariff reductions was the sixth round (known as the Kennedy round), which achieved a 35 percent reduction.[6] GATT's coverage also expanded until it came close to the much more comprehensive coverage of the original Havana Charter. By 1993, at the conclusion of the Uruguay Round, the international community reached important new agreements on services and on intellectual property rights, as well as bringing agriculture into the system for the first time. These agreements were presented as a single package: countries could no longer "opt out" of "side codes" as they could at the Tokyo Round of the late 1970s.

The Uruguay Round also set up an agenda for ongoing negotiations, which has ensured the continuing expansion of multilateral trade agreements. Three significant agreements were concluded in 1997, eliminating customs tariffs on information technology, liberalizing telecommunications services, and, most importantly, liberalizing financial services by dismantling market access and foreign investment barriers. All these agreements are, of course, subject to WTO dispute settlement procedures, discussed further below.[7]

Despite this expanding coverage of trade law, and the potentially disruptive processes of adjustment entailed by the concomitant expansion of trade, most countries have complied with their obligations under international trade law most of the time.[8] This achievement is even more impressive given that participation in GATT also expanded over time, creating an extraordinarily heterogeneous group of states.[9] As of April 2003, membership of the WTO had reached 146 states, accounting for 97 percent of world trade, and is growing, with additional states negotiating membership.[10] Unlike some other areas of international law, many types of trading restrictions (such as tariffs or quotas) are not only clearly visible, but also are unambiguously under the control of the national government, since control of movements across borders is one of the most basic functions of governance and attributes of sovereignty. In the case of tariff cuts, for example, implementation *is* compliance.[11]

However, there are three arguments that, particularly in the context of the contentious 1999 Seattle WTO meetings, undercut this optimistic picture of generally high compliance. First, critics have been concerned that powerful countries have been able to manipulate GATT/WTO regulations in order to effectively evade them. For example, although the European Economic Community (EEC) did not appear to satisfy the letter of the law, it was nonetheless granted an Article XXIV exception to GATT rules against preferential trading arrangements. Second, there have been accusations that reductions in tariff barriers have been matched by a growth in nontariff barriers to trade, and that certain areas, such as agriculture, remain stubbornly resistant to change, as Chung-in Moon's chapter in this volume attests in the Korean case.[12] In addition to administrative barriers to certain products or services, these actions also include unilateral retaliatory measures against so-called unfair trade practices, such as antidumping rules or countervailing duties. Countries that have made use of the latter measures, chiefly the United States, justify their actions by claiming that they are supporting the international trade regime by punishing countries which violate its rules. Such unilateral claims should be harder to support now that the WTO has enhanced enforcement procedures, although the WTO's main method of enforcement—permitting the plaintiff to undertake retaliatory action—effectively legitimates unilateral action.

Finally, there have been a wide range of trade disputes, both high and low profile. When thinking about compliance, it is worth considering whether this indicates the fragility of the trade system or the health of its laws and norms. If violators are ignored, international law is probably weak, but if violators are at least subject to public scrutiny and/or criticism, then that may be good news for the system. Indeed, many of these recent disputes have been resolved within the dispute settlement mechanism of the WTO. Even member states accused of a breach of trade law have agreed to adjudication, suggesting a deeper level of compliance. The following section describes the dispute settlement process and analyzes the data so far.

The Dispute Settlement Process and Judicialization in the World Trade Organization

The deeper institutionalization of the WTO is a path-breaking development in international rulemaking. The idea of allowing an international arbitrator to decide on the international rule of law runs directly counter to the deeply held view of the international system as an anarchical one without legitimate hierarchy of governance. The WTO, therefore, represents a significant step forward in the institutionalization of international law. However, as will be discussed below, it is not clear that the net effect on management of the global political economy will be positive.

The biggest change from the GATT years has been the increased automaticity of the dispute settlement process. The appointment of a panel and the adoption of the panel report can only be blocked if there is a consensus against it. The WTO also has significant new powers of enforcement, although this ultimately rests on the states, since the real sanction is the power to unleash retaliation by the plaintiff. If adequate satisfaction (reform or recompense through other concessions) is not forthcoming, then the plaintiff is automatically granted the authorization to suspend trade concessions equivalent to the damage it is suffering.

The increased judicialization of dispute settlement is potentially a great equalizer: in theory it gives all WTO members equal weight and WTO members do not have the option to opt out of the process. Although the developed countries still have significant powers of dissuasion, which may prevent developing countries from bringing some issues before the WTO, the developing countries have begun to use the dispute settlement system regularly, which was not the case under the GATT.

To evaluate the dispute resolution process, we can examine the results of cases filed up to 2000 to get a sense of how the system is developing.[13] As of 2000, 110 cases had been filed, of these, 47 went to panels, or 43 percent.[14] This compares with 53 percent of disputed cases going to a panel in the less developed GATT system of the 1980s, so we observe that a somewhat smaller percentage of WTO cases have been carried to the stage of appointing a panel.[15]

Given the relative youth of the system, it would be premature to try to assess the efficacy of WTO dispute resolution. If usage is a valid measure of success, then the WTO's dispute settlement mechanism has been even more "successful" than the GATT's, as:

> [T]he volume of cases during the first three years of the WTO disputes procedure is almost 90 percent greater than the highest volume ever achieved by the GATT disputes procedure—the volume achieved during the last four full years of normal GATT operations. The volume of WTO complaints is about 60 percent higher than the old GATT procedure would have achieved if its caseload had continued to increase at the rate of the past 14 years. Measured either way, the increase in volume has certainly been large enough to be considered a significant event.[16]

Unfortunately, Hudec's analysis and most of the rest of the rather sparse literature on dispute settlement focus on the procedural outcomes (i.e., whether the dispute resulted in settlement, withdrawal, or a ruling), rather than following up on the degree of implementation of rulings.[17] However a survey of the state of play on WTO disputes is available on the WTO's website (www.wto.org), which includes information on the implementation status of adopted reports. Of the thirty-eight cases completed as of September 2000, the implementation status was as follows: (1) in seven cases there was no implementation issue due to the result and, in one further case, the original panel was reconvened;[17] (2) in twenty-three cases the respondent had either complied, announced measures that would bring it into compliance, or announced its intention to implement the recommendations of the dispute settlement body; and (3) in four of the more recent cases the respondent was still "studying ways in which to implement the recommendations of the DSB [Dispute Settlement Board]." So, overall, compliance has been achieved in the majority of cases, although the current sample is rather small.

What of the four remaining cases in which some form of noncompliance is manifest? In two cases the defendants (Australia and Brazil) did take action to implement the findings of the DSB, but the WTO then determined that their action was insufficient. In one of these cases, the WTO has also determined that the plaintiff, Canada, may impose countermeasures against Brazil for noncompliance, suspending concessions on Can. $344.4 million of Brazilian imports. The other two cases involve a heavyweight clash between the EU and U.S. export interests. In the bananas case, the EU is moving to a tariff system (and hence compliance) in a two-stage process but, in the meantime, the WTO has granted the United States and Ecuador the right to impose countermeasures against a total of U.S. $393.0 million of EU imports. The EU has been more recalcitrant in the case involving hormone treated beef, publicly backing down on an initial announcement that it would comply. As a result, the WTO granted the United States and Canada the right to impose countermeasures against EU imports amounting to $202 million and Can. $75 million, respectively.

How should we evaluate these cases in terms of compliance? In the cases involving Australia and Brazil, both countries claimed to have implemented the findings of the DSB and, indeed, took some measures in that direction, although the DSB found the measures to be insufficient. They also accepted the WTO's authority to determine the level of sanctions imposed against them. As for the two EU cases, both might seem to demonstrate noncompliance, as the EU has failed to implement the findings of the authoritative body. However, the EU has accepted that the WTO has the authority to impose sanctions against it for its noncompliance and, in the beef hormones case, the EU attempted to offer compensation to the plaintiffs for its noncompliance. Therefore, the plaintiffs have clearly submitted to the authority of the WTO. As in the case of domestic law, the submission of defendants to the penalty of law does not weaken the judicial system, but rather implies the continued legitimacy of that legal system.

Though the data are not yet conclusive, the general picture on judicialization and compliance in the international trade regime remains a relatively positive one. Simple statistics, however, do not provide a complete picture of the state of the WTO's dispute settlement mechanism. Perhaps the biggest question hanging over it is whether the success of the process is dependent on the restraint of plaintiffs in not pushing controversial cases in which defendants would reject a ruling against them. For example, the EU and other potential plaintiffs have resisted pursuing their case against Washington's "Helms Burton" restrictions on trade against Cuba, even though the provisions of this bill would appear to violate WTO regulations. To assess fully the effectiveness of the WTO and to gauge the level of compliance, it would also be helpful to have a better sense of whether some important disputes are not being brought up for consideration. If power politics rather than international law is driving the pattern of trade policies and trade outcomes, then the inclusion of these cases would presumably present a different picture of compliance.

Emerging Issues in Trade and Compliance

Perhaps the most challenging development in the area of international trade law
has been the rise of "trade and" issues, in which trade law has become involved
in new areas of policy, for example, "trade and the environment." This is a result, in part, of the dynamic effects of increased globalization and legalization of
the trade regime. As trade liberalization has overcome barriers at the border (tariffs, quotas), there has been a rising awareness of the impact of internal barriers
(competition law, national standard setting). There has been a growth as well in
the political activities of domestic advocacy groups seeking to limit trade liberalization in order to protect the environment or workers. However, this expansion of trade law could ultimately threaten the legitimacy and effective functioning of the international trade regime, as it pushes the WTO into new areas in
which it lacks both the expertise and the political authority to regulate. While the
WTO offers a new and deepened institutional mechanism for extending law, it is
not yet clear how or whether it will succeed in getting states to actually comply
with its regulations and settlements. The expansion of its powers may yet backfire, a danger that grows as the expansion of its remit leads it into ever more
controversial areas of regulation. Simultaneous change on two dimensions, its
powers and scope, make the future of the WTO particularly hard to predict.

Dunoff argues that these "trade and . . ." issues are not only taking the WTO
into contentious territory where it lacks expertise and institutional competence,
but they also could jeopardize the political understandings supporting the trade
regime and thereby undermine its continued viability.[18] In other areas, such as
competition, intellectual property, and investment, there is pressure on the WTO
to expand its activities into areas where there is little consensus on what the underlying principles should be. For example, in the area of competition policy
there are significant divisions within the developed world, including divergent
approaches to competition policy in the EU and in the United States. American
competition policy basically consists of stringent antitrust law with semiprivat-
ized enforcement mechanisms (private individuals and corporations can sue for
damages if they have been adversely affected by anticompetitive practices). The
EU's approach to competition law, on the other hand, has been conditioned,
from the outset, by its drive to create a single market among its member states.[19]
In contrast, there is as yet no clear and committed consensus among the global
trade regime participants on acceptable, common rules in the area of competition
policy.

One area where the developing and the developed world seem intractably
divided is intellectual property. The agreement on Trade Related Intellectual
Property (TRIPs) does not mask the continuing divergence between the interests
of the developed countries, which seek to protect a large range of intellectual
property rights, and the less developed, which do not. Critics of the TRIPs
agreement point out that, "unlike domestic legislation, which seeks to balance
the economic interests of owners of intellectual property against the public in-

terest in having access to new knowledge, the TRIPs Agreement is concerned primarily with protection and not, as such, with dissemination."[20] This imbalance could even render the TRIPs agreement impotent. Even if states have laws on their statute books which formally comply with the TRIPs agreement, the intent of the agreement can easily be evaded by a failure to enforce these laws. For example, Indonesia has good copyright laws, yet its inability or unwillingness to enforce them renders them meaningless and ensures that it is relatively easy to purchase pirated products there. Chung-in Moon's chapter in this volume details the obstacles to compliance in the Korean case as well.

Goldstein and Martin make a related argument about the increased legalization of the WTO, arguing that the deepening and broadening of trade law may be creating a political backlash that will ultimately undermine support for the regime.[21] The link for them is in the effects of increasing legalization on interest group mobilization. They hypothesize that the change in the nature of information generated through the WTO process, in contrast to the GATT regime, may change the political balance by increasing mobilization of anti-trade groups. They note, however, that it is not yet possible to say a priori what the overall policy effect on trade may be, as it might also prompt increased mobilization on the part of pro-trade groups. However, their insight, that increased legalization may not automatically mean more cooperation toward freer markets, dovetails with Dunoff's claims about the difficulties inherent in the deepening of the trade regime and its ambitions.

In sum, the extension of the trade regime into a more legalized, formalized institution creates a range of potential obstacles to compliance. The introduction of nontraditional trade issues beyond tariff barriers will tend to increase pressures to come to an agreement even when there is no policy consensus across national settings. It may also undermine the ideational basis for the existing consensus by bringing in noneconomic values, usually with strong domestic constituencies, that challenge free trade. The WTO lacks the resources and legitimacy to set global priorities among competing goals beyond a straight commitment to economic efficiency through the dismantling of barriers to trade. "Trade and" issues raise important distributive questions, which undermine the idea that an international trade regime is desirable as a way of providing for some aggregate optimal level of welfare. Finally, the extension of the trade regime raises the question of the proper linkage between international and domestic legal regimes, moving far from the commitment to protection of national social policy which underpinned the postwar Bretton Woods arrangement.[22] From this perspective, the current expansion of the trade regime endangers the regime itself by pushing it into areas that are highly contested in the domestic polity, even as it lacks the capabilities to deal with such repercussions adequately. Unless institutional strategies are devised for addressing these issues, a broadening of the agenda is likely to widen the "compliance gap" and undermine support for the WTO.

International Finance and Compliance

The management of international financial relations is much less judicialized than is trade. The key institution for the regulation of international financial matters is the IMF, which is not as legally formalized in its capacities as the WTO.[23] Only the agreement to maintain current account convertibility, which enables trade flows, is embodied in the original IMF treaty and is currently applicable to states, but compliance is voluntary and has no legal consequences.[24] In general, the IMF has expanded the purview of its activities beyond these treaty-based, exchange rate and monetary regime activities to areas which span training and technical assistance, macroeconomic policy surveillance, structural adjustment programs for the developing states, postcommunist transition programs in the East, and the regulation of financial markets and the management of financial crises.[25]

The basis for the IMF's regulation of the international financial system might be thought of as a combination of ideological power, the ability to provide credibility, and incentives in terms of the material benefits the IMF can offer to those ready to comply with its standards. While there is assessment of policy compliance in the form of the IMF judgments and market reactions, there is no judicial system of third-party review and adjudication as in the trade regime. The following section thus discusses the issues raised by the IMF's role in norm setting, and the market and institutional incentives for states to comply with these norms. The section concludes with a discussion (1) of more conventional compliance issues regarding the use of sanctioning practices in IMF programs, and (2) of some recent work on the more limited question of compliance and the legal rules for current account convertibility.

The international financial regime is faced with the same institutional dilemmas that confront the trade area, as negative integration (the increase in capital mobility and the merging of financial markets) is creating a demand for more positive integration at the same time as it creates political divisions which make global governance more difficult. However, the nature of the compliance challenge appears to differ across trade and money in important ways. It is generally thought that, while the collective action problem in trade is to get states to "resist the protectionist temptation," capital mobility has a market-driven dynamic towards liberalization. Although in recent years there has been a growing normative commitment to capital mobility, most political leaders and business elites also believe that some international regulation and/or laws are necessary to promote system stability through crisis prevention and management. The collective action problem, therefore, is "who will act to stabilize the system?" The answer has overwhelmingly been: "the United States." In times of crisis, U.S. officials repeatedly have played a key role in coordinating financial resources to calm financial markets.

A key overarching norm in the international financial realm is that of "good housekeeping" on the part of national governments, which is viewed by many as the best way to ensure the stability of the system. This entails following neoliberal policies emphasizing balanced national budgets, low inflation, central bank independence, transparency in national accounting, and a sustainable balance of payments position. Although IMF loan conditionality plays an important role, the incentives for compliance with these norms in the area of finance are also reinforced by the perception that markets favor these policies. However, markets, in turn, rely on information and economic ideas that originate, in large part, from international organizations, political elites, and the larger expert consensus among policy economists underlining the endogeneity of this process and the important standard-setting role played by such groups. Over the years, the IMF has created and deliberately expanded its role in this regard through the gradual expansion of the scope and depth of "surveillance" and the publicity accorded to this process.[26]

In the case of its lending programs, the IMF not only sets standards and provides publicized assessments of performance; it also decides the penalties and rewards for compliance. IMF conditionality is an important tool for encouraging compliance with norms of economic governance, but, since it is invariably imposed on countries in the throes of severe economic difficulties, it is not surprising that many IMF loan programs have experienced compliance problems. These have not been restricted to the problems that inevitably attend the IMF's short-term lending programs (due to the desperate nature of the economic situations in which such programs are initiated). Edwards draws attention to the fact that "of the thirty EFF [Extended Fund Facility] programs initiated prior to January 1, 1985, twenty-four were either renegotiated or had payments interrupted. Sixteen of the twenty-four were canceled outright by the Fund." Moreover, only one-quarter of the Extended Structural Adjustment Facility arrangements have been completed without interruption.[27]

The combination, in a single organization, of the functions of standard setting and assessment is problematic. The IMF sometimes has an incentive to interpret standards "creatively" when it is assessing a country to which it is going to lend money (it is easier to lend money if the IMF says that Brazil is meeting standards, even when it is not). If the assessment standards and criteria are transparent, on the other hand, then the market can use them as a guide for evaluation as well. In this sense, assessment is part of enforcement. This relationship creates an incentive to keep the assessment criteria opaque to allow room for maneuver in those cases with geopolitical implications.

Perhaps the easiest place to discern the level of compliance is in the more limited area of current account convertibility. As Simmons points out, this is the only area in that there is an actual legal requirement for IMF members, that is, to keep their current account free from restrictions, in order to facilitate trade across national borders.[28] Other financial areas are ruled by norms of good economic governance that are not clearly laid out, and which are, moreover, subject to constant revision and renegotiation. Simmons is currently undertaking a detailed empirical study on compliance.[29] Despite the incentives for noncompliance, such as to pursue developmental objectives or to deal with balance of payments problems, most countries have complied with their obligations in the area of current account convertibility. It is true, however, that a large number of countries have chosen to retain a "transitional" status that absolves them from the obligation to liberalize their current accounts.

Nonetheless, the record of compliance is reasonably impressive. Of the 110 countries in Simmons' data set (i.e., those countries that had undertaken the obligation from 1967 to 1995), only twenty-five have some period of noncompliance and in five of those cases it was relatively brief (less than 20 percent of the total time period). Given the severity of balance of payments problems experienced by many of these countries over this time period (e.g., many suffered debt crises), this is an impressive record of compliance. Furthermore, Simmons' preliminary findings suggest that, while states are not always capable of or willing to comply with the law on current account convertibility, commitment to the rules does influence state behavior in this area. Moreover, current account policies are only one aspect of the monetary regime embodied by the IMF, although they are a key to removal of barriers to global transactions.

The IMF has also been called on to play a part in the management of financial crises, most recently the debt crisis of the 1980s, the Mexican peso crisis of 1994, and the Asian crisis of 1997-1998. However, the very occurrence of these crises in states purported to be following many of the precepts of the IMF and the difficulty of reversing their course have prompted some rethinking of the models used by economists in promoting liberalization. The crises have slowed the effort to expand the realm of international norm setting by making capital account convertibility part of the IMF's remit. The crises have also provoked a debate about what further measures need to be undertaken to preempt future crises and added to the ongoing debate about the best way to deal with economic crises, given that they cannot be entirely prevented.

The response to the Asian crisis, in particular, brought forth a slew of proposals for reforming the "international financial architecture."[30] One widely touted conclusion was that international financial markets can only be stabilized if domestic financial regulation is improved (e.g., standards of reporting for banks) and many of the proposals include measures to allow greater international scrutiny or even supervision of domestic financial regulation. However, as with the "trade and" issues, any move to expand international oversight of nationally controlled policy arenas is bound to arouse controversy and is likely to be difficult to implement. As Chung-in Moon's chapter on Korea indicates, however, the incentives to comply with IMF standards can be strong if both the public sense of crisis and the domestic willingness to reform are deep enough.

Conclusion: Global Governance in Trade and Finance

Despite the publicity given to trade disputes and financial crises, compliance with the international laws and norms that govern economic life is relatively high. Building on the foundations established at Bretton Woods, a mixture of norms, formal institutions, and legal mechanisms has promoted rapid market integration in goods, services, and money through the postwar era.

Nonetheless, while the removal of barriers to market transactions, or negative integration, has proceeded apace, the necessary corollary, the proactive management and regulation of those markets, or positive integration, has proven problematic. As markets become more and more integrated, disparate voices have called for more attention to the distributional, social, and environmental effects of global capitalism. The existing institutional pillars, the WTO and the IMF, on which the system rests may not be ready to provide a suitable foundation for the building of a more comprehensive institutional framework for global economic governance, however. At this point, they lack the legitimacy, authority, and institutional capacity to weigh competing values across nations and to make difficult decisions regarding regulatory and redistributive policies that could affect the stability of both international markets and national societies. This makes creating new policies difficult and the likelihood of ensuring compliance with new and farther-reaching global norms, standards, and laws rather low. There would appear to be a number of alternative policy paths forward, depending on whether nations choose to adopt an incremental or reformist approach.

An incremental approach would essentially accept the status quo and do little to seek to change it. It would allow the international economic system to reach its own political limits, in the process slowing the pace of globalization and reorienting trade and finance toward national regulation. The tensions, as described in this chapter, between the policy challenges presented by globalization and the mandates of the existing international institutions may force retrenchment in the reach and purview of the WTO and the IMF. The WTO protests in Seattle, after all, did correspond with a considerably scaled back schedule for further trade rounds, and it may be that the most likely course will be a much slower and more incremental movement forward in terms of liberalization of nontariff barriers in any case. However, the WTO dispute resolution program has taken on a dynamic of its own, and, while the political environment will affect the types of cases brought before the court, it is difficult to predict how this will play out. If the WTO takes on too many controversial cases, however, its own legitimacy may well be weakened, perhaps resulting in a reluctance on the part of litigants to use the WTO option.

In the case of the IMF, what evolves from a "do nothing" scenario may depend on the economic context: as long as growth remains strong and financial stability seems secure, political pressure for the reform of IMF programs may abate. When financial stability is again threatened, however, more pressure and scrutiny will be put on the IMF, from both the developed and developing states. Some change might be possible at the margins in both the IMF and the WTO, but it is unlikely that such pressures will on their own produce deep organizational reform. As Finnemore and Barnett note, the tendency for most international organizations is to embrace stasis rather than reform, and Stiglitz's account of the problematic culture and operation of the IMF does not reassure us otherwise.[31]

A reformist approach, on the other hand, would accept the need for international governance, while seeking to improve the existing institutions and to create others to address gaps in governance. One key criterion for achieving such ambitious goals would be to devise a way of broadening societal representation within the trade and finance regimes, a step that would enhance their democratic legitimacy.

Providing a place and giving a voice to social groups traditionally underrepresented in the dominant international regimes would go some way toward establishing a more inclusive dialogue on what constitutes good governance of the international economy. At present, there is a widely held perception that the interests of big business have been effectively represented in the WTO and IMF, while workers and members of various social movements have not. Some labor unions claim that the WTO and the IMF have placed inordinate burdens on workers.[32] They argue that the WTO disallows certain barriers to trade that function to protect workers by retarding unfair trade, while the IMF pursues structural adjustment programs that disproportionately affect the working poor. Environmental groups protest the lack of attention to the ecological effects of WTO and IMF policies, from rulings against trade discrimination based on environmental grounds to the effects of heavy debt loads on the resource policies of developing nations.[33]

One strategy would be to provide more avenues for input in policy formation on the part of labor representatives and nongovernmental organizations (NGOs), an approach that seems to have improved both the policy record of the World Bank and public perceptions of it. A second strategy would be to strengthen those international organizations designed to deal with these issues, such as the International Labor Organization, and to create stronger channels of communication between them and the WTO and IMF. Since the United Nations is more representative of the world's peoples and nations, it may be able, at least theoretically, to adjudicate across a broader set of claims than can those bodies focused solely on traditional trade and finance issues. As in the domestic setting, the various specialized policy instruments need effective interlocutors in other areas of policy. In recent years, however, most U.N. agencies have not enjoyed as much or as consistent political support from the national governments of some developed countries as have the WTO and IMF. It would presumably take a severe crisis of confidence in the current global governance scheme for states to consider moving toward this model.[34]

The development of a more inclusive dialogue and a broader social base for trade and financial policy at the level of international organizations is a necessary step toward the resolution of the institutional dilemmas created by rapid and deep market integration across national borders. However, these international organizations will have to work hard to provide the democratic accountability necessary for more proactive regulatory policymaking of the sort demanded by the critics of the current regime. Increased transparency and communication will be necessary, but even the European Union, with its panoply of institutions designed to address many of the quandaries discussed in this chapter, is not immune from widespread criticism about its alleged democratic deficit.[35] At the start of the twenty-first century, compliance with the existing international market opening rules promoting globalization may be relatively high, but this globalization has also posed new and difficult challenges to the WTO and the IMF, as well as to the international community as a whole.

Notes

1. Jeffrey Sachs and Andrew Warner, "Economics Reform and the Process of Global Integration," Brookings Papers on Economic Activity 1 (1998); Michael Bordo, Barry Eichengreen, and Douglas Irwin, "Is Globalization Today Really Different than Globalization a Hundred Years Ago?" National Bureau of Economic Research (NBER) Working Paper 7195 (June 1999); and Richard E. Baldwin and Philippe Martin, "Two Waves of Globalisation: Superficial Similarities, Fundamental Differences," NBER Working Paper 6904 (January 1999).

2. Stephen D. Krasner, "Structural Causes and Regime Consequences: Regimes as Intervening Variables," in Stephen D. Krasner, ed., *International Regimes* (Ithaca, NY: Cornell University Press, 1983), 1.

3. See Kenneth W. Abbott, Robert O. Keohane, Andrew Moravcsik, Anne-Marie Slaughter, and Duncan Snidal, "The Concept of Legalization," *International Organization* 54, no. 3 (Summer 2000) for an alternative typology for assessing the relative legalization of international regimes.

4. Judith Goldstein and Lisa L. Martin, "Legalization, Trade Liberalization, and Domestic Politics: A Cautionary Note," *International Organization* 54, no. 3 (Summer 2000); Alec Stone Sweet, "Judicialization and the Construction of Governance," *Comparative Political Studies* 32, no. 2 (April 1999): 147-84.

5. Ethan Kapstein, "Between Power and Purpose: Central Bankers and the Politics of Regulatory Convergence," *International Organization* 46, no. 1 (Winter 1992).

6. Joan Spero and Jeffrey Hart, *The Politics of International Economic Relations* (New York: St. Martin's Press, 1997), 57.

7. See Charles Owen Verrill, "International Trade," *International Lawyer* 32, no. 2 (1998).

8. It is also true that many countries have made, or are making, full use of the leeway that the system grants them, whether it is a grace period in which to implement their obligation or an opportunity to opt out of some subset of obligations.

9. Twenty-three countries participated in the 1947 Geneva round, 120 participated in the Uruguay round.

10. Information was retrieved from www.wto.org/wto/inbrief/inbr02.htm.

11. This is not, of course, true of all other areas of trade law.

12. See Jagdish Bhagwati, *The World Trading System at Risk* (Princeton, NJ: Princeton University Press, 1991).

13. The most recent cases are excluded as they have not had time to be resolved.

14. Annual Report (2001), *Overview of the State of Play of WTO Disputes*, Dispute Settlement Body, World Trade Organization, WT/DSB/26/Add. 1, October 12, 2001.

15. Robert E. Hudec, "The New WTO Dispute Settlement Procedure: An Overview of the First Three Years," *Minnesota Journal of Global Trade* 8 (1999).

16. Hudec, "The New WTO Dispute Settlement Procedure."

17. Keisuke Iida does include substantive outcomes in his measure of the degree of "satisfaction" obtained by the plaintiff but, as his focus is elsewhere (on the influence of power over outcomes), he simply uses the variable in his regression analysis without giving any breakdown of its distribution. See Iida, "Between Power and Principle: Multilateral Trade Dispute Settlement Revisited," paper delivered at the APSA Annual Meeting, September 2-5, 1999.

18. Jeffrey Dunoff, "'Trade and:' Recent Developments in Trade Policy and Scholarship and Their Surprising Political Implications," *Northwestern Journal of International Law and Business* 17, no. 2/3 (Winter-Spring 1996-97): 579-74. See also Jeffrey Dunoff, "The Death of the Trade Regime," *European Journal of International Law* 733 (1999).

19. There is also significant variation within the EU on certain issues of competition policy. Recent reforms in EU member states highlight the way in which different varieties of capitalism are supported by different forms of competition policy, which suggests the difficulty or inadvisability of formulating a global competition policy. See Amanda Dickins and Valerie Hahn, "Competition Policy and 'Varieties of Capitalism' in the European Union: Putting Recent Reform in German and UK Competition Policy into Comparative Perspective," paper presented to the APSA Annual Meetings, September 2-5, 1999.

20. Ruth Gana, "Prospect for Developing Countries under the TRIPs Agreement," *Vanderbilt Journal of Transnational Law*, 29 (1996): 742.

21. Goldstein and Martin, "Legalization, Trade Liberalization, and Domestic Politics."

22. John Gerard Ruggie, "International Regimes, Transactions and Change: Embedded Liberalism in the Postwar Economic Order," in Krasner, *International Regimes*, 195-232.

23. This discussion does not examine the activities of the G-7 in the financial realm. The G-7 has traditionally dealt with financial stabilization in a less systematic and perhaps less effective way. See Michael Webb, *The Political Economy of Policy Coordination* (Ithaca, NY: Cornell University Press, 1995) for an assessment of the G-7 process.

24. Beth Simmons, "International Law and State Behavior: Commitment and Compliance in International Monetary Affairs," *American Political Science Review* 94, no. 4 (December 2000): 819-35.

25. Robert O'Brien, Anne Marie Goetz, Jan Aart Scholte, and Marc Williams, *Contesting Global Governance: Multilateral Economic Institutions and Global Social Movements* (Boston: Cambridge University Press, 2000), 159.

26. For an authoritative account of the development of IMF surveillance, see Harold James, "The Historical Development of the Principle of Surveillance," IMF Staff Papers 42, no. 4 (1995).

27. See Martin Edwards, "Crime and Punishment: Understanding IMF Sanctioning Practices," paper delivered at the APSA Annual Meeting, September 2-5, 1999; Stephen Haggard, "The Politics of Adjustment: Lessons from the IMF's Extended Fund Facility," in Miles Kahler, ed., *The Politics of International Debt* (Ithaca, NY: Cornell University Press, 1986); and "The ESAF at Ten Years: Economic Adjustment and Reform in Low-Income Countries," Occasional Paper no. 156 (Washington, D.C.: International Monetary Fund, 1997).

28. Simmons, "International Law and Behavior."

29. For details, and references for the data in this paragraph, see Beth Simmons, "The Legalization of International Monetary Affairs," *International* Organization 54 (Summer 2000): 573-602.

30. For a useful survey of the various proposals by national governments, academics, analysts, international organizations, and the G-22, see Appendix A: Architecture Scorecard in Barry Eichengreen, *Toward a New International Financial Architecture: A Practical Post-Asia Agenda* (Washington, D.C.: Institute of International Economics, 1999).

31. Martha Finnemore and Michael Barnett, "The Politics, Power, and Pathologies of International Organizations," *International Organization* 53 (Autumn 1999): 699-732; Joseph Stiglitz, "The Insider: What I Learned at the World Economic Crisis," *The New Republic*, April 17-24, 2000.

32. O'Brien, Goetz, Scholte, and Williams, *Contesting Global Governance*, 159, 164.

33. O'Brien, Goetz, Scholte, and Williams, *Contesting Global Governance*, chapters 4 and 5.

34. For example, on the difficulties of establishing effective global governance of labor markets, see Daniel Gitterman, "Discretion, the Ally; Commitment, the Enemy. Global Governance and Labor Markets," paper prepared for a Workshop on Globalization and Governance (Institute on Global Conflict and Cooperation: University of California, San Diego, June 22-25, 2000).

35. Sheri Berman and Kathleen R. McNamara, "Bank on Democracy: Why Central Banks Need Public Oversight," *Foreign Affairs* 78, no. 2 (March/April 1999).

3

South Korea and International Compliance Behavior: The WTO and IMF in Comparative Perspective

Chung-in Moon

Traditionally, South Korea was known as a mercantile state that engaged heavily in the practice of free riding, often circumventing the norms, principles, and rules of international economic regimes. Such practices were tolerated as long as it was labeled a developing country. As South Korea graduated from the status of developing country, however, it began to face growing pressure to comply with international regimes. Two waves of globalization have further heightened the importance of compliance with international organizations. The first wave involved a voluntary, managerial globalization, initiated by former president Kim Young Sam through the ratification of the Uruguay Round (UR) and Seoul's admission to the Organization for Economic Development and Cooperation (OECD) during 1994-1997.[1] The second wave resulted from the economic crisis in 1997 and from the subsequent bailout by the International Monetary Fund (IMF) and its imposition of conditionalities for macroeconomic stabilization and structure reforms.[2] While the former was proactive and anticipatory, the latter was reactive.

In both cases, the process of globalization required South Korea to address outstanding issues of compliance with international organizations. The first wave entailed the ratification of, compliance with, and enforcement of norms, principles, rules, and procedures embodied in the Uruguay Round and later the

World Trade Organization (WTO). Arrangements predicated on the liberalization of members' manufacturing, agricultural, and service sectors, as well as on the strengthening of the governance structure of the international trading regime. Meanwhile, in return for $57 billion in rescue financing, the IMF forced South Korea to comply with eight conditionalities involving macroeconomic stability, financial sector restructuring, prudential financial regulations and supervision, corporate governance reform and restructuring, trade liberalization, capital account liberalization, labor management reform, and transparency and accuracy in economic data reporting.[3]

Compliance with these global trade and finance regimes has posed quite daunting challenges to South Korea not only because of its entrenched mercantilist tradition, but also because of vested interests organized around the mercantile template. Despite such structural barriers, South Korea has shown relatively good compliance behavior with both regimes. But there were also some interesting divergences in its compliance behavior. While South Korea literally obeyed IMF conditionalities, its compliance behavior with the WTO has been less consistent.[4] Two areas have been particularly problematic in the latter case: rice and intellectual property rights. South Korea has stubbornly resisted liberalization of agricultural products, especially rice. Although it has formally complied with the WTO's new requirements regarding intellectual property rights, Seoul's enforcement has been rather weak, lagging far behind what would be required for full compliance.

As Kate McNamara notes in this volume, South Korea's compliance behavior appears to defy conventional wisdom, which links the degree of formalization or institutionalization of international organizations to the compliance behavior of individual countries: greater formalization is supposed to produce higher compliance rates. The WTO is highly institutionalized with its own dispute resolution mechanism, whereas the IMF is much less legally formalized. In addition, the domestic political and social costs of complying with IMF conditionalities were greater than those of complying with mandates of the WTO. Nevertheless, South Korea has complied more fully with the IMF than with the WTO, posing an interesting anomaly.

The chapter explores this apparent anomaly by tracing and comparing the factors that have determined South Korea's compliance behavior with international organizations in each case. The findings of this chapter suggest that South Korea's relatively poor compliance behavior with the WTO with regard to rice and intellectual property rights can be attributed by and large (1) to the rather loose enforcement mechanism of the WTO; (2) to the social construction of Korean cultural norms underlying the issue areas, which led to intense political opposition to compliance steps; and (3) to a lack of political will to insist on strict domestic enforcement. Meanwhile, Seoul's compliance behavior with the IMF in the areas of corporate and financial reforms was initially satisfactory because (1) of the acuteness of the economic crisis, which resulted in a relatively swift building of a national consensus for action; (2) of the structure of the incentives and disincentives, as well as the tight enforcement mechanism, embedded in the IMF; and (3) of the leader's political commitment to accommodate its conditionalities, contrasted with the fragility of the domestic political opposition. It should be noted, however, that initial compliance does not necessarily guarantee its sustainability over time. For example, successful compliance and the resulting economic improvement can produce complacency, which in turn can delay or deform the process of further compliance, allowing a "compliance gap" to reemerge (see the introduction and conclusion to this volume).

The findings of the chapter also suggest that, contrary to the Kantian liberal expectation, states have an inherent tendency to defy or neglect international laws or regimes when so dictated by important domestic factors. Neither moral obligation nor the liberal democratic structure of a state, including transparency and the rule of law, can ensure compliance behavior. Despite adopting new norms associated with deepening democratic consolidation and globalization, South Korea has revealed a propensity to slip away from complying with international regimes. The case of South Korea suggests that reducing the compliance gap entails (1) developing well-defined incentives and disincentives, along with tight and sustaining international enforcement mechanisms; (2) undertaking constant and conscious efforts to internalize international norms, principles, and rules through transnational networks and learning; and ultimately (3) engaging sufficient leadership commitment to pacify domestic opposition, to forge a national consensus, and to implement compliance with international regimes on a continuing basis.[5]

Uneasy Compliance with the WTO:
Rice and Intellectual Property Rights

An Overview of South Korea's Compliance with the WTO

South Korea has been notorious for its mercantile practices. Despite its apparent transition from an era of import-substituting industrialization to an export-led growth strategy in the early 1960s, South Korea continued to rely on a subtle form of protectionism. Its trade profile has long been characterized by an import license system, by high tariff escalation over finished goods, by export subsidies, and by the protection of agricultural products. Since the early 1980s, such mercantile practices invited enormous bilateral pressures from the United States. Although the Chun Doo-hwan government undertook measures to liberalize import markets, trade liberalization did not proceed very far during the 1980s. Rather than aiming to enhance liberal international trade and market competition, liberalization steps were much more reactive to American pressures than proactive. The prevailing mercantile ethos (wrapped in the ideology of "rich nation and strong army"), bureaucratic inertia, and social resistance combined to undercut reform efforts in the 1980s.[6]

The Uruguay Round, starting in 1986, provided an impetus for deeper change. At the outset, the South Korean government did not have clearly defined policy objectives for the negotiations. By 1989, however, the South Korean government realized the importance of the negotiations for trade liberalization and for producing positive spin-off effects in terms of the enhancement of international competition through industrial adjustment, the reduction of excessive bilateral trade pressures from the United States and other OECD countries, the minimization of selective import restrictions by advanced industrial countries, and the enhancement of tools to manage trade conflicts.[7] To advance these ends, the South Korean government outlined four major policy objectives regarding the UR negotiations: (1) contribution to successful settlement of the UR negotiations; (2) minimization of discretionary import restrictions by advanced industrial countries; (3) maximum resolution of difficulties involving structural adjustment in negotiations over the agricultural and service sectors; (4) proactive pursuit of market opening within limits of structural adjustment; (5) strengthening of the General Agreement on Tariffs and Trade (GATT) and dispute resolution functions to enhance effectiveness of multilateral trading regime.[8]

After six years of negotiations, South Korea agreed to comply with the outcomes of the UR negotiations in the following areas: an average 8.1 percent tariff reduction of manufactured imports; ten years' suspension of tariffication of rice; minimum market access (MMA) in rice (2 percent of domestic consumption during 1995-1999 and 4 percent during 2000-2004); acquisition of developing country status in tariff reduction; delayed implementation of liberalization of agricultural products; continuation of farm subsidies for structural adjustment; incremental liberalization of the service sector; partial opening of the financial service sector; nonconcession in legal, educational, medical, postal, mass media, and cultural services; gradual enforcement of protection of intellectual property rights; and establishment of multilateralism and deterrence of unilateralism through the WTO.[9]

Through these steps, South Korea has accommodated most of the requirements of the newly established WTO trading regime. Import liberalization of the manufacturing sector has almost reached the level of advanced industrial countries, and liberalization of the service sector has been satisfactory by international standards. South Korea has also made big concessions in agricultural liberalization with the exception of rice markets. At the same time, South Korea turned out to be a major beneficiary in the areas of textiles and apparel, antidumping, and emergency import relief. Having suffered immense bilateral trade pressures from the United States under its principle of strategic reciprocity, the launch of the WTO as a more binding, rule-based multilateral trading regime with a strong dispute resolution mechanism was also a positive factor for South Korea. From its perspective, multilateral muddling through the WTO was perceived to be preferable to bilateral bargaining with such a strong trade partner as the United States. South Korea has achieved its policy goals, however limited, in the UR negotiations. From the perspective of international compliance, however, two troublesome spots remain. One is the unfailing resistance to the liberalization of the rice market, and the other is the loose enforcement of protection of intellectual property rights.

Uneasy Compliance: Rice Market Liberalization

South Korea has one of the most protected rice markets in the world. Despite declining international competitiveness, the rice sector has been sustained by tight market protection and extensive farm subsidy. This protectionist posture has provoked the United States to persistently pressure South Korea to open its rice market since the mid-1980s. Throughout various stages of the UR negotiations over the agricultural sector—from the Punta del Este Ministerial Declaration of September 20, 1986, the Montreal Mid-term Review from January 1987 to April 1989, to the Dunkel Draft Final Act in December 1991— advanced industrial countries consistently called for the unexceptional tariffication of agricultural products and the complete elimination (United States' position) or gradual reduction (European Union position) of farm subsidies. Resisting such pressures, South Korea achieved an exceptional treatment of rice, while liberalizing other agricultural products, including livestock.

In a significant concession, South Korea agreed to reduce tariff rates on agricultural products by 24 percent for ten years between 1995 and 2004. Departing from its earlier position of absolutely no concession on rice market liberalization, it also complied with the principle of unexceptional tariffication of rice but was able to delay its tariffication for ten years by taking advantage of minimum market access and current market access. While the minimum market access rate was increased from 1 percent of an average domestic consumption of rice during 1986-1988 to 4 percent, the current market access rate was set at the import rate of the 1986-1988 period. Here again, a basic foodstuff such as rice was exempted. It was allowed to increase tariffs in the case of emergency injury. South Korea also agreed to reduce farm subsidies by 13.3 percent over ten years, from 1995 to 2004. Yet it was allowed to grant various forms of subsidies for structural adjustment, regional development, environmental preservation, and compensation for idle lands. Most of these subsidies were concentrated in the rice sector. Subsidies for exports were also permitted.[10]

The agreement, however, has proven problematic, as South Korea has since violated the fundamental norms and principles of the WTO. The new multilateral trading regime is framed around the principles of non-discrimination, tariff concessions, prohibition of quantitative restrictions, transparency, and market opening. At least in spirit, South Korea has violated two outstanding principles, namely nondiscrimination and tariff concession.

Equally important is that South Korea has defied the principle of market competition by protecting the rice sector, which had already lost comparative advantage.[11] More troublesome are a series of backlash effects emanating from the delayed tariffication of rice for ten years. The delay has bred another round of stiff domestic political opposition, undercutting the potential for compliance with the WTO. Prior to the third WTO conference, which was held in Seattle in November 1999, the Ministry of Agriculture and Forestry officially announced that the South Korean government would stand firm against increasing pressure from the WTO to completely open its doors to foreign rice producers. The South Korean delegation raised other issues too: South Korea's right to retain control over its agricultural sector; guarantee of a reasonable rice price in the global market; support for South Korea in adopting the direct subsidy payment system; and the need for guidelines on genetically modified (GMO) food. The spokesman of the Ministry of Agriculture and Forestry stated that the Korean government would do its best in meeting the WTO's expectations, where they were considered to be reasonable. This attitude contradicted Seoul's earlier pledge to the WTO that it would liberalize domestic rice markets starting from 2004.[12]

South Korea's noncompliance behavior further resurfaced in the area of structural adjustment of the agricultural sector. From 1992 to 1999, the South Korean government invested almost $50 billion in restructuring the agricultural sector in the light of the liberalization of the agricultural market, but its effects have been rather limited.[13] For example, while rice consumption declined by 3.4 percent in 2000, its production rose from 4.7 million tons in 1995 to 5.5 million tons in 2001. And the area (1.05 million hectare) devoted to rice farming has remained almost unchanged between 1996 and 2002. More shocking is that the price of rice is more than eight times higher than it is in the United States.[14] Although South Korea was granted a ten-year probation period in order to prepare for rice market liberalization through structural adjustment, it has not made any significant progress, underscoring difficulties in compliance with the WTO. The South Korean government has set a new goal of slowing down the pace of rice market liberalization through progressive, rather than substantive, openings in its renegotiation with the WTO, scheduled in 2004, by claiming non-trade concerns, such as food security, as well as maintaining the status of developing country.[15] All this indicates that its compliance with the WTO agreements has been rather dismal.

Why has South Korea shown such behavior? First, it can be attributed partly to the decentralized nature of the enforcement mechanism of the WTO.[16] Even though the WTO has incorporated a dispute resolution mechanism into its governance structure, it still lacks an immediate and compelling set of sticks and carrots for inducing South Korea's compliance with its norms and principles. The aborted Seattle WTO meeting and the power and influence of non-governmental organizations (NGOs) have already fueled domestic political opposition to the scheduled liberalization of rice markets starting from 2004. Farmers' groups and NGOs sympathetic with their plight have initiated political campaigns to defy the original schedule of opening rice markets in 2004.[17] Prior to the establishment of the WTO, American bilateral pressures were crucial in altering South Korea's behavior, but the primacy of multilateralism has diluted its intervening power. Multilateral outside pressures, devoid of the power of concurrent bilateral ones from the United States, have proven less effective in fostering South Korea's compliance behavior.

Second, the social meaning of rice matters. As with Japan, rice has secured a special symbolic status in Korean society not only because of its cultural tradition, but also because of its dietary pattern, which relies heavily on rice. In South Korea's cultural tradition, the agricultural sector has been regarded as the foundation of all industries, and rice has constituted its mainstay, often being treated as sacred. Furthermore, the liberalization of the rice market was equated with threats to food security. These social perceptions elevated rice to a privileged position in South Korea, forging a pattern of socialization where urban consumers are willing to pay the social costs of protection of rice markets. Indeed, rice exceptionalism has been deeply embedded in Korean society and culture, serving as a powerful and effective deterrent to compliance behavior with the WTO.[18]

Such social sentiments directly translate into political coalitional dynamics. While rice farmers account for less than 5 percent of the Korean population, their political support base has been quite extensive and formidable. A great majority of the urban population in South Korea are of rural origins, and they still support the protection of rice markets despite its high social costs.[19] Politicians, civic organizations, and the mass media have all patronized the protectionist position. Those opposing rice market protection have been limited largely to exporters of manufactured goods, liberal economists, and some bureaucrats. Opponents could not engage in effective lobbying or a public campaign because of the adverse public mood.[20] The electoral consequences were much more grave. Former president Kim Young Sam featured the protection of the rice market as one of his major presidential election pledges. He adhered to the nonconcession policy until the last moment of negotiations. But threats of retaliation from the United States eventually forced him to make concessions on the principles of market opening and tariffication, while gaining some benefits, such as an extended period of suspension of tariffication and in the rate of minimum market access. Despite these benefits, his popularity rapidly declined because of his failure to stick to the position of no concession in tariffication and in the market opening of rice. The same can be said of the Roh Moo-hyun government, which was inaugurated in February 2003. President Roh pledged during his presidential election campaign that he would not allow rice market liberalization until proper measures are undertaken to minimize juries on rice farmers. His government also promised the maximum delay of effective tariffication of rice scheduled in 2004.[21] Both cases illustrate how adversely domestic politics can affect compliance behavior.

Finally, bureaucratic fragmentation also played a role. The Economic Planning Board, the Ministry of Commerce and Industry, and the Ministry of

Foreign Affairs supported rice market opening and tariffication for several justifiable reasons: changing patterns of comparative advantage, negative macroeconomic consequences, such as the fiscal burden of farm subsidies and concerns over inflation, and the potentially adverse effects on exports of manufactured goods. But the Ministry of Agriculture, Forestry, and Fishery, which had been widely perceived as a weaker government agency, was able to undercut the mainstream bureaucratic position both by forming an alliance with farmers and sympathetic nongovernmental organizations and by spurring massive popular protests.[22]

Given the current political outlook in South Korea, compliance with the country concession schedule submitted to the WTO is not likely to be observed as planned. The decentralized WTO structure, with its consensus-driven decision making and weak enforcement mechanism, has done little to discourage South Korea's noncompliance behavior, but the key factors can be found in domestic politics. For example, the fragmented political party structure, increased electoral sensitivity, persistent public opposition, the organizational and mobilizational capacity of the Federation of Korean Agricultural Cooperatives, and bureaucratic divisions all cloud the prospects for future compliance with the WTO. Increased farmers' debts could further complicate the process of compliance. In the wake of the ratification of the Uruguay Round agreements, the South Korean government offered extensive structural adjustment loans to rice farmers. But the results have been dismal, with farm debts accumulating phenomenally. Rising farm debts and the farmers' plight could act as a formidable deterrent to South Korea's concession schedule. The South Korean government's attitude of noncompliance with rice market liberalization during the 1999 Seattle WTO meeting was an accurate reflection of domestic political dynamics. Such behavior resurfaced in March 2003, during the Doha Development Agenda (DDA) negotiation over modality of agricultural tariffs and subsidies.

Between Compliance and Enforcement: Intellectual Property Rights

The Uruguay Round negotiations have resulted in an agreement on Trade-Related Aspects of Intellectual Property Rights (TRIPs), which comprised the Paris Convention for the Protection of Industrial Property and the Berne Convention for the Protection of Literacy and Artistic Works. In contrast with rice, the South Korean government has fully complied with the agreement in all areas. In accordance with Article 63.2 of the TRIPs, the South Korean government notified its council of laws and regulations covered by the agreement. Eight main intellectual property laws and regulations (the Copyright Act, the Computer Program Protection Act, the Trademark Act, the Patent Act, etc.) and other related laws were amended and entered into force as of 1999, consistent with the four years' delay of application stipulated by the agreement.[23] South Korea has also encouraged active multilateral diplomacy in the area of intellectual property rights. In May 1996, South Korea joined the World Intellectual Property Organization (WIPO), and it was elected as the chair country of its Paris alliance on September 30, 1996. The Republic of Korea Customs Agency also entered a Memorandum of Understanding (MOU) with the European Union Chamber of Commerce on the protection of intellectual property rights on October 10, 2000.[24]

Problems with intellectual properties, however, arose from the enforcement side. Although South Korea had provided notification of its legal compliance ahead of agreed schedules and had set up special teams to deal with the protection of intellectual property rights in the Ministry of Justice, overall enforcement records have remained rather poor. According to government statistics, the frequency of violations of intellectual property rights increased by 4.6 times, from 2,254 cases in 1989 to 10,423 in 1993. Five years later, in July 1998, more than 80 percent of respondents to another survey replied that they still engaged in the illegal practice of copying computer software programs.[25] In May 1999, the prosecutor's office and the police jointly conducted a nationwide investigation of the violation of intellectual property rights, especially copyright violations involving computer software programs, by raiding universities, government offices, and big business conglomerates. Although the police and the prosecutor's office provided advance notice to these organizations, 406 cases of copyright violation were detected. It was also revealed that 15 percent of those government agencies and state enterprises raided were using illicit software programs. Another survey, by the American Business Software Association, indicates that the rate of South Korea's piracy of foreign software decreased from 76 percent in 1995 to 50 percent in 1999. But the figure is still high compared to a world average of 36 percent, implying that one in every two software programs was pirated.[26]

There are several salient examples that point to the difficulty of enforcing the protection of intellectual property rights. According to the Ministry of Justice, the number of those violating the intellectual property rights rose by more than three times from 13,693 individuals in 1995 to 42,798 in 2000. The steep rise can be attributed partly to an actual increase in the violations of intellectual property rights, and partly to the South Korean government's active enforcement efforts through the "War Against Illicit Copying" campaign since 1999.[27] Another survey, conducted by the Korean Association of Intellectual Property Rights Protection on November 11, 2002, revealed that more than 60 percent of software used in 500 Internet cafes around the nation was illicit.[28]

Even more striking is the widespread practice of piracy of foreign textbooks. Pirated foreign textbooks are openly used in South Korean colleges by professors and students alike. Application of TRIPs notwithstanding, violations of intellectual property rights, especially copyright, are so rampant in South Korea that effective enforcement is likely to be extremely difficult. In the area of performing arts, such as dance, music, and drama, piracy is even more serious. The five-year probation period of the copyright law, which was amended in 1995, came to an end in 2000. No official statistics on the violation of copyrights in the performing arts have yet been released, however, and its frequency is likely to increase.[29]

A recent measure by the United States Trade Representative (USTR) underscores the dismal performance in the enforcement of protection of intellectual property rights in South Korea. On May 1, 2000, the USTR downgraded the status of South Korea's compliance with protection of intellectual property rights from a country on the watch list (WL) to one on the priority watch list (PWL). It cited several reasons for this step: extensive ambiguities in the recently amended Computer Program Protection Act and Copyrights Act; legal permission of "reverse analysis" in the Computer Program Protection Act; and lapse provisions in the Copyrights Act, such as those that allow the transmission and copying of databases among libraries.[30] Ironically, the USTR came up with this recommendation to the U.S. Congress just as the South Korean government was beginning to strengthen its compliance with TRIPs through internalization of their norms, principles, and rules. In May 2001, the United States upgraded South Korea's status by placing it on the watch list. But the USTR has warned that, if South Korea does not accept its additional demands, such as patent protection in movie and music through out-of-cycle review in fall 2003, then it would re-downgrade South Korea to the status of PWL).[31]

Why has the enforcement of TRIPs been so weak in South Korea? Several factors explain the lapse enforcement. The first stems from the nature of the enforcement mechanisms of the WTO and WIPO. As noted above, the WTO does not have a centralized enforcement mechanism. It relies solely on notification of new codification or amendment of related laws by member countries. By ignoring how these laws are carried out, it leaves local or national enforcement vulnerable to political forces. In fact, it was not the WTO but the United States that had a profound influence on South Korea's enforcement behavior in protecting intellectual property rights. American bilateral pressures, through the maintenance of a watch list and a priority watch list that take into account South Korea's performance, have been the primary factors in altering its compliance behavior. In this case, bilateral pressures and multilateral commitments worked in the same direction.

But, as in the case of rice, more critical are widespread social and cultural norms and customs that undercut the enforcement of TRIPs. In Korea, for example, plagiarism has long been tolerated. The Chinese intellectual tradition permitting plagiarism has penetrated deeply into Korean society. In a similar vein, the violation of intellectual property rights has not been considered a crime, but a virtue. Knowledge is to be shared, and free riding in knowledge is socially acceptable and even encouraged. That is why the concept of consulting fees has remained foreign to Koreans until very recently. The sharing of such norms among the enforcers and the enforced makes it extremely difficult to implement TRIPs in South Korea. A culture of accomplice among Koreans in the violation of intellectual property rights is likely to impede the effective implementation of the TRIPs.

But there has been a positive development. A nationwide investigation of the violation of copyrights, that began in May 1999, reflected a growing self-awareness of changing interests in the protection of intellectual property rights. In the past, South Koreans believed that most intellectual property rights belonged to rich Northern countries and, therefore, that it was all right for them to engage in free riding at the expense of TRIPs. But the widespread practice of illicit copyrights caused extensive damage to domestic computer software firms. For instance, a leading South Korean computer software firm, Hangul and Computer, was on the verge of bankruptcy because of piracy of its computer software programs, leading Microsoft to attempt to acquire the firm for only $20 million. The plight of Hangul and Computer triggered a nationwide campaign to prevent illegal copying of computer software. Though the growth of the Korean software industry and a recalculation of self-interests have encouraged South Koreans to comply with TRIPs, its strict enforcement seems to be a long way off.

Finally, there are also problems with the domestic enforcement mechanism. Those government agencies, such as the prosecutor's office and the police, that are in charge of enforcing TRIPs-related laws and decrees are ill equipped. They are short on funds, staff, and technical expertise, each reflecting a lack of political will and commitment by the leadership. Thus, most violations of intellectual property rights are being brought to the court through civil litigation rather than criminal cases. As long as such trends persist, it will be quite difficult for South Korea to enforce the protection of intellectual property rights in accordance with TRIPs.

In view of the above, South Korea's compliance with the WTO in rice market liberalization and the protection of intellectual property rights has been less than satisfactory. While the former directly raises the issue of a compliance gap, the latter touches on the related issue of the effectiveness of domestic enforcement of international regimes. Several factors are responsible for the compliance and enforcement gap: the decentralized decision making structures and loose enforcement mechanisms of international regimes; the social and cultural context of each issue area, as it affects the subsequent intensity of domestic political opposition; and a relatively weak leadership commitment and institutional capacity. Prospects for compliance with the WTO and WIPO are not likely to be bright unless there are concurrent realignments in the governance structure of the international regimes, in the deconstruction and re-socialization of the social and cultural foundation, and in the leadership's commitment to overcoming domestic political opposition.

IMF Conditionalities and Compliance Behavior:
Financial Reforms and Corporate Restructuring

Economic Crisis, IMF Conditionalities, and Compliance Behavior: An Overview

South Korea's dramatic pathway from the periphery of the international economy seemed to be capped by its ascension to membership in the OECD in 1995. But the Korean miracle was soon shattered. In 1997, South Korea encountered its worst economic crisis since national independence in 1945. While foreign reserves declined from $33.2 billion in 1996 to $12.4 billion in 1997, foreign debt rose from $43.9 billion in 1993 to $153 billion in 1997. At the height of the currency crisis on December 2, 1997, usable foreign reserves were less than $6 billion, signaling an outright default.[32] In the wake of the currency crisis, the Korean won was devalued by more than half from US$1:KW808.1 in 1993 to KW1,415 in December 1997 and KW1,920 in mid-January 1998. The stock index fell from 1,027.4 in 1994 to 375 in December 1997, and nonperforming loans doubled from 2.4 trillion won in 1993 to 4.8 trillion in 1997.[33]

South Korea was able to avoid the ultimate humiliation of a moratorium through rescue financing by the IMF. But, in turn, the IMF imposed tough conditionalities on the Korean government. In approving a $57 billion bailout plan for South Korea, the IMF memorandum set three major objectives:

> The [Korean] government's program should be built around: (i) a strong macroeconomic framework designed to continue the orderly adjustment in the external current account; build up international reserves; and contain inflationary pressures, involving a tighter monetary stance and significant fiscal adjustment; (ii) a comprehensive strategy to restructure and recapitalize the financial sector, and make it more transparent, market oriented, and better supervised; (iii) measures to reduce the high degree of reliance of corporations and financial institutions on short-term debt and allow a better diversification of risks in the economy.[34]

Within these broadly defined objectives, the IMF specified detailed conditionalities. They included: tight monetary policy and high interest rates; a flexible exchange rate policy with minimal intervention; tight fiscal policy with increased revenues through tax reforms; comprehensive financial restructuring through a clear and firm exit policy, strong market and supervisory discipline, and increased competition; liberalization of the trade and capital accounts, such as elimination of trade-related subsidies as well as restrictions on foreign ownership; restructuring corporate governance structures through the adoption of consolidated financial statements, the prevention of cross-payment guarantees among affiliates of *chaebols*, and allowance of mergers and acquisitions of domestic firms by foreign firms; enhancement of labor market flexibility by easing dismissal restrictions under mergers and acquisitions and corporate restructuring, which continue to rely on time-consuming court rulings; and fuller transparency in the government's economic data.

Ironically, most of the conditionalities imposed by the IMF were embodied in the economic adjustment measures under the previous government. Since the Chun government in the early 1980s, South Korea had been trying to implement them but had failed to do so. These failures of implementation were directly related to political and policy gridlock. Although globalization provided the government with a clear justification for structural reforms, at the same time democratization, accompanied by the rise of pluralistic politics and bureaucratic fragmentation, impaired the scope and rate of structural adjustment. More importantly, political actors in South Korea failed to reconcile the new democratic institutions with the mandates for economic reforms. While the collective egoism of social forces, such as labor, farmers, and even corporate owners, undercut reform efforts, deformed political processes associated with legislative gridlock emerged as an additional hurdle.[35]

Remarkably, despite these obstacles, the South Korean government was able to implement most of the conditionalities within two years of the bailout agreement.[36] As table 3.1 illustrates, compliance with IMF conditionalities has been quite impressive. Although there were some delays in implementation, most of the conditionalities were observed.[37] As the IMF requested, the South Korean government lifted ceilings on the fluctuation of interest and foreign exchange rates. As a way of ensuring fiscal soundness, it slashed government

Table 3.1. A Comparative Overview of Compliance with IMF Conditionalities

Macroeconomics	Succeeded in achieving stabilization
Financial Sector Restructuring	First phase completed, second phase delayed
Prudential Regulations and Supervision	Achieved, but still troublesome
Capital Account Liberalization	Achieved in advance of required schedule
Trade Liberalization	Accepted requests
Corporate Governance and Restructuring	First phase completed, second phase delayed
Transparency, Monitoring, Data Reporting	Delayed, but achieved
Flexible Layoff	Achieved, but still troublesome

spending by 4 trillion won, a 10 percent reduction, while introducing new tax revenues, such as a special consumption tax and a transportation tax. Banking and financial reforms were also expedited. While the government suspended the operations of fourteen merchant banks that were in trouble, several security and investment firms were allowed to go bankrupt. In addition, the "big bang" policy, which is designed to restructure the banking and financial sector through mergers and acquisitions, is underway. The government has also allowed foreign investors to acquire domestic banks, which was prohibited in the past. The most remarkable measures involved capital market liberalization. Mergers and acquisitions of domestic firms, including hostile takeovers by foreign investors, were permitted without any major restrictions. Even the defense industrial sector, in which foreign entry was banned for national security reasons, is now open to foreign investment.

In order to foster foreign investment, labor reform has also been expedited. After a lengthy negotiation, the government, business, and labor reached an agreement to amend the existing labor law so as to enhance flexible labor market conditions. As a result of the amendment, management is now allowed to lay off workers without going through court action. Reforms in corporate governance are also under way. Cross-payment guarantees and cross-ownership among affiliates of business conglomerates are now banned. In conjunction with this, *chaebols* are now required to enhance their corporate transparency by introducing consolidated financial statements and by placing outsiders on the board of directors and as nonstanding auditors. The government is also squeezing *chaebols* by obligating them to reduce their debt equity ratio from the current level of 400 percent to 200 percent within two years. Neither government bailouts nor blank-check lending by banks are likely to be available, which in turn is forcing *chaebols* to downsize and to restructure themselves by selling their affiliates. Revolutionary changes are taking place in South Korea. Major structural reforms, which the Kim Young Sam government and its predecessors could not accomplish over the past two decades, have now been undertaken within the period of two years. What is particularly interesting is that this success has been achieved in the two areas, namely, financial and corporate reforms, which showed the least progress over the past two decades.[38] The dynamics of South Korea's compliance behavior can be elucidated by examining these reforms in detail.

Financial Reform and Compliance Behavior

The South Korean economic crisis was triggered by and large by the proliferation of nonperforming loans (NPLs), which severely impaired the financial health of banking institutions. Thus, one of the important IMF conditionalities involved financial rationalization, which required South Korean commercial and merchant banks to satisfy the 8 percent capital adequacy ratio of the Bank for International Settlement (BIS). Most South Korean banks satisfied the BIS 8 percent rule. An average capital adequacy ratio of South Korean banks increased from 7 percent at the end of 1997 to 8.2 percent a year later,[39] accomplished through an injection of public funds and a reduction of bank assets. But the BIS 8 percent rule changed the overall landscape of the banking sector in South Korea by forcing liquidation, mergers and acquisitions, and restructuring in the banking and financial sector.

As a result of the imposition of the BIS 8 percent rule, the number of commercial banks declined from thirty-three in the precrisis period to twenty-two in the postcrisis period, and the number of their employees fell by one-third (see table 3.2). There was an extensive assessment by the Financial Supervisory Commission of the twelve commercial banks that did not meet the BIS 8 percent rule, and, of these, five commercial and regional banks (Daedong, Donghwa, Dongnam, Kyonggi, and Choongchung) were liquidated and later merged with healthy commercial banks. Two of the leading national commercial banks, the Korea First Bank and the Seoul Bank, underwent major restructuring. The South Korean government acquired 94 percent of the equity of the Korea First Bank in January 1998 and arranged for a foreign financial institution (Newbridge Capital) to acquire it. Meanwhile, the Seoul Bank was subject to extensive restructuring and rehabilitation through an official injection of public funds. A more profound change took place in the merchant banks, which are wholesale financial institutions engaged in underwriting primary capital market issues, leasing, and short-term unsecured lending. Eighteen merchant banks were closed and three were merged with their operations being suspended, leaving only nine merchant banks in normal operation. In all, 70 percent of existing merchant banks were subject to rationalization measures (see table 3.2). As table 3.2 illustrates, nonbanking institutions, such as insurance firms, securities companies, investment companies, lease companies, and savings and loans also underwent an extensive restructuring.[40]

Table 3.2. Restructuring of Financial Institutions (as of the end of August 2000, %)

Institutions	Total Number of Institutions (A) as of the end of 1997	Liquidation (B)	Liquidation Percentage (B/A)	Contents
Commercial Banks	33	11	33.3	License revoked 5, mergers 5, foreign sales 1
Merchant Banks	30	21	70.0	License revoked 18, mergers 3 (suspension of operation)
Securities	36	6	16.7	License revoked 6

(Continued)

(Table 3.2.—*Continued*)

Institutions	Total Number of Institutions (B) as of the end of 1997	Liquidation (B)	Liquidation Percentage (B/A)	Contents
Investment Trusts	31	7	22.6	License revoked 6, mergers 1
Insurance Firms	50	13	26.0	Contract transfer 5, mergers 1, sales 5, voluntary exit 2
Lease	25	9	36.0	Suspension 9
Savings and Loans	231	78	33.8	License revoked 43, mergers 19, sale to third party 16
Credit Unions	1,666	340	20.4	License revoked 2, mergers 101, dissolution 97, bankruptcy 140
Total	2,102	485	23.1	

Another other important factor underlying the banking and financial crisis in South Korea was a lapse in regulations and supervision, which had led to extensive moral hazard. In order to prevent moral hazard in the banking and financial sector, the IMF imposed tougher conditionalities in the area of standards in prudential regulations and supervision. As table 3.3 illustrates, the South Korean government complied with most of the IMF conditionalities ahead of schedule. While mark-to-market for corporate bonds was introduced in June 1998, loan classification procedures were revised to reflect capacity to repay and not simply past performance. The BIS capital ratio calculation was significantly improved through deduction from tier 2 capital of all provisions except those with respect to assets classified as normal and precautionary. Prudential rules for foreign exchange liquidity and exposure were enforced, whereas a new trust account system was introduced. And in 1999, the Financial Supervisory Commission, which is in charge of regulating and supervising all banking and nonbanking financial institutions, decided to apply the Basle Committee's twenty-five core principles of banking supervision, which emphasize strict enforcement of rules on transparency and financial soundness. The commission even went beyond the original IMF recommendation by imposing a BIS 10 percent rule.[41]

Table 3.3. Standards in Prudential Regulations and Supervision

Objective	Measures	Schedule
Mark-to-market for corporate bonds	Introduction of mark-to-market for corporate bonds. Changes in securities' classification from categorization by currency (domestic, foreign currency) to maturity (investment securities, marketable securities)	June 1998: completed
Banking sector disclosure	More information to be disclosed to meet the international accounting standard	December 1998: completed
Loan classification and provisions	Revision of loan classification to fully reflect capacity to repay and not simply past performance	June 1999: effective from December 1999
Improvement on BIS capital ratio calculation	Deduction from tier 2 capital of all provisions except those with respect to assets classified as normal and precautionary	January 1999: completed
Prudential rules for foreign exchange liquidity and exposure	Risk management for short-term foreign currency risk (short-term assets classified as normal and precautionary) Report maturity mismatches for sight: 1 day to 7 days; 7 days to 1 month; 1 to 3 months; 3 to 6 months; 6 months to 1 year; and over 1 year Management of country exposures (set exposure limits for each country based on international credit ratings)	July 1998: completed
Trust account	Introduction of rules providing full disclosure to trust beneficiaries and precluding any possibility of payment by managing banks to make good or guarantee any loss	January 1999: completed
	Introduction of restrictive rules to be applied to all trust accounts, ensuring segregation for management as well as accounting purposes	January 2000

Source: Seung-min Yoo, *Assessments of Chaebol after Crisis and Its Tasks* (Seoul: Korea Development Institute, 2000).

The banking and financial sector reform has also entailed extensive institutional changes. Since signing an MOU with the IMF on December 2, 1997, the South Korean government enacted fifteen major legislative bills on institutional and regulatory reform, laying the foundation for a new governance structure for financial institutions. These included the General Banking Law, the Financial Industry Restructuring Act, and a refinement of the Depositor Protection Act. Along with this, the South Korean government, by establishing the Financial Supervisory Commission, has vested supervising power in a single agency. In addition, the Korea Asset Management Corporation (KAMCO) was established to deal with the task of purchasing impaired assets resulting from nonperforming loans. And, most importantly, the Korea Deposit Insurance Corporation (KDIC) was created to ensure greater accountability in the banking industry.

As these steps document, the South Korean government was very successful in its efforts to comply with, and enforce, IMF conditionalities on the banking and financial sector. Seen in the context of the vested interests and inertia of the developmental state, which were framed around collusive relationships among the government, banking and financial institutions, and private firms, the IMF-induced financial reforms appear no less than revolutionary. Both the rate and the extent of the reforms were more than what the IMF had requested, presenting a stark contrast to the vicious cycle of bailout, delayed big bang, and dismal banking performance that has gripped Japan.

Corporate Reforms and Compliance Behavior

Beyond the woes of the banking and financial sector, weaknesses in the corporate sector constituted another crucial cause of the economic crisis of 1997. Even when facing declining international competitiveness, many South Korean firms, especially big business, undertook ambitious corporate expansions with borrowed money rather than downsizing and restructuring. Excessive investment and corporate expansion, coupled with declining corporate profits, resulted in the amassment of delinquent loans, precipitating the economic crisis. Such corporate behavior was possible not only because of cozy state-business relationships, which created a myth of "too big to fall," but also because of a loose corporate governance structure. In imposing its conditionalities, the IMF paid utmost attention to two aspects of corporate reform: (1) the overhauling of corporate governance and (2) the restructuring of big business to reduce economic concentration.[42]

As table 3.4 demonstrates, the IMF has imposed a long list of conditionalities on corporate governance and restructuring, involving transparency, shareholder rights, company directors, intragroup relations, insolvency procedures, foreign investment, and other issues. Here again, the South Korean government has been quite successful in complying with, and en-

Table 3.4. Measures for Corporate Governance and Restructuring

Topic	Actions Taken
Transparency	• *Chaebols* are required to prepare combined financial statement beginning in 1999. • External auditors and corporate accounting officers are subject to stiffer penalties.
Shareholder Rights	• Minority shareholders' rights strengthened by lowering the shareholder threshold for various initiatives. • The shadow voting requirement for institutional investors was abolished.
Company Directors	• Listed companies were required to fill one-fourth of their board of directors with outsiders beginning in 1999. The requirement will gradually be expanded to half of the total members. • De facto directors, including controlling shareholders, face the same liability as elected directors. • The fiduciary duty of corporate directors was explicitly mandated. • Cumulative voting for directors was made possible.
Intragroup Relations	• New debt guarantees between *chaebol* subsidiaries were prohibited in 1998; existing guarantees are to be eliminated by March 2000. • The 25 percent ceiling on equity investments by *chaebol* subsidiaries was temporarily lifted and then revised in 1999. • Investigation of improper intragroup transactions led to the imposition of fines. • Holding companies were subjected to restrictive conditions.
Insolvency Procedures	• Introduced economic criteria in evaluating applications for corporate reorganization and introduced time limits
Foreign Investment	• Ceiling on foreign shareholdings in individual companies was abolished in May 1999. • All forms of M&A, including hostile takeovers by foreigners, was permitted. • Number of business lines where foreign direct investment is restricted was reduced from 53 to 24.
Others	• The ceiling on banks' equity investments in individual companies was boosted from 10 to 15 percent. • The corporate tax system will not allow interest payment on any debt exceeding five times the equity capital to be deducted from taxable income. • The corporate Restructuring Fund was established in October 1998 with W 1.6 trillion to assist SMEs.

Source: *The Way to Reform Chaebol* (Seoul: The Ministry of Finance and Economy, 1999).

forcing, the IMF conditionalities. *Chaebols* or business conglomerates were required to prepare combined financial statements of all affiliated firms, starting from 1999. And external auditors and corporate accounting officers are subject to stiffer penalties. Minority shareholders' rights have been significantly improved and, as of 1999, listed companies are required to fill one-fourth of their board of directors with outsiders. At the same time, minimal ownership rights have considerably improved (see table 3.5).

Major changes have also been introduced in the intragroup relations of *chaebols*. Cross-payment guarantees, cross-investment, and cross-ownership among affiliates, which had served as the principal vehicles for the octopus-like corporate expansion of South Korean *chaebols*, were prohibited. In fact, the investigation of improper intragroup transactions led to the imposition of huge fines to such *chaebols* as Samsung, Hyundai, and LG. Another remarkable development took place in foreign investment regimes. As of May 1999, the ceiling on foreign shareholding in individual companies was abolished, and all forms of mergers and acquisitions, including hostile takeovers by foreigners, were permitted. The number of business lines where foreign direct investment is restricted was reduced from fifty-three to twenty-four. In addition, the new cor-

Table 3.5. Minimum Ownership to Exercise Rights (Share of Common Stock in Percentages)

	Unlisted Corporations		Listed Corporations	
	Former	New	Former	New
Judicial removal of a director	5	3	0.5	0.25
Right to injunction	5	1	0.5	0.25
Right to file derivative suit	5	1	0.01	0.01
Shareholder's proposal in statements	–	3	1	0.5
Demand for convocation of SGM	5	3	3	1.5
Right to inspect account books	5	3	1	0.5
Right to inspect affairs and company property	5	3	3	1.5
Removal of liquidator	5	3	0.5	0.25

Note: Small companies are those with paid-in capital of less than W 100 billion.
Source: *Economic Restructuring in Korea: An Overview of Reforms since the Crisis* (Seoul: Korea Development Institution, 1999).

porate tax system will not allow interest payment on any debt exceeding five times the equity capital to be deducted from taxable income.

Radical corporate restructuring has also taken place. First, the Financial Supervisory Commission made it obligatory for five top *chaebols* to reduce their debt-equity ratio to 200 percent by the end of 1999. All five complied with the 200 percent debt-equity ratio by the deadline. Samsung reduced its debt equity ratio from 366 percent in 1997 to 96 percent in 1999, while Hyundai, LG, and SK reduced their debt-equity ratio to 199 percent. Second, in order to reduce their debt-equity ratio, these *chaebols* were urged to sell some of their subsidiaries. Such administrative guidance, in which President Kim Dae-jung himself intervened, led to a sharp reduction in the number of affiliated firms. As table 3.6 illustrates, the Hyundai Group, the largest business conglomerate in South Korea, downsized the number of its subsidiaries from sixty-three in 1998 to twenty-six in 1999, exceeding its original objective of thirty, whereas the Samsung Group reduced its number from sixty-five in 1998 to forty in 1999. To meet the government guideline on the debt-equity ratio, LG and SK undertook drastic measures to reduce the number of their affiliates. The most drastic step involved the bankruptcy and dismantling of the Daewoo Group, which had been the third largest business conglomerate in South Korea. No one would have believed that the Daewoo Group would go bankrupt, since it was too big to fall. Thus, the Daewoo case was a kind of litmus test to gauge the South Korean government's will toward corporate restructuring. Grave political and economic risks notwithstanding, the government did not bail Daewoo out, allowing its demise in 1999. Finally, prior to Daewoo's collapse there was an overall corporate restructuring to avoid duplication and excess capacity by realigning the core industries of the five top *chaebols* (see table 3.6).

Table 3.6. Restructuring Plans of the Top Five Business Groups

Groups	Core Industries	Number of Subsidiaries	
		End-1998	Objective
Hyundai	Car, construction, electronics, chemicals, and financial services	63	30
Samsung	Electronics, financial services, and trade/service	65	40
Daewoo	Cars, heavy industry, trade, construction, and financial services	41	10

(Continued)

82 Chung-in Moon

(Table 3.6—*Continued*)

Groups	Core Industries	Number of Subsidiaries	
		End-1998	Objective
LG	Chemical/energy, electronics/ telecommunications, construction, distribution, and financial services	53	30
SK	Energy, chemicals, telecommunications, construction, distribution, and financial services	42	20

Note: Based on the agreement between the government, the top five *chaebols*, and their creditor banks; signed on December 7, 1998.
Source: Seung-min Yoo, *Assessments of Chaebol after Crisis and Its Tasks* (Seoul: Korea Development Institute, 2000).

As with banking and financial reform, the South Korean government was successful in complying with IMF conditionalities on corporate reform, in this case despite formidable resistance. While *chaebols* engaged in extensive lobbying efforts to minimize the negative effects of the new guidelines for corporate governance and restructuring, conservative forces, united around the old mercantilist ideology, claimed that the imposition of those global standards was part of an American imperialist conspiracy to undercut South Korea's international competitiveness through the dismantling of its *chaebol* system. The bankruptcy and dismantling of the Daewoo Group, in particular, involved enormous political risks for the Kim Dae-jung government, faced with handling the massive unemployment and $50 billion in debts left behind. Even such constraints did not prevent the South Korean government from complying with IMF conditionalities.

What facilitated such compliance behavior? The IMF's centralized enforcement mechanism was an essential element. The IMF is not an international agreement, and its program results from mutual consultation between the IMF and the beneficiary of its standby loans. The beneficiary does not have any legal duty to implement the program, but the IMF can withdraw the standby loan agreement at any time. This combination of a very centralized enforcement mechanism and the existence of credible sticks and carrots was vital to South Korea's compliance with IMF conditionalities. Equally important was the process of monitoring and consultation that minimized the danger of moral hazard. The IMF set up its standing office in Seoul and monitored South Korea's compliance behavior on a quarterly basis through the verification of letters of intent submitted by the South Korean government. At the same time, IMF officials became deeply engaged in the crafting of the letters of intent by lending their technical expertise. Such a circular consulting process has bred a sense of epistemic community between IMF officials and South Korean economic technocrats. Likewise, the normative nature of the IMF enforcement mechanism played an important role in inducing South Korea's compliance behavior. But the role of the IMF was a necessary, not a sufficient, condition. Episodes of failed IMF programs abound elsewhere. In fact, the South Korean success was an exception rather than the rule.

This difference illustrates the importance of domestic factors.[43] First, the sense of acute crisis widely shared by Koreans, as well as the intensity of outside pressures embodied in IMF conditionalities, virtually demolished the domestic political gridlock. All three of the main vested interests, the *chaebols*, labor unions, and bureaucrats, were heavily criticized for their role in contributing to the economic crisis, and they could not openly resist the reform mandates. On the one hand, the severity of the crisis helped people to see structural reform as a positive-sum rather than as a zero-sum situation. It was widely believed, on the other hand, that a failure to comply with the IMF mandate would bring about negative-sum outcomes for all parties concerned. Thus, the severity of the crisis contributed to the removal of collective action dilemmas that had been embedded in South Korean society since the democratic transition in 1987.

Second, the transfer of power from Kim Young Sam to Kim Dae-jung at the time of the crisis also facilitated the implementation of IMF conditionalities. If a candidate from the ruling Grand National Party had won the presidential election on December 18, 1997, it might have been more difficult to carry out the conditionalities in a speedy manner. Opposition from the labor bloc, as well as political debts to big business, could have hampered the process of structural reform. But Kim Dae-jung won strong labor support, while not being captured by big business. At the same time, he was not associated with the causes of the economic crisis. Accordingly, President Kim Dae-jung was relatively free from structural constraints at the time of implementing reform programs.

Third, Kim's leadership capacities mattered. Immediately after winning the presidential election, President-elect Kim Dae-jung and his transition team took away economic policymaking power from incumbent President Kim Young Sam and engaged in day-to-day economic crisis management. His commitment to neoconservative reforms, his command of economic matters, and his powers of persuasion proved to be vital assets in dealing with international banking and financial institutions, as well as with domestic audiences.[44]

Finally, democracy has also provided opportunities for structural reforms. While Kim Dae-jung's commitment to democracy and a market economy helped him win much goodwill and support from foreign investors and allies, especially the U.S. government, the democratic transition of power following a presidential election endowed him with legitimacy and credibility. He was also able to overcome some of the complications of democratic decision making, such as indecisiveness and special interests, by including business and labor in the policymaking process. Furthermore, democratic values encouraged the Kim

Dae-jung government to challenge the power of the *chaebols* and to introduce greater transparency across the board. It is also noteworthy that the proliferation, political activism, and legal interventions of NGO movements, such as those by the People's Solidarity for Participatory Democracy (Chamyeoyondai) and the Coalition for Social and Economic Justice (Kyungsilyon), facilitated the government's efforts to reform corporate governance.

Postcompliance Era and Newly Emerging Challenges

In general, South Korea's compliance with IMF mandates was remarkable in the first phase from 1998 to 1999. The reform drive contributed significantly to the revival of the economy in a short period. As table 3.7 demonstrates, the GDP growth rate rose from -6.7 percent in 1998 to 10.7 percent in 1999 and 9.0 percent in 2000, while the rate of industrial productivity increased from -7.3 percent in 1998 to 20 percent in 1999. The current account balance went from deficits of $23 billion in 1996 and $8.2 billion in 1997 to surpluses of more than $24.4 billion in 1999 and $10.2 billion in 2000. Foreign reserves rose from a meager $7.2 billion in November 1997 to $93.2 billion by the end of November 2000. At the same time, the rates of dishonored corporate bills also returned to precrisis levels, recording 0.10 percent since January 1999. The unemployment rate was also drastically reduced from a high of 8.6 percent in February 1998 to 4.3 percent in late 2000. The stock index also rose, from 376.3 in 1997 to 1,028 in 1999, and the exchange rate has stabilized at the level of US$1:KW1,130 since 1999.[45]

Indeed, South Korea has performed the most impressively of those nations affected by the foreign exchange crisis of 1997. While most Asian countries were still wrestling with economic hardship, South Korea was able to reverse its economic downturn in less than two years. Most international credit-rating agencies, such as Moody's and Standard and Poor's, began to upgrade South Korea's credit ratings. More importantly, on August 23, 2000, the IMF formally announced that, despite some lapses in the implementation of structural reforms, South Korea had made remarkable progress in overcoming the crisis and that it would no longer hold its biannual board of trustees' meetings to oversee the progress of Seoul's reform efforts. As a matter of fact, South Korea paid back $13.5 billion of a total standby loan of $19.5 billion from the IMF ahead of schedule, and it also pledged to pay back the remaining $6 billion by January 2001.[46] By the end of September 2000, South Korea's foreign reserves reached a record high of $92.5 billion, the fifth largest in the world.[47] The sheer size of foreign reserves and the impressive macroeconomic indicators suggested that South Korea had emerged from the tunnel of economic crisis.

Table 3.7. Major Economic Indicators during and after the Crisis

	1997	1998	1999	2000
Real Growth Rate (%)	5.0	-6.7	10.7	9.0*
Unemployment Rate (%)	2.6	6.8	6.3	4.3*
Consumer Price Index (%)	4.5	7.5	0.8	2.6*
Current Account Balance (hundred million US$)	-81.7	403.7	244.8	102.0*
Stock Index (year-end)	376.3	562.5	1,028.1	538.9
Exchange Rate (W/$, year-end)	1,695.0	1,204.01	1,138.0	1,130.0

Note: * Estimated. The stock index and exchange rate are as of November 13, 2000.
Source: *Three Years of the IMF and Changes in the South Korean Economy* (Seoul: Samsung Economic Research Institute, 2000)

Despite this impressive turnaround, South Korea began to encounter another round of economic difficulties during the second half of 2000. The growth rate declined sharply from 11.1 percent in the first half to 7.3 percent in the second half of 2000. The level of short-term overseas loans rose to $46.8 billion, accounting for 33.3 percent of total overseas loans. Most troublesome has been the resurfacing of a severe credit crunch, driving many private firms to the brink of bankruptcy, as sources of corporate financing have begun to dry up. Stock and corporate bond markets, the two primary sources of corporate direct financing, have become virtually frozen. While the stock index declined from 1,059 points in January 2000 to 539 points in December 2000, the corporate bond markets became literally paralyzed as secondary financial institutions, including investment and trust companies, became increasingly delinquent due to mounting nonperforming loans. As sources of direct corporate financing have dried up, private firms have rushed to commercial banks. But they have been reluctant to lend not only because of the BIS 8 percent rule, but also because of fear of corporate defaults and the growth of nonperforming loans. The domestic credit crunch and the uncertain corporate performance have in turn depressed private consumption, reviving an acute recession and the specter of a second economic crisis. Panic behavior has gradually replaced cheers of economic recovery, clouding the prospects for the Korean economy.

What went wrong? South Korea has complied with the IMF mandates, but it failed to implement them in a consistent and durable manner. Compliance with the structural adjustment mandates requires a long-term commitment, but the

South Korean government did little to sustain and deepen the measures. The current economic difficulties can be attributed primarily to a delay in the second phase of corporate reforms. Despite their impressive initial reform steps, the *chaebol* did not reduce their borrowing, improving their debt to equity ratios simply by reevaluating existing assets through inflated stock prices. Most importantly, the government failed to apply market discipline to the corporate sector in a consistent manner. For example, the government has kept seventy-six nonviable large firms alive through workout programs instead of letting them go bankrupt. In addition, several subsidiaries of failed *chaebols*, such as Daewoo, Kia, Hanbo, and Samsung Motors, were allowed to remain in markets. Sustaining these firms through bank loans and corporate bonds aggravated the problem of nonperforming loans, further straining the banking and financial sector. In addition, despite corporate reforms and low interest rate policies, the profitability of private firms remained dismal. The average interest coverage ratio of one-third of the firms in the manufacturing sector was less than 1.0.[48] The failure to allow market discipline to operate, coupled with dismal corporate performance, fueled another round of nonperforming loan crises for major banks and secondary financial institutions.[49] The current credit crunch could have been avoided if the banking and financial reforms had been undertaken more aggressively. As table 3.2 illustrates, however, 485 banking and non-banking financial institutions, only 23.1 percent of the total, were either liquidated or consolidated since the crisis. Instead of seeking a more aggressive restructuring, the government prolonged the survival of troublesome banking and financial institutions by injecting 109 trillion won in the banking and financial sector as public bailout funds. Consequently, the banking and financial sector has become weakened, undermining the smooth circulation of credits. Furthermore, the strict application of the BIS 8 percent rule and the fear of liquidation or merger have deterred banks and secondary financial institutions from providing loans to private firms, precipitating a severe credit crunch. A vicious cycle of poor corporate performance and mounting nonperforming loans, of defensive practices by the banking and financial sector, and of a contrived credit crunch has precipitated a second round of the acute liquidity crisis.[50] South Korea is paying a high price for failing to implement the second phase of corporate and financial reforms.

The delayed implementation of the structural reforms is closely associated with a widespread complacency in Korean society. The cycle of crisis, response, improvement, and complacency is victimizing the South Korean economy. As South Korea starts to show signs of recovery and improvement, no social group is willing to bear the pain of the second phase of structural reforms. Private firms begin to defy the mandates of corporate reforms and to engage in old patterns of corporate expansion with borrowed money. Workers, questioning the necessity of structural reforms by citing the achievements of economic recovery, refuse to cooperate with a second round of reform. The banking and financial sector has also returned to the old way of doing business, reviving moral hazards. Most importantly, political gridlock has again set in. While the government and the ruling party delayed the second phase of corporate and banking reforms because of the potential adverse effects on the general election in April 2000, opposition parties have failed to cooperate in passing critical reform bills related to the injection of additional public funds to normalize the banking and financial sector, prepackaged bankruptcy of troublesome private firms, and the establishment of the banking holding company in the National Assembly. A collective action dilemma, emanating from this widespread complacency, has held the entire second phase of corporate and banking reform at bay. Although the Kim Dae-jung government has pledged to complete the second phase of reform, including the privatization of state enterprises, by the end of February 2001, it does not appear to have broad public support. The government's failure to implement the whole reform package has severely undercut the people's trust in the government and market, fueling panic behavior. The South Korean case clearly shows that while the initial crisis fostered its compliance behavior, the resulting public mood of complacency has revived the collective action dilemma, obstructing the deepening of compliance with international regimes.

Conclusion: Comparative Implications and Policy Prescriptions

The comparative analysis of South Korea's compliance behavior with the WTO and the IMF renders some interesting theoretical and policy conclusions. First, the nature of an enforcement mechanism seems to be more influential in determining compliance behavior than the degree of formalization or institutionalization of the relevant international organization and/or regime. While its centralized enforcement mechanism, with available sticks and carrots, allowed the IMF to induce South Korea's compliance behavior, the WTO's generalized normative structure and voluntary and decentralized enforcement mechanism undermined South Korea's compliance and enforcement behavior.

Second, on some issues cultural underpinnings and the patterns of political socialization can be an important factor in shaping compliance and enforcement behavior. Through the process of globalization, international standards in the financial and corporate sector have become substantially internalized norms in South Korea. Such shared norms facilitated South Korea's compliance with IMF conditionalities concerning financial and corporate reforms, defying domestic political and social resistance. In contrast, rice and intellectual property rights have created their own niches in the social and cultural fabric of contemporary Korea. When the norms and principles of international regimes contradict the preservation of cultural and social values and affect underlying political dynamics, compliance with international regimes could well be compromised. Thus the cultural and social context of international compliance deserves careful attention in accounting for compliance gaps.

Third, the South Korean case also shows that compliance behavior cannot be separated from the political calculus of contending actors. Compliance with international organizations is frequently predicated on institutional changes, which in turn shift the structure of incentives and disincentives within societies, reshaping winners and losers in domestic politics. To the extent that compliance behavior is perceived as posing zero-sum outcomes, it will precipitate intense domestic political conflicts, portending an uncertain future. Thus, it seems essential to look into the political calculus of economic agents in accounting for the nature and direction of compliance and related domestic reforms. What is important here is not only domestic political configurations, but also the overall domestic political ambiance and leadership competence. The Kim Dae-jung government was able to comply with IMF conditionalities in such a short time span due to the crisis mentality shared widely by South Koreans and the competence of its new leadership, which was able to exploit such public sentiments. Meanwhile, the Kim Young Sam government found it hard to comply with the WTO request of tariffication of rice simply because the issue had taken on political saliency, holding the government at bay. And lack of leadership prudence also aggravated the situation. One important lesson can be drawn here: democratic governance can impede the process of compliance because of collective action dilemmas, but an acute sense of crisis can remove such dilemmas, facilitating international compliance behavior.

Fourth, compliance with international regimes should be understood in an iterated fashion rather than by a snapshot approach. There can be a huge gap between initial compliance and sustained enforcement. As the case of intellectual property rights illustrates, compliance may not ensure effective enforcement. The case of corporate and banking reforms also reveals that the complacency resulting from the completion of the first phase of compliance can then obstruct the deepening of further compliance. Thus, the enforcement gap can be as problematic as the compliance gap.

Fifth, South Korea's compliance with the WTO and the IMF could have been more problematic were it not for strong bilateral pressures from the United States. South Korea was forthcoming in both the liberalization of the rice market and the enforcement of intellectual property rights because of strong American pressures before, during, and after the Uruguay Round negotiations. The financial and corporate reforms embodied in IMF conditionalities have also been pressed by the United States. Though such pressures by as hegemonic a leader as the United States risk the appearance of imperial imposition, it does appear that third-party intervention, by influential governments or by nongovernmental actors, can facilitate compliance behavior. This experience suggests that domestic changes and compliance with international regimes are most likely to be achieved when multilateral pressures are conjugated with bilateral or transnational pressures. While multilateral processes set global standards and norms (and provide legitimacy), bilateral or transnational pressures can transform themselves into new political forces directly affecting domestic political processes. In fact, the South Korean government effectively capitalized on American bilateral pressures in persuading the legislative branch and mass media to accept reform.

Finally, international compliance behavior is closely associated with learning. South Korea's eventual decision to accommodate the provision of tariffication of rice was affected partly by Japan's decision to do so. The domestic political opposition to liberalization of rice markets in Japan was perceived to be stronger than that in South Korea, so Japan's concession implied no other choices for South Korean policymakers. Failed episodes of Latin American countries refusing to comply with IMF conditionalities and then suffering economic hardship also offered a valuable reference for South Koreans in weighing whether to enhance their compliance behavior. In addition, the formation of an epistemic community between IMF officials and South Korean economic technocrats also eased compliance with the IMF. Likewise, learning from other countries' compliance behavior and the formation of epistemic communities between international organizations and the officials of individual countries could aid the understanding of how to reduce the compliance gap elsewhere.

What kinds of policy prescriptions can be drawn from the South Korean case? First, international organizations need to enhance their enforcement mechanisms with clearly defined incentives and disincentives. In reducing the compliance gap, enforcement mechanisms can be more crucial than the degree of formalization or institutionalization.

Second, international organizations need to pay constant attention to the characteristics of the enforcement gap in individual countries. Compliance with international regimes does not necessarily guarantee its sustaining implementation. New measures for monitoring, sanctioning, and enforcement should be devised.

Third, international organizations should take into account the social and cultural contexts of compliance efforts. Otherwise, pressures on individual countries, if domestic cultural and social factors are disregarded, can backfire, delaying the process of international compliance. At the same time, individual countries should render additional efforts to induce cultural and normative reorientation in ways conducive to successful compliance behavior.

Fourth, the process of international compliance should not be elongated. The longer the process of ratifying international compliance, the more divisive domestic politics may become, weakening the prospects for international compliance.

Fifth, leadership commitment and competence seem to be an essential element of international compliance. Thus, it is recommended that international organizations try to win leadership support in the process of negotiating compliance behavior in individual countries.

Sixth, multilateral pressures from international organizations might not be sufficient to foster compliance behavior. Such multilateral pressures should be combined with bilateral pressures from hegemonic states and with transnational pressures involving international NGOs and multinational corporations.

Seventh and finally, intraregional or interregional learning and the formation of epistemic communities between international organizations and individual countries should be encouraged as valuable assets in the fostering of international compliance behavior.

Notes

1. Chung-in Moon, "Globalization: Challenges and Strategies," *Korea Focus* 3, no. 3 (1995): 62-79.

2. See Chung-in Moon, "In the Shadow of Broken Cheers; Globalization Strategy in South Korea," in Jeffrey Hart and Aseem Prakash, eds., *Responding to Globalization* (New York: Routledge, 2000); and Chung-in Moon and Mo Jongryn, "Korea after the Crash," *Journal of Democracy* 10, no. 3 (1999): 150-64.

3. "Republic of Korea: Request for Stand-by Arrangement" (Washington, D.C.: International Monetary Fund, December 1997, internal document).

4. Harold H. Koh identifies four possible "relationships between stated norms and observed conduct: coincidence, conformity, compliance, and obedience." According to his definition, South Korea's compliance with the IMF can be seen as an obedience behavior because most of its conditionalities have become parts of its domestic legal structure. See Harold H. Koh, "Why Do Nations Obey International Law?" *Yale Law Journal* 106, no. 9 June (1997): 2599-2659 and chapter 2 in this volume by George Downs and Andrea Trento.

5. For details, see Downs and Trento in this volume. They identify seven schools of international compliance behavior: realist, Kantian liberal, democratic process, strategic, managerial, transformationalist, and transnationalist schools.

6. Jongryn Mo and Byung-il Choi, "Multilateral Market Opening: The Case of Agricultural Negotiation in the Uruguay Round," paper presented to a conference on "Economic Reform in South Korea," Yonsei University, Seoul, November 18, 1999.

7. See Mo and Choi, *Multilateral Markets Opening*, and *The Assessment of Implementation of the Uruguay Round Agreements and Preparation for the New Round* (Seoul: Korea Institute for International Economic Policy, 1999).

8. *Uruguay Round Negotiations and Measures to Cope with UR* (Seoul: Economic Planning Board, 1999).

9. *The Results of the Uruguay Round Negotiations and Its Assessment* (Seoul: Ministry of Foreign Affairs, 1994).

10. *The Results of Agricultural Negotiations in the Uruguay Round* (Seoul: Ministry of Agriculture, Forestry, and Fisheries, 1993).

11. Mo and Choi, "Multilateral Markets Opening."

12. *Korea Times*, August 13, 1999.

13. *Maekyung*, January 28, 2002.

14. *Maekyung*, December 26, 2002.

15. *Understanding WTO Agricultural Negotiation* (Seoul: Ministry of Agriculture and Forestry, 2003)

16. See chapter 2 in this volume.

17. *Collection of Materials on Preparation for WTO New Round* (Seoul: Committee on New Round Negotiations, 1999, in Korean).

18. Song-min Kim, *The Politics of the Two-Level Game: U.S.-Korea Agricultural Trade Negotiations* (Seoul: Yonsei University Press, 1997).

19. Sang-ae Park, "Public Opinion and Protectionism in South Korea: The Uruguay Round Negotiations," Masters Dissertation (Seoul: Graduate School of International Studies, Yonsei University, 1998).

20. Eun-sun Hwang, "Business and Agricultural Market Liberalization: The Role of the FKI during the UR Negotiations," Masters Dissertation (Seoul: Graduate School of International Studies, Yonsei University, 1999).

21. *Maekyung*, December 26, 2002.

22. See Mo and Choi, "Multilateral Markets Opening" and Kim, *The Politics of the Two-Level Game.*

23. "The Notification of Law of WTO/TRIPs and the Meeting for Review and Counter-measure" (Seoul: Ministry of Foreign Affairs and Trade, 2000, mimeo).

24. *Hankuk Gyungje*, October 11, 2000.

25. *Chosun Ilbo*, July 16, 1998.

26. *Joongang Ilbo*, May 30, 2000.

27. *Daehan Maeil*, July 12, 2001.

28. *Hankuk Gyungje*, November 12, 2002.

29. *Joongang Ilbo*, February 12, 2000.

30. *Joongang Ilbo*, May 2, 2000.

31. *Hankuk Gyungje*, May 3, 2003.

32. "Republic of Korea: Request for Stand-by Arrangement," 4.

33. Moon, "In the Shadow of Broken Cheers."

34. "Republic of Korea: Request for Stand-by Arrangement," 5, and Hyung-soo Chang and Yung-jong Wang, *The Korean Economy under the IMF Administration* (Seoul: Korea Institute for International Economic Policy, 1998).

35. Jongryn Mo and Chung-in Moon, eds., *Democracy and the Korean Economy* (Stanford, CA: Hoover Institution Press, 1999); and Jongryn Mo and Chung-in Moon, *Democratization and Globalization in South Korea* (Seoul: Yonsei University Press, 1999).

36. For a more detailed analysis of compliance with IMF conditionalities, refer to Chung-in Moon and Jongryn Mo, *Economic Crisis and Structural Reforms in South Korea: Assessments and Implications* (Washington, D.C.: Economic Strategy Institute, 2000).

37. *The First Year of the Government of the People: Outcomes and Tasks of Its Economic Policy* (Seoul: Ministry of Finance and Economy, 1999).

38. For a detailed analysis of banking and financial and corporate reforms, see Moon and Mo, *Economic Crisis and Structural Reform in South Korea.*

39. *Economic Restructuring in Korea: An Overview of Reforms since the Crisis* (Seoul: Korea Development Institute, 1999).

40. *Economic Restructuring in Korea* and *Three Years of the IMF and Changes in the South Korean Economy* (Seoul: Samsung Economic Research Institute, 2000).

41. *Economic Restructuring in Korea.*

42. Seung-min Yoo, *Assessments of Chaebol Policy after Crisis and Its Tasks* (Seoul: Korea Development Institute, 2000); and *The Way to Reform Chaebol* (Seoul: Ministry of Finance and Economy, 1999).

43. Moon and Mo, "Korea after the Crash" and Moon and Mo, *Economic Crisis and Structural Reforms*, 37-42.

44. Moon and Mo, "Korea after the Crash."

45. *Three Years of the IMF* and Moon and Mo, *Economic Crisis and Structural Reforms.*

46. Joongang Ilbo, August 25, 2000.

47. Joongang Ilbo, October 4, 2000.

48. The average interest coverage rate is derived from dividing current corporate profits by interest payments. If the ratio is less than 1.0, it can be seen as problematic.

49. Moon and Mo, *Economic Crisis and Structural Reforms*, 56-7.

50. *Three Years of the IMF* and Moon and Mo, *Economic Crisis and Structural Reforms*.

4

Compliance with Multilateral Environmental Agreements: The Climate Change Regime

Philippe Sands and Jan Linehan

In this chapter we address current issues relating to compliance with multilateral environmental agreements (MEAs), with particular reference to the arrangements emerging under the 1992 United Nations Framework Convention on Climate Change and its Kyoto Protocol of 1997.[1] We also consider, more broadly, how traditional dispute settlement arrangements fit in with emerging arrangements for improving compliance with international environmental agreements, and the extent to which the institutions that currently exist may assist in achieving compliance.

Background

Over the past twenty years states have adopted a large number of MEAs. These address a broad range of substantive and procedural issues, from atmospheric protection to the disposal of hazardous wastes, from environmental impact assessment to citizen participation in environmental decision making.[2] These MEAs impose increasingly onerous obligations, with growing impacts on a wide range of economic activities. Today, compliance with obligations arising under MEAs has become a matter of interest and concern, spawning academic studies and increased governmental attention.[3] This trend began with instruments adopted in the run up to the 1992 United Nations Conference on Environment and Development (UNCED) and continued with MEAs subsequently negotiated or further developed.[4] These developments are accompanied by a growing recognition that environmental concerns are related to broader issues of international peace and security, as affirmed by the U.N. Security Council in January 1992, and that they cannot be treated in hermetic isolation form broader societal concerns and objectives.[5] The response to stately and privately expressed concerns relating to compliance with MEAs has been twofold: *first*, to develop existing or create new institutional arrangements to address implementation, enforcement, and dispute settlement;[6] and *second*, to ensure that financial resources are made available to developing countries to assist them in meeting the incremental costs of meeting their obligations under some MEAs.[7] Compliance and the provision of financial resources have become intertwined in MEAs; the design of recent noncompliance arrangements, for example, under the 1987 Montreal Protocol on Ozone Depleting Substances, makes a formal connection between the two issues.

Three factors appear to be catalyzing concern about compliance with MEAs. First, as already noted, the extent of international environmental obligations has been transformed in recent years as states take on more environmental commitments under MEAs. These impose increasingly onerous burdens for states. Second, growing demand for access to natural resources, coupled with a finite, and perhaps even shrinking, available resource base provide the conditions for increasing conflict over environmental resources. This concentrates minds on the need to enhance compliance with MEAs and, relatedly, address disputes before they arise (UNCED instruments stress this preventive approach). Third, and perhaps most significantly, as international environmental obligations increasingly address fundamental economic interests and needs, states which do not comply with their environmental obligations are perceived to gain unfair, and perhaps unlawful, advantages (in particular economic advantages) from their environmentally harmful activities. These three factors have combined to place the spotlight on compliance (and noncompliance) with MEAs.[8] In summary, in the field of the environment noncompliance is seen as important because it limits the overall effectiveness of the treaties, undermines international legal commitments, and contributes to conflict and instability in the international order.

In assessing the institutional arrangements which have been put in pace to address noncompliance with MEAs, it should be noted that noncompliance can occur in a number of different ways, and for different reasons.[9] These include the failure to give effect to substantive norms (for example, to limit atmospheric emission of sulphur dioxide or greenhouse gases as required by treaty); the failure to fulfill procedural requirements (for example, to carry out an environmental impact assessment or consult with a neighboring state on the construction of a new plant); or the failure to fulfill an institutional obligation (for example, to submit an annual report to an international organization). In this regard, for the traditional international lawyer compliance raises three separate, but related questions. These are:

(a)   what formal or informal steps must a state or an international organization take to implement its international legal obligations? ("*implementation*");

(b) what legal or natural person may seek, or has the right, to enforce at the international level the international environmental obligations of a state or international organization? (*"enforcement"*); and

(c) what institutions and procedures exist under international law *to assess compliance* and resolve conflicts or settle disputes over alleged non-compliance with international environmental obligations? (*"institutional aspects"*).

In this chapter we focus on the institutional aspects of noncompliance, the third element. And we do so particularly by reference to the obligations of states under MEAs as opposed to freestanding environmental obligations under general international law. With regard to the first element—implementation—we note simply, by way of background, that states implement their international environmental obligations in three distinct, but related, phases: (a) by adopting national implementing legislation, policies, and programs; (b) by ensuring that such national environmental legislation, policies, and programs are complied with by those subject to its jurisdiction and control; and (c) by fulfilling any obligations to the relevant international organizations, such as reporting the measures taken to give effect to international obligations. The reporting requirement is one that has received considerable attention, and most environmental treaties require parties to report certain information to the international organization designated by the treaty.

With regard to the second element—international enforcement—we note that once evidence has become available that a state, or a party to a treaty, has failed to implement an environmental obligation established by international law, the question arises as to which entities or persons may seek to enforce that international environmental obligation on the international plane, rather than before national courts and invoking domestic law. [10] The available options include international enforcement at the instigation of states, international organizations, or nonstate actors (including the corporate sector and nongovernmental organizations [NGOs]). As we shall see, in the environmental field the preferred option remains interstate enforcement; unlike the human rights field, individuals and associations do not, except in the most limited exceptions, have recourse under MEAs to enforcement processes. As we will show, the question of standing to enforce becomes especially pertinent in the climate change context since the Kyoto Protocol expressly envisages a role for the private sector. Related to this issue is the question of enhancing enforcement in the national courts, an issue which lies beyond the scope of this chapter but which attracts increasing attention.

Institutional Responses

It is the institutional mechanisms of the third element which are now available or emerging to assist in assuring compliance with MEAs. Traditionally, a range of international processes and mechanisms are available to assist in the pacific settlement of environmental disputes (taking the traditional terminology of international law) arising from noncompliance with MEAs. Article 33 of the U.N. Charter identifies the traditional mechanisms:

> The parties to any dispute, the continuance of which is likely to endanger the maintenance of international peace and security, shall, first of all, seek a solution by negotiation, enquiry, mediation, conciliation, arbitration, judicial settlement, resort to regional agencies or arrangements, or other peaceful means of their own choice.

These different techniques can be divided into two types: *diplomatic* means according to which the parties retain control over the dispute insofar as they may accept or reject a proposed settlement (negotiation, consultation, mediation, conciliation); and *legal* means which result in legally binding decisions for the parties to the dispute (arbitration and judicial settlement). Recourse to international organizations (regional and global) as mediators and conciliators provide something of a middle way, and one that is emerging as a preferred choice in the environmental context. As we shall see, MEAs now favor a mix of "diplomatic" and "legal" options; a typical MEA will provide for the full range of techniques, from consultation and information exchange, to noncontentious administrative style noncompliance mechanisms, and finally traditional arbitral and judicial arrangements. What the MEAs do not do, however, is indicate the relationship between these different techniques, a point forcefully made by Professor Koskenniemi.[11]

Some History

Many of the earliest MEAs did not provide for any dispute settlement or compliance mechanisms.[12] As "dispute settlement" began to be addressed, the preference was for the use of informal and nonbinding mechanisms, such as negotiation and consultation. This came to be supplemented by the more formal mechanisms, such as conciliation, arbitration, and judicial settlement. More recently, there has been a move toward the development of new techniques that aim at establishing noncontentious mechanisms that allow the intervention of a third party or a body internal to the regime which is established to assist in bringing about compliance through a process of "assessment" and "persuasion."[13] The practice of the most recent treaties has been to provide parties with a range of options for dispute settlement and encouraging implementation avenues.[14]

Negotiation and Consultation

Interstate negotiation as a technique of dispute settlement has early roots in the environmental sphere. As early as 1866 the three Treaties of Bayonne, which were the subject of interpretation in the award by the arbitral tribunal in the Lac Lanoux Case concerning a dispute over the use of natural resources shared by France and Spain, required the highest administrative authorities of the bordering departments and provinces to "act in concert in the exercise of their right to make regulations for the general interest and to interpret or modify their regulations whenever the respective interests are at stake, and in case they cannot reach agreement, the dispute shall be submitted to the two Governments."[15] In the Fisheries Jurisdiction Case the International Court of Justice set out the basic conditions for the conduct of future negotiations.[16] Against this background, MEAs refer, more or less as a matter of standard practice, to the need to ensure that parties resort to negotiation and other diplomatic channels to resolve their disputes before making use of other more formal approaches.[17] Since negotiations of this type invariably take place behind closed doors, it is difficult to identify specific examples involving the successful resolution of claims and disputes by negotiation.[18] Consultation between states is also encouraged by environmental treaties as a technique to avoid and resolve disputes and potential disputes between states.[19]

Mediation, Conciliation, and International Institutions

Where negotiation and consultation fail, a number of environmental treaties provide for the use of mediation,[20] conciliation[21] (or the establishment of a Committee of Experts[22]) to resolve disputes. Mediation and conciliation involve the intervention of a third person. In the case of mediation, the third person is involved as an active participant in the interchange of proposals between the parties to a dispute, and may even offer informal proposals of his or her own. With conciliation the third person assumes a more formal role and often investigates the details underlying the dispute and makes formal proposals for the resolution of the dispute. Examples of conciliation include the role of the International Joint Commission established by Canada and the United States in the 1909 Boundary Waters Treaty, which fulfills a combination of quasi-judicial, investigative, recommendatory, and coordinating functions.[23] The Dispute Settlement Panels established under the World Trade Organization (WTO)—and previously the General Agreement on Tariffs and Trade (GATT)—perform a similar function.[24] Under the 1985 Vienna Convention, the 1992 Climate Change Convention, and the 1992 Biodiversity Convention, conciliation will be used if the parties to the dispute have not accepted compulsory dispute settlement procedures by arbitration or the International Court of Justice (ICJ).[25] In a related fashion, the political organs of international institutions and regional agencies also play a role in the settlement of environmental disputes, either by express mandate, or, as is more usually the case, on an ad hoc basis in a particular dispute.[26] One such example is the 1985 decision of the Conference of the Parties to the Convention on International Trade in Endangered Species of Wild Fauna and Flora (CITES) concerning the application of the convention to endangered species acquired prior to the entry into force of the convention.[27] It is also becoming apparent that the secretariats established to service the Conference of Parties are playing an important role in advising, and putting pressure on, states on compliance. This is happening whether or not secretariats are given explicit powers or functions.[28]

This approach has given rise to the establishment in some multilateral environmental agreements of specialized subsidiary bodies to deal with compliance issues and disputes relating to noncompliance. The most important example of this is the noncompliance procedure established under the 1987 Montreal Protocol (an approach now taken up in several other MEAs), which includes an implementation committee established in 1990.[29] Briefly, any party that has reservations about another party's implementation of its obligations under the protocol, may express its concerns in writing to the secretariat, with corroborating information.[30] The secretariat will then determine with the assistance of the party alleged to be in violation whether it is unable to comply with its obligations under the protocol, and will transmit the original submission, its reply and other information to the implementation committee.[31]

The function of the Montreal Protocol Implementation Committee, which consists of ten parties (originally five) elected by the Meeting of the Parties, is to receive, consider, and report on submissions made by any party concerning reservations regarding another party's implementation of its obligations under the protocol, and any information or observations forwarded by the secretariat in connection with the preparation of reports based on information submitted by the parties pursuant to their obligations under the protocol.[32] The committee may, at the invitation of the party concerned, undertake information gathering in the territory of that party, and will also maintain an exchange of information with the Executive Committee of the Multilateral Fund related to the provisions of financial and technical cooperation to developing country parties.[33] The committee is to try to secure "an amicable resolution of the matter on the basis of respect for the provisions of the Protocol" and report to the Meeting of the Parties, which may decide upon and call for steps to bring about full compliance with the protocol.[34] In its report, the implementation committee is to identify "the facts and possible causes" of noncompliance and make appropriate recommendations.[35] The Fourth Meeting of the Parties also adopted an indicative list of measures that might be taken by a Meeting of the Parties in respect of noncompliance, which comprise:

(a) appropriate assistance;
(b) issuing cautions; and
(c) suspension (in accordance with the applicable rules of international law concerning the suspension of the operation of a treaty) of specific rights and privileges under the protocol, including with respect to trade and the financial mechanism created by the protocol.[36]

The committee may engage in confidential consultations with parties, but its report is not to contain any confidential information and is to be made available to any person upon request.[37] Significantly, resort to the noncompliance procedure is without prejudice to the dispute settlement provisions available under Article 11 of the 1985 Vienna Convention, including negotiation, good offices, mediation, arbitration, submission to the International Court of Justice, and the establishment of a conciliation commission.

In practice, the implementation committee has provided a nonadversarial and noncontentious forum, with no cases alleging violations being brought by another party and most cases resulting from the reporting process or through a party raising its own potential noncompliance. The committee has made a number of recommendations to the Meeting of Parties dealing with noncompliance, the most controversial against the Russian Federation in 1995.[38] On the basis of the Implementation Committee's recommendations, the Seventh Meeting of the Parties decided to recommend that international assistance by bodies such as the Global Environment Fund should only occur if the Russian Federation met certain conditions and it imposed limited, somewhat ambiguous, trade restrictions. The Russian Federation initially rejected the findings, but subsequently attempted to comply. The implementation committee has developed a practice of recommending individual country phaseout programs backed by the threat (sometimes expressed as a "caution") of a finding of noncompliance accompanied by "conditionality" of funding and trade restrictions.[39]

In related fashion, a number of multilateral development banks have recently established inspection panels, to receive claims from citizens or other persons affected by a bank project alleging noncompliance by the institution with its internal operating requirements, including environmental requirements. The best-known example is the World Bank Inspection Panel, which has now received a significant number of claims and, on occasion, found violations by the bank of its environmental obligations. The mechanism is of interest because it allows nonstate actors to institute the process, and because it leads to a nonbinding recommendation or finding, rather of the character of a conciliation process, which the bank may then decide to implement.

Arbitration

International arbitration has as its "object the settlement of disputes between states by judges of their own choice and on the basis of respect for the law. Recourse to arbitration implies an engagement to submit in good faith to the award."[40] It is characterized, generally, by its ad hoc nature. Arbitral awards have played a limited but nonetheless significant role in the development of international environmental law. Three international arbitral awards have contributed to the development of substantive rules on environmental protection and use of natural resources: the 1893 Fur Seal Arbitration, the 1941 Trail Smelter Arbitration, and the 1957 Lac Lanoux Arbitration. In recent years, states negotiating environmental treaties have favored the inclusion of specific language providing for the establishment of an arbitration tribunal, with the power to adopt binding and final decisions, to settle disputes. These had not been used until recently. However, in July 1999 Australia and New Zealand commenced arbitration proceedings against Japan under the 1982 United Nations Convention on the Law of the Sea (UNCLOS) to challenge Japan's unilateral experimental fishing program for bluefin tuna in the South Pacific. In August 2000 the arbitral tribunal ruled that it did not have jurisdiction over the dispute, which was more properly centered on a 1993 convention that did not provide for compulsory adjudication by arbitration or judicial settlement.[41]

International Courts

International environmental disputes, including under MEAs, may also be referred to international courts, which are permanent tribunals competent to deliver a legally binding decision. In relation to environmental disputes a number of international courts have played a particularly important role: the ICJ, the European Court of Justice (ECJ), the courts established under the various regional human rights treaties (including in particular the European Court of Human Rights), the International Tribunal for the Law of the Sea, and the Appellate Body of the World Trade Organization. With the exception of the ECJ and the human rights courts, access to these bodies is only open to states. It used to be said that states were unwilling to resort to these bodies to raise or resolve environment issues, and it is certainly true that over the past century only a small number of cases have been reported. However, it is noteworthy that in each of the past five years there has been a major international environmental dispute that has been brought to these courts, in particular:

- In 1995 New Zealand brought proceedings to the ICJ (supported by Australia, Samoa, Solomon Islands, Marshall Islands, and Federated States of Micronesia) to challenge the resumption by France of underground nuclear testing (alleging inter alia noncompliance by France with its obligation to carry out an environmental impact assessment (EIA) under the 1986 Noumea Convention for the Protection of the Natural Resources and Environment of the South Pacific Region);
- In 1996 forty-one states argued the (il)legality of the use of nuclear weapons before the ICJ, including environmental aspects, and invoking obligations under various MEAs (including the 1992 Biodiversity and Climate Change Conventions);
- In 1997 the ICJ gave judgment in the Case Concerning the Gabcikovo/Nagymaros Project between Hungary and Slovakia, which raised important environmental issues, including the relationship between environmental norms and the law of treaties and the law of state responsibility;

- In 1998 the WTO Appellate Body gave its decision in the Shrimp Turtles Case, brought by Malaysia, India, Thailand and Pakistan against the United States (and in so doing invoking a number of MEAs);
- In 1999 the International Tribunal for the Law of the Sea ordered provisional measures requiring Japan to stop its scientific fishing program for Southern Blue-Fin Tuna, a case instigated by Australia and New Zealand under UNCLOS (invoking also the 1993 Convention on Southern Blue-Fin Tuna); and
- In 2001 the International Tribunal for the Law of the Sea ordered provisional measures requiring the United Kingdom and Ireland to cooperate for the prevention of pollution in relation to the operation of a new Mixed Oxide Fuel (MOX) facility at Sellafield.

It appears that the traditional reluctance of states to have resort to contentious, dispute settlement procedures has given way to a new willingness to have recourse to international adjudicatory bodies, a number of which are now active in environmental matters. However, this new willingness is unlikely to be replicated across the broad range of MEAs, many of which concern "global" rather than "bilateral" interests.

International Court of Justice (ICJ)

The International Court of Justice is the principal judicial organ of the United Nations. It has a contentious and an advisory jurisdiction. Until recently the ICJ—like its predecessor the Permanent Court of International Justice (PCIJ)—had never dealt fully with a major international environmental dispute. Early PCIJ cases touched upon environmental and natural resource issues: see Diversion of the Waters of the River Meuse[42] and the Territorial Jurisdiction of the International Commission of the River Oder.[43] Before the ICJ some early cases have influenced the development of international environmental law. These include the Corfu Channel Case (affirming "every state's obligation not to allow knowingly its territory to be used for acts contrary to the rights of other states");[44] the Fisheries Jurisdiction Case (setting out basic principles governing consultations and other arrangements concerning the conservation of shared natural resources);[45] the Nuclear Tests Cases;[46] and Certain Phosphate Lands in Nauru (addressing inter alia the physical destruction of an island as a unit of self-determination accompanied by a failure to rehabilitate the land, as well as the nature and extent of obligations relating to permanent sovereignty over natural resources and entitlement to the costs of rehabilitation).[47]

European Court of Justice (ECJ)

The European Court of Justice is the judicial institution of the European Community (EC) and is required to ensure that in the interpretation and application of the European Economic Community (EEC) Treaty "the law is observed."[48] Environmental cases reach the ECJ in a number of ways. The EC commission has brought more than 100 cases to the ECJ alleging the failure of a member state to comply with its EEC environmental obligations. The procedure is a rare example of the way in which an international organization can challenge noncompliance by a state. Interstate cases between members are also possible, but to date no member state has challenged another before the ECJ. The ECJ can also judicially review the legality of acts of the EC council and commission. Actions may be brought by a member state, the council or the commission, and by any legal or natural person provided that the act concerned is a decision addressed to that person or is of direct or individual concern to it.[49] In *Greenpeace and Others v. the Commission*, the ECJ effectively precluded actions by nongovernmental organizations and individuals by severely curtailing their locus standi to bring environmental claims.[50] The ECJ also considered environmental questions on the basis of its jurisdiction under Article 177, the "preliminary reference procedure."

Human Rights Courts

The human rights courts established under the various regional human rights conventions are more frequently exercising jurisdiction over environmental matters, at the instigation of individual victims.[51] Within the past five years the European Court of Human Rights has ruled that excessive pollution may give rise to an environmental nuisance violating the right to privacy (*Lopez Ostra v. Spain*, 1994) and that citizens are entitled to access to information on environmental hazards in their neighborhood (*Guerra v. Italy*, 1998). Although these cases do not relate directly to multilateral environmental agreements, the approaches they take may affect proceedings in other contexts.

International Tribunal for the Law of the Sea (ITLOS)

ITLOS became operational in 1996. Established under UNCLOS, it is an independent international judicial body that forms an integral part of the regime established under Part XV of UNCLOS for the peaceful settlement of disputes concerning the interpretation and application of the convention and other agreements related to its purposes. The tribunal is open to states parties and, in specific circumstances, to other states, international organizations and entities other than states, including private persons and corporations. Even in the limited time in which it has been operational the tribunal has faced arguments relating to the protection of the environment and the conservation of natural resources, both in relation to its "prompt release" jurisdiction and more generally. In its provisional measures order in the Southern Blue-Fin Tuna case it applied a far-reaching and precautionary approach to order a halt to a Japanese experimental fishing program pending the determination of the case on its merits by an arbitral tribunal, indicating that it may emerge as an important new forum for the resolution of environmental disputes. [52]

WTO Appellate Body

The WTO Appellate Body is a standing body established by the 1994 Agreement Establishing the World Trade Organization, under the WTO's Dispute Settlement Body. The Appellate Body receives cases by way of appeal on points of law from ad hoc panels established by the Dispute Settlement Body to resolve disputes between WTO members (states and the European Community) arising under the WTO agreement and related instruments. Since 1995, the Appellate Body has had the opportunity to address a number of disputes having an environmental component, and has indicated that the WTO rules are not to be interpreted and applied in clinical isolation from the rules of public international law. In a 1998 case concerning the import prohibition imposed by the United States on Certain Shrimp and Shrimp Products from India, Malaysia, Pakistan, and Thailand, on the grounds that they were harvested in a manner which adversely affected endangered sea turtles, the Appellate Body relied upon a number of MEAs to support its conclusion that the United States was provisionally entitled to take measures to protect endangered sea turtles from harvesting activities even within the territory of the four complainant states (even if ultimately it ruled that the U.S. measures were unlawful because they had been imposed in an arbitrary and discriminatory manner). [53] Several cases touching on environmental issues in the GATT and the WTO have generated considerable controversy, and this has in turn led to calls for greater access to WTO dispute resolution by environmental groups. There is little prospect that such groups will be given standing as parties, but the Appellate Body has indicated that there is nothing to prevent panels or itself from seeking information from such groups and has invited such submissions. The WTO Appellate Body is likely to emerge as an important forum for the resolution of trade disputes with an environment aspect.

Against this background we turn now to consider the specific case of the 1992 Climate Change Convention and its 1997 Kyoto Protocol.

Compliance with Climate Change Treaties

The development of dedicated procedures and institutions to deal with compliance is part of the so-called unfinished business of the 1997 Kyoto Protocol negotiations.[54] The 1992 Climate Change Convention established a framework and a set of new institutions to address climate change. The protocol to that convention provides for legally binding emissions commitments for the parties listed in Annex B in respect of six greenhouse gases with respect to the "first commitment period" of 2008-2012.[55] However, it leaves critical rules, principles, guidelines, and methodologies to be developed. In November 2001, after difficult and prolonged negotiations, the parties to the Climate Change Convention adopted a series of decisions known as the Marrakesh Accords. While at the time of writing some elements are still under negotiation, the final package is expected to be formally adopted by the first meeting of the Conference of Parties serving as the Meeting of Parties to the Protocol (COP/MOP) after the protocol enters into force. However, it is not clear when the protocol will enter into force, following its rejection by the United States in 2001 and doubts about early Russian ratification.[56]

The compliance committee proposed for the Kyoto Protocol will be the most far-reaching nonjudicial institution for assessing compliance yet agreed in an MEA.[57] The committee will involve a mix of "facilitative" and "enforcement" strategies," with the first drawing on the experience of noncompliance procedures (NCPs) and institutions which have a "managerialist" rationale and the latter going beyond any dispute resolution precedents. The experience under the convention has shown a marked reluctance to accept institutions that would "assess" compliance. Nonetheless, the move to consider an "enforcement" model under the Kyoto Protocol is understandable given the onerous nature of the commitments and the risk of free riding.[58] However, as discussed below, there is still a question mark over whether the committee will be able to impose consequences that are binding under international law. Before turning to look at the protocol, it is necessary to examine the experience under the convention both as background and because it is of continuing relevance so long as the protocol has not entered into force and while significant emitters such as the United States refuse to ratify the protocol.

The 1992 Climate Change Convention

During the negotiation of the convention, numerous proposals were considered for "monitoring and verification."[59] However, the failure to include binding emissions targets removed the urgency to agree on such procedures, a task that was proving difficult given the reluctance of many of the negotiating parties to agree to any kind of dedicated review or compliance procedures.[60] Although several states put forward detailed compliance proposals, apparently motivated by fears of leakage and free riding (i.e., the potential loss of industries and markets to parties with weaker compliance), most states—particularly developing countries—rejected this approach, citing sovereignty concerns.[61] In the end there was only agreement to create a suborgan of the Conference of Parties—the Subsidiary Body for Implementation—and to undertake the future negotiation of a "multilateral consultative process, available to Parties at their request, for the resolution of questions regarding the implementation of the Convention" (Article 13, Multilateral Consultative Process [MCP]).

In addition to a "hortatory" commitment to aim to return greenhouse emissions to 1990 levels for developed country parties listed in Annex 1, the convention requires all parties to formulate and implement national mitigation plans and engage in elaborate data collection and reporting about national circumstances and policies.[62] The mandate of the Subsidiary Body for Implementation (SBI), which comprises delegates/representatives of all parties, is to assist the Conference of Parties in "the assessment and review of the effective implementation of the Convention."[63] While broadly expressed, the powers of the Conference of Parties and the SBI would at best appear only to authorize a political assessment of the "performance" of the parties. Nonetheless, efforts to review the collective performance of the parties as mandated by convention have proved controversial and any suggestion of institutional assessment of individual performance has been strongly resisted. [64] However, there was early agreement to establish a secretariat-led "in-depth review" process for Annex 1 party national communications. The review process is to be conducted in a "facilitative, non-confrontational, open and transparent manner."[65] The secretariat conducts paper reviews and may, at the invitation of the relevant party, send expert teams to "clarify" aspects of a report. All Annex 1 parties have agreed to visits by expert teams. So far there appears to have been little controversy in the review process.

Settling the terms of the "multilateral consultative process" under Article 13 has proved more problematic. The terms of reference of the MCP have not been formally approved by the Conference of Parties owing to disagreements about the size and geographic representation of its membership. However, there is apparent agreement that the MCP is to be "facilitative, co-operative, non-confrontational, transparent and non-judicial"; that it may be invoked by any party concerning a question of implementation (i.e., its own or that of another party); and that it has the power to make a report to the COP that may include recommendations.[66] While the terms of the proposed MCP do not distinguish between Annex 1 (developed) and non-Annex 1 (developing) country parties, it is to be assumed that it will be limited to providing advice to the latter.

Finally, the convention contains a dispute resolution provision of the kind that follows several other MEAs.[67] Under Article 14, disputes about "interpretation or application of the Convention" are to be settled through negotiation or other peaceful means. Recourse to the International Court of Justice or a dedicated arbitration tribunal can only occur in effect where both parties agree. A decision of the International Court of Justice would be binding on the parties to the dispute. The status of a decision by an arbitration commission is still to be decided as the Conference of Parties has yet to settle the terms of the arbitration annex. However, such a decision would ordinarily be binding on the parties to the dispute.[68] Where recourse to arbitration or an arbitration panel is not available, any party to a dispute that remains unsettled after twelve months may invoke the provision for the creation of a conciliation commission. This body may only make a recommendatory award. Only one party has accepted the ICJ and arbitration provisions.[69] The limited acceptance of these provisions can be attributed to the traditional aversion of many states to compulsory dispute resolution. It is also likely that many states regard the limited nature of the commitments in the convention as inappropriate for judicial review. The Conference of Parties has yet to settle the terms of the arbitration and conciliation procedures. The delay is not surprising given the competing priorities of developing the new climate regime and the negotiations leading to the Kyoto Protocol.

The Kyoto Protocol

The Kyoto Protocol draws on the experience and institutions of its parent framework convention. However, it goes much further in terms of substantive obligations as it provides for legally binding emissions controls for developed countries and economies in transition (Annex B parties) in respect of the period 2008-2012. The protocol allows the parties to use a variety of "flexible" means to meet these obligations, such as collective action (e.g., through "bubbles" like the European Union states) and the so-called Kyoto mechanisms. Under the Kyoto mechanisms of international emissions trading and extraterritorial emissions reductions projects (joint implementation [JI] and the clean development mechanism [CDM]), Annex B parties will be able respectively to trade portions of their assigned amounts of emissions and to generate emissions credits through undertaking mitigation projects.[70] Private actors are expected to be significant participants in the Kyoto mechanisms as buyers of carbon credits and investors in the project-based mechanisms. The CDM will involve developing countries as the hosts of projects that assist in achieving local sustainable development and mitigation of climate change. These projects will generate carbon credits— "certified emissions reductions"—for Annex 1 parties to use in meeting their emissions commitments. Under Article 12, certified emissions reductions generated between 2000 and 2007 may be used in the first commitment period. Compliance-related issues, therefore, potentially arise before entry into force and the start of the first commitment period, distinguishing this regime from other MEAs.

The Kyoto Protocol has numerous provisions relating to reporting and review that build on the convention. Annex B parties are required by 2007 to have in place national systems to estimate emissions and removals by sinks, as well as to provide detailed inventory and other information.[71] The convention practice of in-depth reviews of individual party information is developed in Article 8. Expert review teams, coordinated by the secretariat, comprising government-nominated experts and, "as appropriate, intergovernmental organizations," are to undertake "a thorough and comprehensive technical assessment of all aspects of the implementation by a Party to the Protocol." The teams are to report to the

COP/MOP with their "assessment of the implementation of commitments, identifying any potential problems in, and factors influencing, the fulfillment of commitments." The COP/MOP is to consider the information submitted by the parties, reports of the review teams, questions of implementation listed by the secretariat and any questions raised by the parties. The COP/MOP also has a power to "take decisions on any matter required for the implementation of this Protocol."[72] The Marrakesh Accords provide for the elaboration of the basic data reporting requirements in Articles 5 and 7 and expert review team process in Article 8 with some aspects still to be finalized.[73] Disagreements between affected parties and expert review teams will be considered by the compliance committee.[74]

A range of other institutions and bodies will also be involved in monitoring and certifying/verifying information in relation to the Kyoto Mechanisms. For example, the CDM is made subject to the authority and guidance of the COP/MOP, but it is to be "supervised by an executive board," which will also have the capacity to provide guidance in respect of the participation of private and/or public entities.[75] "Operational entities" designated by the COP are to validate CDM projects and certify emissions reductions from each project.[76] There is provision for detailed monitoring plans and independent assessment, as well as national registries to track Certified Emission Reduction (CER) credits generated and subsequently traded as part of the emissions trading regime. Participating governments and private participants will be subject to these controls. The compliance committee is given a mandate to resolve disputes about compliance issues that affect a party's eligibility to participate in the CDM, as well as the dedicated CDM institutions.[77] It appears likely the system of certification and validation will somehow have to interact with a range of other regulatory arrangements, such as national laws, other international agreements (bilateral and multilateral) and contractual arrangements.

A Dedicated Compliance Regime

During the negotiation of the Kyoto Protocol, it seems to have been accepted that the terms of any new compliance institutions would have to be deferred to the future. The main controversy concerned the possible inclusion of "consequences" (beyond the predictable list of cautions, suspension of privileges, etc.).[78] In the subsequent negotiations there was a clear early consensus that any dedicated compliance procedures and institutions would include a strongly "facilitative" aspect to provide assistance and advice to parties during the course of the commitment period, as well as the ability to deter noncompliance by imposing "consequences" for noncompliance.[79] However, the negotiation of the compliance procedure proved to be one of the most difficult and controversial issues, with some parties refusing to accept that the compliance committee should be able to impose binding consequences.

Under the compliance procedure, the compliance committee is to have a plenary and two branches, a facilitative branch and an enforcement branch. The two branches will each have ten members elected by the Conference of Parties. Members are expected to be independent experts, and members of the enforcement branch must have legal experience.[80] The enforcement branch will be "responsible for determining when a Party included in Annex 1 is not in compliance" with its emissions targets, certain issues relating to adjustments to inventories and compliance with the eligibility requirements for participation in the Kyoto mechanisms.[81] The facilitative branch is to provide advice and facilitation to parties, principally non-Annex 1 parties and address "questions of implementation" with respect to how an Annex 1 party is striving to minimize adverse impacts on developing countries and whether the use by such a party of the Kyoto mechanisms is "supplemental" to domestic action as required by the protocol. It can also provide "an early warning of potential non-compliance with emissions targets, before and during a commitment period."[82]

The enforcement branch will be involved in considering a party's compliance with its emissions target at the end of the commitment period and its actual or potential noncompliance during the commitment period. The compliance procedure provides that an Annex 1 party has an additional period after the end of the commitment period where it can bring itself into compliance, for example, through emissions trading, failing which the enforcement branch is to impose certain consequences. The most serious of these is the carryover of the responsibility for meeting the target to the next commitment period with a 30 percent penalty. In addition, a party declared to be in noncompliance would have to develop a compliance plan setting out how it would meet its target and would be suspended from using the Kyoto mechanisms. The enforcement branch would also consider a failure to comply with reporting and inventory requirements, as well as disputes about eligibility to use the Kyoto mechanisms.[83]

In terms of procedure, "questions of implementation" may be raised by any party with respect to itself; any party about another party, with supporting corroborating information or through the Article 8 expert review process.[84] A nonparty may not initiate a proceeding before the compliance committee, but competent intergovernmental and nongovernmental organizations may submit relevant factual and technical information.[85] The bureau of the Compliance Committee will be responsible for allocating questions to the appropriate branch and the branch concerned will conduct a preliminary examination to determine whether, for example, the question is supported by sufficient evidence, based on the requirements of the protocol and is not *de minimis* or ill-founded.[86] Where a question is referred to the enforcement committee, a detailed procedure, including time limits, is to be followed, with the party concerned being given the opportunity to make written submissions and have a hearing, which will usually be in public. The enforcement branch is then to make a preliminary finding of non-compliance or decide not to proceed. The party concerned will have the opportunity to respond to any preliminary finding of noncompliance before it becomes "final."[87] An "expedited procedure" is provided for questions concerning eligibility requirements for the Kyoto mechanisms.[88] Where there is a final finding that an Annex 1 party is not in compliance with its target under Article 3 (1), the party may appeal to the COP/MOP, which will decide the issue by a three-quarters majority. If the COP/MOP "overrides" the decision of the enforcement branch, it must refer the matter back to that branch.[89]

The most contentious issue in the negotiations was the "indicative list of consequences" that could be imposed by the enforcement branch and their effect. In fact, on the critical point of compliance with the emissions target at the end of the commitment period, the compliance procedure *requires* the enforcement branch to impose particular consequences, such as development by the party of a compliance plan with a carryover penalty regarding noncompliance with an emissions target. On other questions of implementation, such as noncompliance with the reporting and inventory requirements in Articles 5 and 7, the committee must make a declaration of noncompliance and the party must have a compliance plan, but the committee would seem to have more flexibility.[90] While ensuring that the environmental outcome of the protocol met is critical, the compliance procedure must deal with the fact that the project of climate mitigation is a work in progress and there will be mistakes made by parties that are not the result of willful disobedience or even incapacity.[91] Some flexibility will be important in ensuring the long-term credibility of the climate regime. The facilitative branch cannot examine matters within the mandate of the enforcement branch. The consequences that it can apply include the provision of advice, facilitation of financial and technical assistance, and recommendations, taking into account the situation of non-Annex 1 parties as provided for in Article 4 (7) of the convention.[92] On their face, the compliance procedures and mechanisms with respect to the enforcement branch under the 1997 Kyoto Protocol are the most far-reaching of any MEA.

At the Marrakesh meeting, the negotiators were not able to agree on whether the consequences will be "binding" on the parties. The EU and the Group of 77 (G-77)/China took the view that there was already agreement that the consequences would be legally binding and that only the form of adoption of the compliance procedures was in issue. Several members of the Umbrella Group of countries, such as Australia, Canada, Japan, and the Russian Federation, took the view that the issue should be deferred first to COP/MOP. The compromise was the inclusion in the preamble to the compliance procedures of language, noting that it "is the prerogative of the parties to the Kyoto Protocol to decide on the legal form of the procedures and mechanisms relating to compliance." The argument is not a technical treaty issue nor a semantic one. In the absence of a resolution of this issue, there is a real risk that the scheme of the compliance procedures could be undermined. The last sentence of Article 18 of the protocol requires that any "binding consequences" be adopted in an amendment to the protocol and so the issue of the "binding" quality under international law of the compliance procedures is still to be resolved. However, even if the COP/MOP decides on the amendment, it follows that the compliance procedures will only be binding on parties that have adopted a later amendment to the protocol and this could potentially lead to two categories of parties. For those parties that did not accept the amendment, there would be few pressure points beyond shaming, suspension of membership, or denial of access to the mechanisms, or whatever limited countermeasures are permitted under international law. These could be powerful disincentives, as would the political risk of a harsher approach from other parties in negotiating targets for future commitment periods. However, given the high risk of noncompliance and concerns about potential free riding in this kind of MEA, there may need to be some greater assurance that all protocol parties would adopt the amendment in a contemporaneous manner. The effort to ensure a "binding" quality would also address the concern about the lack of power on the part of NCPs and the Conference of Parties to impose "binding" determinations and sanctions that are properly within the purview of traditional dispute resolution and general international law—a concern that is rarely raised in development of NCPs.[93]

Little attention is being given to the relationship of noncompliance procedures and mechanisms with the dispute resolution provisions under Article 14 of the convention as applied *mutatis mutandis* by Article 19. There appears to be a consensus that Montreal Protocol language to the effect that the compliance procedures and mechanisms will apply "without prejudice" to the dispute resolution provisions is sufficient. However, such a formula leaves unclear whether a party may invoke the Article 19 procedures while a matter is before the compliance committee or by way of indirect challenge or appeal.[94] It seems to be generally assumed that resort to these provisions is unlikely since there is not sufficient interest on the part of complying parties to generate a bilateral dispute with a noncompliant party. This assumption ignores the high stakes in this particular agreement, the considerable scope for dispute over the meaning of key provisions and the untested nature of the new institutions. The real constraint on resort to the dispute resolution provisions is more likely to come from the limited acceptance of the jurisdiction of the ICJ and arbitration tribunal, which is unlikely to change in the short term.

Private Actors and Extra Regime Assurance

The involvement of private actors in emissions trading, JI, and CDM raises interesting issues in looking at compliance. Given the sensitivities of the parties to perceived intrusions on sovereignty and the state—state bias of international dispute resolution—there is no provision for private actors to be given a role in formal compliance proceedings. Under the current proposal, such actors may only be able to bring "information" before the compliance committee via intergovernmental organizations or nongovernmental organizations. However, it is not unprecedented to allow private actors access to dispute resolution directly or with the support of a state party of nationality. The involvement of private actors, along with state parties, in transnational contracts and agreements relating to the

Kyoto mechanisms, will call into play a range of national and transnational legal rules and institutions where such actors may have standing. This potential multiplicity of institutions may help to promote compliance. However, multiple institutions could also increase confusion and introduce the potential for disparate actors to be involved in "judging compliance" outside the protocol institutions. So far as NGOs are concerned, the proposed dedicated compliance procedures and mechanisms do not depart from the usual denial of standing, but the information provisions are an explicit acknowledgment of the potentially important role that such bodies play in tracking compliance.

Finally, it is worth noting that the protocol and the rules under negotiation envisage detailed provisions at a national level for accounting and tracking purposes for the carbon credits involved in the Kyoto mechanisms, but they do not prescribe any particular form of national compliance approach. Nonetheless, it is to be expected that many states will enact domestic compliance regulations with strong sanctions to ensure domestic controls and avoid potential compliance problems at the international level. There may also be pressure for this from those involved in emissions trading and ancillary markets that have an interest in ensuring the integrity and value of trading in carbon credits.

Trends and Future Directions

From this survey a number of themes and tendencies emerge:

First, in the environmental field institutional arrangements for ensuring compliance with MEAs and other environmental obligations are generally open only to states; unlike the area of human rights, there is little if any scope for nonstate actors to invoke international procedures to challenge noncompliance. However, in many MEAs nonstate actors (industry and NGO) play an important role in providing information to treaty bodies about the performance of contracting parties.

Second, MEAs have tended to offer a range of institutional options for addressing noncompliance, involving both managerial approaches (such as the noncompliance mechanism of the Montreal Protocol, or conciliation) and traditional arbitral and judicial settlement of disputes (although there appears to be a preference for managerial, noncontentious mechanisms).

Third, states have been reluctant to agree to include provision in MEAs for unilateral recourse to binding dispute resolution (the 1982 UNCLOS is a notable exception) and there is a general perception that the global nature of commitments in most MEAs are not suited to bilateral and confrontational dispute resolution. Formal dispute resolution is seen as a last resort.

Fourth, negotiators of MEAs have been reluctant to create new institutions to address compliance, and a preference has been expressed for existing institutions. That said, while some inspiration has been drawn from the mechanisms established under trade, human rights, and arms control regimes (in particular reporting), the new institutions which have been established are peculiar to the environmental field and do not replicate the design of institutional arrangements in these other areas.

Fifth, the whole area is fragmented, in the sense that each MEA provides for its own particular institutional response to noncompliance (although certain general tendencies are now emerging).

Sixth, states have been reluctant to give institutions in MEAs explicit power to impose outcomes or resolve disputes over interpretation, but the linkage between compliance and funding for developing countries and economies in transition has become a significant aspect of MEAs and a de facto method securing "compliance."

Seventh, it is difficult to generalize about the role that the newer non-compliance institutions at the international level play in promoting compliance. Clearly, they enhance transparency and provide opportunities for pressure to comply, as well as a generally nonconfrontational forum to discuss genuine compliance difficulties. Nonetheless, such bodies have the potential to blur the distinction between a process-oriented form of negotiation and traditional dispute resolution and there are still unresolved legal questions about the status and operation of such bodies.

Eighth, in the case of the Kyoto Protocol the most ambitious compliance and enforcement institutions of any MEA are under consideration. However, it would be premature to speculate about whether these proposals will ultimately form part of the final package, given that the suspicion of powerful international institutions in this area is likely to be a serious constraint. Moreover, it may be that the Kyoto Protocol is *sui generis* and not likely to be a precedent for the development of other MEAs.

These themes and tendencies provide a framework against which to assess whether there exists a "compliance gap." It is apparent that states and other international actors are now giving considerable attention to compliance with MEAs, a subject that has only been addressed within the past decade. To the extent that a "compliance gap" implies generally a lack of awareness of the importance of compliance, or more specifically of the practical and real-world consequences of one or more international legislative efforts in the field of the environment, then there is no such gap. But of course mere awareness of issues of "compliance" will not be sufficient to conclude that there exists no gap. It is additionally necessary to be able to ascertain, first, whether those persons to which international environmental norms are addressed are in fact complying with their obligations, and, second, where they are not complying whether the MEAs provide for institutional or other arrangements to assist in bringing these actors into compliance. As to the first element the various empirical studies that have been made of MEAs reveal that this is a complex question.[95] There is some empirical evidence that in relation to some MEAs compliance—that is to say the adoption of measures that directly or indirectly bring an actor into a situation which the MEA requires as a matter of law—has been very effective. For example, the various protocols to the 1979 U.N. Economic Commission for Europe (UNECE) Convention on Long-Range Transboundary Air Pollution have brought down emissions of sulphur dioxide within the limits defined by the instruments. On the other hand, it is readily apparent that other kinds of agreements, particularly in the fields of biodiversity and fisheries conservation, have been, for the most part, of limited effect. But even here the failure to achieve the objectives of the instrument may reflect less on the issue of compliance than on the nature of the norms established and the techniques that marshaled to achieve them.

As to the second element, this chapter has demonstrated that practice among the various MEAs and other instruments varies greatly. Where MEAs have been ineffective—for example, in relation to biodiversity and fisheries conservation— there is not necessarily a correlation between ineffectiveness and the absence of institutional means for bringing about compliance. The Biodiversity Convention, for example, has a conciliation procedure that has never been invoked, notwithstanding the abundant evidence that many states are not complying with their obligations. The critical factor here seems to be the manner in which the procedure is invoked: in an interstate system, the actors (states) have a mutual interest in acting with restraint and not invoking bilateral, contentious proceedings. And even where they are invoked—as in the proceedings brought by Australia and New Zealand in relation to southern bluefin tuna—the institutions concerned (in that case an arbitral tribunal) often act with similar restraint in seeking not to overextend their jurisdictional reach. In our view it is simply not possible to draw broad conclusions about the relationship between substantive compliance and the existence of institutional arrangements for achieving compliance. The relationship turns on a range of other factors, including the subject matter which the MEA addresses and the nature of the obligations imposed (these two elements are often closely connected) and the identity of the party or parties concerned, including the presence and level of engagement of interested third parties, including states, international organizations, NGOs, and the corporate sector.

Nonetheless, it seems possible to make some general observations. In many instances, access to institutions that can provide guidance to states, particularly developing counties and economies in transition, as well as technical assistance and capacity building, is likely to promote compliance. It is apparent that traditional dispute settlement (i.e., international courts and arbitral bodies) can play an important, if complementary role, to the diplomatic means of dispute settlement, and that they form part of the general "armory" of encouraging compliance-even if only as a deterrent. However, it is to be noted that the circumstances in which these bodies are invoked where a dispute as to compliance arises remains very much the exception, and we are aware of only a very small number of cases. Practice under the emerging noncompliance mechanisms— such as that under the 1987 Montreal Protocol and the various inspection panels of the multilateral development banks—is already far more extensive. These kinds of institutions routinize scrutiny, dialogue, and transparency, notwithstanding that they are not unproblematic. This suggests that the current trend towards designing an array of institutional means to address compliance with MEAs is sensible. Finally, our sense is that compliance is likely to be enhanced by allowing the new international actors—international organizations, NGOs, and corporations—to play a formal role.

Notes

1. 1992 United Nations Framework Convention on Climate Change, *International Legal Materials*, 31: 849-73; and the 1997 Kyoto Protocol, *International Legal Materials* 37: 22-42.

2. See, generally, Philippe Sands, *Principles of International Environmental Law*, 2nd ed. (Cambridge, United Kingdom: Cambridge University Press, 2003).

3. Abraham Chayes and Antonia Handler Chayes, *The New Sovereignty: Compliance with International Regulatory Regimes* (Cambridge, MA: Harvard University Press, 1995); James Cameron, Jacob Werksman, and Peter Roderick, eds., *Improving Compliance with International Environmental Law* (London: Earthscan Publications Limited, 1996); David G. Victor, Kal Raustiala, and Eugene B. Skolnikoff, eds., *The Implementation and Effectiveness of International Environmental Commitments: Theory and Practice* (Cambridge, MA: MIT Press, 1998). See also Edith B. Weiss, "Understanding Compliance with International Environmental Agreements: The Baker's Dozen Myths'," *University of Richmond Law Review* 32 (1998-1999): 1555-89.

4. See, for example, the Survey of Existing International Agreements and Its Follow-Up, Report by the Secretary-General of the United Nations Conference on Environment and Development, A/Conf.151/PC/103 and Add. 1, January 20, 1992 and December 9, 1991, respectively. In particular the 1987 Montreal Protocol on Substances that Deplete the Ozone Layer, *International Legal Materials* 154: 1541-61; the 1992 Climate Change Convention; the 1992 Convention on Biological Diversity (the Biodiversity Convention), *International Legal Materials* 31: 822-48; and the development of noncompliance mechanisms and the current negotiations under the 1997 Kyoto Protocol described in the text accompanying endnotes 31 and 60 below.

5. See Note by the President of the Security Council, on "The Responsibility of the Security Council in the Maintenance of International Peace and Security," S/23500, January 31, 1992, 2, declaring that "non-military sources of instability in the . . . ecological fields have become threats to international peace and security."

6. For example, the decision in July 1993 by the International Court of Justice to establish a Chamber for Environmental Matters in Sands, *Principles of International Environmental Law*, 215.

7. This topic, while closely related to compliance, lies beyond the scope of this chapter; see, generally, Sands, *Principles of International Environmental Law*, chapter 20.

8. Noncompliance by states and international organizations with their treaty and other international legal obligations can be considered as the failure to give effect to obligations under the rules of international environmental law.

9. Noncompliance with international environmental obligations can occur for a variety of reasons, including a lack of institutional, financial, or human resources, and differing

interpretations as to the meaning or requirements of a particular obligation. Instances of "deliberate" noncompliance seem to be unusual. For an examination of theories about "why" states comply, see Benedict Kingsbury, "The Concept of Compliance as a Function of Competing Conceptions of International Law," *Michigan Journal of International Law* 19 (Winter 1998): 345-72.

10. In this context "enforcement" means the right to take measures to ensure the fulfillment of international legal obligations or to obtain a determination by an appropriate international court, tribunal, or other body, including an international organization, that such obligations are not being fulfilled.

11. Martti Koskenniemi, "Breach of Treaty or Non-Compliance? Reflections on the Enforcement of the Montreal Protocol," in Günther Handl, ed., *Yearbook of International Environmental Law* (London: Grahm and Trotman, 1992): 123-62, esp. 155-62.

12. See, for example, 1940 Western Hemisphere Convention, U.N. Treaty Series 161: 193-204; 1946 International Whaling Convention, U.N. Treaty Series 161: 72-110.

13. See Martti Koskenniemi, "New Institutions and Procedures for Implementation and Control and Reaction," in Jacob Werksman, ed., *Greening International Institutions* (London: Earthscan Publications Ltd., 1996), 236-48, esp. 237. See also Chayes and Chayes, *The New Sovereignty*, 25.

14. For example, as discussed below, the 1992 Climate Change Convention, Articles 10, 13, and 14. See also 1985 Vienna Convention for the Protection of the Ozone Layer, U.N. Treaty Series 1513: 322-447, Article 11; 1989 Convention on the Control of Transboundary Movements of Hazardous Wastes and Their Disposal (Basel), *International Legal Materials* 28: 657-86, Article 20; 1992 Biodiversity Convention, Article 27 and Annex II.

15. Additional Act to the Treaties of Bayonne (1866), Article 16, in 24 I.L.R., p.104.

16. The court said that negotiations should be conducted "on the basis that each must in good faith pay reasonable regard to the legal rights of the other . . . thus bringing about an equitable apportionment of the fishing resources based on the facts of the particular situation, and having regard to the interests of other states which have established fishing rights in the area. It is not a matter of finding simply an equitable solution, but an equitable solution derived from the applicable law." Id., 33. The court also invoked its earlier statement in the North Sea Continental Shelf cases, that ". . . it is not a question of applying equity simply as a matter of abstract justice, but of applying a rule of law which itself requires the application of equitable principles": Fisheries Jurisdiction Case: *United Kingdom v. Iceland* (1974), ICJ Report 3, July 25, 1974, esp. 47.

17. 1973 Convention on International Trade in Endangered Species of Wild Fauna and Flora (CITES), U.N. Treaty Series 993: 243-417, Article XVIII; 1973 International Convention for the Prevention of Pollution from Ships, *International Legal Materials* 12: 1319-1444 and its 1978 Protocol, *International Legal* Materials 17: 546-78 (MARPOL 73/78), Article 10; 1972 Convention on International Liability for Damage Caused by Space Objects, U.N. Treaty Series 961: 187-261, Article IX; 1974 Convention on the Marine Environment of the Baltic Sea Area, *International Legal Materials* 13: 546-90, Article 18 (1); 1979 Convention on Long-Range Transboundary Air Pollution (LRTAP), *International Legal Materials* 18: 1442-55, Article 13; 1985 Vienna Convention, Article 11 (1) and (2); 1992 Climate Change Convention, Article 14; 1992 Biodiversity Convention, Article 27 (1).

18. One example, however, involves the settlement between Canada and the U.S.S.R. concerning damage caused by the disintegration over Canada of Cosmos 954, a nuclear powered satellite launched by the U.S.S.R. By a protocol dated April 2, 1981, the U.S.S.R. agreed to pay, and Canada agreed to accept, Canadian $3,000,000 in a final settlement of the claim: see Sands, *Principles of International Environmental Law*, chapter 18.

19. For example, the 1979 LRTAP Convention requires early consultations to be held between parties "actually affected by or exposed to a significant risk of long-range transboundary air pollution" and the parties in which a significant contribution to such pollution originates: 1979 LRTAP Convention, Article 5.

20. See, for example, the 1968 African Convention on the Conservation of Nature and Natural Resource, U.N. Treaty Series 1991: 4-18, Article XVIII; 1982 Convention on the Law of the Sea (UNCLOS), *International Legal Materials* 21: 1261-1354, Article 284 and Annex V, Section 1; 1985 Vienna Convention, Article 11 (2).

21. See, for example, the 1985 Vienna Convention, Article 11 (4) and (5) providing for the establishment of a conciliation commission; 1992 Biodiversity Convention, Article 27 (4) and Annex II, Part 2; 1992 Climate Change Convention, Article 14 (5) to (7).

22. See, for example, 1952 International Convention for the High Seas Fisheries of the North Pacific Ocean, Protocol, paras. 4 and 5 (special committee of scientists), www.oceanslaw.net/texts/nphs.htm.

23. 1909 Treaty Relating to the Boundary Waters and Questions Arising along the Boundary between the United States and Canada, 36 Stat. 2448, T.S.No.548, especially Articles VIII and IX.

24. See also dispute settlement under the North American Free Trade Agreement (NAFTA), Sands, *Principles of International Environmental Law*, chapter 18.

25. 1985 Vienna Convention, Article 11; 1992 Biodiversity Convention, Article 27; 1992 Climate Change Convention, Article 14.

26. See, for example, the 1982 Regional Convention for the Conservation of the Red Sea and the Gulf of Aden Environment (Jeddah), 9 EPL 56 (1982), Article XXIV (2); 1988 Agreement on the Network of Aquaculture Centres in Asia and the Pacific, Article 19 (1).

27. CITES Conference of Parties Resolution 4.27 (April 1983). See generally on the role of the organs created by MEAs, Robin Churchill and Geir Ulfstein, "Autonomous Institutional Arrangements in Multilateral Environmental Agreements: A Little-Noticed Phenomenon in International Law," *American Journal of International Law* 94, no. 4 (October 2000): 623-59.

28. For an example of an explicit power, see 1973 CITES Convention, Articles XII, 2 (d) and (e) and X.

29. See Decision II/5 (noncompliance), Report of the Second Meeting of the Parties to the Montreal Protocol on Substances that Deplete the Ozone Layer, UNEP/OzL.Pro.2/3, June 29, 1990; see now Decision IV/5 and Annexes IV and V, adopting the noncompliance procedure; Report of the Fourth Meeting of the Parties, UNEP/OzL.Pro.4/15, November 25, 1992, *International Legal Materials* 32: 874-87 and the later amendments in Decision X/10 and Annex II, Report of the Tenth Meeting of the Parties; UNEP/OzL. Pro. 10/9, December 3, 1998. See also 1992 Climate Change Convention, Article 13; 1994 U.N. Protocol to the LRTAP Convention, *International Legal Materials* 33: 1540-54 (1994), Article 7 (1); 1994 U.N. Convention to Combat Desertification in those Countries Experiencing Serious Drought and/or Desertification, Particularly in Africa, *International Legal Materials* 33: 1328-82, Article 27.

30. UNEP/OZL.Pro.4/15, Annex IV, para. 1.

31. Annex, IV, paras. 2 to 4.

32. Annex IV, para. 7(a) and (b), Decision IV/5 and Annex IV.

33. Annex IV, paras. 7(d) and (e).

34. Annex IV, paras. 8 and 9.

35. Annex IV, para. 7(d).

36. Annex IV, Decision IV/5.

37. Annex IV, paras. 15 and 16.

38. See Jacob Werksman, "Compliance and Transition: Russia's Non-Compliance Tests the Ozone Regime," *Heidelberg Journal of International. Law (ZaOrv)* 56 (1996): 750-73; David G. Victor, "The Operation and Effectiveness of the Montreal Protocol's Non-Compliance Procedure," in *The Implementation and Effectiveness of International Environmental Commitments*, 137. Similar decisions were made with respect to Belarus and Ukraine, but only the Russian Federation had a major domestic production and recycling capacity.

39. See, for example, the Report of the Implementation Committee under the Non-Compliance Procedure for the Montreal Protocol on the Work of Its Twentieth Meeting, UNEP/OzL. /Imp. Com/20/4, July 9, 1998, paras. 30-33. On the role of financial assistance in MEAs, see Phillipe Sands, "Carrots without Sticks? New Financial Mechanisms for Global Environmental Agreements," *Max Planck Yearbook of United Nations Law* 3 (1999): 363-88, esp. 364.

40. 1907 Hague Convention on the Pacific Settlement of International Disputes, Article 37.

41. Southern Bluefin Tuna Case, *Australia and New Zealand v. Japan*, August 4, 2000, *International Legal Materials* 39: 1359-1401.

42. PCIJ Series A/B, No. 70 (June 28, 1937): 76-7

43. PCIJ Series A, No. 23 (September 10, 1929): 27.

44. *United Kingdom v. Albania*, April 9, 1949, ICJ Report 4.

45. 1974 Fisheries Jurisdiction Case, *United Kingdom v. Iceland*, ICJ Report 3, 31.

46. 1973 ICJ Report 135; 1974 ICJ Report 253.

47. *Nauru v. Australia*, 1992 , ICJ Report 240.

48. 1957 EEC Treaty, Article 164. The ECJ also has competence in relation to the interpretation and application of the 1950 European Coal and Steel Community (ECSC) Treaty and the 1957 European Atomic Energy Community (Euratom).

49. 1957 EEC Treaty, Article 173.

50. Judgment of April 2, 1998.

51. The relevant courts are the European Court of Human Rights and the Inter-American Court of Human Rights.

52. Supra note 43.

53. *US-Import Prohibition of Certain Shrimp and Shrimp Products*, Report of the Appellate Body, World Trade Organization, Decision AB-1998-4, WTO/DS58/AB/R, October 12, 1998; *International Legal Materials* 38 (1999): 118-75.

54. See Henry D. Jacoby, Ronald G. Prinn, and Richard Schmalenesee, "Kyoto's Unfinished Business," *Foreign Affairs* 77, no. 4 (July/August 1998): 54-66.

55. See, generally, Michael Grubb with Christiaan Vrolijk, and Dunan Brack, *Kyoto Protocol: A Guide and Assessment* (Washington, D.C.: Brookings Institution Press, 1999); Clare Breidenich, Daniel Magraw, Anne Rawley, and James W. Rubin, "The Kyoto Protocol to the United Nations Framework Convention on Climate Change," *American Journal of International Law* 92, no. 2 (April 1998): 315-31.

56. Entry into force will occur when fifty-five states, representing at least 55 percent of the total emissions in 1990 of the parties listed in Annex B (developed country and economies in transition), become parties: Article 25.1. As of September 25, 2003, 119 states had become parties, which represents 44.2 percent of Annex 1 party emissions: www.unfccc.int/resource/kpthermo.html. In the absence of U.S. participation, Russian participation is probably necessary to meet the 55 percent emissions limit. For the U.S. position, see Greg Kahn, "The Fate of the Kyoto Protocol under the Bush Administra-

tion," *Berkeley Journal of International Law* 21 (2003): 548-71. In late 2003, doubts emerged about early Russian ratification: "Russia Puts Global Climate Pact in Doubt," *New York Times*, September 30, 2003.

57. See Procedures and Mechanisms Relating to Compliance under the Kyoto Protocol, Annex to Decision 24/CP.7 in FCCC/CP/2001/13/Add.3, January 21, 2002, the Marrakesh Accords, supra note 56 (hereafter "Compliance Procedure"). See also Report of the Joint Working Group on Compliance on its work during the second part of the thirteenth session of the subsidiary bodies, FCCC/SB/2000/CRP.15/Rev.2, November 20, 2000; Jacob Werksman, "Compliance and the Kyoto Protocol: Building a Backbone into a 'Flexible' Regime," *Yearbook of International Environmental Law* 9 (1998) 49-101; and Jutta Brunnée, "A Fine Balance: Facilitation and Enforcement in the Design of a Compliance Regime for the Kyoto Protocol," *Tulane Environmental Law Journal* 13, no. 2 (Summer 2000): 223-70.

58. Werksman, supra note 58, 25.

59. Daniel Bodansky, "The United Nations Framework Convention on Climate Change: A Commentary," *Yale Journal of International Law* 18, no. 2 (1993): 451-558, esp. 546.

60. Bodanksy, "Commentary," 546-47.

61. Jacob Werksman, "Designing A Compliance System for the UN Framework Convention on Climate Change," in *Improving Compliance with International Environmental Law*, 85-112, esp. 122.

62. 1992 Climate Change Convention, Articles 4.1, 4.2, and 12. Annex 1 parties also have commitments toward different categories of non-Annex parties: for example, Articles 4.3.-10. Note special provision is also made for the "differentiated" responsibilities of developing countries: Articles 4.3, 12.5, and 6.

63. See Article 7, and note Article 7.2 (e); Article 10.1 of the 1992 Climate Change Convention.

64. The second review of commitments was not completed by December 31, 1998, as provided for in Article 4.2.d.

65. Report of the Conference of Parties on its First Session, FCCC/CP/1995/7/Add.1, Decision 2/CP.1, Annex 1, June 6, 1995.

66. Report of the Ad Hoc Group on Article 13, FCCC/AG13/1998/2, July 10, 1998.

67. See, for example, Article 11 of the 1982 Vienna Convention.

68. For an explicit provision to this effect see Article 15 of the arbitration annex to the 1982 Vienna Convention: Report of the Conference of Parties to the Vienna Convention UNEP/ OzL.Conv. 1/5, Annex II, April 28, 1989.

69. The Solomon Islands at the time of ratification.

70. See for joint fulfillment, Kyoto Protocol: Article 4; emissions trading: Articles 17, 3 (10), and 3 (11); Joint Implementation/JI: Articles 6, 3 (10), and (11); and the clean development mechanism/CDM: Articles 12 and 3 (12).

71. See Articles 5 and 7 (Kyoto Protocol).

72. Articles 8.5 and 8.6 (Kyoto Protocol).

73. Marrakech Accords, supra note 56, Decisions 21-23, FCCC/CP/2001/13/Add.3, Section 2.

74. Compliance Procedure, supra, note 58, at section V, paras. 5 (a) and (b).

75. Articles 12.4 and 12.9 (Kyoto Protocol); Marrakesh Accords, supra note 56, Modalities and Procedures for the Clean Development Mechanism, as defined in Article 12 of the Kyoto Protocol, Decision 16/CP.7 (FCCC/CP/2001/13/Add.2, January 21, 2002). The CDM Board is in operation, but modalities and definitions for projects are

still being elaborated.

76. Article 12.4 (Kyoto Protocol).

77. Section V, para. 4 (c).

78. See Joanna Depledge, "Tracing the Origins of the Kyoto Protocol: An Article-by-Article Textual History, FCCC/TP/2000/2, November 25, 2000, paras. 396-402. See Article 18: "The Conference of Parties serving as the Meeting of the Parties to this Protocol shall, at its first session, approve appropriate and effective procedures and mechanisms to determine and to address cases of non-compliance with provisions of this Protocol, including through the development of an indicative list of consequences, taking into account the cause, type, degree and frequency of non-compliance. Any procedures and mechanisms under this Article entailing binding consequences shall be adopted by means of an amendment to this Protocol."

79. See, for example, para. 4 of the proposed Procedures and Mechanisms Relating to Compliance under the Kyoto Protocol: Elements of a Compliance System and Synthesis of Submissions, Note by the Co-Chairs of the Joint Working Group on Compliance, FCCC/SB/1999/7, September 17, 1999.

80. Compliance Procedures, supra note 58, paras. II.6, IV.3, and V.3.

81. Section V, paras. 4 and 5.

82. Section IV, paras. 4-6..

83. Section XIII and XV, paras. 5 and 6 (regarding the additional period and non-compliance with an emission target); section XV, paras. 1 and 2 (regarding non-compliance with reporting and inventory requirements); section XV, para. 4 and section X, paras. 2-4 (regarding the Kyoto mechanisms).

84. Section VI, paras. 1-3.

85. Section VIII.

86. Section VII.

87. Section IX.

88. Section X.

89. Section XI.

90. Contrast Section XV para. 1 and para. 5.

91. Ronald B. Mitchell, "Institutional Aspects of Implementation, Compliance, and Effectiveness," in Urs Luterbacher and Detlef F. Sprinz, eds., *International Relations and Global Climate Change* (Cambridge, MA: MIT Press, 2001), 232 and 240.

92. Compliance procedures, Section XIV.

93. Martti Koskenniemi, "Breach of Treaty of Non-Compliance?" 146.

94. Compliance procedures, Section XVI.

95. See the studies in endnote 3.

5

Crises and Conflicts in the African Great Lakes Region: The Problem of Noncompliance with Humanitarian Law

*James R. Katalikawe, Henry M. Onoria,
and Baker G. Wairama*

The Compliance Gap—Some Factual Observations

In this study, we analyze several national and international factors that may help to explain the causes of the compliance gap and how to close it. The choice of factors is based on their crosscutting nature, that is, they are to a large extent shared by the states most affected by humanitarian problems in the Africa Great Lakes Region. First is the "dereliction" of most of the states in the region when it comes to fulfilling their humanitarian obligations under international law. State dereliction or virtual collapse is attributed to the very nature of the state in Africa, especially its conceptual and juridical foundations. A major problem seems to be lack of national identity in these multiethnic states. National identity is a fundamental factor in modifying and moderating state behavior in an increasingly nation-based, rather than state-based, international system.[1]

The first factor, state dereliction or collapse, has amplified the effects of the second factor: a colonial legacy of ethnoreligious schism and repressive undemocratic governments that has drastically weakened most states in the region or rendered them dysfunctional. Closely related is the absence of an effective civil society to bridge these schisms and to counter those actions of state and nonstate actors that violate humanitarian law. Third is the amorphous and intractable nature of conflict in the region. Over the past several decades, local conflicts have become more protracted in their blend of intrastate and interstate dimensions. Fourth is the seeming absence of effective mechanisms for holding individuals accountable for crimes against humanity and for violations of humanitarian law that are being committed, with increasing frequency, by state and nonstate actors. Fifth, and interrelated to the preceding factor, has been the inaction or evasion of responsibility on the part of regional and international bodies that have lacked the political will to prevent humanitarian violations. The overall dilemma of noncompliance in the region is compounded by hegemonic power politics that are played out by the region's statesmen and the Western powers. As a result, compliance and enforcement are too often left to these statesmen, who broker peace, conjure up peace pacts and alliances, and seek to carry out peacekeeping in the territory of their neighbors, while pleading that state sovereignty should bar outside interference in their own domestic conflicts.

This chapter opens with overviews of the region's history of conflict and of its record of noncompliance with the provisions of the Geneva conventions. These overviews are followed by a review of the five factors noted above and then by a series of specific recommendations for closing the gap in compliance with humanitarian norms in the conflicts that abound in the Great Lakes Region. It is important to note that unless concerted regional and international action is taken to address the issues raised in this chapter, the region is likely to experience extended destabilization and humanitarian disasters far worse than the calamities of the 1990s.

Crises and Conflicts in the Region: A General Overview

The African continent has experienced thirty wars during the last three decades.[2] With regard to the particular conflict situation in the Great Lakes Region, the endemic cycle of conflict has gradually spiraled out of control from the 1960s, when most of the states in the region attained independence, to the current unprecedented "regional conflict" that has involved most states in the region since 1998. Soon after independence in the 1960s, conflict was largely internal to each multiethnic state, as competition for power turned into competition for sovereignty over ethnic rivals, leading to marginalization of many groups in each state.[3] This process increasingly led toward internal anarchy and, as conflicts grew more violent, international intervention became harder, especially because the concept of "state sovereignty" increasingly became associated with inequality and discrimination.

The above can be exemplified by one of the earlier and larger deployments of a United Nations peacekeeping mission: the operation in the Belgian Congo between 1960 and 1964.[4] The mission, the first involvement of the United Nations in an African conflict for humanitarian purposes, was largely ineffective in dealing with the effects of an army mutiny, Belgian military intervention to protect the remaining Belgian residents, and the secession of the province of Ka-tanga under Moise Tshombe. It failed, in short, to restore order in the country. A succession of events, as the U.N. watched, led to Colonel Joseph Mobutu's (later Mobutu Sese Seko) first coup in 1960 and his decisive final overthrow of the government in 1965. From 1965, the Belgian Congo (now the Democratic Re-public of Congo) underwent numerous violent conflicts and gross human rights violations until Mobutu was removed from power by a Ugandan and Rwandan led armed intervention. In 1998, a full-fledged regional war flared up and con-tinues to simmer in spite of numerous ceasefires, peace accords, and resolutions of the United Nations.[5]

While conflicts on the continent have been numerous, the United Nations has continued to play an uncertain and inconsistent role in their resolution. In some cases, the previous colonial powers have been allowed to carry out what-ever unilateral interventions they deemed necessary, that are then justified as interventions by members of the U.N. Security Council. In the aftermath of the Somalia debacle, the United Nations has tended to take a distanced position, preferring to make exhortations upon belligerent parties from New York, though it has sent peacekeepers or observers to Liberia, Sierra Leone, the Congo, and Ethiopia-Eritrea. Clearly these efforts have been inadequate and taken under inappropriate intervention timetables.

As a result, at the start of the twenty-first century, the Great Lakes Region is draped in conflict in almost every state in the region and the compliance with humanitarian law is deplorable. First, the situation in the Democratic Republic of Congo (DRC) outlined above has been described as "Africa's first War" for the involvement of at least seven regional states.[6] Until recently, Angola was gripped by a persistent Movimento Popular de Libertacao de Angola (MPLA)-Uniao Nacional para Independencia Total de Angola (UNITA) conflict, rooted in a struggle for political power and for control over petroleum resources. In Southern Sudan, the conflict between the Islamic Khartoum government and the Christian and animist Sudanese Peoples Liberation Army (SPLA) guerrillas rages against a background of clamors for self-determination. In Uganda, the Museveni government is faced with rebel insurgency in the northern and west-ern parts of the country, while Rwanda and Burundi are engrossed in a histori-cally long-running Tutsi-Hutu ethnic conflict. Somalia has, since the botched U.N. peacekeeping operation, been without effective government, as the warring between the clans and warlords has reduced the country to a wasteland.

Some of these regional conflicts have lasted the lifespan of the independent state, as in Angola, or for decades, as in the Sudan and Uganda. Significantly, the persistence and ferocity of these conflicts has left the region littered with failed, collapsed, or fragmented states—from Somalia to the Democratic Repub-lic of Congo—incapable of exercising effective authority over large parts of their territories or meeting the most basic needs of their populations.[7] More fun-damental, though, has been the blatant disregard and nonrespect of principles of humanitarian law in these conflicts, as reflected in the butchery of the Rwanda genocide, the mutilation and abductions of the Lord's Resistance Army (LRA) and the Allied Democratic Forces (ADF) rebel groups in northern and western Uganda, the recruitment of child soldiers in the Congo, and so on.

Noncompliance: Tearing Apart the Geneva Conventions in the Region's Conflicts

The depth of the brutality in the Great Lakes Region over the last two decades of the twentieth century is incomprehensible. The initially commonplace tenor of human rights violations there, although in most cases on a massive scale, has in the last two decades given way to the most gruesome and telling violations of humanitarian norms as conflict ripped through the region's states. From the "human rights" violations of the dictatorial regimes of Amin, Bokasa, Habre, Mobutu, Nguema, and Barre, the region has since become mired in broad-based "humanitarian crises" of unprecedented levels. While the human rights abuses of the dictatorial regimes shocked the conscience of the world, the post-1980 humanitarian crises in the region, especially the Somalia clan-based violence and the Rwanda genocide, reflected deliberate and mass noncompliance with normative regimes. The 1994 Rwanda genocide stands as the most horrendous event in our contemporary times since the massacre of Jews during World War II.

In Uganda, situations of insurgency, from the Luwero conflict (1980-1985) to the ongoing conflict in northern and western parts of the country (1986-present), have in most instances entailed gross disrespect for humanitarian law. During the conflicts, both the government and the insurgents have ignored the provisions of the 1949 Geneva Conventions, though these form part of Ugandan law.[8] Abductions, mass murder, mutilation, forced labor and conscription, rape, torture, extrajudicial executions, and forced displacement of civilians into "reception centers" (in the Luwero conflict) or "protected villages" (in the Northern Uganda conflict) have been regular features of violations of humanitarian law.[9] In the Sudan, there have been numerous incidents of indiscriminate air and ground attacks against the civilian populations in the South by the Khartoum government.[10] In the background of the conflict between government and insurgents, interethnic conflict and slavery flourish.[11] In Angola, where the MPLA-UNITA conflict persisted into its third decade, the laying of landmines, apart from other deliberate wanton acts on the part of both belligerents, has wrought a humanitarian disaster on both human life and the environment.[12] In Rwanda, the genocide—in which an estimated one million people were mass murdered—was the definitive humanitarian tragedy. As discussed below and in Luc Côté's chapter in this volume, the violations of humanitarian law there have since become the subject of prosecution of the perpetrators at the criminal tribunal at Arusha.[13] Even then, in refugee crises in Eastern Zaire following the genocide, the humanitarian situation remained dismal, with the refugees being used as human shields and as a source of insurgency by the Hutu extremists, while the international community idly looked on. Regarding the noncompliance with humanitar-

ian law during the crisis in Eastern Zaire, the Director of Oxfam's Community
Aid Abroad, Jeremy Hobbs, lamented:

> What we are seeing right now is more than a humanitarian disaster—it is the
> tearing-up of the Geneva Convention. International law is being flouted on a
> massive scale. The refugees and the displaced are being denied the right to pro-
> tection and assistance enshrined in the Convention . . . . Hundreds of thousands
> of refugees and displaced have been abandoned by the international community
> and are now moving deeper into Zaire, out of sight, spreading unrest and desta-
> bilisation.[14]

Since then, many of these thousands have reportedly been killed by disease
or during ethnic conflict fanned by various states or have been raped, murdered,
or suffered other casualties of war between governments.[15]

In the more protracted conflict in the Democratic Republic of Congo, the
scale of the humanitarian crisis is reflected both in the loss of life and in the
plunder of the territory's resources. Following the fighting between the armed
forces of Uganda and Rwanda in Kisangani in June 2000, the International
Court of Justice was requested to indicate provisional measures of protection. In
the court's decision, it was remarked:

> The Court is of the view that persons, assets and resources present on the terri-
> tory of the Congo, particularly in areas of conflict remain vulnerable, and that
> there is a serious risk that the rights at issue in this case . . . may suffer irrepa-
> rable prejudice.[16]

In the Great Lakes Region, the warring belligerents have increasingly relied
on illegal means and methods of warfare that often place civilians in the center
of conflict. These practices have included the laying of landmines; indiscriminate bombing; attacks on, abductions of, and the use of civilians as war shields;
reprisals against populations in rebel-infested areas; disruption of relief supplies;
etc. An enduring consequence of these conflicts and of noncompliance with international norms has been hundreds of thousands of refugees, internal displacement, food crisis and hunger, and the loss and destruction of life and property.[17]

Understanding Noncompliance with Humanitarian Law during Conflict in the Region

Dereliction of the State: Legacy of Ethnoreligious Schism and Nonrespect for Human Rights

The conflicts in the Great Lakes traverse the entire expanse of the landscape of the region—Angola, the Congo, Burundi, Rwanda, Sudan, Somalia, and Uganda. While this chapter concerns itself with the conflict and humanitarian situation in the region, and draws examples, incidents, and lessons from all the region's states, the primary focus will be the situation in the Congo, Uganda, Rwanda, and Sudan. This is because the conflicts in these states epitomize the long-term problems in the region.

Since independence in the 1960s, the history of the Great Lakes Region, as already noted, has been bedeviled with a common legacy of ethnoreligious schism and nonrespect for human rights by successive regimes. In most cases, the origins of postcolonial state-inspired ethnic and religious divisions, as well as violations of human rights, are rooted in the policies of the colonial government—from the undertones of Belgian perpetration of a "hamitic" superiority complex among the Tutsi over the Hutu in the Rwanda-Urundi federation,[18] British encouragement of feelings of superiority in the South and of a labor reservoir in the North in Uganda,[19] and the Arab-African racial and Islamic-Christian religious identity of the peoples of Northern and Southern Sudan.[20] In the Congo, the conflict over the Shaba and Katanga remains largely ethnic based.[21] These deeply ingrained ethnoreligious schisms that characterize conflict in the region are also evident in the clan warlordism in Somalia and the Tutsi-Hutu rivalry in Rwanda and Burundi.

The result has been that since independence, in most of sub-Saharan Africa, the state has been closely linked with particular ethnic or religious groups, whose members form the majority in the close circles of government. Ismagilova has reflected on this aspect of the state in Africa as follows:

> Ethnicity continues to play a significant role in the various spheres of life in African States, mainly in politics . . . [T]here is a growing significance of traditional ethno-cultural values and . . . growth of ethic consciousness, the desire to preserve one's culture, languages, etc. . . . The ethnicity is seen in different spheres of life . . . existing political parties and organizations . . . express the interests of definite ethnic groups . . . in administrative bodies, the majority belongs to the dominating ethos or even a clan . . . attention is paid to the [socio-economic] development of the regions where representatives of the higher echelons of power come from.[22]

In summary, inside each state in the region, competition for power has become a compelling struggle for sovereignty over ethnoreligious rivals, causing a cycle of violence as groups see threats to their existence.[23]

The perpetration of ethnoreligious schisms was paralleled only by the virtual absence of human rights notions in the administrative structures of government introduced during colonial rule. This was apparent from the naked brutality of Leopold II's Congo to the subtlety of the judicious construction of the image of the "homo colonialis" to whom human rights guarantees were considered inapplicable. Indeed, the attitude to the rights of peoples in colonized societies was summed up early in the nineteenth century by a British judge in the terms: "We are not here to consider the case of a civilised and orderly State, such as modern England or the Rome of Cicero's time, but the administration of a barbarous or, at least, semi-barbarous community."[24]

The failure to inculcate a culture of respect for human rights was, in fact, worsened by the enactment of legislation extensively limiting rights as well as their possible vindication. In this regard, the legacy of the laws on deportation and unlawful assemblies cannot be overstated.[25] While the colonial government had its own intentions, the legacy of nonrespect for human rights continues to characterize government in most of the region's states—and, in the conflict-ridden situation that obtains, has only assumed the catastrophic proportions of a humanitarian disaster. The genocide in Rwanda and the atrocities of northern and western Uganda, Eastern DRC, Angola, and so on attest to this. Further, the virtual absence of any democratic tradition in the political landscape of colonial rule translated, on independence, into the dictatorial regimes of Africa's states. The Great Lakes Region has had more than its share of these regimes, from Mobutu (Zaire), Amin (Uganda), Banda (Malawi), Nguema (Equatorial Guinea), Bokasa (Central African Republic), Said Barre (Somalia), to name a few of the region's most famous dictators. The failure to develop a clear conception of "democratic governance" on the continent found expression in the Banjul Charter, where no reference is made to the "will of the people,"[26]—a factor underpinned by the predominance of unelected, military, or one-party states at the time in 1981.[27] Apart from Nigeria, the bulk of abuses, in particular for violation of political rights, have involved Zaire (now the DRC) and Malawi.[28] In fact, the conflict in the Democratic Republic of Congo has revolved, among other factors, upon a failure of the post-Mobutu regime to secure more democratic openness.[29] The past and present conflicts in the region have been exacerbated by the widely perceived lack of political legitimacy of the governments in power.

Furthermore, the forty years of independence in Africa, and in particular the Great Lakes Region, have with time bred another feature in the character of the state: the militarization of government and politics. A number of post-independence leaders found themselves either forcefully removed by the armed forces, as was the case of Lumumba, or dependent on the might of the military to remain in power, as in the instances of Obote and Mobutu, and, more recently, of Museveni, Kagame, the late Desire Kabila, and now his successor in power, Joseph Kabila.

Most African states have, since the 1960s, been governed by military regimes or by leaders installed in military putsches.[30] Supported by the Kelsenian theory of the legality of extraconstitutional changes in government by coup d'états,[31] the ascent to the echelons of political power by the *barrel* rather than the *ballot* has meant that the issue of legitimacy has become a pivotal element of conflict. For the Great Lakes Region, with the divisions that abound, the eth- noreligious group in power often dominates the military.[32] This has resulted in what are essentially "predator states" that survive by purges upon the opposition, resulting in violations of human rights—and, in extreme instances, genocidal conduct in violation of humanitarian norms. The control of the armed forces by a nondemocratic government places conflict situations on a different plane, as both its forces and the rebel groups become involved in violations of human rights and humanitarian law.

The absence of a democratic tradition has invariably stifled the emergence of a viable civil society in the region. While there have been civic groups of a religious character, those with political leanings have generally been absent or, where they are present, have been subject to harassment by functionaries of the state. In this regard, the Africa Peace Forum has observed:

> In general, civil society in the Great Lakes region does not present a solid united sphere able to engage governments on issues of social justice or act as a powerful 'check' on regimes of the day. It has been easily manipulated and co- opted, falling prey to ethnic and regional animosities fanned by political elite.[33]

From the above, it is clear that the state in postcolonial Africa has been left at the mercy of its own dereliction, ethnoreligiously divided and militarized. In the Great Lakes Region, moreover, the prevailing geopolitical and hegemonic power relations have nurtured and ensured the intransigence of conflict.

Dysfunctional Nation-States and Power Relations in Their Internal Political Ordering

The greatest burden on Africa has been the nature of the "nation-state" that was cast upon it at the moment of independence.[34] The new states were invariably bundles of peoples of differing ethnoreligious or national identities. Lovelace precisely sums up this state of affairs thus:

> The formation of the state system in Africa is primarily the result of a process of destruction of the native social and political systems and of the imposition of artificial constructs, concerning boundaries, population, and governmental in- stitutions. Political de-colonization was not meant, and could not possibly mean, to erase such legacy. When the Organization of African Unity endorsed the principle of *title to territory—uti possidetis* juris—as the basis for the de- limitation of territorial boundaries, in agreement also with the pattern which was emerging in that respect in the jurisprudence of the International Court of Justice, it did so for the good reason that an alternative approach aiming at a comprehensive revision of what the colonial powers had done, entailed basi- cally launching the continent in a free fall of absolute uncertainty. That does

not mean the principle, as applied to the African context, was comparatively sound or just. On the contrary, the compulsive nature of the decision amounted to a sanctioning, by Africa itself, of its own loss of identity.[35]

The consequence of the above process has been a continent bedeviled by intrastate conflicts, as particular groups seek to assert independence, as was the case with Katanga in the Belgian-Congo (1960-1961) and with Biafra in Nigeria (1967-1970). The more protracted conflicts have been those involving Eritrea, then as part of Ethiopia, and Cabinda in Angola. As already noted, this splitting process has in the end come to manifest itself in "failed" or "collapsed" states, such as Somalia and the Congo, in which conflict rages on and the scale of the humanitarian tragedy is paralleled by the ethnoreligious schism. With ethnoreligious conflicts dividing country after country, most of the region's states are unable to exercise any kind of effective authority over large parts of their territory. This lack of competence exacerbates the compliance gap, since the monitoring of human rights and the enforcement of humanitarian norms require the state to exercise such authority throughout its territory.[36] The near total dysfunction of the states in the region thus invariably bodes ill for the respect or enforcement of human rights and humanitarian law. The populace in those parts that are without effective state authority are often left at the mercy of warring bands of rebels and insurgents. Compliance with humanitarian norms in the circumstances becomes virtually nonexistent.

In practice, a serious outcome of the dysfunctional state is that it abdicates its role of providing law and order and security; yet it is supposed to ensure that rights are properly protected during times of war or states of emergency in a manner that is in conformity with international humanitarian standards. Too often the state takes on repressive measures, by legislation or naked force, to deal with the upsurge of discontent and rebellion. In effect, a government, dominated by a particular ethnoreligious group, tends to so concern itself with the prevailing situation of national politics, that is, with holding onto state power, as to fail to significantly observe or comply with humanitarian principles. Consequently, the state may even allow purges and victimization against those civilian populations believed to be lending support to groups opposed to the government. In the region, one finds numerous instances of this treatment of civilian populations as "proxy" targets of conflict, such as the military purges in the wake of rebel activity in Luwero in Uganda,[37] military expeditions of the Khartoum government in the Southern Sudan (1983-present),[38] and the MPLA-UNITA conflict in Angola.[39] In the intractable conflicts that presently prevail in the region, noncompliance with humanitarian norms has become commonplace on the part of both state and rebel (nonstate) groups.

In the schema of power politics, defined along the ethnoreligious schisms in the state, enforcement is often a postmortem exercise, in the character of the prosecution of the individuals accused of gross violations of human rights and humanitarian norms.[40] This has been the case since the Nuremberg and Tokyo trials, with the most recent manifestation in the Yugoslav and Rwanda trials.

More significantly, though, is the fact that in a conflict situation, governments are often keen to prosecute individuals belonging to the "opposition," while its own supporters are given immunity from any trial and punishment for "criminal acts" committed on their part. Thus, captured members of political opposition or rebel groups will readily be prosecuted for treason by the government in power, as has been the case in Uganda. Conversely, the vanquished members of a previous government will be tried by the new government, as has been the case in Rwanda. This fact of a "victor's justice" defines the power relations and ethnoreligious divisions that underpin the region's states, rendering it that much more difficult to resolve a prevailing or simmering conflict, as there may be substantial mistrust of the efforts of the government at political reconciliation and restoration of peace.[41]

The Amorphous and Intractable Nature of Conflict

The nature of conflict in the Great Lakes Region is a further major obstacle to the application of, and therefore to compliance with, humanitarian law. This has similarly affected its possible enforcement. Where the conflicts had, in the 1980s, largely been intrastate in the sense of internally organized guerrilla or rebel activity, the 1990s witnessed the introduction of interstate elements as well, producing a volatile situation of "intractability." This aspect is evident in the Sudan-Uganda support of LRA and SPLA rebel groups in each other's territories, in the seven-nation "war" in the Democratic Republic of Congo, and in Uganda's support for the RPF incursion into Rwanda prior to the 1994 genocide. The political and military maneuvering in terms of ideology, deployment of troops, and support to rebel groups greatly complicates the web of conflict in the region. An ironic example of the outcome of this convoluted process was the fighting that erupted between Ugandan and Rwandan troops in eastern DRC. In legal terms, the best that can be made of the situation in the region is to regard the conflicts there as both internal and international—in effect, the *corpus* of the humanitarian principles comprised in the Geneva Conventions and Protocols is applicable.[42]

The intractability of the conflicts is further accentuated by a number of other factors. First, the apparent collapse or absence of governmental authority in parts of the territory of a state producing a void that is often filled by warring bands of rebel groups, as in the case of eastern Congo, or of warlords in Somalia. Second, governments in power, as already noted, tend to be primarily concerned with retaining the reigns of power at any cost, and so they adopt a militaristic response to any upsurge of rebel activity. The detrimental effects of this tendency are evident in the conflicts in Angola, Southern Sudan, the Congo, and northern and western Uganda. Third, the proliferation of light and medium weaponry, through the extensive arms trafficking going on in the region, has placed more potent military arsenals at the disposal of the rebel groups than ever before.[43] The ultimate consequence of the amorphous and intractable conflicts is a struggle for hegemonic superiority fueled by the personal political ambitions of the region's statesmen at the expense of severe violations of humanitarian law against civilian populations.

Against this background of the intractability of conflicts in the region, attacks upon civilian populations have become a standard practice on the part of both governments and rebels, particularly in Angola, Uganda, the Congo, and Sudan. In Angola, the perennial MPLA-UNITA conflict has left a country with probably the highest numbers of amputees in the aftermath of sporadic laying of landmines.[44] In Uganda, conflict in Luwero and in the north and west has resulted in a humanitarian disaster of killings, extrajudicial executions, mutilation, rape, and the abduction of children and women.[45] The conflict in Sudan has entailed military expeditions into the South by the Khartoum government, often with civilian casualties.[46]

In eastern Congo, the infighting between rebel groups or their backing states, Uganda and Rwanda, has occasioned collateral damage of loss of life and property.[47] The attacks on civilian populations in the region have inflicted indiscriminate and unnecessary suffering, as all manner of weapons are used during the attacks, in clear contravention of a "cardinal" principle of humanitarian law that states (and by extension other belligerents) "must *never* make civilians the object of attack, and must consequently *never* use weapons that are incapable of distinguishing between civilian and military targets."[48]

An interrelated aspect of the amorphous and fluid character of conflicts in the region concerns the *status* of rebel or insurgent groups. In the region, there are over twenty such groups: SPLA in the Sudan; UNITA in Angola; ADF, Holy Spirit Movement (HSM), LRA, and West Nile Bank Front (WNBF) in Uganda; Alliance of Democratic Forces for the Liberation of Congo-Zaire (ADFL), Conseil de Resistance et la Liberation du Kivu (CRLK), ex-Forces Armees Rwandaises (FAR), *Interahamwe*, Lendu, Mai-Mai, Movement for the Liberation of Congo (MLC), Movement Revolutionnaire pour la Liberation du Congo-Zaire (MLR), Rassemblement congolais pour la democratic (RCD)-Goma, and RCD-Kisangani in the Congo, Front Democratique du Burundi (FRODEBU), and Parti pour la Liberation du People Hutu (PALIPEHUTU) operating from Tanzania; not to mention the clan warlords in Somalia. In most instances, the governments in power are reluctant to accord any sort of recognition to these rebel groups, often only referring to them as bandits or terrorists—in essence, criminal elements. Coupled with a militaristic approach that is often taken in response to insurgency, this attitude makes any reconciliation process difficult and serves as a rationale for harsh tactics against them.

In any event, the status of "rebel" groups in international law is itself wrought with difficulties given the multifarious actors involved in these conflicts. In the first place, certain instances of violations of humanitarian law occur as a result of situations of conflict between the rebel groups. This situation was not contemplated under Additional Protocol II, since it does not deal with cases in which neither of the conflicting parties is a state. Additional Protocol II is envisaged to apply to "internal armed conflicts" taking place in the territory of a state party,

> . . . between its armed forces and dissident armed forces or other organised armed groups which, under responsible command, exercise such control over a part of its territory as to enable them to carry out sustained and concerted military operations and to implement this Protocol.[49]

Second, many of the rebel groups involved in conflicts in the region would not meet these criteria. Most of these groups deplorably lack a responsible—or even any—command and do not exercise effective control over a defined part of the territory. Although the SPLA in the Sudan and certain of the rebel groups in Eastern Zaire can be said to meet those criteria, the same cannot be said of the Mai-Mai and Lendu in the Congo or, for that matter, the LRA and ADF rebel groups in northern and western parts of Uganda. The latter groups are ineffectual in controlling any territory, often resembling underground bandit-like groups that carry out sporadic, cross-border, hit-and-run attacks upon civilian populations to pillage, murder, rape, and abduct. The applicability of the regime of Protocol II in this respect would seem to be minimal or none at all. Third, and more worrying, is the fact that most peace-directed efforts are undertaken without participation of these rebel groups, making it difficult to get these groups to then comply with the terms of cease-fire agreements entered into by the regional states.[50]

Incapacity and Unwillingness to Prosecute Perpetrators of Humanitarian Law Violations

A major factor of noncompliance concerns the prosecution of individuals and groups that have participated in the commission of "crimes against humanity" and "violations of humanitarian law." This is as much a problem in the Great Lakes Region as it is in any other part of the world, for atrocities from Pol Pot's Cambodia to Pinochet's Chile have largely gone unpunished. In the Great Lakes Region, one need only recall the brutality of the regimes of Amin, Banda, Barre, Bokasa, Habre, Mobutu, and Nguema. There has never been a concerted effort to apprehend and prosecute most of these individuals and their regimes' henchmen. Although Habre has since been arrested and indicted in the wake of the Pinochet saga, dictators like Mengistu escaped the net when authorities failed to respond to calls for his arrest when he visited South Africa for medical treatment.[51] In this regard, the legacy of the Nuremberg and Tokyo trials seems too distant a memory to act as a deterrent to today's institutionalized violations of human rights and humanitarian law by governments. It was not until the extremity of the violations in the former Yugoslavia and later in Rwanda shook the international community out of its slumber that concerted attention was readdressed to the issue of criminal trials as a means of enforcement of humanitarian law. The impact of these tribunals, in the sense of enjoining compliance by the threat of sanction of prosecution, is in itself yet to be definitively seen.

As already stated, the Great Lakes Region had been a hotbed of humanitarian law violations without any significant measures toward ensuring accountability. The situation in the region had thus been defined by the murderous and kleptocratic elements of its statesmen and security organizations, with no accountability ever asked of overthrown or former governments. Perhaps the only instance where an attempt was made to bring perpetrators of crimes against humanity to justice came at the end of the Amin regime in Uganda. By then, in 1979, several security organizations, whose members had kidnapped, raped, murdered, and committed all manner of human rights violations against Ugandans, came to be classified as prohibited organizations.[52] In 1980, a Human Rights Court was proposed for the prosecution of individuals accused of commission of "offenses against humanity" during the Amin regime.[53] These two facets of the aftermath of the overthrow of the Amin regime recall the post-Nazi proscription of "criminal organizations" and the Nuremberg trials, only that this had been contemplated at a national level. The problem was that this well-conceived idea never materialized. Since then the efforts at prosecution of perpetrators of violations of humanitarian law has been half-hearted, and the atrocities committed during the Luwero and northern and western conflicts in Uganda have largely gone unpunished.[54] However, a major problem has been the prevalent mistrust of the judicial process by the peoples in the conflict areas obtaining from the weakness of criminal investigation and the perception that the government is not up to addressing the conflict. In effect, the national forum is looked at with skepticism:

> Few people have the confidence that the . . . courts will deliver justice . . . [and] take it as given that human rights violators will walk free. . . . Further evidence of official disinterest at the level of government in solving the problems that underlie the war. Justice . . . is neither a possibility for people in the north nor a priority for those in high authority.[55]

The use of national courts as the forum for prosecution of individuals is always wrought with suspicion, for the tendency is for the victorious party in a conflict or the government in power to try the vanquished or opposition, while their own who have been involved in criminal conduct go scot-free.[56] On the other hand, as already noted, international tribunals are a postmortem exercise in effecting "justice": Rwanda did in fact raise objections to the establishment of the Arusha Tribunal as likely to be "ineffective" and as being only an attempt to appease the conscience of the international community for its inaction during the genocide.[57] And the absence of political will in the early years of the tribunal did not help matters.

Therefore, while legalistic steps have been taken in the last decade to ensure that individuals are held accountable for violations of humanitarian law, a very wide spectrum of acts of previous governments in the region—has been, and will probably—remain, uncensored. Apart from the numerous reports by nongovernmental organizations, like Amnesty International and Human Rights Watch, there have been investigations by Special Rapporteurs under the United Nations' mandate in, for instance, Angola, Sudan, and the Congo. The end result seems to have been the production of reports on the humanitarian situations in those states with little subsequent processes or mechanisms for accountability or enforcement.

Ineptness and Inaction by International Community with Regard to Crises in Africa

The primary function of a world community, at least as conceived in 1945, is the maintenance and restoration of international peace and security.[58] Although the United Nations has with credit pursued this function since then, the fate of the Great Lakes Region seems to have become a nonissue insofar as efforts at peacemaking are concerned. Since the Somalia fiasco in 1993-1995 and, more recently, the hostage taking of peacekeepers in Sierra Leone, the United Nations has given the continent a wide berth. The occurrence of the 1994 genocide in Rwanda has often been attributed to the inaction of the United Nations.[59] By then, the United Nations had already demonstrated a lack of interest in dealing with humanitarian situations in the region until they got out of hand, as evident in Liberia and Angola. To this end, Hiltermann has critically observed:

> The approach the United Nations has taken to severe humanitarian crises has, especially in Africa, been shortsighted, half-hearted and, if I may throw in another bodily function, weak-kneed. In the hour of greatest need, in April 1994, as unspeakable horrors began to unfold in Rwanda, the institution that represents the consensus of the international community left the scene with its tail between its legs. Even if one thinks of tough measures short of direct military action, like sanctions, the UN has failed miserably, not once but time and again—in Rwanda, Angola, Liberia and, of course, Somalia.[60]

In the void left as a result of the inaction on the part of the United Nations, former European colonial powers have thrown in their lot by intervening when and how they deem as befitting in each crisis. In regards to Rwanda, Hiltermann notes for instance of the French response:

> The French effort to carve out a 'safe zone' in western Rwanda under Operation Turquoise, which was launched as the Rwandan Patriotic Front had begun its military rout of the *génocideurs*, provides a fine example of the international community granting default power to the pre-eminent neo-colonial overlord in the face of gross indifference on the part of just about every other major player outside the African continent.[61]

It may be mentioned here that the consequences of failure by the international community to act become most obvious during periods of short but intense mass violations, such as during the Rwanda genocide. During long drawn-out conflicts, humanitarian problems in Africa are generally given a casual response. Thus as regards the conflict in the Congo, the United Nations has largely been passive, by taking on a *distanced* role of issuing exhortations to the belligerent states from New York. Since the conclusion of the Lusaka Peace agreement, it has only deployed a modest peacekeeping operation that perhaps does not meet the forces required under the agreement.[62] But it may well be pointed out that there have been intransigence on the part of the Congo government in previous instances when the United Nations has sought entry into its territory in order to investigate allegations of violations of human rights. Herein the extreme effects of sovereignty in a collapse state. While sovereignty helps to reduce international conflict and discourage conquest, weak states use the doctrine to justify anarchy, often until it is too late. Sovereignty has also been used by Uganda and Rwanda to claim a right to intervene in the Congo purportedly to prevent genocide and defend national security interests.[63] Thus the plea of state sovereignty continues to undermine any attempts at ensuring compliance with humanitarian norms.[64] Nonetheless, the evolution of international attitudes in the past two decades or so has demonstrated that sovereignty is no longer a viable shield to noncompliance, and in certain circumstances, such as in Iraq, Bosnia-Herzegovina, and Kosovo, a "community of states" may employ force to secure compliance. The change of international attitudes has, however, been implemented when dealing with hot spots in Europe and not Africa.[65] For Africa, international action still largely takes the form of a postmortem process of setting up ad hoc international criminal tribunals to prosecute those guilty of gross violations of humanitarian law. Even then, the latter is not often accompanied by the requisite "political will" in the effecting of arrests of the perpetrators of violations of humanitarian law.[66]

Revisiting the "Compliance Gap": An Agenda for Its Closure with Regard to Humanitarian Crises in the Region

In light of the foregoing realities of the humanitarian situation in the Great Lakes Region, there is undeniably a serious problem of "noncompliance." There is an urgent need to address the problem of the compliance gap that is so apparent with respect to humanitarian norms. In the first place, the inevitable question is the adequacy of the present normative regime itself to deal with the protracted and fluid character of today's conflict situations, in which there is a proliferation not only of nonstate actors but also of armaments. But the more fundamental questions are undoubtedly rooted in the nature of the sovereign entities that ultimately will decide the future of the Great Lakes Region—that is, the nation-states. We have noted the core problem of derelict nation-states in the region, which greatly complicates the prospects for compliance. Under these conditions, as Jeffrey Herbst has also noted in this volume, a great weakness of international law, including humanitarian law, is its "state-centered" nature, that is, its dependence on states for compliance and respect. Furthermore, removed from its abstractness, the state is composed of individuals who are the primary subjects of humanitarian law. Hence, the failure or inability to prosecute perpetrators of violations is a critical factor fueling noncompliance. Finally, the attitude of the international community remains crucial in effecting compliance, as its role has been grossly wanting.

In this section, we examine ways in which some of the factors that underpin the problem of noncompliance with humanitarian law in the Great Lakes Region can be addressed.

Chimera of the Nation-State and Democratic Governance in Africa

A major challenge for Africa generally, and for the Great Lakes Region in particular, is "transforming the colonial legacy."[67] Thus, while the Congolese people do not desire to do away with the integral entity of the Congo as a nation-state, they nonetheless call for great changes in its internal political ordering.[68] Whether this will remain the case is unclear given the protracted conflict, in which the government has no effective control over more than half of its territory and thus can be considered to be a "disintegrating" or "failed" state. The situation does, nonetheless, underline the need to redefine the role of the nation-state in Africa as the unit of political ordering on the continent. For the very ethnoreligiously divided character of the states in the region has been the cause of the bulk of the intrastate conflicts that largely define the political scene of Africa. In this regard, the need to define forms of social and political ordering within states that accommodate the interests and aspirations of various ethnoreligious groups has assumed great significance. In fact, the *Human Development Report 2000* warns: "The multiple layers of people's identity and loyalty—to their ethnic group, their religion and their state—have to be recognised and given fair play in democratic institutions or explode into conflict."[69]

The breadth of conflict in the Great Lakes Region and the growing cognizance of its causes have resulted in attempts at defining new approaches to ethnoreligious relations in the composition of states. First, there have been arguments for reexamining the application of the principle and right of self-determination in Africa, beyond the parameters to which it was confined in the wake of the Katanga and Biafra incidents in the early years of independence.[70] Although it has been observed that "there is controversy. . . as to the definition of peoples and the content of the right" of self-determination,[71] it has nonetheless been admitted that a variant of the right compatible with the territorial integrity of states may be exercised.[72] This has been seen to embrace "self-government, local government, federalism, confederalism, unitarism or any other form of relations that accords with the wishes of the people."[73] Second, the attempts at reconstituting the states in the region imply a need to reconceive the effectuation of the right of self-determination.

Under the confusion of conflicting self determination demands, conflicts in the region have, in the past decade or so, taken on a new perspective: from Angola, Sudan, Ethiopia to Somalia.[74] In the Sudan, for instance, the Sudanese Peoples Liberation Movement/Army (SPLM/A) leader, John Garang, has construed self-determination in the sense of a transitional process embracing initially a confederalist idea:

> We have a specific suggestion that in the interim period we have a confederate arrangement, whereby the north will have a separate constitution, the south a separate constitution. At the end of the interim period, the people of the southern Sudan and other areas, Nuba mountains and Funj areas of southern Blue Nile will exercise the right of self-determination to choose between whether to continue this form of union, confederate union, or go for outright independence.[75]

In fact, determination of the applicability of the doctrine of self-determination as part of a solution to the conflict in the Sudan is being undertaken under the auspices of the Inter-Governmental Authority on Drought and Development (IGADD).[76] Elsewhere, in Ethiopia, a new constitution was promulgated in 1994 embracing a federalist structure as well as a right to self-determination.[77] (Invariably, the exercise of self-determination is governed by certain procedures and majorities, as well as by a time frame for its ultimate realization.[78]) In the other African states, the trend is to give cognizance to the interests and aspirations of ethnoreligious groups through constitutional provisions guaranteeing rights to culture and identity as well as equal participatory rights.[79] While these are only recent developments and their success is to be seen, they mark positive and hopefully definitive steps toward diffusing the very ethnoreligious tensions that have so often flared up into conflict in the region. Interrelated, as a consequence, is the factor of equal participation in the political affairs of the state,[80] which poses the necessity of securing more democratic governance in the region. This factor has taken root in some of the states in the region, for instance, Malawi, but in the majority it has yet to find genuine expression.[81] The post-Mobutu Congo is perhaps the best example of a failure at experimentation in this regard, and this failure explains the persistence of conflict on the part of the various rebel groups and their supporters.[82]

In effect, there is a need for more pluralist-conscious and democratic states in the region. With the current prevalence of undemocratic and ethnoreligiously divided states, noncompliance is bound to remain a major feature of conflict situations in the region.

Peacemaking in the Region: Defining the Role of Nonstate Actors and Detaching the Process from Hegemonic Politics

A major feature of conflicts in the Great Lakes Region, as identified above, has been the impunity with which nonstate actors engage in acts and conduct that are obviously gross violations of humanitarian law. Most nonstate actors there are insurgents or "rebels," but a new category has emerged in conflicts in the region, that is, persons and entities that are created by the state or are an offshoot of its security agencies but that have no official or legal relationship with the state itself. These actors have no definitive status under the existing legal regime on humanitarian law, yet undoubtedly individuals belonging to this amorphous category should be made accountable for violations. But it may be necessary first to bring this category into the ambit of the law. This would then allow for defining a role for these nonstate and quasi-state actors in the process of conflict resolution. In this regard, a definitive status should inure to these nonstate and quasi-state actors not only in terms of application of humanitarian law, but also of participation in interstate peacemaking efforts. The tendency to exclude these actors—often dismissed by states as no more than "criminals"—from the negotiating table or from the conclusion of peace and cease-fire pacts has often had very negative effects.

In recent years, there have been some attempts to involve nonstate actors in peacemaking processes, for example, in the mediation efforts in Burundi under Nelson Mandela and in Sudan under IGAAD auspices. In fact, an aspect of the Sudan conflict has been the ability of the various rebel and political groups to evolve a vision for the state.[83] In the efforts toward resolution of the Congo conflict, a key factor envisaged by the United Nations is engagement of the various dissenting (insurgency) groups in the process of mapping out the political future for the country, but the late Desire Kabila's politics of exclusion of such groups, including primarily the MLC and RCD, did not augur well for such a process.

Furthermore, in light of the peacemaking efforts in the region, it may be said that there is a need to shelter such efforts from the hegemonic politics and power relations of the states in the region. Admittedly, gross violations of humanitarian law undermine a state's claim to sovereignty, but the difficulty in the Great Lakes has been the role given by default to individual states (neighboring and Western) to undertake censure. This tendency reflects the prevailing institutional weaknesses of international monitoring mechanisms, especially those of the United Nations and the Organization of African Unity (OAU). In the default situation noted above, attempts at the resolution of regional disputes are often militaristic or tied to the intertwined interests of states. Such is the case with the Lusaka cease-fire agreement, which has been a demonstrable failure for a number of reasons. First, it is biased in favor of particular states, for the demand is made of the United Nations to dismantle the *ex*-FAR/*Interahamwe*, ADF, and UNITA rebels, while no such demand is made of the various rebel groups fighting the Congo government.[84] Second, its efficacy is premised upon the deployment of peacekeeping forces by the United Nations, a factor that has not been effectuated for much of the country. Third, there is a demonstrable history of nonrespect for contractual obligations on the part of the region's statesmen. Peacemaking in such a scenario is likely to be futile, as cease-fire pacts have often been concluded as a tactic to gain time to mobilize additional resources towards the further prosecution of the conflict.

There is thus a very pressing need to revamp the regional organization, the OAU, to make it a viable vehicle for peacemaking in Africa. It is imperative that the Africans make and keep the peace themselves, preferably under the multilateral auspices of the OAU.[85] In this regard, the institutional structures of the OAU need to be revisited, especially as regards collective security, peacekeeping, and "early warning."[86] The ongoing efforts to resuscitate the African dream of a politically united continent under an "African Union" reflect recognition of this need.

Making Accountability Practical: Beyond Doctrinal Regimes on Responsibility of Individuals

The existence of normative and doctrinal regimes on crimes against humanity is not in doubt. Nor is there doubt regarding the principle of jurisdiction over perpetrators of crimes against humanity or violations of humanitarian law. The jurisdiction, which is conceived as "universal," is contemplated at both national and international fora. The latter has largely entailed the creation of ad hoc tribunals, as in the instance of the Nuremberg and Tokyo tribunals in the aftermath of the World War II, and the Yugoslav and Rwanda tribunals to deal with genocide and other humanitarian violations in the 1990s.[87] The Rwanda tribunal, like its Yugoslav counterpart, was considered by the United Nations to be a means to bring "to an end" serious crimes such as genocide and to "take effective measures to bring to justice the persons responsible for them."[88] The jurisdiction of international tribunals is seen, nonetheless, as complementary to that of national courts.[89]

No doubt the creation of these tribunals has had the effect of making the individual the subject of international prosecution.[90] The problem that has beleaguered the Yugoslav and Rwanda tribunals, however, has been the apprehension of accused individuals. It has been difficult to try and punish perpetrators because of political or logistical difficulties in their apprehension.[91] The creation of the tribunals, especially in the case of Rwanda, has also been widely seen as being no more than a pathologist's postmortem, in the sense that it follows on the heels of inaction on part of the world community to avert a foreseen humanitarian tragedy. Even if the Rwanda tribunal was to be a success, that will never compensate for the inaction of the international community as the genocide took place. While this has been a nemesis of the ad hoc tribunals, the situation with

Table 5.1. States Where Individuals Were Arrested before Subsequent Transfer for Trial at the Rwanda Tribunal in Arusha

Angola	1	Namibia	1
Belgium	6	Netherlands	1
Benin	2	South Africa	1
Burkina Faso	1	Senegal	1
Cameroon	10	Switzerland	2
Cote d'Ivoire	2	Tanzania	6
DRC	2	Togo	2
Denmark	1	United Kingdom	1
France	2	United States	1
Kenya	14	Zambia	3
Mali	2		

Source: ICTR Detainees: Status on 26 May 2003, www.ictr.org/as.

the national courts has not been any better, for, as already pointed out, they are prone to the *injustice* of prosecution of only the vanquished while the victors go scot-free.[92]

While these criticisms of the efficacy of the normative regime on accountability have been well founded, it should be noted that over the past six to seven years there have been great leaps in making accountability "practical." First, there has been increased cooperation on the part of states in the apprehension and committal of perpetrators to international tribunals. While progress has been slower in the case of the Yugoslav tribunal, cooperation has become a marked feature of the Rwanda tribunal. Growing cooperation among seventeen states in Africa, Europe, and America since 1996 has enabled the Rwanda tribunal, as of May 2003, to have jurisdiction over a total of sixty-five individuals.[93] The numbers depict demonstrable political will and cooperation by states, in particular African, in the apprehension and transfer of perpetrators to the Rwanda tribunal in Arusha. In 1994, when the Tribunal was established, and again in 1995, there were no transfers made, but, as table 5.2 indicates, there has since been a change in the attitude of states, which has in itself gone a long way toward giving a sense of practicality to the element of accountability.

Table 5.2. Numbers of Individuals Arrested and Transferred for Trial at the Rwanda Tribunal in Arusha between 1996 and 2003

1994	0	1999	11
1995	0	2000	6
1996	7	2001	12
1997	14	2002	6
1998	6		

Second, states in the region have demonstrated increasing readiness to invoke the principle of "universal" jurisdiction[94] in a number of ways: (a) apprehension and exercise of that jurisdiction over an individual who has come within a state's territory in respect of crimes committed in another state; (b) issuance of arrest warrants for individuals accused of committing crimes in any particular state; and (c) conduct of trials in absentia with regard to such individuals. These steps do suggest that states are increasingly ready to take on the challenge of invoking the universal jurisdiction principle with regard to crimes and other humanitarian law violations. In fact, in light of the DRC-Belgium dispute over the April 11, 2000, arrest warrant, ad hoc Judge van den Wyngaert remarked:

> The case concerning the Arrest Warrant of 11 April 2000 . . . is the first modern case which confronts two States on the issues of extraterritorial jurisdiction . . . arising from the application of a domestic statute implementing international core crimes . . . International law now calls upon States to prosecute and punish international core crimes, but leaves some uncertainty as to the practical implications of this proposition as far as the enforcement of domestic implementation laws is concerned. For the sake of legal certainty, it is important that the International Court of Justice decides on the merits of the present case with expedition.[95]

While the above indicates a growing awareness of the need to limit, or better yet abolish, impunity as a step toward inculcating a culture of compliance, several imperfections remain in the process. First, the entire process, of course, still remains shrouded in state-centric processes involving the existence of extradition treaties (and procedures) and is dependent on a particular state having territorial jurisdiction over the particular individuals. Secondly, as the defeated Hutu have argued, their lack of state protection after loss of political power has exposed them to trial, while those who might have provoked or even perpetrated the crimes but are in power, now remain untouched. Thirdly, the penal regime of international law is not seen to have sanctions that are effective and therefore does not act as an effective deterrent. Furthermore, in this regard, most states in the region have not adopted legislation to provide national courts with jurisdiction over violations of human rights. In the same vein, no obligation is placed upon states, without reservation, to transmit persons accused of atrocities to international tribunals. In effect, therefore, safe havens still exist for persons accused of crimes against humanity.

Alternative Approaches to Conflict Resolution: Retributive Justice versus Conciliatory Processes

A critical issue about conflict in society is the manner in which the violators of its norms are treated. As we have noted above, the normal course of conflict is for the victor or government in power to employ national institutions for the trial and prosecution of the vanquished or opposition. The postgenocide Rwanda has been accused of retributive justice against the Hutu, while in most of the states in the region governments have relied on the penal law provisions on treason. This approach does not augur well for efforts at reconciliation,[96] for it tends to reinforce the opposition's determination to carry on the fight, leading in most instances to further flagrant noncompliance with humanitarian norms. It is, therefore, argued that there is a need for more reconciliation-oriented approaches to conflict resolution to tame acrimonious feelings and vengefulness between peoples in the ethnoreligiously and racially divided states of Africa. This perspective underpinned postapartheid South Africa's constitution of a Truth and Reconciliation Commission.[97] The experience in South Africa called for reconciliation with the perpetrators of apartheid, which had been declared a "crime against humanity." In the post-1993 constitutional period, the idea of reconciliation has been seen in South Africa as imbued in the concept of *ubuntu*:

> The post-amble to the [1993] Constitution gives expression to the new ethos of the nation by a commitment to "open a new chapter in the history of our country," by lamenting the transgressions of "human rights" and "humanitarian principles" in the past, and articulating a "need for understanding, but not for vengeance, a need for reparation but not retaliation, a need for *ubuntu* but not for victimization" . . . The need for *ubuntu* expresses the ethos of an instinctive capacity for and enjoyment of love towards our fellow men and women; the joy and the fulfillment involved in recognizing their innate humanity; the reciprocity this generates in interaction within the collective community; the richness of the creative emotions which it engenders and the moral energies which it releases both in the givers and the society which they serve and are served by.[98]

In the Great Lakes Region, apart from the mediation efforts and other regional peacemaking initiatives, reconciliation is being sought as part of a way forward in state reconstruction. The necessity to diffuse the ill feelings that the Hutu might harbor against the Tutsi-dominated government and peoples has placed the issue of forgiveness and reconciliation on the political agenda. Such reconciliation will undoubtedly take time to take root in Rwanda as the scars of genocide and other humanitarian violations heal. However, the creation of a National Reconciliation Commission indicates that there may be some hope in this direction for Rwanda's future.[99] The efforts toward reconciliation spurred the Rwanda government's introduction of a concept of *gacaca*, derived from and having its roots in a traditional communal justice system in Rwanda. The *gacaca* system is:

> . . . expected to allow communities to establish the facts and decide the fate of the vast majority of those accused of *lesser* offences, while at the same time addressing *reconciliation* objectives and involving the population on a mass scale in the disposition of justice.[100]

However, the Hutu majority tends to see the *gacaca* system as one that does not conform to modern concepts of justice and fair trial.[101]

In Uganda, where conflict has wrought havoc upon the peoples in the northern and western parts of the country, attempts at a political resolution have entailed the offer of amnesty to the insurgents. In part, this was meant to overcome the cynicism that the government was just engaged in the prosecution of supposed rebel sympathizers for treason and other political offences. In 1987, an amnesty statute was enacted to provide amnesty from prosecution for past activities to persons involved in "acts of war and hostilities against the government."[102] The life of this statute was extended when a new amnesty law was passed in November 1999. The context of the new amnesty statute, moreover, is much wider, encompassing persons who are on trial for treason and other political offences who renounce violence, and it also envisages the reintegration of persons granted amnesty into society.[103]

The above experiences suggest that there are a number of significant features that should be incorporated in the process of reconciliation. First, any forgiveness or amnesty should be predicated upon a formal acceptance of wrongdoing on the part of the perpetrator of the act. There should be an expiation of guilt and its acceptance by the body commissioned to grant an amnesty or by the community of people. Second, the amnesty should reflect the desire of the people, either obtained through popular consultation or expressed by their lawful representatives. As such, amnesties granted by departing dictators to themselves and their cohorts should not count. Third, the amnesty should not extend to "heinous crimes." Apartheid was certainly a crime against humanity, but even the Truth and Reconciliation Commission was never expected to condone instances involving its gross perpetration. In effect, crimes such as genocide, murder, and rape should be expressly excluded from any amnesty legislation.[104] The success of the National Reconciliation Commission, of *gacaca* as a communal system of justice in Rwanda, or of the amnesty law in Uganda waits to be seen. In the latter case, scores of individuals imprisoned on treason charges have since taken advantage of the law,[105] but allegations of government forces acting in a manner dismissive of the law, as well as the logistical difficulties in originally setting up the commission, have left the whole process rather fragile.[106]

Conclusion

This study has addressed a perennial question that applies not only to the Great Lakes, but to all of the hotbeds of conflict worldwide, that is, why there exists a "compliance gap" between the legal regime and the actual behavioral conduct of belligerents. The situation in the Great Lakes Region is particularly alarming, as the belligerents in the region's intractable conflicts have blatantly turned a blind eye to the norms of humanitarian law. Moreover, the region poses factors for noncompliance that are peculiar to it. These are rooted in the political, hegemonic, and socioeconomic elements of the local states. The dereliction and dysfunction of the state have been emphasized, as have the attendant ethnoreligious schisms and lack of a democratic tradition. Further, the practical rendering of accountability of individuals for violations of humanitarian law remains a major concern. On the other hand, the response of the international community to humanitarian crises in Africa has been inept at best. In conclusion, the suggestions for closing the compliance gap can be summed up as:

- Reconstitution of the state so that its political and sociocultural ordering accommodates the interests and aspirations of diverse ethnoreligious groups. In effect, conflict prevention should be viewed within the much broader framework of efforts to address the root causes of conflict.

- Defining an obligation of states to adopt legislation to give effect to jurisdiction over violators of humanitarian law, as well as an obligation in international law for states to transmit without reservation such persons to an international tribunal. This would go a long way toward giving efficacy to accountability for violations of humanitarian law.

- Revamping the institutional structures, mandate, and approach of international and regional organizations, in particular the OAU, regarding collective security, peacekeeping, and early warning of threats to international peace, such as crimes against humanity.

Notes

1. See Stuart J. Kaufman, "The End of Anarchism: The Society of Nations, Institutions, and the Decline of War," paper presented at the 42nd International Studies Association Annual Convention, "International Relations and the New Inequality," Chicago, Illinois, February 20-24, 2001.

2. Report of the secretary-general, "The Causes of Conflict and the Promotion of Durable Peace and Sustainable Development in Africa," A/52/871-S/1998/318, April 13, 1998.

3. Most of the states in the region, except Rwanda and Burundi, are multiethnic in character with borders that were arbitrarily drawn at the Berlin Conference of 1884. Even Rwanda and Burundi, which seem to have two ethnic groups, have minority groups such as the Batwa who are almost totally excluded from political power.

4. See Catherine Hoskyns, *The Congo since Independence: January 1960-December 1961* (London: Oxford University Press, 1965). The United Nations Operation in the Congo (UNOC), deployed in July 1960 and withdrawn in June 1964, at its peak involved about 20,000 military personnel.

5. See, in particular, the Democratic Republic of Congo Ceasefire Agreement, August 1999 (hereinafter the Lusaka Agreement) and Security Council resolutions 1234 of April 12, 1999, and 1304 of June 16, 2000.

6. *Africa's Seven-Nation War* (New York: International Crisis Group, May 21, 1999). Also, see the Security Council debate on the situation in the Democratic Republic of the Congo, S/PV.4902, January 24, 2000.

7. With respect to the Congo, *Armed Activities on the Territory of the Congo* (Democratic Republic of the Congo v. Uganda) (Indication of Provisional Measures), General List No. 116/2000, July 1, 2000, para. 43. See, generally, Michael Stohl and George Lopez, "Westphalia, the End of the Cold War and the New World Order: Old Roots to a 'New' Problem," paper presented at a conference on "Failed States and International Security: Causes, Prospects, and Consequences," Purdue University, West Lafayette, Indiana, February 25-27, 1998. A particular pressing moral, political, and economic issue on the political agenda is the failure of the state to deal with mass poverty. Poverty is linked to the more general issues of equity, equality, and distributive justice both within and across borders. See Philip Nel, "Equity as a 'Global Public Good'?" paper delivered at the 18th World Congress of the International Political Science Association, Quebec City, Canada, August 1-5, 2000.

8. The 1949 conventions are incorporated into Uganda's domestic law by virtue of the Geneva Conventions Act, Cap. 323 (Laws of Uganda, 1964). During the Luwero conflict, the rebel National Resistance Movement/Army (NRM/A) appears to have operated more or less in accord with the Geneva Conventions—this was more by default, given the necessity of wining the support of the local populace, than any particular express awareness of the normative regime. Since ascending to the reigns of government, the NRM/A has not paid due regard to humanitarian norms in carrying out the offensive in the North.

9. See the Final Report of the Commission of Inquiry into Violations of Human Rights, Kampala, Uganda, October 1994; three Amnesty International reports, "Uganda. The Failure to Safeguard Human Rights," AFR 59/05/92, September 1992, "Uganda. Breaking the Circle: Protecting Human Rights in the Northern Zone," AFR 59/01/99, March 1999, and "Uganda. Breaking God's Commands: The Destruction of Childhood by the Lord's Resistance Army," AFR 59/01/97, September 1997. See also, Robby Muhumuza, "A Case Study of Girls Abducted by Joseph Kony's Lord's Resistance Army (LRA) in Northern Uganda," Kampala, Uganda, May 1996.

10. Riek Machar Teny-Dhurgon, "South Sudan: A History of Political Domination—A Case of Self-Determination," www.sas.upenn.edu/African_Studies/ Hornet/sd_machar.html.

11. *Slavery and Slavery Redemption in the Sudan* (New York: Human Rights Watch, March 12, 1999).

12. See John Jolliffe, "Limbless Victims of Angola War," *The Guardian* (London), February 28, 1987; Africa Watch, "Angola: Violations of the Laws of War by both Sides" (London, April 1989).

13. The International Criminal Tribunal for Rwanda was established by Security Council resolution 955 (November 8, 1994). Under Article 6 of its statute, the tribunal has a mandate to prosecute individuals involved in acts of genocide and violations of humanitarian law.

14. Jeremy Hobbs, "More than a Humanitarian Crisis: the Geneva Convention Is Being Torn Apart," www.caa.org.au/world/africa/zaire/zaireop.html.

15. See *Uganda in Eastern DRC: Fueling Political and Ethnic Strife* (New York: Human Rights Watch, 2001).

16. *Armed Activities on the Territory of the Congo*, para. 43.

17. On the food crisis, see "Food and Humanitarian Crisis Looms in Democratic Republic of Congo," FAO/GIEWS Special Alert No. 285, September 3, 1998 and IRIN, "Sudan: Humanitarian Crisis in Bentiu Region," August 11, 2000; on the refugee situation, see UN Consolidated Inter-Agency Appeal for Countries of the Great Lakes Region and Central Africa: Burundi, DRC, Rwanda, Uganda and United Republic of Tanzania, January-December 1998, OCHA/IASB/98/3, February 27, 1998; also see "Uganda: Breaking the Circle"; and on internal displacement and life in camps, see James Komakech, "Life in a Displaced Camp in Gulu District," *Child Trumpet* 1 (April 1999): 10-12.

18. See Edith R. Sanders, "The Hamitic Hypothesis: Its Origins and Function in Time Perspective," *Journal of African History* 10, no. 4 (1969): 521; and Catherine Newbury, *The Cohesion of Oppression: Clientship and Ethnicity in Rwanda (1860-1960)* (New York: Columbia University Press, 1988).

19. See Nelson Kasfir, *The Shrinking Political Arena: Participation of Ethnicity in African Politics: A Case Study of Uganda* (Berkeley: California University Press, 1976); Anthony G. G. Gingyera-Pinycwa, *Northern Uganda in National Politics* (Kampala, Uganda: Fountain, 1992).

20. See Tim Allen, "Ethnicity and Tribalism on the Sudan-Uganda Border," in Katsuyoshi Fukui and John Markakis, eds., *Ethnicity and Conflict in the Horn of Africa* (London: James Curey, 1994).

21. *Katangese Peoples' Congress v. Zaire*, African Committee on Human and Peoples Rights (ACHPR) Commn. No. 75/1992. This is apart from the recent controversy over the Banyamulenge citizenship in the Congo: David Newbury, "Irredentist Rwanda: Ethnicity and Territorial Frontiers in Central Africa," *Africa Today* 44, no. 2 (1997).

22. Roza Ismagilova, "Ethnicity in Africa and the Principles of Solving Ethnic Problems in the Constitutions," a paper presented at the 4th International Conference of the Ethnic Studies Network on "Moving Towards Pluralism," Moscow, Russia, February 8-11, 1999.

23. Stuart J. Kaufman, "The End of Anarchism: The Society of Nations, Institutions, and the Decline of War."

24. *Rex v. Earl of Crewe*, ex parte *Sekgome* [1910] AC 587: 628 (per Kennedy, L. J.) The case involved the detention without trial of a native African in a British Protectorate.

25. In Uganda, the power of deportation under the Deportation Ordinances epitomized the tendencies to clamp down on anticolonial sentiment: cf. *Re GL Binaisa* (1959) EA 997. The legacy of those ordinances became evident in postindependent states. See, for example, *Ibingira and Ors v. Uganda* [1966] EA 305.

26. African Charter on Human and Peoples Rights, 1981, Article 13(3) does not specify that the "will of the people" shall form the basis of government. In effect, it has no equivalent of Article 21(3) of the Universal Declaration on Human Rights, 1948. See, however, endnote 81 on the conceptualization of the import of Article 13 of the African Charter.

27. Makau wa Mutua, "The African Human Rights System in a Comparative Perspective: The Need for Urgent Reformulation," *Nairobi Law Monthly* 44 (1992): 27.

28. See *World Organisation against Torture, et al. v. Zaire*, ACHPR Commn. Nos. 25/89, 47/90, 56/91, and 100/93, paras. 73, 75, *Krishna Achuthan on behalf of Aleke Banda, et al. v. Malawi*, ACHPR Commn. Nos. 64/92, 68/92, and 78/92.

29. In fact, the perception of the DRC as a "disintegrating state" is stated on the basis of the *internal opposition* against its government: *Armed Activities in the Territory of the Congo*, separate opinion by Judge Oda, para. 4.

30. In the Congo, Patrice Lumumba was assassinated in a Mobutu military-backed putsch. In Uganda, militarization was first introduced after the 1964 army mutiny and later involvement of the forces in the 1966 Buganda crisis, during which the riot police used live ammunition to quell a riot at Nakulabye: *Muwonge v. Attorney-General* (1967) EA 57. The process was complete during Amin's regime, with the army given powers of arrest and trial over civilians: see Armed Forces (Powers of Arrest) Decree, 1971 and Trial by Military Tribunals Decree, 1973, respectively. For a more critical analysis, see Ami Omara-Otunnu, *Politics and the Military in Uganda, 1896-1985* (London: St. Martin's Press, 1987). In recent years, in spite of arguments to the contrary, the armies in Congo, Uganda, and Rwanda have largely been personal armies.

31. See the doctrine as expounded in *Uganda v. Commissioner of Prisons* ex parte *Matovu* (1966) EA 514. The theory has been fundamental in legitimizing military regimes in other African states, such as Nigeria, Lesotho, and Sierra Leone.

32. Ismagilova, "Ethnicity in Africa."

33. Africa Peace Forum, "Background Report: Great Lakes Early Warning Network," August/September 1998.

34. Basil Davidson, *The Black Man's Burden: Africa and the Curse of the Nation-State* (London: Currey, 1992), 162-96. The *nation-state* was stamped on Africa in 1964 by the Organization of African Unity. See Resolution on the Intangibility of Frontiers, AGH/Resolution 16 (I), Cairo, July 1964.

35. Leopoldo Lovelace, Jr., "Has International Law Failed Africa?" paper prepared for the 42nd International Studies Association Annual Convention.

36. A state *cannot* thus argue that its failure to protect human rights arises from the fact that it has no control over that part of its territory where the violations are taking place: see cf. *Commission Nationale des Droits de l'homme et des Libertés v. Chad*, ACHPR Commn. No. 74/92, paras. 36-41. In the corollary, a state in illegal occupation of part of the territory of another state is responsible for violations in the occupied territory: see cf. *Chrysostomos v. Turkey* (1991) 12 HRLJ 113. In this regard, Uganda and Rwanda are responsible for any violations of humanitarian law in the eastern part of the Congo. See *Armed Activities on the Territory of the Congo*.

37. Joseph Oloka-Onyango, "Armed Conflict, Political Violence and Human Rights Monitoring of Uganda: 1971 to 1990," CBR Working Paper no. 12 (1991), Centre for Basic Research, Kampala-Uganda.

38. Teny-Dhurgon, "South Sudan."

39. Africa Watch, "Angola: Violations of the Laws of War," 69-88, 128-43.

40. For a further exposition of this aspect, see the section on "Beyond Doctrinal Regimes on Responsibility of Individuals" in this chapter.

41. See, for instance, on the conflict in Uganda: *Parliamentary Report on the War in the North*, Sessional Committee on Defence and Internal Affairs, Parliament of Uganda, February 1997, 52-6. The distrust was clearly reflected in the electoral results of the 1996 presidential elections, where the incumbent candidate obtained a small percentage of the northern vote.

42. *Armed Activities on Territory of the Congo*, para. 43.

43. The *Interahamwe's* gory hand ax attacks on their victims during the Rwanda 1994 genocide shocked the world but were just a massive example of what rebels, such as Kony's Lords Resistance Army, had been doing on a smaller scale for years. However, modern weapons, such as landmines, assault rifles, tanks, helicopter gunships, etc., are all enthusiastically applied in the region. For an examination of the arms-trafficking in the region, see Francois Misser, "Arms Pour into Great Lakes Region," *New Africa* 347 and "Arms Flows to Central Africa/Great Lakes Fact Sheet" (Washington, D.C.: Bureau of Intelligence and Research, Department of State, November 1999).

44. Africa Watch, "Angola: Violations of the Laws of War," 51-62.

45. See endnotes 7-9, 31-33 on the conflicts in the Great Lakes Region and their consequences.

46. Teny-Dhurgon, "South Sudan."

47. *Armed Activities on the Territory of the Congo*, para. 43.

48. See cf. *Prosecutor v. Martic (Rule 61)*, Case IT-95-11-R61 (1996), paras. 15-7. In applying the principle in common Article I of the 1949 Geneva Conventions, the International Criminal Tribunal for the Former Yugoslavia stated: "no circumstances would legitimise an attack against civilians even if it were a response proportionate to a similar violation perpetrated by the other party."

49. Additional Protocol II to the Geneva Conventions, 1977, Article 1 (1).

50. This is typified by the Lusaka and Victoria summits on the Congo conflict (July-August 1999) and the Nairobi meeting on the Uganda-Sudan conflict (November 1999) from which the rebel groups were excluded or not called upon to participate.

51. "More 'Pinochet Style' Prosecutions Urged: Senegal's Habre Arrest a Precursor" (New York: Human Rights Watch, March 3, 2000). A recent development in the Pinochet saga has been the Santiago Appeals Court dismissal of the charges and order of house arrest against the dictator. This confirms the baffling immunity that national courts tend to confer upon individuals and that make compliance difficult. See "Chilean Court Blocks Pinochet Arrest, Trial," *Reuters*, December 11, 2000.

52. The list included the State Research Centre, the Public Safety Unit, the Military Police, the Military Intelligence, the Anti-Corruption and Anti-Smuggling Units.

53. Human Rights Court Statute, 1980. The statute catalogued offences regarded as "crimes against humanity" in line with those of the Nuremberg trials, the Genocide Convention, or any of the recent instruments establishing the international Tribunals of Yugoslavia and Rwanda. The envisaged court was to deal with crimes committed between 1971 and 1979.

54. Between 1986 and 1993, the government commissioned an inquiry into violations of human rights under the previous regimes: Report of the Commission of Inquiry into Violations of Human Rights. It was never acted upon as a basis for any subsequent arrests and prosecution. The violations that occurred after 1986 have been the subject of several Amnesty International reports since 1987. The present constitutional organ, that is, the Uganda Human Rights Commission, has largely not been effective in addressing violations of human rights and humanitarian law in the areas of conflict. See "Northern Uganda: Justice in Conflict," *Africa Rights* (February 2000), 75-8.

55. Amnesty International, "Uganda: Breaking the Circle," 49.

56. This has been the case with the trials before the Rwanda national courts, at least in the eyes of the Hutu. This perception has not been helped by the dispatch with which

executions are shortly carried out upon conviction—the process ceases to be less one of seeking "justice" than of "revenge."

57. See Makau wa Mutua, "From Nuremberg to the Rwanda Tribunal: Justice or Retribution?" unpublished article, 3 (Buffalo, State University of New York, 1996).

58. United Nations Charter, Article 1.

59. *Report of the Independent Inquiry into the Actions of the United Nations During the 1994 Genocide in Rwanda*, December 15, 1999, www.un.org/News/ossg/ rwanda_report.htm; Corinne Dufka, "Rwanda Genocide Survivors Say Annan Part Responsible," *Reuters,* May 8, 1998; J Price, "Why Rwanda Was Ignored; Months of Carnage Passed before Congress Urged Aid," *Washington Times*, July 7, 1994. See also *Life after Death: Suspicion and Reintegration in Post-Genocide Rwanda* (Washington, D.C.: U.S. Committee for Refugees, February 1998) and the testimony of Jeff Drumatra, Africa Policy Analyst, U.S. Committee for Refugees, *Rwanda: Genocide and the Continuing Cycle of Violence: Part II—Genocide Revisited: Review of Information and Inaction*, before the Subcommittee on International Operations and Human Rights, House Committee on International Relations, May 5, 1998.

60. Joost R. Hiltermann, "Post-Mortem on the International Commission of Inquiry (Rwanda)," *Bulletin of Concerned Africa Scholars*, January 26, 1998, www.iansa. org/oldsite/documents/research/res_archive/archive.htm.

61. Hiltermann, "Post-Mortem."

62. An envisaged United Nations' role has essentially been one of lip service. See Nicole Winfield, "UN May Intervene in Congo's War," *Associated Press*, March 19, 1999; or a posture of noncommitment, see Thalif Deen, "UN May Abort Peacekeeping Operations in the Congo," *Inter Press Service*, August 3, 2000.

63. Yoweri K. Museveni, "Conflicts in the Great Lakes Region," paper circulated to the UN Security Council, January 24, 2000, 31 (unreported).

64. An interesting development arose recently, with the Democratic Republic of Congo filing a claim against Belgium before the International Court on account of an order of arrest issued by a Belgian magistrate against Congo's Foreign Minister, on grounds that this was an interference in its sovereignty: *Arrest Order of 11 April 2000 (Democratic Republic of the Congo v. Belgium)*, application instituting proceedings, November 17, 2000.

65. Richard J. Goldstone, "Kosovo: An Assessment in the Context of International Law," 19th Morgenthau Memorial Lecture on Ethics and Foreign Policy (New York: Carnegie Council on Ethics and International Affairs, 2000), 22, 26-7.

66. On this issue, there has been a major outcry as regards the Yugoslav and Rwanda tribunals. See criticism by then Judge Goldstone in this regard: Charles Trueheart, "War Crimes Judge Assails West's Failure to Seize Serb Suspects," *International Herald Tribune*, September 19, 1996.

67. Ernest Wamba dia Wamba, Democratic Republic of Congo Governance Position Papers (DRCGPP) no. 15, www.congorcd.org/political/pospapers.htm.

68. DRC Governance Position Paper nos. 3, 4, 5, 6, and 9, posted at www.congorcd.org/political/pospapers.htm. In any event, "territorial integrity" of the Congo (then as Zaire) had long been affirmed by the African Human and Peoples' Rights Commission. See *Katangese Peoples' Congress*, para. 26.

69. See Jaya Ramachandran, "UNDP Report Criticises Exclusion of Minorities Around the World," Inter Press Service, June 29, 2000, www.oneworld.org/ips2/ june00/21_18_080.html.

70. See, in this regard, UN Secretary-General U Thant's official statement on Biafra's attempt to secede from Nigeria. *UN Monthly Chronicle* (February 1970): 40.

71. *Katangese Peoples' Congress*, para. 24.

72. *Katangese Peoples' Congress*, paras. 26-8.

73. *Katangese Peoples' Congress*, para. 26.

74. See, for example, Anthony J. Carroll and B. Rajagopal, "The Case for the Independent Statehood of Somaliland," *American University Journal of International Law and Politics* 8 (1983): 653; Elizabeth M. Jamilah Koné, "The Right of Self-Determination in the Angolan Enclave of Cabinda," paper presented at the 6th Annual African Studies Consortium Workshop, University of Pennsylvania, October 2, 1998; Proceedings of the Conference on Human Rights in the Transition in Sudan, "Marginalized Areas and Self-Determination," Kampala-Uganda, February 8-12, 1999.

75. *IRIN*, "SPLM for Peaceful Solution but 'Sharia' Key," July 7, 2000.

76. Inter-Governmental Authority on Drought and Development (IGADD) Common Agenda for Peace Talks, January 6, 1994, and Declaration of Principles, May 20, 1994.

77. Constitution of the Federal Republic of Ethiopia, 1994, Article 39 (1). Interestingly, the right of self-determination includes *secession* that is available to every "nation, nationality and people." The constitution also recognizes other *lesser* forms of self-determination, through self-government and political participation (Article 39[3]).

78. Constitution of the Federal Republic of Ethiopia, Article 39 (4) (a) (b) and (5).

79. Ismagilova, "Ethnicity in Africa." See, for Uganda, the Constitution of the Republic of Uganda (1995), Articles 36, 37, and 246.

80. The postgenocide Rwanda has been trying to experiment with a power-sharing arrangement between the Tutsi and Hutu.

81. It may be noted that the African continent human rights watchdog, the African Commission on Human and Peoples Rights has condemned regimes that result from "*forcible take-over* of government by army, civilian or military group" (emphasis added) as being in contravention of "articles 13(1) and 20(1) of the African Charter." Resolution on the Military, ACHPR Meeting, 16th Ordinary Session, October 25-November 3, 1994, preamble, para. 4. Being only a human rights monitoring body, such good-intentioned positions may not effectively change the situation on the continent where there is no political will and enforcement mechanisms against states where undemocratic governments abound or might surface. Sanctions against Burundi imposed in 1994 failed to have the desired effect.

82. DRC Governance Position Papers nos. 3-6.

83. See the political agreement between the Umma Party and the Sudan Peoples Liberation Movement/Sudan Peoples Liberation Army (SPLM/SPLA) on Transitional Arrangements and Self-Determination, Chukudum, December 12, 1994.

84. Lusaka Agreement, Annex, chapter VIII.

85. In this regard, the Africa Crisis Response Initiative (ACRI) is a good idea, although concerns were raised about the risks of the armed contributions of states turning the unit into a military outfit of a few states.

86. See, generally, recent arguments and trends in this regard, Margaret A. Vogt, "The Organisation of African Unity (OAU) and Conflict Management in Africa," paper presented at the International Resource Group Conference, Mombasa-Kenya, November 6-9, 1996, www.ploughshares.ca/CONTENT/BUILD%20PEACE/Vogt.html; Jan Ameen

(Rapporteur), "OAU/IPA Joint Task Force Report on Peacemaking and Peacekeeping," www.ipacademy.org/Publications/Reports/Africa/PublRepoAfriPP98Print.htm.

87. The creation of an International Criminal Court with the adoption of its statute puts in place a *permanent* institution for enforcement of humanitarian law. See the Statute of the International Criminal Court, July 18, 1998.

88. Security Council resolution 955, preamble.

89. See the Statute of the International Criminal Court, Article 1.

90. See C. Peter Maina, "The International Criminal Tribunal for Rwanda: Bringing the Killers to Justice," *International Review of the Red Cross* 321 (1997): 695.

91. This lack of political will has been a major factor that has frustrated the Yugoslav and Rwanda tribunals, see endnote 66. The reality thus dawns that while a permanent court is a welcome development in ensuring a mechanism for jurisdiction over and trial of perpetrators of crimes and humanitarian violations, it is difficult to see it not being hampered by a similar lack of political will. Though the United States signed the Statute at the end of 2000, President Bush has expressed his opposition to it and the prospects for Senate consent to ratification appear bleak in any case. None of this bodes well for the court. Similarly, the framework of the court is primarily state centered, based on acquiescence of the five permanent members of the Security Council to an investigation, request of a state in whose territory violations are said to be taking place, and states opting out of the war crimes jurisdiction of the court. See the Statute of the International Criminal Court, Articles 12, 16, and 124.

92. See endnotes 54-7 and accompanying text.

93. See *ICTR Detainees: Status on 26 May 2003*, www.ictr.org/as.

94. See the Pinochet saga and Senegal's putting ex-Chad president Hussein Habre under house arrest, in "More Pinochet Style." Habre was in fact subsequently indicted on torture charges by a magistrate on February 3, 2000.

95. *Arrest Warrant* case, para. 10, separate opinion ad hoc Judge van den Wyngaert.

96. In this regard, the Arusha tribunal has been criticized as entirely irrelevant to the "reconstructionist" and "normalization" process that should be achieved in Rwanda. See Makau wa Mutua, "From Nuremberg," 3.

97. The commission was created pursuant to provisions of the Constitution of the Republic of South Africa (1993) s. 82(1)(g).

98. *State v. Makwanyane & Ors* [1995] 1 LRC 269, para. 263 (*per* Mahomed, J).

99. The Rwanda National Reconciliation Commission headed by Aloyise Inyumba initiated consultations on the issue of coexistence. Its mandate includes, *inter alia*, to monitor government programs as to their impact on *peace, reconciliation, and national unity*. The success of these efforts remains to be seen, especially since effective participation by the minority Twa or majority Hutu may not be easy to achieve.

100. John Prendergast and David Smock, "Post-Genocidal Reconstruction— Building Peace in Rwanda and Burundi," September 15, 1999, www.usip.org/pubs/ specialreports/sr990915.html. The *gacaca* process has also been perceived as necessitated by the slow progress at the Arusha tribunal.

101. Personal interviews conducted in Rwanda between August and November 2000.

102. Amnesty Statute No. 6 of 1987, Article 1.

103. Amnesty Statute No. 5 of 2000. The statute also establishes an amnesty commission to hear denouncements of violence and armed struggle against the government, and a Demobilization and Resettlement Team.

104. In Uganda, the 1987 Amnesty Statute did not extend amnesty to acts classed as "heinous crimes" Article 1. Article 2 classed as "heinous crimes," (a) acts of genocide; (b) murder; (c) kidnapping with intent to murder; and (d) rape. See also, with regards to Rwanda, for a critique of the apparent failure to penalize rape in indictments before the Arusha tribunal, Yifat Susskind, "Demanding Justice: Rape and Reconciliation in Rwanda," *MADRE* Newsletter (1997/98), www.madre.org/country_rwan_demand.html, October 1997. Interestingly, the Uganda amnesty law of 2000 grants a *blanket* amnesty, which raises questions about instances of the crimes that were excluded under its predecessor. In this respect, an amnesty law passed by Togo in 1994 has been criticized as tending to grant immunity to human rights violators: "Togo: Time for Accountability; No Political Stability without Respect for Human Rights," AFR 57/38/99 (London: Amnesty International, November 1999).

105. Rebels, particularly from the ADF, WNBF, and HSM groups, have demonstrated keenness to apply for amnesty: ANN/IRIN, "Uganda: Rebels Ask Government for Amnesty While Others Are Freed," September 14, 2000.

106. See Edward Ojulu, "Uganda Army 'Not Serious' over Amnesty," *The East African*, February 14-20, 2000. The commission remained financially strapped for a long time: James Moro, "Facilitate Amnesty Commission," *New Vision*, October 2, 2000.

6

Compliance with the Laws of War: The Role of the International Criminal Tribunal for Rwanda

Luc Côté

In early April 1994, the world's attention was riveted on one event taking place on the African continent. The election of Nelson Mandela as president of South Africa closed the book on the apartheid era, thus reducing the compliance gap with respect to a fundamental human right.

At the same time, on the same continent, the international community was turning a blind eye to the Rwandan genocide, where hundreds of thousands of civilians were being massacred in the most horrific violation of international humanitarian law in African history. Over a period of 100 days, a well-planned and quickly executed genocide unfolded, as the United Nations withdrew the majority of its troops.

While the Rwandan genocide clearly represented unspeakably abhorrent violations of international humanitarian law, it was a neither unforeseeable nor isolated tragedy. From the U.N. standpoint, the birth of the International Criminal Tribunal for Rwanda[1] (hereinafter "ICTR") in November 1994 would redress a series of failures towards Rwandans by both the U.N. and the international community. Among these were a failure to prevent, a failure to stop and, at an earlier stage, a failure to acknowledge and denounce.[2] In that context, the seemingly insurmountable skepticism the ICTR must overcome, first from Rwandans, is understandable, as is the need to prove wrong those who see it as yet another exercise in failure.

Given this challenge and faced with the horrors of war, it seems important to study the ability of such a judicial institution to help ensure greater respect for the existing norms regarding armed conflicts. In the following chapter, we look beyond the Rwandan tragedy as such and study the political and legal impact of the two ad hoc tribunals established by the Security Council—the ICTR in particular but also its elder sibling, the International Criminal Tribunal for the former Yugoslavia[3] (hereinafter "ICTY")—regarding compliance with the norms of the laws of war in general, set forth in their respective statutes and general international law. First, after identifying some of the weaknesses or gaps in international humanitarian law, we will examine whether the judicial approach adopted by the Security Council can solve the problems involved in applying the laws of war. Then, using concrete examples taken from the two ad hoc international criminal tribunals (hereinafter "the Tribunals"), we will study their impact on compliance with the laws of war in Rwanda and the former Yugoslavia, from the point of view of political reality and the normative developments they have generated. We will then be in a position to draw some conclusions regarding the impact of the Tribunals on respect for the law of armed conflict.

War Crime Norms: A System of Law Universally Violated and Rarely Punished

Although we readily consider the Middle Ages to be the darkest period of civilization's history, referring to its first phase as the "Dark Ages," the twentieth century was, in fact, the bloodiest and most lethal century of all. Its numerous wars resulted in the deaths of over 100 million people, more than were killed in conflicts of the previous nineteen centuries combined. Paradoxically, it was during the twentieth century that the Charter of the United Nations banned war,[4] proclaiming a prohibition on the use of force in the aftermath of World War II, except in case of self-defense.[5] Although war may have been "just" in the days of Grotius, it was now unlawful. Where once it had been treated with indifference by international law, war was now policed and regulated by what became known as international humanitarian law. In a strangely paradoxical way, utopia[6] gave way to realism and, from The Hague to Geneva, international humanitarian law built an imposing edifice of norms to regulate the now-forbidden use of force. The law penetrated the realm of lawlessness in a bid to take control of a situation where the use of force prevailed over the rule of law. It attempted to control the manner in which wars are conducted and punish any excesses, while protecting its victims. In fact, although it is based on The Hague and the Geneva conventions, which were ratified by almost all states in existence, thus making it a truly universal system, international humanitarian law would also be the most universally violated law, as it was powerless to prevent the most serious violations of its rules and incapable of ensuring punishment.[7] The tragic conflicts of the twentieth century, whether examined from the point of view of *jus ad bellum* (now *jus contra bellum* with the banning of the use of force) or *jus in bello*, which imposes compliance with basic humanitarian principles in times of conflict, bear witness to the miserable failure of the laws of war.

Developed at a time when war was primarily a state prerogative, *"jus in bello"* provided another striking illustration of the principle of state sovereignty, as it was based exclusively on the willingness of the state to submit to it. With the Geneva Conventions, it evolved from a multilateral, state-centric system of law into a more "humanitarian" law in pursuit of universality, whereby all people are recognized as having certain rights,[8] thus following the trend toward international protection of human rights.[9] Despite this, international humanitarian law remained deeply influenced by its origins and gave states a great deal of room to maneuver, making it possible for them, if not to ignore it, then at least to remove any possibility of sanction. Indeed, although the Geneva Conventions introduced an original and sophisticated sanction mechanism by inserting in the realm of international law the notion of individual criminal responsibility for the violation of some of its provisions and by investing national courts with the universal jurisdiction to apply it, it was nonetheless up to individual states to make use of it. Despite that, they did not do so.[10]

The self-enforcing nature of international humanitarian law, relying exclusively on states for its application, is undoubtedly one of its main weaknesses. The events in Rwanda and the former Yugoslavia offer vivid examples of why states are reluctant to enforce international humanitarian law, as they are often directly involved in violating it.[11] International humanitarian law was created by states whose primary goal was to ensure respect for their sovereignty, with disregard for the effectiveness of the system as such. In fact, it may even be possible that the reason the norms are almost universal is that it is almost impossible to punish violations thereof.[12]

A System Ill-Adapted to Deal with Modern Conflicts

The post-World War II conflicts marked the end of the state's monopoly on war-related violence. The world witnessed the appearance of new players on the battlefield: more or less organized and controlled militia and paramilitary groups with a nebulous and uncertain chain of command. Classic warfare, based on territorial interests, gave way to conflicts based on ethnic, religious, or economic differences that often brought about the implosion of the state and put an "ungovernable, chaotic entity"[13] in its place. International humanitarian law was ill-equipped to deal with this change. With the dismembering and "destructuring" of the state that occurred in some conflicts, international humanitarian law no longer had a valid party with whom to negotiate. Moreover, in the absence of an authority with territorial jurisdiction, access to victims was threatened.[14] Further, this type of conflict victimized even more civilians than classic warfare, as they were often targeted or taken hostage. These victims are not, strictly speaking, "protected persons" under international humanitarian law, which is based on the concept of nationality as applied to classic international conflicts. From that perspective, it could be said that international humanitarian law, in addition to losing its prime interlocutor, the state, also lost its purpose, its raison d'être, being unable to protect civilian populations against their own nationals.

Another weakness in the protection mechanisms in international humanitarian law stems from the conventional distinction between international and non-international conflicts.[15] Although it may be true that "in our contemporary world, few conflicts are truly internal, many are at least mixed or internationalized,"[16] the recent evolution of war forces us to acknowledge that what were once considered international conflicts are now becoming "internalized."[17] While international humanitarian law provides a particularly elaborate system of norms for international conflicts, it is poorly equipped to deal with internal conflicts.[18] The provisions of the Geneva Conventions regarding noninternational conflicts are contained in a single article, Article 3 common to the four conventions, and it provides no enforcement mechanism.[19] Although Additional Protocol II of 1977 deals specifically with internal conflicts, it contains very few provisions and has no enforcement mechanism. These few provisions illustrate more the states desire to maintain control over what were still perceived as internal security problems subject to their exclusive sovereignty.[20]

The Security Council's Judicial Approach

Of all the attempts by the international community to remedy the atrocities committed in Rwanda and the former Yugoslavia, the Security Council's approach in establishing an international criminal tribunal was both remarkable and innovative. While the "traditional function of political bodies as regards international criminal law is essentially to ensure compliance with it" by issuing reminders of the existence of the conventions on international humanitarian law and by condemning violations,[21] the creation of the Tribunals "extended the scope of intervention in the matter in a remarkable way."[22]

The use of legal proceedings to apprehend and sanction the norms of international law was a revolutionary step in an area where a form of self-enforcement had always prevailed, in the name of a dubious kind of volunteerism inspired by state sovereignty. In that sense, the establishment of a genuinely international tribunal with binding power was an original approach that could only be regarded as suspect by many states. It is not surprising, therefore, that the establishment of the two ad hoc tribunals was not effected by the states themselves, but rather by an international organization, namely, the U.N. Security Council. Nor is it surprising that the newly established institutions set out to focus entirely on individual responsibility for serious violations of the law of armed conflict. After all, the precedents set by Nuremberg and Tokyo had paved the way[23] and, more importantly, refused to sink into oblivion. Moreover, international humanitarian law had itself proposed such an approach by granting all

States the universal jurisdiction to ensure that serious infractions of its norms were punished, be it by national courts.

The Security Council's approach to the law of war was innovative, in that it clearly reflects a supranationalist logic over statist logic,[24] firmly substituting itself for the states with respect to their obligations under the Geneva Conventions. The classic notion of sovereignty, whereby international law was reduced to a law of coexistence, was thus called into question in favor of an approach inspired by the fundamental human values that transcend states in pursuit of universality and demand a law based on cooperation.[25] By instituting an international tribunal, the Security Council discarded the logic of domination based on national sovereignty and opted for a solution that ostensibly called for higher morals in public life in the name of universal human values. In that sense, the creation of the Tribunals by the Security Council was part of a new trend in international law, which led to an explosion in normative production after World War II, primarily in the area of human rights,[26] and fostered an increase in the number of international judicial bodies.[27]

An Infringement on Sovereignty?

Though it is possible to view the territorial and personal jurisdiction exercised by the Tribunals as a kind of infringement on state sovereignty,[28] it is also possible to see it as the exercising of the "universal jurisdiction" provided for in the Geneva Conventions of 1949 (on grave breaches of international humanitarian law) and recognized by customary international law.

On the other hand, it is true that states are in a weakened position as regards their sovereign right not to act, that is, not to enforce international humanitarian law, notably by exercising their own universal and national jurisdiction. The Security Council has taken their place in order to exercise the material, territorial, and personal power of the Tribunals. The Security Council has assumed the power granted exclusively to states by the Geneva Conventions and, unlike them, is exercising it. Perhaps this is simply the fulfillment of the stated goal of the convention on genocide, which called for the formation of an international tribunal.

Three main aspects of the Security Council's approach help foster greater compliance for the existing norms regarding armed conflict: the use of a "judicial" institution, the enforcement of individual criminal responsibility, and the obligation of states to cooperate.

An International Judicial Institution

The establishment of an institution with a judicial function of "settling conflicts through binding decisions based on rules"[29] is in itself the most important aspect of the Security Council's decision. The judicial function as such is twofold: first, it is a means of settling conflicts, and, second, it is an instrument for the affirmation and development of the law. The Tribunals must not only judge individuals, they must do it according to existing law. "In criminal law, the purpose of the judicial act is to state the law, as per its etymology, 'jus dicere'."[30] In that sense, the Tribunals are crucial tools in the "internalization"[31] of the norms of international humanitarian law. As Professor Abi-Saab explains:

> And it is here that lies the great potential contribution of international criminal tribunals, in their role in the development of humanitarian norm, via the elaboration of the crimes that ensue from their violation; in transporting us from theoretical or doctrinal speculations to concrete determinations of the constitutive elements of these crimes, of the conditions and modalities of their application.[32]

With the Tribunals, judges regained control of international humanitarian law, which had all but eluded them since Nuremberg. And as we shall see, faced with the political obstacles that undermined the establishment of both Tribunals and the lack of interest shown by states and the United Nations in providing them the means to be effective, the judges replied with their favorite weapon, the only one at their disposal, their voices. Through a dynamic interpretation of their statutes and customary international law, they enabled international humanitarian law to evolve in an unprecedented way.

A System of International Criminal Law that Punishes
Individual Violations Directly

With individual criminal responsibility, the Tribunals removed the state from the stage and replaced it with individuals, in order to focus on criminal sanction of international norm violations, two relatively unusual phenomena in international law.[33] We, therefore, witnessed an unlikely union, which, according to former prosecutor Louise Arbour, presented "the extraordinary difficulty of trying to marry together principles of international law (a profoundly consensual body of law that is essentially concerned with regulating conduct between States) with the criminal law (a body of law that is profoundly coercitive), which is primarily concerned with personal liability."[34] The Tribunals are thus the offspring of international law and criminal law, the former known for its lack of means of implementation and sanction, and the latter for exactly the opposite. This new hybrid borrowed from both legal systems to produce a law that can be enforced like criminal law but is left largely to the discretion of states to implement, like international public law.

On the one hand, as international humanitarian law provides for direct sanction of individual violations of its provisions, it is safe to say that, "the advent of international tribunals constitutes a major step forward in 'teething' international humanitarian law and putting an end to individual impunity."[35] In that sense, the exercise of individual criminal jurisdiction contributes to the strengthening of the norms of international humanitarian law and fosters by that very act their greater integration.

On the other hand, although individual responsibility leaves the judicial stage primarily to individuals, the state nonetheless maintains its lead role in executing decisions and orders of the Tribunals based on the principle of sovereignty. Thus, although the court does indeed have the power to issue arrest warrants or summons, it is completely at the mercy of states for their execution.

A Binding Tribunal as a Subsidiary Organ of the Security Council

Legally, the Tribunals are subsidiary organs of the Security Council (Article 29 of the charter) and thus benefit from the binding power inherent in Security Council resolutions (Article 25 of the charter). Before establishing them, the Security Council, acting under Chapter VII of the charter, recognized "the existence of a threat to the peace" (Article 39 of the charter), which made the tribunals, in the words of the United Nations, "measures for maintaining or restoring peace" (Article 41 of the charter).

The use of a Security Council resolution made it possible to establish the Tribunals swiftly and effectively[36] and thus to avoid the lengthy process of a more conventional route, while reflecting the approach of internationalization of enforcement. Through this method, states were placed under a legal obligation, *erga omnes*,[37] to abide by court orders and decisions.[38] Hence, under international law, the Tribunals represent truly supranational binding institutions vis-à-vis states and that is a definite advantage with recalcitrant members, particularly in the conflict in the former Yugoslavia. Thus, refusal by a state to respect an order of the Tribunals constitutes a violation of international law that may result in sanctions by the Security Council.

In conclusion, although international criminal justice, as exercised by an international binding legal institution, can contribute significantly to the normative development of international humanitarian law and sanctions the punishment of violations, be it in a limited manner, it is nonetheless dependent upon states for its implementation. As the first presiding judge of the ICTY, Judge Cassese, stated, "If States are willing and prepared to cooperate, the tribunals are able to fulfill their mission. If, on the other hand, States refuse to enforce orders or warrants, the tribunals are completely powerless."[39]

The Impact of the International Tribunals
on Respect for Norms

Evaluating the impact of the Tribunals on compliance with the norms of the laws of war is not an easy task. Although seven or eight years may seem an eternity to those who suffered the torments of an armed conflict, it is nonetheless too short a period to assess the record of a judicial institution. In the short term, we can examine the effect the Tribunals have had on the conflicts that have broken out and are ongoing in the territories of their respective jurisdictions. In this, we are discussing the political impact of the Tribunals. In the longer term, we can provide a brief analysis of the legal impact of the Tribunals on the norms of international humanitarian law, as they were understood.

Impact of the Tribunals on the Conflicts, Particularly in the Case of Rwanda

The Tribunal for Rwanda came into being four months after the genocide ended. The ICTR thus differs from the ICTY insofar as the conflict in Rwanda was over when it was created, while the war in the former Yugoslavia endured, which explains why the temporal jurisdiction of the former was limited, while that of the latter is concerned with ongoing conflicts.[40] On the other hand, the inclusion of a territorial jurisdiction extending to neighboring states in the ICTR Statute rightly reflected the concerns of the Security Council regarding the situation in the Great Lakes Region.[41]

Indeed, to assess the impact of the ICTR in relation to international humanitarian law, we must consider the Rwanda tragedy in the geopolitical context of the Great Lakes Region (which includes Burundi, the Democratic Republic of Congo, and Uganda), renowned then and now for its instability and poor record of compliance with regard to international humanitarian law and human rights.[42] Although the region was monitored on a continuous basis throughout the 1990s by United Nations organizations such as the U.N. Observer Mission Uganda-Rwanda (UNOMUR), the U.N. Assistance Mission for Rwanda (UNAMIR), the U.N. High Commissioner for Refugees (UNHCR), the U.N. High Commissioner for Human Rights (UNHCHR), numerous nongovernmental organizations (NGOs) and the International Committee for the Red Cross (ICRC), the human rights situation nonetheless deteriorated during that period, as demonstrated so thoroughly by the Rwandan genocide and the protracted and complex war in the Democratic Republic of Congo (involving nearly all the states in the region) that followed it. Consequently, we can state that the arrival of the ICTR on the scene in 1995 appears not to have dampened the ardor of the belligerents in the Great Lakes Region any more than that of the ICTY was able to prevent the massacres in Srebrenica (Bosnia-Herzegovina) and Kosovo.

Some see this as the first case of failure of a judicial institution to ensure short-term compliance with the norms of international humanitarian law in a region still at war. However, the very role handed down to the Tribunals by the Security Council, to be "instruments in the cessation of violations," is itself questionable, given its own lamentable failure to stop the same conflicts on repeated occasions.

The ICTR as a Tool in Restoring and Maintaining Peace

The ICTR was established by Security Council resolution 955 under Chapter VII of the U.N. Charter as a measure that "would contribute to the process of national reconciliation and to the restoration and maintenance of peace" and "contribute to ensuring that such violations are halted and effectively redressed." Although the wording used in the resolution was clearly intended to establish the jurisdiction of the Security Council to create such a judicial body, one can question the real capacity of such an institution, a Tribunal, to contribute effectively to reconciliation and compliance with international humanitarian law. As Wairama, Onoria, and Katalikawe put it in this volume, the creation of the Rwanda Tribunal was "widely seen as being no more than a pathologist's post-mortem, in that it follows on the heels of inaction on the part of the world community to avert a foreseen humanitarian tragedy."[43]

Thus, the creation of the ICTR (and the ICTY) derives directly from an admission of failure by the international community. It bears witness to the powerlessness of the United Nations to guarantee "collective security" and is symptomatic of what some call "la dérive humanitaire"[44] [the humanitarian backsliding] of the Security Council.[45] Given the tragic consequences of its failures in Rwanda and the former Yugoslavia and the serious violations of international humanitarian law that followed, the Security Council once again resorted to solutions, characterized as humanitarian, that, while laudable, simply illustrate its inability to fulfill its primary mission, leading it to react after the fact to bandage the wounds it failed to prevent. By giving the two ad hoc tribunals a peacemaking mandate under the formula, "no peace without justice," the Security Council doomed them to failure from the outset. In that regard, "legal means cannot replace political means," and justice cannot be used as "an alibi for non-intervention."[46] It is in this dismal context that the Tribunals undertook their difficult mandate, tainted from the outset by serious credibility issues. And yet in order to be effective in the face of the conflicts that gave rise to their establishment, the Tribunals required some degree of credibility in the eyes of the warring parties and the international community.

A Credibility Problem

There is no doubt that the Security Council is by nature a political organ. Its decision to establish two Tribunals was first and foremost a political decision by its member states at the time. Although, on the one hand, the necessity of "fighting impunity" was put forth in no uncertain terms, behind the scenes the member states were less decisive[47] regarding the new judicial institution. Some felt it was a dangerous exercise that threatened both the principle of sovereignty[48] and the need to allow diplomatic efforts toward peace talks take their course.[49] This lack of enthusiasm was evident, especially at the beginning, from the insufficient resources and administrative support provided by the U.N. and its member states, the poor transmission of information and the refusal to arrest indicted individuals by some states, and the absence of sanctions by the Security Council against states that refused to cooperate.[50] The tribunals were confined to the political role of acting as a means of pressure or sword of Damocles to serve the purposes of diplomacy, rather than the reverse.[51] This affected the credibility of the tribunals from the outset and cast doubt on their effectiveness and independence.[52]

Further, by creating the ad hoc tribunals for very specific conflicts, "the Security Council indirectly conferred on itself the power of prosecutor—who alone would decide on the appropriateness of establishing the special tribunals. Tainted by this original sin,"[53] which made them instruments of selective international criminal justice, the tribunals were forced to carry out their mandate. They may not be the direct instruments of the victors, as was the case of the Nuremberg tribunal, but they were nonetheless seen as the tool of the powers, who used them to mask their indifference (Rwanda)[54] or renunciation (former Yugoslavia)[55] and to ease their consciences.[56]

The Case of Rwanda

Even before its establishment in Rwanda, the ICTR suffered from its negative perception as a United Nations organ.[57] The changing circumstances of its establishment,[58] with the Rwandan government proposing and then voting against its establishment at the Security Council meeting, were indicative of the relations that would develop between the two, which were marked by disbelief and distrust. The perception of the ICTR by other African states was also tainted by skepticism at the beginning, but it improved greatly with the official support of the Organization of African Unity in June 1997, which urged its member states to assist and collaborate with the Tribunal.[59]

Nevertheless the Rwandan government still considers the ICTR much more as a political rather than a judicial institution and uses political pressure to express its discontent with the Tribunal's decisions. During the first years of existence of the Tribunal, the government of Rwanda saw the ICTR as a competitor as it attempted to obtain the extradition of its main suspects.[60] Then, following a first decision of the Appeal Chamber in the *Barayagwiza* case[61] by which the Judges ordered the release of the accused for abuse of process, the Rwandan government reacted angrily and threatened to suspend all cooperation with the ICTR. In a second decision reconsidering the issue, the Appeal Chamber while strongly asserting its independence vis-à-vis states, reversed its previous judgment.[62] Therein lay a perfect illustration of the fragile relations between the two. Nevertheless, the Rwandan government provided the ICTR with the minimal collaboration necessary for it to function. Without that, it would have been nearly impossible for the ICTR to fulfill its mandate.

Unlike the case of the ICTY, the Office of the Prosecutor of the ICTR is seated in the very country where most of the violations took place and is surrounded by victims and perpetrators on both sides of the conflict. Up to this point, the prosecutor has been investigating the leaders of the former regime and has been accused by some critics of applying victor's justice.[63] Investigation of leaders of the current regime who are believed to have been involved in war crimes or crimes against humanity will enhance the ICTR's credibility among the vanquished by demonstrating its impartiality.[64] There is, however, a concurrent danger that the present government may become increasingly hostile.[65] This was demonstrated by a letter of the president of the ICTR dated August 8, 2002, addressed to the president of the Security Council, alleging that the Rwandan government's noncooperation by imposing new restrictions on witnesses traveling to Arusha stemmed from the "Prosecutor's recent efforts to investigate members of the Rwandan Patriotic Army."[66]

Since the beginning, ICTR has been under strict scrutiny from Rwandan governmental and nongovernmental organizations. It has been criticized for its malfunctioning, its slow pace, its poor consideration of the victims, its treatment of the accused, and so on.[67] While most of the criticism is valid, some simply reflect a misconception of the ICTR's role or exaggerated expectations of its possibilities.

The ICTR's Role in Rwanda

The principal role of a criminal tribunal in this case is to prosecute individuals charged with violations of international humanitarian law. As a Chapter VII measure, the ICTR's main objectives are reconciliation, restoration of peace, and ensuring future compliance. The question is whether the Tribunal can achieve these objectives solely by discharging its mandate to judge individuals responsible for serious violations of international humanitarian law. Certainly, the arrest, imprisonment, and conviction of numerous political and military leaders responsible for the genocide will confer on them a lasting stigma of unsuitability for public office. By arresting those who continue to commit violations of international humanitarian law, notably the military leaders who are still operating in the Democratic Republic of Congo, the ICTR is making a definite, albeit limited, contribution to peace and compliance with the laws of war. It is also likely that the judicial recognition of the Rwandan genocide as a planned and deliberate action by a specific group of persons whose desire was to retain their grip on power will help prevent acts of retribution against the entire ethnic group to which they belong. No one can underestimate the importance of strong judicial condemnation of the use of ethnic discrimination and violence in a region where the potential of ethnic conflict still exists. So, from the outset, it can be said that the basic purpose of the ICTR to judge persons responsible for serious violations of international humanitarian law is in itself contributing modestly to compliance with war laws. On the other hand, considering the prevailing human rights situation in the Great Lakes Region since the establishment of the ICTR, one might be tempted to think that its contribution to fostering compliance with international humanitarian law has been negligible. In reality, both statements contain some truth, even though the Tribunals' political contribution to restoring peace and national reconciliation may appear minor in the short term.

The Tribunals' Political Contribution to Restoring Peace and
National Reconciliation

In an article entitled "Justice as a Tool for Peace-Making," former ICTR prosecutor Richard Goldstone listed some positive contributions which justice can achieve. [68] These contributions may be formulated in light of the ICTR objectives outlined in Security Council resolution 955:

Deterrence: an international deterrent can come only from the strict enforcement of international humanitarian law, thereby "ensuring that such violations
are halted."[69]

Individual responsibility: Individualized guilt serves the very important purpose of preventing a collective guilt syndrome. By diminishing the tendency to
ostracize a specific ethnic or national group and the need for revenge, it contributes "to the process of national reconciliation."[70]

Keeping an accurate record of history: Judicial exposure of the truth is the
only effective way of ensuring that history is recorded more accurately and
faithfully than otherwise would have been the case. This constitutes an effective safeguard against revisionism and "contributes to the restoration and maintenance of peace."

These statements reflect the liberal school of thought according to which
there can be no peace without justice. It contrasts with the realist school of
thought, which sees international criminal justice as a threat to peace efforts.[71]
For the short term, the massive violations of international humanitarian law that
took place after the Tribunals were established, both in the Great Lakes Region
and in the former Yugoslavia, make the dissuasive ability of criminal punishment appear highly doubtful.[72] The scale of the violations, the state and/or military support the many perpetrators enjoyed, and the ethnic ideology that instilled
hatred and violence are all factors that lead us to question the dissuasive capability of international criminal justice. Moreover, in order for deterrence to work,
the punishment must be seen as certain, swift, and just.[73] However, international
criminal justice is slow and can deal with only an extremely limited number of
cases. In addition, the distance between the scene of the crimes and the tribunal,
which is seated in a different country, as well as the differences in the procedural systems adopted, create a problem of perception with regard to the fairness
of the penalty, which thus *loses* "its resonance in the cultural universe in which
the atrocities took place."[74] In fact, if there is any deterrence, it is much more a
question of general deterrence, that is, "in the long run, the establishment of
international norms or law can deter potential war criminals globally."[75]

The extremely limited number of people who may be brought before the
Tribunals also reduces the desired effect of avoiding collective guilt by specifically attributing criminal responsibility to individuals.[76] Certainly, international
criminal justice remains largely symbolic and has limited resources. Nonetheless, it must not be forgotten that by choosing a handful of individuals bearing
"the greatest responsibility" for the crimes committed by a multitude of people,
individual criminal justice paradoxically makes them the representatives of certain groups that are just as guilty in the eyes of the victims. "Thus what is billed
as individual justice actually becomes a de facto way of exonerating many of the
guilty," and "the idea that war crimes tribunals will individualize guilt turns out
to be fraught with ambiguity."[77]

Lastly, the Tribunals make a substantial contribution to establishing the facts in a rigorous manner subject to the strictest requirements of judicial procedure.[78] "Everyone thought they understood the horror of this war, but before the tribunal, undeniably and irrefutably, the truth suddenly emerged, standing out against revisionism."[79] Particularly in conflicts where manipulation of the truth is a weapon of choice, it is important to be sure that the facts will be reported faithfully and not undergo a kind of revisionism that would undermine all efforts to attain a durable peace.

In summary, based on the experience of the Tribunals, it is safe to say that their political contribution to maintaining peace and bringing about national reconciliation cannot be measured in the short term. In response to a question about whether a lasting peace was impossible in Bosnia without justice, Prosecutor Louise Arbour stated:

> Probably. But it's an ambiguous question and will remain that way for some time to come. Justice truly does represent an investment in peace. But it's a long-term investment. Right now, it is not happening in a particular peaceful way. Arrests are often violent and criminal trials on such a painful subject are bound to disturb the people. . . . That is why some people view justice as being contrary to the goal of bringing peace to Bosnia. In the end, people realized that an absence of fighting was really just a semblance of peace. True peace is a society that has reconciled itself and is able to integrate all its conflicting elements.[80]

The Legal Impact of the Tribunals on the Norms of International Humanitarian Law

In this section, we intend to discuss briefly the issue of the Tribunals' normative contribution to the law of armed conflict. This is by far the most important aspect of the work of the Tribunals. Like the Nuremberg and Tokyo tribunals, they make an impressive normative contribution to international humanitarian law as it was understood.[81] Thus, though it maintained a certain control over the Tribunals, particularly by carefully limiting their jurisdiction, the Security Council has been unable to rein in the independent judges called upon to make law in this area for the first time since Nuremberg.

The Tribunals' normative contribution is twofold. First, new norms have been developed, both in the statutes and the rules of the Tribunals and in the judicial decisions that have revealed the existence of customary international norms. Second, due to their jurisprudence, the Tribunals have made it possible to clarify the content of certain existing norms. The nature of the judicial function is precisely to interpret, define, and clarify the law in order to apply it. The Tribunals have been able to put some order to rules that existed well before their creation and present them in a coherent, comprehensible manner.[82]

In that sense, the Tribunals can be considered as "norm entrepreneurs" or "norm promoters," as they establish new rules and provide a clear explanation of the meaning and purpose of existing norms.[83] Further, by providing an institutional framework that makes it possible to punish the violation of norms, the Tribunals are participating in their internalization. Thus, on a theoretical level, the Tribunals' contribution to compliance with the norms of the law of armed conflict is undeniable.

A Brief Overview of the Statutes

The statutes of the Tribunals are normative resolutions of the Security Council addressed to all states, requiring them to cooperate. A quick analysis of the statutes tells us that, in many ways, the normative approach taken by the Security Council is quite original. First, by using the expression, "serious violations of international humanitarian law," in Article 1 of the statutes, it disregarded the restrictive definition of "grave breaches" contained in the Geneva Conventions and opted instead for a broader notion of international humanitarian law that includes both war crimes and crimes against humanity.[84] This is a vision that "appears perfectly justified, as the collective violence that broke out demanded a global apprehension and reaction on the part of the legal order, regardless of the manner in which the violence took place."[85]

Secondly, by including the fundamental legal guarantees provided for in the main international human rights protection instruments, the statutes provided a genuine "international criminal procedural system,"[86] which made it possible to "spell out specific procedures by which norms leaders coordinate disapproval and sanction for norm breaking."[87] Further, the statutes were also innovative in that they reproduced the main United Nations standards for human rights, "not only the ones that are already mandatory, or lex lata, but also the ones that are aspired to as standards of achievement, de lege ferenda, such as the abolition of capital punishment."[88]

As for the ICTR statute specifically, one cannot but salute the bold steps taken by the Security Council by at last adopting a mechanism for punishing individual violations of Article 3 common to the Geneva Conventions and of Protocol II, thus making it possible for the first time in the international arena to punish criminal acts committed during noninternational conflicts.[89] In so doing, the Security Council broke new ground, adding an important chapter to international humanitarian law as regards internal conflicts, which had suffered serious deficiencies.[90] The Tribunal judges would quickly adopt this expansive and dynamic approach of the Security Council[91] and echo it in their decisions.

Jurisprudence of the Tribunals

Although according to the Statute of the International Court of Justice, jurisprudence is just a "subsidiary means for the determination of rules of law" (Article 38(1)(d)), it is nonetheless a source of identification and interpretation of the norm. As stated by Hans Kelsen, "all norms must be interpreted inasmuch as they must be applied."[92] The two go hand in hand, as the norms must be interpreted before being applied to a specific situation. It is, therefore, impossible to deny the normative function of interpretation, which is a process of capturing and identifying the meaning (or meanings) of the content of the law.[93] In that sense, the judicial decisions of the Tribunals foster greater respect for and better integration of norms, by clarifying them and determining precisely their application.

The greatest challenge facing the Tribunal judges, charged by the Security Council to judge those responsible for the crimes committed in Rwanda and the former Yugoslavia, consisted precisely in identifying the norms of the law of armed conflict, a classic and orthodox law, and then applying them to entirely new, complex situations:

> However, the task of the tribunals was far from simple; indeed, of the numerous difficulties they faced, one of the most arduous was the need to adapt the humanitarian norms contained in the Geneva Conventions of 1949 on the protection of war victims and their additional protocols of 1977, as well as the old Annex to The Hague Convention IV of 1907: Regulations respecting the laws and customs of war, to the new context of war to which they had to be applied. This new context bore almost no resemblance to the types of armed conflicts that were common when these instruments were written. As a result, it was necessary to ensure greater protection of civilians, especially when they came under enemy control, using the principle of nullum crime sine lege. The judges adopted a progressive approach in that regard, which quickly enabled the ICTY and the ICTR to start rendering decisions of capital importance for the development of international humanitarian law. Slowly but surely, the decisions formed the basis of a jurisprudence that allowed consolidation of some of the progress made in the long-awaited corpus of norms, notably concerning the protection of civilians.[94]

The normative contribution of the international Tribunals to the law of armed conflict is a rich one and has been the subject of much commentary. A thorough analysis of its contribution is beyond the scope of this chapter. Two examples will suffice to illustrate its importance: the extension of the laws of war to internal conflicts and the dynamic interpretation of the categories of persons placed under the protective umbrella of the law.

Extension of the Laws of War to Internal Conflicts
The judges of the ICTY were quickly confronted with the problem of applying the laws of classic warfare, which governed international conflicts, to the ambivalent situation that followed the breakup of the former Yugoslav state. They quickly found they had a problem with qualifying the conflicts, which had both internal and international aspects and were thus hybrids, depending on who the warring parties were and the territory on which the fighting occurred. In its first decision in the Tadic case, the ICTY Appeals Chamber stated:

On the basis of the foregoing, we conclude that the conflicts in the former
Yugoslavia have both internal and international aspects, that the members of
the Security Council clearly had both aspects of the conflicts in mind when
they adopted the Statute of the International Tribunal, and that they intended to
empower the International Tribunal to adjudicate violations of humanitarian
law that occurred in either context. To the extent possible under existing international law, the Statute should therefore be construed to give effect to that purpose.[95]

Unlike the ICTR statute, however, the ICTY statute contained no explicit
provision for violations of Article 3 common to the Geneva Conventions, which
covers noninternational conflicts. The court thus referred to Article 3 of its statute, which punished violations of the laws and customs of war, interpreting it in
an evolutionary way in order to apply it to all conflicts, whether internal or international, under customary law.[96] It was a spectacular about-face, by which the
court, in stating the customary nature of the norms governing the laws of war
and their application to internal conflicts distanced itself from the conventional
view of international humanitarian law as governing essentially international
conflicts. The decision thus extended protection to civilians and civilian objects
against the effects of wars resulting from internal conflicts.[97] Finally, it stated
that the notion of individual criminal responsibility of the belligerents also fell
under customary law and could be evoked with regard to violation of the laws of
war taking place in internal conflicts.[98] While it cannot be stated that the "international criminalization" of the violations of the laws of war committed in internal conflicts will halt the atrocities perpetrated in the former Yugoslavia and the
Great Lakes Region, it must nonetheless be admitted that it makes a significant
normative contribution to enhancing respect for the laws in that regard.

Dynamic Interpretation of the Categories of Persons Placed under the Protective Umbrella of the Law

One of the functions of international humanitarian law is to protect groups
of people who are particularly vulnerable in times of conflict, notably by punishing war crimes, genocide, and crimes against humanity. Both the ICTR and the
ICTY have been confronted with definitions of persons to be protected mainly
designed to applied to international conflict that, if applied to the letter in an
internal conflict, would have put the protective function of the norms into check.
By rejecting a purely mechanical application of the norms in relation to their
finality, the tribunals reformulated some of the rules in a more general way in
order to adapt them to the reality of the conflicts to which they were to be applied.

Thus, according to the fourth Geneva Convention, persons protected in
times of international conflict are those who find themselves "in the hands of a
Party to the conflict or an Occupying Power of which they are not nationals"
(Article 4, IV). This provision was based on the concept of "nationality," which
was applicable to classic international conflicts, but which becomes devoid of

meaning when applied literally to the hybrid, ethnically motivated conflicts that have torn the former Yugoslavia apart. For instance, a Bosnian native detained in Bosnia by another party to the conflict of the same nationality, but of different ethnic origin, would not have benefited from protection under the convention. Confronted with a contemporary conflict of an ethnic nature, the ICTY Appeals Chamber threw aside the criteria of nationality and instead adopted a more flexible notion of allegiance to a party to the conflict, ruling as follows:

> While previously wars were primarily between well-established States, in modern inter-ethnic armed conflicts such as that in the former Yugoslavia, new States are often created during the conflict and ethnicity rather than nationality may become the grounds for allegiance. Or, put another way, ethnicity may become determinative of national allegiance. Under these conditions, the requirement of nationality is even less adequate to define protected persons. In such conflicts, not only the text and the drafting history of the Convention but also, and more importantly, the Convention's object and purpose suggest that allegiance to a Party to the conflict and, correspondingly, control by this Party over persons in a given territory, may be regarded as the crucial test.[99]

As for the ICTR, it was faced with the problem of defining ethnic identity for the purpose of genocide. Indeed, in the strictest sense of the term, Hutus and Tutsis are not different ethnic groups, because they share the same language and culture. As a result, the massacres that took place in Rwanda could not be characterized as genocide. Once again, the court adopted an effective definition of ethnic identity, which gave greater weight to the sentiment of belonging to a specific group rather than the existence of ethnicity in anthropological terms.

> The Chamber notes that the Tutsi population does not have its own language or a distinct culture from the rest of the Rwandan population. . . . The identification of persons as belonging to the group of Hutu or Tutsi (or Twa) had thus become embedded in Rwandan culture. . . . Moreover, the Tutsi were conceived of as an ethnic group by those who targeted them for killing. . . . As the expert witness, Alison Desforges, summarized: "The primary criterion for [defining] an ethnic group is the sense of belonging to that ethnic group. It is a sense which can shift over time."[100]

These two decisions illustrate how important the Tribunals' contribution was in defining the norms of the law of armed conflict. By interpreting the existing norms in a dynamic way, the Tribunals have broadened their scope to cover the contemporary reality of armed conflict.

Conclusion

> We must neither let the tribunal starve for lack of funds, nor let it suffocate under the weight of exaggerated expectations.[101]

To conclude this chapter, we would like to make a few observations designed to increase the impact of institutions like the ICTR on compliance with the norms of the law of armed conflict in general and on the Great Lakes Region in particular. As we have seen, a judicial institution in itself is not capable of bringing an end to conflict. However, by trying some of those responsible for the most serious violations of international humanitarian law, the Tribunals are unquestionably involved in fighting the impunity that prevailed in those regions. We may question the deterrent power of the Tribunals' decisions, but we cannot deny the importance of the message they send: that such violations will not go unpunished, regardless of the high offices held by the accused. Particularly on the African continent, which has all too often been torn apart by bloody conflicts, the ICTR by its very existence is now making it possible to envision trying the main culprits, despite its limited jurisdiction and the fact that it cannot prevent or stop wars. The indictment of President Charles Taylor of Liberia by the Special Court for Sierra Leone is another important step toward the fight against impunity on the African continent.

Chris Maina Peter, a professor at the University of Dar-es-Salaam in Tanzania, commented on the impact of the ICTR:

> The establishment of the Rwanda Tribunal is even more significant in Africa itself, where its presence on the continent will help raise people's awareness of the importance and value of human life. Serious crimes have been committed against the African people by all sorts of dictators, and so far they seem to be getting away with it. . . . And there are still many others on the continent who are shielded and pampered by the West. The establishment of the Rwanda Tribunal in Arusha has thus come as an unpleasant surprise for the power-hungry leadership in Africa. It is a clear signal from the international community that human life is precarious, that it should be respected and protected, and that those who abuse it will be held responsible and be sought wherever they are hiding.[102]

It is in this context that we must view the recent attempt in Senegal to bring charges against the former president of Chad, Hissène Habré, and similar attempts by an investigating judge in Spain to charge General Augusto Pinochet.

Thanks to the Tribunals, we are witnessing a new awareness on the part of the international community, which is now using national courts to punish the most serious violations of international humanitarian law. Thus, in Belgium and Switzerland, Rwandan victims have succeeded in appealing to the national courts to have Rwandan nationals arrested and tried for crimes falling under international humanitarian law. Some countries, like Canada, have set up special units mandated to prosecute individuals who have committed serious violations of international humanitarian law, notably in Rwanda. In that sense, the Tribunals' contribution to the new momentum of having the most serious violations of international humanitarian law punished through national court systems, although difficult to assess, has certainly not been negligible.

As we have seen, the Tribunals' greatest challenge has been to overcome their lack of credibility, particularly in the eyes of the belligerents involved in the conflicts. We believe it is primarily the responsibility of the prosecutor to take up this challenge. In the case of the ICTR, the Office of the Prosecutor is the only organ of the Tribunal based in Kigali, Rwanda. For most Rwandans, the members of the Office of the Prosecutor *are* the Tribunal. Under Article 15 of the Tribunal statute, the prosecutor is "responsible for the investigation and prosecution of persons responsible for serious violations of International Humanitarian Law." The only limitations on the prosecutor's discretionary powers are those concerning "ratione loci, ratione tempori and ratione materiae," and its duty to act fairly in relation to the fundamental right of the accused to have a fair trial, as provided by Article 20 of the Tribunal statute.[103] Considering the discretion it must use regarding the individuals indicted and the nature of the indictments brought against them, we believe that the Office of the Prosecutor plays the central role in enhancing the credibility of the Tribunal as a whole among the international community and in ensuring that it fulfills its objectives.

The reality of the Rwandan genocide means that the ICTR prosecutor must adopt a highly selective strategy, contrary to national jurisdictions.[104] In fact, a strict application of the Statute's call for "prosecuting persons responsible" to the reality of the Rwandan genocide, implying the direct responsibility of tens of thousands of persons, is impossible. Unlike the case of the former Yugoslavia, almost all of Rwanda's high-level authorities fled the country in the aftermath of the genocide; most are, therefore, accessible to the prosecutor, who can request the states where they seek refuge to arrest and transfer them to the ICTR jurisdiction. These states have proven to be more cooperative with the ICTR than other states have been regarding the tribunal for the former Yugoslavia. Therefore, the prosecutor must exercise discretion. Careful attention must be paid to the selection of the individuals to be indicted in light of the objectives of reconciliation, with a focus on providing a thorough reflection of Rwanda's tragic history. For that reason, it is important that the prosecutor make a serious effort to investigate violations of international humanitarian law committed by members of the current regime during the 1994 war, and thus shed the image of rendering "victor's justice."[105] Reports from various credible organizations and United Nations organs indicate that the Rwandan Patriotic Front (RPF) committed crimes against humanity and war crimes during the ICTR's jurisdictional time frame.[106] As time goes on, this becomes increasingly an issue of credibility and legitimacy for the ICTR.

Apart from the strict legal test of sufficiency of evidence, consideration of the ICTR's larger objectives is also appropriate. The selection of individuals should be based on the specific nature of possible indictments in relation to the objectives already discussed. Where evidence supports it, indictments should cover the broader range of acts of genocide, such as incitement, conspiracy, and sexual aggression. In the Rwandan context, it is also important to demonstrate the use of propaganda in "dehumanizing the enemy, instilling acute fear"[107] and manipulating individual perpetrators, in order to prevent a group guilt stigma and facilitate national reconciliation. The current "media trial," involving individuals responsible for the dissemination of hate propaganda through the use of newspaper and radio broadcasts is, in that perspective, of the utmost importance, particularly in the Great Lakes Region, where such practices are still being used. For the first time, an international court will be asked to define and interpret the norms applicable as regards incitement to genocide by individuals using the media. By directly addressing the key role played by ideology before and during the genocide, the ICTR is dealing with one of the most important aspects of the Rwandan genocide.

In addition, to enhance their credibility among the people affected by the conflicts under their jurisdiction, the Tribunals must at all costs mitigate the inevitable consequences of "justice hors sol" (justice abroad).[108] For Rwandans, the justice rendered by international judges far from their homes using procedures completely foreign to them is of little significance.[109] This distance problem, often cited by Rwandan authorities to criticize the work of the Tribunals, may foster a negative perception of the judicial institutions and thus undermine their credibility. Alison Des Forges has stated with regard to the ICTR:

> Rwandans are accustomed to a court case being heard in one or two days, with few or no witnesses, and being decided soon after. The lengthy presentation of evidence, complicated by the need to observe extensive safeguards for the rights of the accused, is foreign to them. Since neither the tribunal itself nor Rwandan authorities have successfully explained such aspects of tribunal procedure, most Rwandans see the slow pace of trials as simply one more proof of the inefficiency of the U.N., or worse still, of its indifference to Rwandans' needs.[110]

The applications by the prosecutor to have some hearings held in Kigali will certainly help to fill the perception gap felt by the Rwandan citizens towards international justice.[111] Thus, one area requiring vast improvement on the part of the ICTR is publicity.[112] Justice is public and must be communicated to Rwandans in a language and a form accessible to them. The present "coverage" of the trials in Arusha is done partially through Radio Rwanda, a government-controlled radio station. This is far from satisfactory. And yet, it is important to remember as Alison Des Forges stresses:

> Conditioned by long experience of courts which operated only to serve the interests of the powerful, Rwandans could benefit from following the work of an independent tribunal which seeks to operate according to the highest standards of impartiality and respect for all parties.[113]

The Rwandan people need to be kept informed of who is being indicted, for what crimes, committed in what region, etc. Indictments should be translated into Kinyarwanda and made available to the general public. If we want justice to play the important role of national reconciliation under Chapter VII of the U.N. Charter, an appropriate means of dissemination of information is needed.[114]

Also, the Office of the Prosecutor should establish a clear policy on indictments and make it known to the public. This policy should primarily take into account the objectives assigned to the ICTR by Security Council resolution 955. The Office of the Prosecutor could make important parts of its strategy in Rwanda public without jeopardizing its operations; this would contribute to avoiding misunderstanding with the Rwandan government and other states.

Finally, in accordance with the requirements laid out by Security Council resolution 955, the ICTR should establish a program of "cooperation to strengthen the courts and judicial system of Rwanda," in which the Office of the Prosecutor in Kigali could contribute directly. Until now, this aspect of the Security Council resolution has been all but ignored,[115] occasionally giving rise to justifiable criticism from the Rwandan authorities. Copies of the Statute and the Rules of Procedure and Evidence of the ICTR should be given to the Rwandan magistrates responsible for the special chamber in charge of implementing the genocide law. Regular meetings between members of the Office of the Prosecutor and Rwandan magistrates should be held. Any expert evidence, such as forensic reports, establishing the commission of serious violations of international humanitarian law, should be given to the Rwandan judicial authority as soon as available after being used publicly in court.

This chapter would not be complete without stressing the contribution of the Tribunals toward the adoption of the Rome Convention of 1998, which provided for the setting up of an international criminal court. All observers agree that the Tribunal experiment was a benchmark, a critical step toward the creation of a permanent international criminal judicial institution. As to the concrete contribution of the Tribunals to the ICC Statute, Articles 8(2)(c) and 8(2)(e), which deal with individual criminal responsibility for war crimes committed during non-international armed conflicts, are taken directly from the ICTR statute and ICTY appeal chamber rulings. Thus, the state signatories of the statute had to be aware of the undeniable evolution of international humanitarian law driven by the two Tribunals. It is undoubtedly a remarkable normative contribution.

More recently, the United Nations and the Republic of Sierra Leone signed an international agreement[116] setting up the Special Court for Sierra Leone with the mandate:

> to prosecute persons who bear the greatest responsibility for serious violations of international humanitarian law and Sierra Leonean law committed in the territory of Sierra Leone since 30 November 1996, including those leaders who, in committing such crimes, have threatened the establishment of and implementation of the peace process in Sierra Leone.[117]

This treaty-based Tribunal drew heavily upon the experience of the ICTR as illustrated by the adoption of the Rule of Procedure and Evidence of the International Criminal Tribunal for Rwanda, which is "applicable *mutatis mutandis* to the conduct of legal proceedings before the Special Court."[118] It will, therefore, apply the norms of international criminal law to the bloody conflict that ravaged Sierra Leone in the 1990s.

As a final note, we should point out that, though the Tribunals punish individuals, they form nonetheless part of a process of "legalization"[119] of international relations, by interpreting and applying the norms of international humanitarian law through decisions binding on both individuals and states. In so doing, the Tribunals are effectively responding to the traditional limitations of international humanitarian law, whose progress had been checked for far too long by state inertia. The Tribunals will add important nuances to the rhetoric stating that the weaknesses of international law are due to the very structure of international society and that "it is not within the lawyer's power to remedy it,"[120] or that "the absence of judge and police is indeed an evil to which we must resign ourselves without recrimination."[121] Though it may be true that international law was long circumscribed by the diplomatic, political, and military order and that it was limited or even "confiscated" by states, such is not the case today with the "opening of new judicial corridors" to nonstate players.[122] We are now witnessing an increasing reappropriation of international law by these new players who, thanks to the new international courts, will subject it to the judicial control it has all too often escaped.

Notes

1. "International Tribunal for the Prosecution of Persons Responsible for Genocide and Other Serious Violations of International Humanitarian Law Committed in the Territory of Rwanda and Rwandan Citizens Responsible for Genocide and Other Such Violations Committed in the Territory of Neighbouring States, between 1 January 1994 and 31 December 1994," established through Security Council resolution 955, November 8, 1994.

2. "Policymakers in France, Belgium, and the United States and the United Nations all knew of the preparations for massive slaughter and failed to take the necessary steps to prevent it. Aware from the start that Tutsi were being targeted for elimination, the leading foreign actors refused to acknowledge the genocide. To have stopped the leaders and the zealots would have required military force; in the early stages, a relatively small force. Not only did international leaders reject this course, but they also declined for weeks to use their political and moral authority to challenge the legitimacy of the genocidal government." Alison Des Forges, *Leave None to Tell the Story: Genocide in Rwanda* (New York and Paris: Human Rights Watch and International Federation of Human Rights, 1999), 2.

3. "International Tribunal for the Prosecution of Persons Responsible for Serious Violations of International Humanitarian Law Committed in the Territory of the Former Yugoslavia since 1991," established through Security Council resolution 827, May 25, 1993.

4. See Article 2(4) of the U.N. Charter.

5. See Article 51 of the U.N. Charter.

6. "The law of armed conflict . . . is probably the least respected and consequently the most theoretical, if not the most utopian, branch of international law, or even the law

in general!" Éric David, *Principes de droit des conflits armés*, 2nd ed. (Brussels: Bruylant, 1999), 553.

7. "Consider human rights, where the most serious category-wide compliance problem lies. We have seen that in this area more than a dozen and sometimes considerably more states are chronic violators of many of the most important agreements and their violations are often serious. No other regulatory arena is characterized by a compliance gap that even approaches this." George Downs and Andrea Trento, "Conceptual Issues Surrounding the Compliance Gap," published in this volume.

8. See Georges Abi-Saab, "Cours général de droit international public," in *Recueil des cours de l'Académie du droit international de La Haye* 207, VII (1987): 436.

9. See Theodor Meron, "The Humanization of Humanitarian Law," *American Journal of International Law* 94, no. 2 (2000): 239.

10. "The truth is that existing international humanitarian law refuses to make proper arrangements for its own implementation. The truth is that the international community, aside from taking selective, one-off measures, refuses to carry out systematically its duty of ensuring respect for humanitarian rules." Luigi Condorelli, "L'évolution récente des mécanismes visant à assurer le respect du droit international humanitaire," *Mélanges offerts à Hubert Thierry* (Paris: Éditions Pedone, 1998), 127-33.

11. Particularly in the area of ethnic conflicts, we see the state apparatus being manipulated for the purposes of a political elite, which uses it to encourage and participate in violations of international humanitarian law, thus bringing terrible effectiveness to the horrors of war. "If state fragility and group exclusion are sources of security concerns in divided societies, it is opportunistic, predatory political elites who take advantage of these factors. Where dominant state elite misuses governmental power to mobilize its supporters to action, forces are set in motion that can, as in Bosnia, Kosovo, Congo, and Rwanda, lead to fearsome consequences, including massive forced migration, destruction of property, and genocide." Caroline Hartzell, Matthew Hoddie, and Donald Rothchild, "Stabilizing the Peace after Civil War: An Investigation of Some Key Variables," *International Organization* 55, no. 1 (Winter 2001): 186.

12. Downs and Trento, "Conceptual Issues."

13. Charles-Philippe David, "La guerre et la paix/Approches contemporaines de la sécurité et de la stratégie," *Sciences Politiques* (2000): 524.

14. ". . . as regards the definition of the authority having territorial jurisdiction, in situations in which the de facto power is in the hands of entities that are neither legitimate authorities nor effective powers. Clan chiefs and looting bands are not among the authorities mentioned in the relevant provisions of the Conventions and the Protocols. Nonetheless, in many situations, access to the victims depends on the willingness of such players." Marie-José Domestici-Met, "One Hundred Years after The Hague: 50 Years after Geneva—International Humanitarian Law in an Age of Civil War," *International Review of the Red Cross* 834 (June 1999): 282.

15. See Paul Tavernier, "Réflexions sur les mécanismes assurant le respect du droit international humanitaire, conformément aux Conventions de Genève et aux Protocoles additionnels," *Actualité et Droit International*, par. 11, April 2000, www. ridi.org/adi.

16. Theodor Meron, "Is International Law Moving toward Criminalization?" *European Journal of International Law* 9 (1998): 18.

17. "In fact, internal conflicts have multiplied, while inter-State wars have almost disappeared, partially due to the effects of the balance among the super powers, until recently construed as a balance of terror. Thus, over the last two decades, half a dozen of

this type of conflict have arisen, while 'over thirty conflicts . . . over power, land, minorities and religion' were bathing the planet in blood when the 25th International Conference of the Red Cross and Red Crescent Societies opened in December 1995." Marie-José Domestici-Met, "One Hundred Years after the Hague," 277, note 11, quoting a statement from the ICRC president on the opening of the 25th International Conference of the Red Cross and Red Crescent Societies in Geneva in 1995.

18. ". . . most rules of international humanitarian law clearly apply only to international armed conflicts, which are relatively rare; but few rules actually apply to the frequent, cruel and violent non-international armed conflicts." Theodor Meron, "International Criminalization of Internal Atrocities," *American Journal of International Law* 89 (1995): 554.

19. "And it has been the consistent practice of governments struggling with insurgents to deny Article III's applicability on the grounds that they are merely conducting police operations rather than a true armed conflict." Tom Farer, "Restraining the Barbarians: Can International Law Help?" *Human Rights Quarterly* 22 (2000): 90.

20. See Jeffrey Herbst, "International Laws of War and the African Child: Norms, Compliance, and Sovereignty," published in this volume. See also Meron, "International Criminalization of Internal Atrocities."

21. For instance, the Security Council's resolutions on the conflicts in Iran-Iraq, Liberia, Somalia, Afghanistan, Sierra Leone, Rwanda, and the former Yugoslavia.

22. See Églantine Cujo and Mathias Fortheau, "La réaction des organes politiques," *Droit International Pénal* (Paris : Éditions Pedone, 2000), chapter 55, 663.

23. In many respects, the International Military Tribunal of Nuremberg laid the groundwork of modern international criminal law when it proclaimed: "That international law imposes duty and liabilities upon individuals as well as upon States has long been recognized . . . individuals can be punished for violations of international law. Crimes against international law are committed by men, not by abstract entities, and only by punishing individuals who commit such crimes can the provisions of international law be enforced." *The Trial of Major War Criminals: Proceedings of the International Military Tribunal Sitting at Nuremberg* 22, Final Judgment, September 30, 1946, 464-5 (The Avalon Project at Yale Law School, www.yale.edu/lawweb/avalon/imt/proc/09-30-46.htm).

24. "STATIST LOGIC: The predominant ordering logic since the Peace of Westphalia has been associated with the 'will' of the territorial sovereign state . . . The mainstream of international law has evolved out of the predominance of the state and of the states system . . . SUPRANATIONALIST LOGIC: Supranational logic aspires to vertical ordering from above whereas statist logic are based on the horizontal ordering of separate states." Richard Falk, "Theoretical Foundations of Human Rights," in Richard Falk, ed., *Human Rights and State Sovereignty* (New York: Holmes and Meier, 1981), 33-62.

25. See Wolfgang Friedmann, *The Changing Structure of International Law* (New York: Columbia University Press, 1964).

26. ". . . Fourthly, the impetuous development and propagation in the international community of human rights doctrines, particularly after the adoption of the Universal Declaration of Human Rights in 1948, has brought about significant changes in international law, notably in the approach to problems besetting the world community. A State-sovereignty-oriented approach has been gradually supplanted by a human-being-oriented approach. Gradually the maxim of Roman law hominum causa omne jus constitutum est (all law is created for the benefit of human beings) has gained a firm foothold in the international community as well." *Prosecutor v. Dusko Tadic*, No: IT-94-1, Appeals

Chamber, International Criminal Tribunal for the former Yugoslavia, October 2, 1995, para. 97. Also see Meron, "The Humanization of Humanitarian Law."

27. See "Symposium Issue: The Proliferation of International Tribunals—Piecing Together the Puzzle," New York University School of Law, October 1-2, 1998," published in *New York University Journal of International Law and Politics* 31, no. 4 (Summer 1999).

28. See Anne Bodley, "Weakening the Principle of Sovereignty in International Law: The International Criminal Tribunal for the Former Yugoslavia," *New York University Journal of International Law and Politics* 31, nos. 2-3 (1999): 417.

29. See Géraud de Geouffre de La Pradelle, "La fonction des juridictions de l'ordre international," *Journal de droit international* 2 (1998): 389.

30. Pierre Robert, "La procédure du jugement en droit pénal international," in *Droit International Pénal* (Paris : Éditions Pedone, 2000), chapter 67, 823.

31. See Martha Finnemore and Kathryn Sikkink, "International Norm Dynamics and Political Change," *International Organization* 52, no. 4 (Autumn 1998): 887.

32. Georges Abi-Saab, "International Criminal Tribunals and the Development of International Humanitarian Law and Human Rights Law," in Emile Yakpo and Tahar Boumedra, eds., *Liber Amicorum Judge Mohammed Bedjaoui* (The Hague: Kluwer Academic, 1999), 651.

33. "This brings us to the next level of enforcement of international humanitarian law, through criminal jurisdiction: that is through the prosecution and punishment by national or international tribunals of individuals accused of being responsible for violations of international humanitarian law. . . . This method distinguishes itself from the others . . . in that it is concerned with individual criminal responsibility as opposed to state responsibility. Its aim is to enforce the obligations of individuals under international humanitarian law, whereas the preceding methods concentrate on the enforcement of the obligations of states." Antonio Cassese, "On the Current Trends Towards Criminal Prosecution and Punishment of Breaches of International Humanitarian Law," *European Journal of International Law* 9 (1998): 4.

34. Louise Arbour, "Progress and Challenges in International Criminal Justice," *Fordham International Law Journal* 21, no. 2 (1997): 531.

35. Abi-Saab, "International Criminal Tribunals," 651.

36. "As a practical matter and quite apart from the question of whether the establishment of a Tribunal by means of a Chapter VII resolution was the most appropriate mode of establishing an international jurisdiction, at issue was whether in the circumstances of Rwanda, there were any other viable alternatives which could offer an expeditious mode of establishment and powers to enforce compliance. The answer clearly was no." Daphna Shraga and Ralph Zacklin, "The International Tribunal for Rwanda," *European Journal of International Law* 7, no. 4 (1996): 501, 503.

37. "The Security Council, the body entrusted with primary responsibility for the maintenance of international peace and security, has solemnly enjoined all Member States to comply with orders and requests of the International Tribunal. The nature and content of this obligation, as well as the source from which it originates, make it clear that Article 29 does not create bilateral relations. Article 29 imposes an obligation on Member States towards all other Members or, in other words, an 'obligation *erga omnes parte*'." *Prosecutor v. Tihomir Blaskic*, Appeals Chamber, International Criminal Tribunal for the former Yugoslavia, October 29, 1997, para. 26.

38. "23. This approach [Security Council resolution under Chapter VII] would have the advantage of being expeditious and of being immediately effective as all States would be under a binding obligation to take whatever action is required to carry out a decision taken as an enforcement measure under Chapter VII." Report of the Secretary-General under Security Council Resolution 808, S/2504, May 3, 1993.

39. Antonio Cassese, "La répression des infractions internationales: Présentation," in *Droit International Pénal* (Paris: Éditions Pedone, 2000), chapter 53, 621.

40. "Unlike the Yugoslav Tribunal which had been established while the conflict was still underway and as a measure to prevent and deter further atrocities, the Rwanda Tribunal was established at a time when, although peace and national reconciliation had not yet been achieved, the civil war, at least, was virtually over." Shraga and Zacklin, "The International Tribunal for Rwanda," 503.

41. "The end date of 31 December 1994 was fixed, however, on the understanding that if more serious violations of international humanitarian law occurred thereafter, the Council would be entitled to extend the temporal jurisdiction of the Tribunal beyond 31 December 1994." Shraga and Zacklin, The International Tribunal for Rwanda," 504.

42. See chapter 5 by Baker Wairama, Henry Onoria, and James Katalikawe, "Crisis and Conflicts in the African Great Lakes Region: Problem of Noncompliance with Humanitarian Law," published in this volume.

43. Wairama, Onoria, and Katalikawe, "Crisis and Conflict in the Africa Great Lakes Region."

44. See Olivier Russbach, "ONU contre ONU, Le droit international confisqué" (Paris: Éditions de la Découverte, 1994).

45. Despite the ambiguity of the expression, we are definitely talking about a failure—the failure of the United Nations' primary mission, which is its very raison d'être, that is, "to take effective collective measures for the prevention and removal of threats to the peace, and for the suppression of acts of aggression or other breaches of the peace." Article 1(1) of the U.N. Charter.

46. Pierre Hazan, *La justice face à la guerre: de Nuremberg à La Haye* (Paris: Stock, 2000), 77, 261.

47. See David Forsythe, "Politics and the International Tribunal for the Former Yugoslavia," in Roger Stenson Clark and Madeleine Sann, eds., *The Prosecution of International Crimes* (London: Transactions, 1996), 185.

48. See chapter 7 by Jeffrey Herbst in this volume.

49. "The two most powerful realist criticisms of war crimes trials are that such efforts will perpetuate a war, or destabilize postwar efforts to build a secure peace." Gary Jonathan Bass, *Stay the Hand of Vengeance: The Politics of War Crimes Tribunals* (Princeton, NJ: Princeton University Press, 2000), 285.

50. "Cassese formally protested five times, and each time got roughly the same reply from the Security Council. 'We deplore their attitude [to Serbia]; we condemn their attitude. Either deplore or condemn,' Cassese said. 'Maybe next time they'll find a third word.'" Bass, *Stay the Hand of Vengeance*, 223. ". . . the Security Council has not been consistently helpful. Verbal admonitions, even made under Chapter VII, not accompanied by credible sanctions or threats of use of force have not proved adequate to force compliance. The need to back up international criminal tribunals with power, power of enforcement, has been demonstrated once again." Theodor Meron, "Comments in the International Law Association Panel on the Yugoslav Tribunal: November 13, 1998," *ILSA Journal of International and Comparative Law* 5 (1999): 347.

51. "The tribunal was evidently intended by many countries to be just another kind of reprimand, not an actual court with defendants in the dock. Even Albright did not seem confident that anyone would ever be arrested: 'The Tribunal will issue indictments whether or not suspects can be taken in custody. They will become international pariahs.'" Bass, *Stay the Hand of Vengeance*, 215.

52. "[The States] tried to turn international justice into an instrument and use it as a means of pressure, in the same way as they would use the threat of sanctions or aerial attacks. This strategy politicized the image of the Tribunal and was thus bound to hinder it." Hazan, *La justice face à la guerre*, 261.

53. Hazan, *La justice face à la guerre*, 69.

54. "The events in Rwanda and Burundi also confirm this pattern of indifference: only minimal efforts were made by the international community to protect the target of genocide or to punish the main perpetrators. No strategic interests were at stake." Richard Falk, *Human Rights Horizons: The Pursuit of Justice in a Globalizing World* (New York: Routledge, 2000), 180.

55. "The governments wanted to hide their political powerlessness behind the existence of a tribunal," Judge Cassese. And "the ICTY was created as a catharsis, a kind of moral imperative, by a Security Council that refused to intervene politically and militarily in the former Yugoslavia," another ICTY judge. Cited by Hazan, *La justice face à la guerre*, 89.

56. "In reality, the purpose was less one of 'deterring' than it was 'reconciling' . . . assuaging Western public opinion through the prosecution of a few criminals," Hazan, *La justice face à la guerre*, 77.

57. "When the Office of the Prosecutor began its work in Rwanda, its staff encountered an atmosphere of general hostility to the U.N. Rwandans in general were disillusioned with its failure to intervene in the genocide and some authorities were dissatisfied with the ongoing operation of various of its agencies. In 1997 the Rwandan government sharply criticized the tribunal." Alison Des Forges, *Leave None to Tell the Story*, 13.

58. See Payam Akhavan, "The International Criminal Tribunal for Rwanda: The Politics and Pragmatics of Punishment," *American Journal of International Law* 90, no. 3 (1996): 505.

59. See Djiena Wembou, "Le Tribunal Pénal pour le Rwanda : Rôle de la cour dans la réalité africaine," *International Review of the Red Cross* 828 (1997): 738-9.

60. "Those difficulties reached a climax when the Rwandan government demanded that I withdraw a request to the Cameroons to have Colonel Theoneste Bagasora transferred for trial to Arusha. . . . Unwilling to compromise, I said I would prefer the tribunal to cease its activities rather than defer to the national courts of Rwanda." Richard Goldstone, *For Humanity: Reflections of a War Crimes Investigator* (New Haven, CT: Yale University Press, 2000), 112.

61. *Jean-Bosco Barayagwiza v. The Prosecutor*, Appeal Chamber, Case No: ICTR-97-19-AR72, November 3, 1999.

62. *Jean-Bosco Barayagwiza v. The Prosecutor No. 2*, Appeal Chamber, Case No: ICTR-97-19-AR72, March 31, 2000. See the comments of William Schabas in the *American Journal of International Law* 94 (2000): 563.

63. See chapter 5 by Wairama, Onoria, and Katalikawe in this volume.

64. "As yet the prosecutors have taken no action against RPF soldiers who might be accused of such crimes [crimes against humanity and violations of the Geneva Conventions], a circumstance which has provoked little commentary from major international

actors but which risks undermining the credibility of the tribunal." Des Forges, *Leave None to Tell the Story*, 744-5.

65. "The Tribunal would certainly face political difficulties in maintaining good co-operation with the Rwandese Government while investigating reports of crimes by the RPF. It is nevertheless essential that it fulfils its mandate with respect to all crimes, maintains its independence and delivers justice to all." "International Criminal Tribunal for Rwanda: Trials and Tribulations," (London: Amnesty International, IOR 40/03/98, April 1998), 17.

66. See the letter dated August 8, 2002, from the president of the ICTR addressed to the president of the Security Council, S/2002/842, August 13, 2002. See Marieke Wierda, "Procedural Developments in International Criminal Courts," in *The Law and Practice of International Courts and Tribunals: A Practitioner's Review* (The Hague: Kluwer Law International, 2002), 631.

67. See the Amnesty International report, "International Criminal Tribunal for Rwanda." See also the report of the secretary-general on the activities of the Office of Internal Oversight Services, A/51/789 (1997).

68. Richard Goldstone, "Justice as a Tool for Peace-Making: Truth Commissions and International Criminal Tribunals," *NYU Journal of International Law and Politics* 28, no. 3 (1996): 485.

69. See Todd Howland and William Calathes, "The UN's International Criminal Tribunal, Is It Justice or Jingoism for Rwanda. A Call for Transformation," *Virginia Journal of International Law* 39, no. 1 (1998): 135-67.

70. See Richard Goldstone, "The United Nations' War Crimes Tribunals: An Assessment," *Connecticut Journal of International Law* 12 (1997): 227.

71. "Liberals are well aware of the risks of backlash, too; and yet they still argue that the benefits of war crimes tribunals outweigh them. Realists see justice as dangerous to a durable peace; liberals argue that there is no durable peace without justice. . . . Liberals argue that international war crimes tribunals build up a sturdy peace by, first, purging threatening enemy leaders; second, deterring war criminals; third, rehabilitating former enemy countries; fourth placing the blame for atrocities on individuals rather than on whole ethnic groups; and, fifth, establishing the truth about wartime atrocities." Bass, *Stay the Hand of Vengeance*, 286.

72. "So long as violence continues to perpetuate and exacerbate ethnic tensions, international lawyers need to identify more precisely which one of their goals—from deterrence to national reconciliation—is truly being furthered by international trials." José Alvarez, "Crimes of States/Crimes of Hate: Lessons from Rwanda," *Yale Journal of International Law* 24 (1999): 459.

73. "The fact that cases are handled in a slow and circuitous manner contravenes the axiom that for deterrence to work, punishments must be meted out with swiftness and certainty. Studies have shown it is necessary to have a process that is perceived to be fair and which efficiently metes out punishment to achieve a significant deterrent impact." Howland and Calathes, "The UN's International Criminal Tribunal," 151.

74. Hazan, *La justice face à la guerre*, 240.

75. Bass, *Stay the Hand of Vengeance*, 295.

76. "The wounds opened by this war will heal much faster if collective guilt for atrocities is expunged and individual responsibility is assigned." Madeleine Albright, as cited in Bass, *Stay the Hand of Vengeance*, 297.

77. Bass, *Stay the Hand of Vengeance*, 300-301.

78. "In effect, although such a tribunal was established in an atmosphere of overall ambivalence, it can at this stage be used at the very least to document the horrors of genocide and to provide a measure of solace to survivors." Richard Falk, *Human Rights Horizons*, 171-2.

79. Hazan, *La justice face à la guerre*, 133.

80. See "Un procureur contre la raison d'État," in *Politique Internationale* 79 (Spring 1998): 305.

81. See Theodor Meron, "The Normative Impact on International Law of the International Tribunal for former Yugoslavia," in Yoram Dinstein and Mala Tabory, eds., *War Crimes in International Law* (The Hague: Martinus Nijhoff, 1996).

82. "This is not to mention the potentially major contribution of international criminal tribunals in the long run—of integrating, through their jurisprudence, the disjointed and overlapping concepts we inherited from Nuremberg and Tokyo into a coherent normative system of international criminal law." George Abi-Saab, "Fragmentation and Unification: Some Concluding Remarks," *New York University Journal of International Law and Politics* 31, no. 4 (Summer 1999): 919.

83. Finnemore and Sikkink, "International Norm Dynamics," 887.

84. "The part of conventional international humanitarian law which has beyond doubt become part of international customary law is the law applicable in armed conflict as embodied in: the Geneva Conventions of 12 August 1949 for the Protection of War Victims; the Hague Convention (IV) Respecting the Laws and Customs of War on Land of 18 October 1907; the Convention on the Prevention and Punishment of the Crime of Genocide of 9 December 1948; and the Charter of the Military Tribunal of 8 August 1945." Report of the Secretary-General Pursuant to Paragraph 2 of Security Council Resolution 808, S/25704, May 3, 1993, para. 35.

85. Luigi Condorelli, "Le Tribunal penal international pour l'ex-Yougoslavie et sa jurisprudence," *Cours Euro-Méditerranéens*, Bancaja de Droit international, 1, Castellón, (1997): 247.

86. Ilias Bantekas, "Study on the Minimum Rules of Conduct in Cross-Examination to be Applied by the International Criminal Tribunal for the Former Yugoslavia," *Revue Hellénique de Droit International* 50 (1997): 207.

87. Finnemore and Sikkink, "International Norms Dynamics," 899.

88. Abi-Saab, "International Criminal Tribunals," 651.

89. "The new Statute constitutes an extremely important development in international humanitarian law with regard to the criminal character of internal atrocities in Rwanda . . . this development has enormous normative importance. Meron, "The International Criminalization of Internal Atrocities," 558.

90. See the section on "A System Ill-Adapted to Deal with Modern Conflicts," in this chapter.

91. "The Security Council has elected to take a more expansive approach to the choice of the applicable law . . . and included within the subject-matter jurisdiction of the Rwanda Tribunal international instruments regardless of whether they were considered part of customary international law or whether they have customarily entailed the individual criminal responsibility of the perpetrators of the crime. Article 4 of the statute. . . for the first time criminalizes common article 3 of the four Geneva Conventions." Report of the Secretary-General Pursuant to Paragraph 5 of Security Council Resolution 955, S/1995/134, February 13, 1995, par. 12.

92. Hans Kelsen, *Théorie pure du droit* (Paris: Bruylant L.G.D.J., 1999), 335.

93. Abi-Saab, "Cours général de droit international public," 215.

94. Julio Jorge Urbina, "Protection of Civilian Persons in the Power of the Enemy and the Establishment of an International Criminal Jurisdiction," *International Review of the Red Cross* 840 (September 2000): 857.

95. *Prosecutor v. Dusko Tadic*, Preliminary Decision (Jurisdiction), Appeals Chamber, International Criminal Tribunal for the former Yugoslavia, October 2, 1995, par. 77.

96. "In the light of the intent of the Security Council and the logical and systematic interpretation of Article 3 as well as customary international law, the Appeals Chamber concludes that, under Article 3, the International Tribunal has jurisdiction over the acts alleged in the indictment, regardless of whether they occurred within an internal or an international armed conflict." *Prosecutor v. Dusko Tadic*, para. 137.

97. "So far we have pointed to the formation of general rules or principles designed to protect civilians or civilian objects from the hostilities or, more generally, to protect those who do not (or no longer) take active part in hostilities. We shall now briefly show how the gradual extension to internal armed conflict of rules and principles concerning international wars has also occurred as regards means and methods of warfare." *Prosecutor v. Dusko Tadic*, para. 119.

98. "All of these factors confirm that customary international law imposes criminal liability for serious violations of common Article 3, as supplemented by other general principles and rules on the protection of victims of internal armed conflict, and for breaching certain fundamental principles and rules regarding means and methods of combat in civil strife." *Prosecutor v. Dusko Tadic*, para. 134.

99. *Prosecutor v. Dusko Tadic*, No: IT-94-1, Merits, Appeals Chamber, International Criminal Tribunal for the former ex-Yugoslavia, July 15, 1999, para. 166.

100. *Prosecutor v. Jean Paul Akayezu*, No. ICTR-96-4-T, First Chamber, September 2, 1998, paras. 170-2. See José Alvarez, "Lessons from the Akayezu Judgment," *ILSA Journal of International & Comparative Law* 5 (1999): 350.

101. Adam Roberts, "The Law of War: Problems of Implementation in Contemporary Conflicts," *Journal of Comparative and International Law* 6 (1995): 73.

102. Chris Maina Peter, "The International Criminal Tribunal for Rwanda: Bringing the Killers to Book," *1997 International Review of the Red Cross* 828 (1997): 747.

103. "Because the Prosecutor has the authority to commence the entire legal process, through investigation and submission of an indictment for confirmation, the Prosecutor has been likened to the 'engine' driving the work of the Tribunal. . . . Consequently, once the Prosecutor has set this process in motion, she is under a duty to ensure that, within the scope of her authority, the case proceeds to trial in a way that respects the rights of the accused." *Jean-Bosco Barayagwiza v. The Prosecutor*, Case No: ICTR-97-19-AR72, November 3, 1999, paras. 91-2.

104. "Domestic prosecution is never really seriously called upon to be selective in the prosecution of serious crimes. In the ICTR, the prosecutor has to be highly selective before committing resources to investigate and prosecute," Louise Arbour, "Progress and Challenges in International Criminal Justice," *Fordham International Law Journal* 21, no. 2 (1997): 531.

105. See chapter 5 by Wairama, Onoria, and Katalikawe in this volume.

106. "In defeating the interim government and its army, the RPF ended the genocide. At the same time, its troops committed grave violations of International Humanitarian Law by attacking and killing unarmed civilians. . . . They killed some in the course of their military advance, but they executed most in the days and weeks after combat had finished." Des Forges, *Leave None to Tell the Story*, 13.

107. See Goldstone, "The United Nations' War Crimes Tribunals," 230.

108. "Despite the distance between the scene of the crime and the seat of the Tribunal . . . international justice has made punishment possible; however, due to this distance, justice is an obstacle to the process of integration and memory for the people concerned. This is both the strength and the weakness of 'justice hors sol': it reproduces the conditions of a State of law that were lacking, but at the same time loses its resonance in the cultural universe in which the atrocities took place, by removing from the countries of the former Yugoslavia the ability to judge." See Hazan, *La justice face à la guerre*, 240.

109. "Distant in location, the tribunal is also alien in procedure. Rwandans are accustomed to presenting their own complaints to persons in authority, whether in formal court or before the local burgomaster." Des Forges, *Leave None to Tell the Story*, 746.

110. Des Forges, *Leave None to Tell the Story*, 747.

111. Applications made by the prosecutor in *Nzabirinda* and *Seromba* in June 2002.

112. "For example, dissemination of detailed accounts of the trials has been fairly limited inside Rwanda. . . . There is a disconnection between the ICTR trials and the internal social process. . . . The common person in Rwanda must certainly feel a lack of connection to the ICTR's process. This lack of connection is a serious problem that needs to be addressed." Howland and Calathes, "The UN's International Criminal Tribunal," 155.

113. Des Forges, *Leave None to Tell the Story*, 746.

114. See Akhavan, "The International Criminal Tribunal for Rwanda."

115. "Thus, the ICTR is called upon to play an active and constructive role in assisting the Rwandan judicial system. Unfortunately, the Tribunal has not effectively performed either of its tasks." Robert F. Van Lierop, "Rwanda Evaluation: Report and Recommendations," Report of the American Bar Association, *The International Lawyer* 31, no. 3 (Fall 1997): 901.

116. Agreement between the United Nations and the Government of Sierra Leone on the Establishment of a Special Court for Sierra Leone, January 16, 2002, www.sierraleone.org/specialcourtagreement.html.

117. Statute of the Special Court for Sierra Leone, January 16, 2002, Article 1.

118. Statute, Article 14.

119. "The definition of legalization adopted in this issue contains three criteria: the degree to which rules are obligatory, the precision of those rules, and the delegation of some functions of interpretation, monitoring, and implementation to a third party." Judith L. Goldstein, Miles Kahler, Robert O. Keohane, and Anne-Marie Slaughter, "Introduction: Legalization and World Politics," *International Organization* 54, no. 3 (Summer 2000): 387.

120. Prosper Weil, *Vers une normativité relative en droit international?* (Paris: RGDIP, 1982).

121. Antonio Cassese, *Violence et droit dans un monde divisé* (Paris: Presses Universitaires de France, 1990).

122. Olivier Russbach, *ONU contre ONU, Le droit international confisqué* (Paris: Éditions de la Découverte, 1994).

7

International Laws of War and the African Child: Norms, Compliance, and Sovereignty

Jeffrey Herbst

The Convention on the Rights of the Child of 1989 is one of the most prominent international humanitarian treaties. It entered into force with, at the time, unprecedented speed and currently only two countries (the United States and Somalia) have not ratified it.[1] Carol Bellamy, executive director of the United Nations Children's Fund (UNICEF), says that the convention has become "the centerpiece of a global movement, a movement that reflects a growing awareness of the importance of safeguarding human rights—and child rights in particular."[2] Similarly, Lisbet Palme claimed, after traveling to some of the worst conflict zones in Africa, that, "for many of the children I have met and talked with, the Convention takes on a very meaningful reality."[3] Yet, during the 1990s, more children in Africa became victims of, and combatants in, war than at any time in history. Partially as a result, a bitter Human Rights Watch report assessing the state of children's rights ten years after the Convention on the Rights of Children came into force was entitled *Promises Broken*.[4] Indeed, to enhance further international humanitarian law protecting children during war, governments agreed in January 2000, after six years of negotiation, to an Optional Protocol to the Convention on the Rights of the Child that seeks to raise the minimum age of combatants to eighteen.

This chapter analyzes the politics of international humanitarian law that attempts to protect children in Africa during armed conflict. Examining how the international community attempts to protect the least powerful when normal political institutions have broken down and the rule of the gun prevails is the ultimate test for international humanitarian law. Indeed, the dichotomy between the law of war and the nature of war has been called "probably the must acute point of tension between law and life."[5] Children have often been a central focus of international humanitarian law: the first global charter protecting a particular sector of society was the 1924 Geneva Declaration on the Rights of the Child that was prompted by concerns over young people affected by conflict in the Balkans.[6] There has since been a succession of international instruments seeking to protect children.

Despite the widespread enthusiasm for protection of children via international law and the seemingly palpable failure to affect behavior that hurts youngsters, there has been remarkably little critical analysis of the large compliance gap between norms and practices in this area. Most of the discussion of these new international humanitarian instruments has been by what Finnemore and Sikkink call "norm entrepreneurs"[7] who are deeply vested in the promulgation of ever more elaborate international legal instruments.

Yet, as Finnemore and Sikkink note, understanding how norms become law and the patterns of compliance with those laws are critical topics at the nexus of international relations and law.[8] As the toughest case for international humanitarian law, the new rules protecting children have already encountered challenging enforcement problems. However, their lofty ambitions can help tell us if the international community should continue to set law which, while noble, has little chance of enforcement in the near future because of implementation problems. Or is setting the goals high an important effort in and of itself by helping chart the course that international society should eventually travel?

Africa is a particularly challenging region to examine the evolution of international humanitarian law. In addition to rapidly adopting the Convention on the Rights of the Child, African states were the first to have their own regional instrument focusing on the rights of the child: the African Charter on the Rights and Welfare of the Child that was agreed to in 1990. At the same time, Africa is home to a large proportion of the conflicts that most endanger children: civil wars where the battlefield is dynamic and largely undefined; where guerilla groups are often inchoate bands whose primary goal sometimes appears to be pillage; and where civilians take up arms to protect themselves. Two million of the estimated three million civilian casualties in the 1980s were in Africa, a change from previous decades when most civilian war deaths were in Asia.[9] When the tallies for the 1990s are finished, the wars in Angola, Liberia, Mozambique, Rwanda, Sierra Leone, Somalia, Sudan, Uganda, Zaire/Democratic Republic of the Congo, and elsewhere will ensure that Africa was again the most dangerous continent for civilians, especially children.

Finally, examining how international humanitarian law can affect children is especially informative in understanding how sovereignty may evolve. Laws of war, especially laws that hope to regulate the prosecution of domestic conflicts, are a potential challenge to sovereignty. As Chadwick notes, "when autonomous state competence to interpret authoritatively the nature of organized domestic violence is in question, the legal expression of the continuing fact of sovereignty is placed in doubt."[10] In fact, some of the new provisions affecting children are being promoted precisely by networks of nongovernmental organizations (NGOs) that want to reform an international system that privileges state actions. As an influential book on human rights activists claimed, "All of our networks challenge traditional notions of sovereignty. . . . Much international network activity presumes. . .[that] it is both legitimate and necessary for states or non-state actors to be concerned about the treatment of the inhabitants of another state."[11] Yet, to add to the complexity of the political processes, the new international humanitarian law that nongovernmental organizations want is developed by conferences of sovereign states, albeit with NGO help and participation. That activists celebrate new international law as diminishing sovereignty after the provisions have been adopted by conferences consisting of states exemplifies the confused nature of sovereignty in the twenty-first century.

Again, Africa is the best region to understand how the continuing development of international norms concerning human rights affects sovereignty. As the weakest group of countries in the world, African states are, by necessity, vitally concerned about their sovereign status. In particular, laws of war that affect children are often explicitly aimed at altering the behavior of rebels. African states obviously want as much assistance as possible in regulating the behavior of such groups. However, they want to avoid, at almost any cost, having any type of international recognition, especially in the form of a legal personality, bestowed on rebel groups, viewed by African states as criminals and thugs rather than as participants in a belligerency as classically understood in international law. Nat Colletta, the head of the World Bank's postconflict unit, and Taies Nezam seem to affirm the fears of African states when they argue that, "'international norms and values' (human rights) further inadvertently supplant the state, reducing the capacity of the state to impose its will."[12]

Regulating rebel entities without recognizing them is an extraordinary conundrum. Yet for international humanitarian law, developed primarily to regulate war between states, to be relevant in the twenty-first century, it must come to grips with the fact that almost all warfare in the world is domestic. The challenge to sovereignty is likely to only increase in the future as people across Africa become frustrated with the slow progress of conflict resolution. A 1995 conference in West Africa focusing on the rights of children during conflict concluded that, "The flexible interpretation of the principle of 'non-interference' in the internal affairs of member States—which has enabled OUA to undertake creative initiatives in peace-building and resolution—should be strengthened to reflect the dynamism of African common bonds and traditional norms of shared responsibility for the welfare of every member of the community, be it intra- or across borders."[13]

The international effort to use humanitarian law to protect African children during times of war is, therefore, at the center of a number of theoretical and policy concerns related to the compliance dilemma: What is the role of international norms in affecting state action? Can these norms get so ahead of state behavior that they only produce cynicism or does the international community do best by setting the bar high and then pressuring states and other parties to conflicts to follow? Finally, how do states and nongovernmental actors reconcile claims to sovereignty with the increasing intrusiveness of international humanitarian law? Given that other international efforts to affect domestic behavior in trade, environmental protection, and other aspects of the law of war (e.g., landmines) are also being propounded by activists through international conferences of sovereign states, this chapter explores how the relationship between compliance and a critical aspect of sovereignty is likely to evolve in the twenty-first century.

Wars and Children in Africa

War as a public health threat to African children is a relatively recent phenomenon. The traditional concern for the child south of the Sahara has related to material deprivation and disease. For instance, in an account of the International Conference on African Children held in Geneva in 1931, Evelyn Sharp noted, "Children in Africa suffer cruelties, but not because people are cruel to them."[14] Similarly, UNICEF's major 1963 study *The Needs of Children* did not even list armed hostilities as a significant threat to children.[15]

However, since the mid-1980s, two phenomena—the dramatic increase in civil unrest in Africa and increasing likelihood for most casualties of war to be civilian—have combined to endanger African children. As is now widely recognized, the clear trend in combat since World War II has been for civilians to suffer an increasing share of total casualties. The proportion of civilian deaths and casualties has risen from less than 10 percent in World War I to over 50 percent in World War II to more than 75 percent in the current period.[16] In the 127 armed conflicts between World War II and 1990, twenty-two million people are estimated to have died, of whom one and a half million were children. A further four million children have been physically disabled and ten million psychologically traumatized. The nature of civil wars in Africa causes civilians to be especially prone to victimization. Indeed, a review of conflict in West Africa concluded,

> "total war" is increasingly being waged within national boundaries. Nothing is spared in the quest for power and control—not crops, not women, children, schools, health-care facilities or places of worship. . . . Children and women constitute the overwhelming majority among the uprooted millions in the [West African] subregion and other trouble spots in Africa. These wars are characterized by the indiscriminate destruction of lives and property and unprecedented numbers of human rights violations against children and women.[17]

The disembowelment of pregnant women to kill their fetuses in Rwanda, the use of amputation as a terror tactic in Sierra Leone, cannibalism and desecration of bodies in Liberia, the destruction of whole communities in Sudan, and the forced recruitment of civilians to promote the war aims of rebels in Mozambique and Angola are only some of the most glaring examples of how civilians are no longer collateral casualties during war but, rather, the major targets.[18]

In particular, the last decade has seen the emergence of the child soldier in Africa as a particularly devastating phenomenon. The advent of advanced technology weapons means that even small boys and girls (although they are overwhelmingly boys) can handle weapons like the AK47 assault rifle.[19] These weapons are also now widely available at a low cost: in Uganda an AK47 costs no more than a chicken and in northern Kenya it is the price of a goat.[20] A rough estimate suggests that there are currently 120,000 children under eighteen in armed conflicts across Africa, some no more than seven or eight years old.[21] Children are used because they are obedient and expendable, and because they often do not even realize that they are killing other people. They can also be brutally exploited because they are so vulnerable. For instance, in Mozambique, a typical Mozambican National Resistance (RENAMO) tactic was to force children to return to their home village and kill someone. They, therefore, had to fight for RENAMO because they had no home to go back to.[22] Finally, it is estimated that there will be ten million orphans in Africa due to the AIDS epidemic early in the twenty-first century.[23] These children will be especially vulnerable to being coerced into fighting.

Children sometimes form a significant portion of those at war in Africa. For instance, it is estimated that of the 40,000 to 60,000 fighters in the Liberian civil war (1989-1997), 10 percent were under fifteen and another 20 percent were between fifteen and seventeen. In that war, children as young as nine or ten armed with automatic rifles manned checkpoints, where they often terrorized and killed civilians for no obvious reason.[24] The Sudanese Peoples Liberation Army is said to have taken 12,500 children who it thought were ready to fight (as indicated by the presence of two molar teeth) across 1,200 miles of desert in the late 1980s and early 1990s.[25] Thousands of young child soldiers, known as "kadogo" (the little ones), were used by Laurent Kabila's Alliance of Democratic Forces for the Liberation of the Congo when he was fighting to overthrow Mobutu Sese Seko in 1996 and 1997.[26] In the war in Sierra Leone, in just 1998, members of the Armed Forces Revolutionary Council and the Revolutionary United Front abducted thousands of civilians, including a high percentage of children, to use as combatants, forced labor, or sexual slaves.[27] In Uganda, the Lord's Resistance Army (LRA), a rebel group trying to overthrow the government of Yoweri Museveni, has kidnapped several thousand children, some after watching their parents be killed, to be used in combat, to raid and loot villages, as porters, and as sex slaves for LRA commanders.[28]

International Law and Rebellion in Africa

Early humanitarian law toward children, including the 1924 Geneva Declaration and the Declaration of the Rights of the Child adopted in 1959, focused on their material needs.[29] The effort to protect children during times of war is, therefore, fairly recent and has collided with the long and confused effort to humanely regulate how men kill each other. The immediate problem confronting activists and states that seek to provide greater protection to children is that large parts of international humanitarian law that govern the conduct of war, including The Hague Regulations, apply to wars between states. Most of the Geneva Conventions only applies to contracting parties and, therefore, does not apply to most situations of domestic conflict.[30] To rectify this situation meant working through the United Nations system and through conferences of sovereign states. Of course, this is a system biased clearly toward preserving the rights of states, since states founded the U.N. and are the principal actors in conferences designed to write new international law.

Article 3 of the Geneva Conventions

In 1949, nations did adopt common Article 3 to all four of the Geneva conventions, which bound signatories to observe humanitarian principles in "armed conflicts not of an international character." The article prohibited each party to a conflict from "a) violence to life and person, in particular murder of all kinds, mutilation, cruel treatment and torture; b) taking hostages; c) outrages upon personal dignity, in particular, humiliating and degrading treatment." [31]

However, governments have resisted the application of Article 3 because it limits, perhaps severely, their ability to prosecute a civil war and to use domestic and municipal law to try what they see as criminals and bandits. As a result, "the applicability of the Article has been skirted in even the most massive internal conflicts since 1949. Governments . . . have sought to preserve maximum flexibility, in the national interest, in dealing with internal armed conflict by avoiding such formal international legal obligation . . . (as) might . . . attach in favor of a challenging group . . . by virtue of their treatment by the incumbent in any manner as a legal personality."[32]

However, even had states chosen to obey Article 3, its protections with regard to children are suspect. As Cohn and Goodwin-Gill have observed, "Common Article 3 places no limits on recruitment or participation of children, the breaches of rules are committed by NGE's [non-governmental entities], the level of strife is debatable, the applicability of human rights provisions is in doubt, and their enforcement, for various reasons, impossible."[33] As a result, "whether or not there is a lacuna in the law and what this consists of, there is certainly a lacuna in practice."[34]

The flaws inherent to Article 3 are hardly accidental. Having been forced by the weight of international opinion to accept that Article 3 did apply to a wide range of conflicts, states have done very little to enhance the protection offered so that their sovereignty is not impinged upon. As a result, it was understood by the 1970s, even before civil wars came to be the predominant type of conflict, that Article 3 by itself simply was an inadequate guide to the protection of civilians, including children, during warfare.

The Optional Protocols to the Geneva Convention

It is a telling lesson that the impetus for the Optional Protocols to the Geneva Conventions came from Sean MacBride in his role as chair of the International Commission of Jurists. MacBride argued before and during the 1968 United Nations human rights conference in Tehran that there should be much greater international regulation of domestic conflicts. He, therefore, proposed a sudden and wholesale revision of international doctrine regarding the laws of war. His was a dramatic early example of the representatives of a nongovernmental organization attempting to redraft international humanitarian law through a conference of sovereign states.[35]

While most of MacBride's ambitions were not realized, in 1977 two optional protocols were added to the Geneva Convention. Protocol I addresses international conflicts. It strengthens the protection of civilian populations, especially by requiring that parties to conflicts at all times distinguish between civilian and military objectives and only attack the latter; by providing protection to cultural objects and houses of worship; by protecting the natural environment and civilian infrastructure; and by making provision for demilitarized zones that all parties must respect. There is also a much greater elaboration of the fundamental rights of each person.[36] Finally, there are articles (77 and 78) designed to give special protection to children. In particular, children under the age of fifteen are not to take part in combat and should not be recruited. For those recruited between the ages of fifteen and eighteen, priority is given to the latter when sending soldiers into combat. Finally, special protection is still to be offered to children under fifteen even if they fight and are captured by the enemy.[37]

This new protocol governing international conflict posed an interesting but complex opportunity for those African countries that in the 1970s were heavily engaged in supporting the wars against the remaining white minority regimes. The African countries and their sympathizers throughout the third world desperately wanted the laws of international war to extend to national liberation struggles occurring in, among other places, Angola, Guinea-Bissau, Mozambique, Namibia, and Rhodesia (Zimbabwe). However, they did not want the laws of war to apply to all domestic disputes because they understood that they were themselves extremely vulnerable to rebellion, including secessionist threats. In an extraordinary political win, third world countries were able to get Protocol I to extend the definition of international armed conflict to include conflicts in which "peoples are fighting against colonial domination and alien occupation and against racist regimes in the exercise of their right of self-determination."[38] However, the protocol does not apply to armed conflicts within a country that was not governed by a colonial regime.

To ensure that Protocol I could only be used against colonial regimes, regional organizations were appointed the gatekeepers to international recognition. Thus, the Organization of African Unity (OAU) has to recognize African rebel groups before they can gain an international personality.[39] The Arab League had a similar role in certifying the Palestinian Liberation Organization. This filter was a further reification of sovereignty because the OAU and other regional organizations are composed of sovereign states. Indeed, the raison d'être of the OAU has been, despite its name, to preserve the sovereign status of African countries.[40]

Protocol II of 1977 to the Geneva Convention does apply to internal conflicts other than national liberation struggles against a colonial power. Many of the same protections are offered to the civilian population, including essentially similar guarantees for children in combat (Article 4).[41] However, for the protocol to be invoked, a classic belligerency has to be recognized. Under commonly accepted international law, a belligerency is said to occur where there is "the existence of civil war within a state, beyond the scope of mere local unrest; occupation by insurgents of a substantial part of the territory of the state; a measure of orderly administration by that group in the area it controls; and observance of the laws of war by the rebel forces, acting under responsible authority."[42] Not surprising, states generally have jealously guarded their prerogative to fight domestic opponents and have refused to recognize that a belligerency is occurring in their country. Cohn and Goodwin-Gill note, "relatively few states involved in internal hostilities have been willing to abandon their presumptive claim to a free hand in dealing with local threats, so that the applicability of Additional Protocol II is resisted, even where the objective criteria are satisfied. . . . The scope for *legal* protection in a non-international armed conflict or violent internal strife situation is thus much less than in a traditional inter-State conflict."[43] Schindler concluded that, "in no civil war since 1945 has belligerency been recognized. . . . The disappearance of the recognition of belligerency coincides with the decline of neutrality. Most States today, both in international and civil wars, prefer not to be bound by the rules of the law of neutrality."[44] Thus, even in El Salvador, where there was a brutal and long-running civil war, the government was unwilling to apply the provisions of Protocol II despite the fact that it had ratified the instrument.[45]

No state would want to recognize a belligerency within its borders. However, Protocol II provided a particularly inappropriate set of incentives to states to treat an insurgency according to the new laws of war, because a state could only be worse off if it tried to apply humanitarian provisions. Therefore, once African states had reclassified those conflicts they wanted to receive extra protection as "international," they were content to see that the effective regulations that might govern internal conflict were as weak as possible. In particular, the possibility of providing a legal personality to rebels other than through the improbable route of recognition as a classical belligerency was foreclosed.

The failure to better regulate domestic conflict at a time when guerrilla war was becoming the predominant form of conflict was ultimately a reflection of who made international law. As Suter notes, international humanitarian law was not "effectively extended to cover guerrilla warfare because there was insufficient political commitment by the governments, by the NGOs, by the U.N. Secretariat or by the International Committee of the Red Cross (ICRC)."[46] As a result, "when it came to the crunch" states were not willing to create a powerful international instrument for the type of war that really mattered.[47] The conservatism of diplomats, especially in conferences of sovereign states, where maintaining consensus is critical to achieving some kind of final product, made such new thinking impossible. Suter concluded that pressure by NGOs on conferences of sovereign states is unlikely to succeed because of the interests of the states themselves. Therefore, nongovernmental organizations "must look beyond simply creating the issue and maintaining pressure on governments" but, instead, inject that new thinking themselves in order to change the nature of the debate.[48]

Convention on the Rights of the Child

The Convention on the Rights of the Child came about because of the agitation of many nongovernmental groups and the success of UNICEF, and particularly of its then executive director James Grant, in focusing attention on the plight of children. Certainly, one of the major motivations for the convention was the critique of international humanitarian law as it had developed up to that point. Western states were the principal drafters of the convention and only three African countries (Algeria, Morocco, Senegal) even attended the working group sessions. The failure of African countries to engage during the long drafting process was probably due less to a lack of interest than to their limited diplomatic personnel resources compared to the very large delegations western countries maintain in New York and Geneva. However, African states were among the quickest in ratifying the convention.[49] The quick ratification was due to enthusiasm for the convention and because many African states, always concerned about their international status, view ratifying such international documents as one more reaffirmation of their sovereignty.

The convention covered a wide range of child rights, including naming, rights to speech and assembly, protection from neglect, and rights to a variety of social services. However, the protections offered to children in armed conflict were not impressive. Article 38 first asked states to apply international humanitarian law, something they were already required to do. Second, the convention reaffirmed that children under the age of fifteen should not take part in hostilities and that there was a presumption against recruiting children between the ages of fifteen and eighteen. Finally, the convention again asked states to protect children in armed conflict according to their existing international obligations. Article 39 on the responsibilities of states to promote physical and psychological recovery from violence, including armed conflict, did break new ground, but these provisions obviously did not affect the actual conduct of hostilities.[50]

The convention, as with most international law, was clearly a reaffirmation of the sovereignty of African countries. This was hardly a surprise given that the convention was written by sovereign states, but the notion of new rights for children gave further prominence to the false idea that international humanitarian law in practice is a threat to sovereignty. The convention made it clear that responsibility for implementing international human rights law lies first and foremost with the state. In the Convention on the Rights of the Child, state parties are charged to undertake to "respect and ensure" the rights in the convention.[51]

Optional Protocol to the Convention on the Rights of the Child

There was especially great unhappiness that the convention had not raised the age of recruitment of children for combat. Indeed, African countries were in some ways ahead of the convention because they had already negotiated a raise in the minimum age to participate in conflict to eighteen. The Charter on the Rights and Welfare of the African Child, signed in 1990, defined a child as under eighteen years old and states were directed in Article 22(2) to "take all necessary measures to ensure that no child shall take a direct part in hostilities and refrain in particular, from recruiting any child" and in Article 22(3) to protect civilian populations in conflict, especially children. In a further innovation, the African Charter on the Rights and Welfare of the Child extends protection to children not only to international and internal armed conflict but also to "lower levels of violence and to "tension and strife.""[52] However, only states parties are recognized as responsible for guaranteeing child rights. There is nothing in the charter about rebel groups, continuing the African allergy to any recognition of rebels that have challenged African states.

Over six years, between 1994 and 2000, there was a tremendous grassroots effort by international nongovernmental organizations to redress what were seen as flaws in the convention, especially as they related to protection of children during conflict. The rise of the phenomenon of child soldiers in the 1990s, especially in the wars in Liberia and Sierra Leone, helped focus international attention on the problem, as did an important report for the United Nations by Graça Machel, widow of the former president of Mozambique and now the wife of Nelson Mandela.[53] In addition, the effort gained further impetus when the statute for the newly created International Criminal Court included using children under fifteen in combat as a war crime.[54]

The International Coalition to Stop the Use of Child Soldiers included many of the world's most prominent nongovernmental organizations, including the African Coalition to Stop the Use of Child Soldiers, Amnesty International, Defence for Children International, Human Rights Watch, International Federation

Terre des Hommes, the International Save the Child Alliance, the Refugee Service, the Latin American Coalition to Stop the Use of Child Soldiers, the Quaker U.N. Office, and World Vision International.[55] These organizations were outraged by the child soldier issue and undoubtedly helped in their campaigning by the opposition of the U.S. government (already the recipient of international opprobrium because of its failure to sign the treaty on landmines), which feared that the voluntary recruitment of seventeen year olds could be adversely affected. Finally, these organizations justify their existence, in part, through their work on international humanitarian law, so that it was useful for them to keep the pot boiling. The impressive degree of mobilization around the child soldier issue certainly validates Keck and Sikkink's argument that transnational advocacy networks have organized most effectively when the "issues involve bodily harm to vulnerable individuals, especially when there is a short and clear causal chain" or when issues involve legal equal opportunity.[56]

The new Optional Protocol to the Convention on the Rights of the Child was agreed to in January 2000 and came into effect in February 2002. It raises the age for participation in hostilities from fifteen to eighteen, but allows recruiting of seventeen year olds as long as "all feasible measures" are taken to keep them out of conflict. However, the protocol continues the practice of international humanitarian law of respecting, to an extraordinary degree, the rights of sovereign states. The Optional Protocol (Article 4[1]) prohibits armed groups opposing a government from even recruiting children under eighteen, a stronger provision than is applied to states. In addition, the Optional Protocol (Article 4[3]) notes that if armed rebel groups accept this higher standard of action, "The application of the present article under this Protocol shall not affect the legal status of any party to an armed conflict."[57] Thus, third world countries managed to have it both ways: they seemingly made it more difficult for rebels to fight than for governments and they explicitly declared that even if the rebels do follow international law, they would not have a legal personality.

There are other important developments in international law, including the advent of the International Criminal Court and the special tribunals for Rwanda and Sierra Leone. It is simply too early to speculate how these initiatives will affect the international humanitarian law of children and war.

Compliance

Given the international humanitarian law that now exists, the obvious question is how to promote compliance. The development of new international human rights law just as the child soldier problem seemed to worsen makes this question especially pertinent. As de Berry notes, "There is, then, a large gulf between the lives of thousands of children who take part in armed conflict and the standard set for their protection in the Convention on the Rights of the Child."[58] Similarly, Olara Otunnu, Special Representative of the U.N. Secretary-General for Children and Armed Conflict, has argued "the impact of these [human rights] instruments remains woefully thin on the ground. Words on paper cannot save children and women in peril. We must therefore shift our energies from the juridical project on the elaboration of norms to the political project of ensuring their application and respect on the ground. This can be accomplished if the international community is prepared to employ its considerable collective influence to this end."[59]

Inevitably, much of the actual pressure that the international community can bring to end the problem of child soldiers revolves around moral suasion. A study for UNICEF argues that the value of the successive documents lies in the realm of moral suasion: "It is worth re-emphasizing that the power of humanitarian law does not lie only in the fact that its principles are in the form of legal instruments. This only adds additional weight. The power of humanitarian principles arises from the fact that they form a moral code rooted in a concept of the common good in the public conscience of men, women and children around the world and that those who violate them do so at the expense of their own legitimacy in the minds of humankind."[60] Thus, the argument for raising the age of combatants to eighteen in the Optional Protocol was that it would send a strong signal that the international community found it unacceptable under any conditions for children to be in armies, much less in combat.

Of particular interest is the problem of influencing rebel groups—the same ones that the international codes have gone to some length to not recognize and to disadvantage—to behave better. The Machel report argued, "Many non-state entities aspire to form governments and to invoke an existing Government's lack of respect for human rights as a justification for their opposition. In order to establish their commitment to the protection of children, non-state entities should be urged to make a formal statement accepting and agreeing to implement the standards contained in the Convention on the Rights of the Child."[61] After bluntly posing the question on his own website, "How come all those international treaties aren't working," U.N. Special Representative Otunnu has also stated:

> [W]hile various warring parties have made personal commitments to me that they will honour international treaties, I am well aware that commitments are one thing, compliance another. It is up to the international community to mobilise a movement of political pressure: naming, shaming and refusing support for armed groups that continue to abuse children. We must also reinforce the other pillar of protection: local standards that say that the abuse of children as a routine part of war is simply unacceptable.[62]

The groups promoting the Optional Protocol to the Convention on the Rights of the Child—which treats rebel groups particularly poorly—also argued that, "the desire for international recognition by some of those groups would curb the most extreme cases of putting children into combat."[63]

The moral suasion argument is potentially useful to limiting the number of children fighting wars because it gets around the sovereignty issue by justifying setting high humanitarian norms that might not actually be implemented in the near future but which could serve as an eventual goal. However, what is continually striking about the pronouncements of NGOs, international organizations, and foreign governments is that there is relatively little evidence of a nuanced understanding of how moral suasion can be used as a tactic. In the various human rights campaigns in favor of children, there has not been any pressure on governments to declare that their internal conflicts justify international regulation. Human rights groups often proclaim that Article 3 of the Geneva Convention applies to a particular situation, but usually there is no discussion of how the international community will reward countries for recognizing the application of international humanitarian law or will be delegitimated if they do not. In his 2002 report on children and armed conflict, U.N. Secretary-General Kofi Annan broke new ground by actually naming governments and rebel groups in five countries (four in Africa: Burundi, Democratic Republic of the Congo, Liberia, and Somalia) that recruit or use child soldiers.[64] However, this information was already well-known and, more importantly, it is not clear what was to happen now that these governments (and rebel groups) had been named.

The same tactical problem applies to rebels. What is the incentive for rebels to follow international norms? It might be some type of international recognition, but international organizations inevitably do not want to recognize rebels. For instance, U.N. Special Representative Otunnu does not list rebel groups as one of the key actors to engage with when promoting norms against child soldiers, although he certainly has had many discussions with individual rebel groups.[65] Many of the nongovernmental organizations that have been critical to the development of international human rights law do not have, as part of their mandate, the ability to promote such recognition and generally try to stay as far away as possible from such explicit political considerations. For instance, Human Rights Watch's recommendations to the LRA in Uganda were, in their totality, to: "immediately stop abducting children; immediately stop killing children; immediately stop torturing children; immediately stop sexually abusing children; immediately release all children remaining in captivity; ensure that Lord's Resistance Army combatants respect the human rights of civilians in areas of conflict." Human Rights Watch does not specify what type of international recognition or other benefit the LRA would get if it were to take these actions. Nor in its recommendations to the Ugandan government or the international community does Human Rights Watch suggest what type of recognition should be given to the LRA if the rebels were to carry out these reforms.[66] It can, of course, be argued that these norms should be respected no matter what the international community does, but the justification for setting relatively high international norms was that moral suasion could then be used to accelerate compliance.

Human Rights Watch, and other nongovernmental organizations, apparently do not feel that they have the mandate to advocate actions beyond adherence to international humanitarian law. For instance, Human Rights Watch does not urge the Ugandan government to do the one thing that would appear logical if the LRA is, in fact, an inherently evil entity that really will not stop killing civilians: win an outright military victory. Instead, Human Rights Watch asks the Ugandan government to be careful while fighting, but it does not urge that the LRA be defeated. Human rights groups face a paradox: they are willing to provide advice on how combat should proceed, but they shy away from any conclusion about how combat should end, even when, as is the case of the LRA, they have clearly implied that the atrocities committed against children and other civilians are absolutely unacceptable.

Other campaigns directed at rebel groups and governments demonstrate a similarly perplexing use of the moral suasion argument. For instance, Human Rights Watch urged all warring factions in Liberia to "disarm and demobilize immediately all fighters under the age of eighteen, and to refrain permanently from enlisting children under eighteen in the conflict."[67] However, it does not indicate if the warring parties would receive some sort of recognition for these highly desirable reforms.

Other NGOs have the same problem. For instance, World Vision's position paper on children in armed conflict states that "ensuring respect for and compliance with international standards both by state and non-state actors must be a priority" and it goes on to express enthusiasm for the Optional Protocol to the Convention on the Rights of the Child. However, World Vision does not actually say how states or rebel movements are to be enticed to comply with international standards, especially what they will get if they comply.[68] The Coalition to Stop the Use of Child Soldiers condemns numerous rebel groups (including the National Union for the Total Independence of Angola (UNITA) and the Front for the Liberation of the Cabinda Enclave (FLEC) in Angola, Hutu opposition groups in Burundi, the LRA in Uganda, and the Sudan People's Liberation Army) but also does not say what international recognition these rebel groups will receive if they comply with international law.[69] Again, NGOs do not see it as their role to make such recommendations, although a subtle use of moral suasion would, it would seem, demand that the incentives and punishments available to the parties being criticized be well understood. Otherwise, moving to an era of compliance with the laws of war as they regard children will be very difficult.

New Ideas for International Humanitarian Law

It seems that there is a wide gap between norms and compliance when international humanitarian law is applied to children in armed conflict. The problem is not that the norms have necessarily been set too high. It does seem reasonable that children under eighteen in almost all circumstances should not be involved in hostilities. Nor is the problem one of norm "overload": international attention to the issues of children in conflict seems justified by the enormity of the human rights abuses. The heart of the problem is that the international community has no way of getting around sovereignty.

What is clearly needed, as Suter recognized when the Optional Protocols to the Geneva Convention were adopted, is new international approaches to domestic armed conflict. Such new international practices would allow the international community to determine what sort of international regulation should apply to domestic conflict, including whether some form of recognition to rebels should be extended as a reward for complying with international norms. If the international community actually wants to remain neutral during a civil war, as is implied by the default position of many NGOs and foreign governments to support outright military victories by African governments, then new practices should be developed which would allow for true neutrality. For the norms to be effective, new methods to promote compliance will have to be developed.

During the 1960s and early 1970s, a sophisticated intellectual effort was made to try to distinguish between different types of civil conflict, so that a more fine-grained version of international humanitarian law could be applied.[70] This effort was no doubt propelled by the wars in Southeast Asia, where scholars were often in favor of international recognition of domestic combatants, and by concerns of others that national liberation movements be recognized. That effort ended in part because the Optional Protocols to the Geneva Convention were adopted and, in part, because the wars in Southeast Asia subsided.

However, there clearly needs to be a new effort to differentiate among conflicts so that the international community can apply the now comprehensive set of international laws relating to conflict and begin to relate to rebels. This effort might center around reviving classical understandings of international recognition of a belligerency, so that outside parties could help determine the nature of the conflict and possibly develop some relationship with rebels. The African Charter on the Rights and Welfare of the Child is a slight indication that the time for such an approach has come in Africa, given that sovereignty in parts of the continent is collapsing. The role of the OAU (and now, presumably, the successor African Union) as a gatekeeper to the international recognition of domestic parties during armed conflict provides the ideal avenue for Africans to begin to think about new approaches to relating to parties during domestic armed conflict.

Part of the new thinking about sovereignty will have to include new approaches to developing international norms and practices. Having all the states of the world come together to adopt international humanitarian law toward domestic conflict is like recruiting criminals to write gun control laws. New ways of developing international practice will have to be developed to promote compliance with the sensible norms being propounded. At the very least, these new international efforts should include investigating the possibility of involving groups outside the state, including rebels, in adopting new practices. Hopefully, such an approach could prove to be the first step toward getting rebels to actually comply with international norms.

Jeffrey Herbst

Conclusion

There is nothing inevitable about the current state of the laws of war. Despite prevalent rhetoric about how human rights law challenges sovereignty, it is important to recognize that the laws of war were actually more effective in the past. For instance, Quincy Wright found that international law with regard to the "status of rebels, the conduct of hostilities, and the rights and duties of neutrals" was continually referenced by both the protagonists and neutral governments during the American civil war.[71] In the current legal context, much more attention will have to be given to compliance, including the difficult questions of who determines the nature of an armed conflict and how to relate to rebel groups during conflict. The international community—including governments, international organizations, and NGOs—has now proclaimed for a decade how committed it is to African children. It is time to go beyond just stipulating that the commitment exists and to begin the difficult job of investigating how to enforce the norms. The ultimate test of seriousness will be if the international community no longer values state sovereignty, in every case, above the welfare of African children.

Notes

1. Geraldine van Bueren, *The International Law on the Rights of the Child* (Dordrecht, The Hague: Martinus Nijhoff, 1995), 15.

2. Speech by Carol Bellamy, "10th Anniversary of the Adoption of the Convention on the Rights of the Child," www.unicef.org/exspeeches/99esp51.html.

3. Lisbet Palme, "Introduction: Personal Reflections on the New Rights for Children in War," in Cole P. Dodge and Magne Raundalen, eds., *Reaching Children in War: Sudan, Uganda and Mozambique* (Uppsala, Sweden: Scandinavian Institute of African Studies, 1991), 1.

4. Human Rights Watch, *Promises Broken: An Assessment of Children's Rights on the 10th Anniversary of the Convention on the Rights of the Child*, December 1999, www.hrw.org/campaigns/crp/promises.htm.

5. Heather A. Wilson, *International Law and the Use of Force by National Liberation Movements* (Oxford: Clarendon Press, 1988), 35. She is quoting G. I. A. D. Draper.

6. Geraldine van Bueren, "The Historical Framework of the International Documents on Children," in Geraldine van Bueren, ed., *International Documents on Children* (Dordrecht, The Hague: Martinus Nijhoff, 1993), xv.

7. Martha Finnemore and Kathryn Sikkink, "International Norm Dynamics and Political Change," *International Organization* 52, no. 4 (Autumn 1998): 895.

8. Finnemore and Sikkink, "International Norm Dynamics," 916.

9. *Children and Development in the 1990s: A UNICEF Sourcebook* (New York: UNICEF, 1990), 194.

10. Elizabeth Chadwick, *Self-Determination, Terrorism and the International Humanitarian Law of Armed Conflict* (Dordrecht, The Hague: Martinus Nijhoff, 1996), 134.

11. Margaret E. Keck and Kathryn Sikkink, *Activists Beyond Borders: Advocacy Networks in International Politics* (Ithaca, NY: Cornell University Press, 1998), 35-6.

12. Nat J. Colletta and Taies Nezam, "From Reconstruction to Reconciliation," *Development Outreach* 1 (1999): 8.

13. Statement of the Third Regional Consultation on the Impact of Armed Conflict on Children in West and Central Africa, November 7-10, 1995 (Abidjan), A/51/306/Add. 1, September 9, 1996), 25.

14. Evelyn Sharp, *The African Child: An Account of the International Conference on African Children, Geneva* (Westport, CT: Negro Universities Press, 1970), 93.

15. *The Needs of Children: A Survey of the Needs of Children in the Developing Countries* (New York: Free Press, 1963).

16. Statistics in this paragraph are from *Children and Development in the 1990s*, 193-4.

17. Statement of the Third Regional Consultation, 23.

18. See, respectively, Gérard Prunier, *The Rwanda Crisis: History of a Genocide* (New York: Columbia University Press, 1995), 256; Ibrahim Abdullah and Patrick Muana, "The Revolutionary United Front of Sierra Leone," in Christopher Clapham, ed., *African Guerrillas* (Oxford: James Currey, 1998), 190; Stephen Ellis, *The Mask of Anarchy: The Destruction of Liberia and the Religious Dimension of an African Civil War* (New York: New York University Press, 1999), 146; Ann Mosely Lesch, *The Sudan: Contested National Identities* (Bloomington: Indiana University Press, 1998), 162; and William Minter, *Apartheid's Contras: An Inquiry into the Roots of War in Angola and Mozambique* (Johannesburg: Witswatersrand University Press, 1994), 173.

19. Ilene Cohn and Guy S. Goodwin-Gill, *Child Soldiers: The Role of Children in Armed Conflict* (Oxford: Clarendon Press, 1994), 23.

20. Report of the Expert of the U.N. Secretary-General, Graça Machel, *Impact of Armed Conflict on Children*, A/51/306, August 26, 1996, 14.

21. Coalition to Stop the Use of Child Soldiers, *Executive Summary: The Use of Child Soldiers in Africa: An Overview*, August 1999, www.child-soldiers.org/Afr_exesum.htm.

22. Cohn and Goodwin-Gill, *Child Soldiers*, 27.

23. See "AIDS Becoming Africa's Top Human Security Issue, UN Warns," Joint U.N. Programme on HIV/AIDS Press Release, January 10, 2000, www.unaids.org/whatsnew/press/eng/pressarc00/ny10100.html.

24. *Easy Prey: Child Soldiers in Liberia* (New York: Human Rights Watch/Africa, 1994), 2-3.

25. Cohn and Goodwill-Gill, *Child Soldiers*, 28.

26. *The Use of Child Soldiers in the Democratic Republic of the Congo* (New York: Human Rights Watch, 1999), 1, www.hrw.org/hrw/campaigns/crp/congo.htm.

27. *New Regime, but Continued Human Rights Violations* (New York: Human Rights Watch, 1999), 1, www.hrw.org/hrw/campaigns/crp/sierra.htm.

28. *The Scars of Death: Children Abducted by the Lord's Resistance Army in Uganda* (New York: Human Rights Watch, 1997), 1, www.hrw.org/hrw/reports97/uganda/recommend.htm.

29. van Bueren, "International Documents on Children," xv.

30. William Walker, "The International Law Applicable to Guerrilla Movements in Internal Armed Conflicts: A Case Study of Contra Attacks on Nicaraguan Farming Cooperatives," *New York University Journal of International Law and Politics* 21 (Fall 1988): 149-150.

31. Common Article 3(1) to the Geneva Conventions. The conventions and other critical documents of international humanitarian law may be found at www.icrc.org.

32. Chadwick, *Self-Determination*, 82. She is quoting E. D. Fryer, "Applicability of International Law to Armed Conflicts: Old Problems, Current Endeavors," *International Lawyer* 11 (1977): 567, 570.

33. Cohn and Goodwin-Gill, *Child Soldiers*, 66.

34. Carolyn Hamilton and Tabatha Abu El-Haj, "Armed Conflict: The Protection of Children Under International Law," *International Journal of Children's Rights* 5 (1997): 32.

35. MacBride's effect on international humanitarian law is described well by Keith Suter, *An International Law of Guerrilla Warfare: The Global Politics of Law-Making* (New York: St. Martin's Press, 1984), 24-35.

36. See the review in Suter, *An International Law of Guerrilla Warfare*, 160-1.

37. See van Bueren, "International Documents on Children," 528.

38. van Bueren, *The International Law on the Rights of the Child*, 331.

39. Malcolm Shaw, "The International Status of National Liberation Movements," in Frederick E. Snyder and Surakiart Sathiratha, eds., *Third World Attitudes toward International Law* (Dordrecht, The Hague: Martinus Nijhoff, 1987), 142.

40. See Jeffrey Herbst, *States and Power in Africa: Comparative Lessons in Authority and Control* (Princeton, NJ: Princeton University Press, 2000).

41. See van Bueren, "International Documents on Children," 530.

42. Yair M. Lootsteen, "The Concept of Belligerency in International Law," *Military Law Review* 166 (December 2000): 109.

43. Cohn and Goodwill-Gill, *Child Soldiers*, 60. Emphasis in the original.

44. Dietrich Schindler, "State of War, Belligerency, Armed Conflict," in Antonio Cassese, ed., *The New Humanitarian Law of Armed Conflict* (Naples: Editoriale Scientifica, 1979), 5-6.

45. Judith Gail Gardam, *Non-Combatant Immunity as a Norm of International Humanitarian Law* (Dordrecht, The Hague: Martinus Njihoff, 1993), 179.

46. Suter, *An International Law of Guerrilla Warfare*, 184.

47. Suter, *An International Law of Guerrilla Warfare*, 177.

48. Suter, *An International Law of Guerrilla Warfare*, 184.

49. Lawrence J. LeBlanc, *The Convention on the Rights of the Child: United Nations Lawmaking on Human Rights* (Lincoln: University of Nebraska, 1995), 33, 49.

50. van Bueren, "International Documents on Children," 19.

51. Bo Viktor Nylund, "International Law and the Child Victim of Armed Conflict—Is the 'First Call' for Children?" *International Journal of Children's Rights* 6 (1998): 45.

52. Reprinted in Maria Rita Saulle and Flaminia Kojanec, eds., *The Rights of the Child: International Instruments* (Irvington, NY: Transnational, 1995), 768.

53. See Machel, *Impact of Armed Conflict on Children*.

54. See Rome Statute of the International Criminal Court, 1998, Article 8(2)(b)(26), www.un.org/icc.

55. See the coalition's website at www.child-soldiers.org.

56. Keck and Sikkink, *Activists Beyond Borders*, 27.

57. The Optional Protocol can be found at www.child-soldiers.org.

58. Jo de Berry, "Child Soldiers and the Convention on the Rights of the Child," *The Annals of the American Academy of Political and Social Science* 575 (May 2001): 93.

59. Olara Otunnu, "Innocent Victims: Protecting Children in Times of Conflict," October 20, 1999, www.un.org/special-rep/children-armed-conflict.

60. Everett M. Ressler, Joanne Marie Tortorici, and Alex Marcelino, *Children in War: A Guide to Provisional Services* (New York: UNICEF, 1993), 54.

61. Machel, *Impact of Armed Conflict on Children*, 65.

62. See www.un.org/special-rep/children-armed-conflict.

63. Steven Lee Myers, "After US Reversal, Deal Is Struck to Bar Using Child Soldiers," *New York Times*, January 22, 2000.

64. *Report of the Secretary-General on Children and Armed Conflict*, S/2002/1299, Annex A, November 26, 2002.

65. Otunnu, "Innocent Victims," 5.

66. Human Rights Watch, *The Scars of Death*, 5.

67. Human Rights Watch, *Easy Prey*, 55.

68. World Vision, *Position Paper: Children in Armed Conflict*, June 1999, www.crin.org.

69. See Coalition to Stop the Use of Child Soldiers, *Executive Summary: The Use of Child Soldiers in Africa: An Overview*, August 1999, www.child-soldiers.org/soldiers.org/Africa%20report.htm.

70. The most important work was Richard Falk, "Toward a New International Law for Civil War," in Richard Falk, ed., *The International Law of Civil War* (Baltimore, The Johns Hopkins University Press, 1971). See also, Rosalyn Higgins, "International Law and Civil Conflict," in Evan Luard, ed., *The International Regulation of Civil Wars* (London: Thames and Hudson, 1972).

71. Quincy Wright, "The American Civil War, 1861-1965," in Falk, ed., *The International Law of Civil War*, 103.

8

Dilemmas of Compliance with Arms Control
and Disarmament Agreements

Harold A. Feiveson and Jacqueline W. Shire[1]

During the past year and a half, between the time that the compliance project began in 2001 and the latest revision of this paper in mid-2003, questions of compliance with international agreements and Security Council resolutions to stop the proliferation of weapons of mass destruction were settled dramatically in Iraq and vividly underscored by recent actions by North Korea and Iran. Also, during this same period, the United States withdrew from the 1972 Anti-Ballistic Missile Treaty (ABM) and scuttled the verification protocol that had been worked out by an international group to strengthen the 1975 Biological and Toxin Weapons Convention (BWC). This last step was justified partly on grounds that the protocol would not be able to secure compliance from recalcitrant states. So there has been a real-world laboratory to test assumptions concerning compliance that had been largely ignored until the recent crises of Iraq, North Korea, and Iran, and the concurrent dismissal by many in the U.S. administration of reliance on international agreements. We draw upon these recent events and ongoing developments in the following analysis, though first we give a general overview of how compliance is achieved (or not) for different classes of arms control and disarmament agreements.

Is There a Compliance Gap?

Arms control agreements range from those bearing on the most formidable weapons—the nuclear arsenals of the nuclear weapon states—to those addressing less destructive conventional small arms (at least per weapon); and they include agreements that restrict actions by only a few states as well as those that potentially bind almost all states. There are three broad categories of agreements:

1. Bilateral, or mostly bilateral, agreements involving primarily the United States and Russia, such as the ABM Treaty, the 1987 Intermediate Nuclear Forces Treaty (INF), the Strategic Arms Reduction Treaties, START I (1991), START II (1993), and the more recent Strategic Offense Reductions Treaty (SORT);
2. Multilateral treaties and conventions restricting the proliferation and/or eliminating weapons of mass destruction, including the 1968 Treaty on the Non-Proliferation of Nuclear Weapons (NPT), the 1996 Comprehensive Nuclear Test Ban Treaty (CTBT), the 1992 Chemical Weapons Convention (CWC), and the BWC; and
3. Measures and conventions to control missiles, conventional arms, small arms, and landmines, such as the 1987 Missile Technology Control Regime (MTCR) and the 1997 Ottawa Convention on Landmines, among others.

With respect to the first category, the task of ensuring compliance with arms control agreements has been largely one of "regime management" rather than coercion through the use of force or sanctions.[2] Parties to the agreements often ascribe actions appearing to be noncompliant to ambiguity and indeterminacy of treaty language, a lack of transparency, or limitations on the capacity of parties to carry out their undertakings, rather than willful disobedience. In this deliberative, management model, coercive enforcement appears generally misguided and even futile. Not surprisingly, the bilateral agreements have mostly been complied with. When a treaty becomes too cumbersome for a country, it has the option of simply withdrawing from the treaty, as of course did the United States from the ABM Treaty. But, as we discuss later, withdrawal is not always easy for a country, which is one reason why several officials in the Bush administration oppose U.S. participation in treaties in the first place.

The third category—international regimes to control dual use and conventional arms—has been less developed. Some of the agreements there, notably the Landmines Convention, however, do employ intriguing compliance strategies.

The middle category, where arguably there have been serious gaps in compliance, is the most interesting. It is certainly the most timely, with events in Iraq, North Korea, and Iran still unfolding, and with the United States asserting, and to some extent acting upon, controversial new nonproliferation policies, such as counterproliferation. This is where we will focus most attention.

The first step is to ask whether there are notable compliance gaps in each of these categories, beginning with the first and third.

Superpower Arms Control

As already noted, for bilateral U.S.-Soviet/Russian arms control, compliance has largely been an issue of "regime management." With management as the mutual goal, it was necessary and practical for the root of actions appearing to be non-compliant to be attributed to ambiguity and indeterminacy of treaty language, a lack of transparency, and limitations on the capacity of parties to carry out their undertakings. That is, the principal source of noncompliance was to be seen not as "willful disobedience but the lack of capability or clarity or priority."[3] Thus, not surprisingly, these superpower treaties contain no provisions for enforcing compliance, whether through sanctions or other means. The two states reserve only the extreme options of playing "tit for tat" or withdrawing from the agreement. They contain withdrawal clauses allowing a country to withdraw with six months notice on grounds of extraordinary events jeopardizing the supreme interests of the state.[4]

Revealingly, (disregarding SORT), the central treaties on arms control between the Soviet Union and the United States, and, since 1991, Russia and the United States, establish technical consultative committees designed explicitly to work out issues of compliance that might arise. Thus, the ABM Treaty and its follow-on protocols established the Standing Consultative Commission (SCC) to resolve disputes related to compliance or treaty interpretation. The INF Treaty established a verification regime, based largely on on-site inspections and data exchanges, and a Special Verification Commission (SVC), which meets regularly to resolve compliance-related questions. START I established the Joint Compliance and Inspection Commission (JCIC) to resolve questions surrounding treaty implementation. To date, there have been some forty agreements reached under the JCIC framework clarifying the original treaty. And START II, which has not entered into force (and will probably never do so), calls for a Bilateral Implementation Commission (BIC), similar to the JCIC, which would meet at the request of either party to resolve compliance-related questions.

The agreements contain elaborately detailed verification measures and prescriptions of what is and is not permitted. Verification is critical for two reasons: it reassures both sides that the other is adhering to the agreement, and, by elaborating technical details, it creates spaces for negotiating differences that can allow for bargaining and adjustment to changing circumstances. By taking this bargaining process into an expert domain, the agreements are insulated from the effects of passing political crises that could damage them.[5]

Recent U.S. efforts to develop a national missile defense (NMD) posed the first real crisis for this model of regime management. In December 2001, President Bush announced that the United States was withdrawing from the ABM Treaty, and the withdrawal was effected in June 2002 after the required six months notice. The administration characterized the ABM treaty as a "relic" of the Cold War; and with the treaty no longer standing in the way, the United States has begun work on a site at Fort Greeley, Alaska, which would be equipped with five interceptors. It could be operational by August 2004 as an emergency missile defense site.[6] In fact, since the work in Alaska could, stretching matters somewhat, be considered a test site and has been characterized as such by the United States, the United States might have been able to secure Russian agreement with the work, while remaining inside the treaty. So regime management could have again described the mode of operation within a treaty, but in this case, the administration clearly wanted to end the treaty altogether.

As the United States moved toward withdrawal, Russia's President Putin first hinted at dire consequences, including Russian withdrawal from START II and other agreements related to the limitation and control of strategic and conventional weapons. Russia also moved beyond the bilateral expert management model of eliciting compliance by involving the larger international community. In October 1999, Russia submitted a resolution to the First Committee of the U.N. General Assembly seeking "Preservation of and Compliance with the Anti-Ballistic Missile Treaty."[7] The resolution reaffirms the need for compliance with the ABM Treaty and was supported by eighty states, with only four opposed— the United States, Israel, Latvia, and Micronesia. Russia also actively lobbied Western European states and China to raise the political stakes for the United States over its ABM policy.

But once the U.S. decision to withdraw was final, Russia's response was, in fact, muted.[8] This may be explained in part by the terrorist attacks on the United States of September 11, 2001 and President Putin's desire not to jeopardize Russia's larger relationship with the United States. Along with Russia, most of the European states also sought to restrain the United States, raising the specter that U.S. actions could lead not only to a breakdown of bilateral arms control, but also to a weakening of multilateral efforts to stem proliferation. Thus, for example, Camille Grand, a French arms control expert, has written that the recent United States shift away from arms control provides an easy rationale for those reluctant to join or comply, and risks a "conceptual decoupling" whereby Europe pursues arms control while the United States reinforces its military or defense options.[9] But European concerns also faded rapidly once the withdrawal happened.

Despite the outcome where the sky did not fall, it is striking how much continued pull the ABM Treaty exerted on the United States. The Clinton administration went to considerable lengths to preserve the treaty in some modified form even as it tentatively contemplated deployment of a limited system. And despite the disdain shown toward the treaty by the Bush administration, it found it no easy matter to abandon it, initially at least. Such compliance pressure is indeed clearly recognized by Bush administration officials. In a study done in late 2000, under the auspices of the National Institute for Public Policy, coauthored by several analysts now in prominent positions in the administration, the authors flagged the issue in no uncertain terms.[10] Acknowledging the powerful lure of compliance with established treaties—"no democratic government wants to be viewed as opposed to peace and goodwill"—the study's authors state that arms control treaties can become "a political straitjacket," as illustrated by U.S. efforts to seek relief from the ABM Treaty. To the authors of this statement, the lesson to be learned from the ABM Treaty is that the United States should be wary of treaty commitments, for fear that they will lock in the United States to unwanted constraints because of a "domestic norm that views arms control commitments as sacrosanct." They fear what others might welcome— that apart from any sanctions and other compliance measures built into treaties, the treaties themselves create compliance inertia beyond the real security interests of the parties.

The way the U.S. withdrawal from the ABM Treaty has so far played out— that is, that no one seems to care very much—leaves one critical compliance question unanswered. This is whether the withdrawal will make it significantly easier down the road for other countries to justify withdrawal from other treaties, such as the NPT.

Ballistic Missiles, Conventional Arms, Small Arms, and Landmines

In this category, we include the Missile Technology Control Regime, a few agreements seeking to limit conventional weapons, and the Landmine Convention. We address the compliance issues raised by these agreements only briefly.

The MTCR, which seeks to restrict the export of certain categories of missiles, unlike most of the other multilateral treaties discussed here, is a regime of limited membership (now with thirty-two members). It has developed a common set of export guidelines and a shared list of items to be controlled, but enforcement relies on each state independently taking responsibility for implementation, including national legislation codifying the regime's guidelines for technology transfers and enforcing it through national sanctions if necessary.[11] The regime contains no formal provisions for enforcement, though, as noted, members could impose unilateral sanctions. Decisions are consensus based, and noncompliance among members is often seen as unintentional and based on differing interpretations of ambiguous, highly technical language.

The unilateral sanctions called for have been exercised by the United States. Thus, for example, in response to alleged Chinese transfers of missile technology to Pakistan and possibly also to Syria and Saudi Arabia, the United States has imposed sanctions on China several times,[12] in accord with the U.S. Arms Control Export Act. However, the sanctions specified in this act for violations of the MTCR guidelines appear quite mild prima facie—they prohibit for two years all U.S. government contracts with the sanctioned entity, licenses for the transfer of all items on the U.S. Munitions List, and the importation of products produced by the sanctioned individual or entity. Furthermore, even these sanctions have often been waived after only one year;[13] and in 2000, the United States agreed to waive economic sanctions for China's past sales of missile parts and equipment to Pakistan and Iran altogether in exchange for China's agreement to adopt an export control regime for missile-related dual-use items.[14]

The network of arms control treaties, regimes, and norms grows noticeably thin when it comes to conventional weapons.[15] The most significant conventional arms control agreement is the 1990 Treaty on Conventional Armed Forces in Europe (CFE), which entered into force in 1992 and aims "to strengthen stability and security in Europe through the establishment of a secure and stable balance of conventional armed forces at lower levels."[16] The CFE, which has thirty member states, does not restrict arms sales, but limits the numbers of tanks, artillery, armored combat vehicles, aircraft, and attack helicopters from the Atlantic Ocean to the Ural Mountains. There have been efforts to further tighten the CFE, most notably by Russia, to include various other kinds of military combat aircraft and restrictions on upgrading infrastructure with military importance, such as airfields, harbors, and railways.[17] As with other U.S.-Soviet treaties, the CFE has a strong managerial focus, with an emphasis on data exchange, inspections and a Joint Consultative Group. This has allowed it to survive the collapse of the Soviet Union and the Warsaw Pact alliance, and more recently the eastward expansion of the North Atlantic Treaty Organization (NATO).

In addition to the CFE, there are other agreements which seek to limit conventional arms sales and to establish registers of arms that might be used to constrain arms sales and exports. These include the Wassenaar Arrangement of predominantly western industrialized countries, which promotes export controls worldwide on munitions and dual-use items;[18] the U.N. Conventional Arms Register, established in 1991 by a U.N. General Assembly resolution calling for greater transparency in arms transfers;[19] a U.N.-sponsored "Program of Action" to combat illicit small arms trafficking;[20] the Inter-American Convention Against the Illicit Manufacturing of and Trafficking in Firearms of the Organization of American States; and other similar initiatives. None of these arrangements have significant enforcement mechanisms.

More interesting in terms of compliance is the 1997 Ottawa Convention on Landmines. This convention is remarkable for being a major multilateral arms control treaty that was negotiated and entered into force without being initiated or supported by the great powers. Rather it is the product of a small group of states and an international network of nongovernmental organizations (NGOs), most notably the International Campaign to Ban Landmines (which represents over 1100 groups and received the 1997 Nobel Peace Prize).

The Ottawa Convention bans the use, development, production, stockpiling, and transfer of antipersonnel landmines and mandates the destruction of existing stockpiles within four years of the treaty's entry into force.[21] States may retain mines only for the purpose of training in mine clearance and the development of mine destruction techniques. The convention contains no explicit verification or compliance provisions, although a state party may raise concerns about non-compliance with the U.N. secretary-general.[22] A majority of parties can also request a special inspection, and a two-thirds majority "further action." States-parties must also submit annual reports detailing the location, quantities, and types of stockpiled and deployed mines. The United States has not signed the treaty, maintaining that the use of landmines is still critical in some areas, in particular along the demilitarized zone (DMZ) in South Korea. Under the 1996 and 1998 Presidential Decision Directives, the United States is seeking "smart" alternatives to mines before ceasing to deploy them.[23] Russia and China are also prominent nonsignatories, along with Israel, India, and Pakistan.

The most innovative compliance mechanism for the convention is to involve both citizen and government-based monitoring.[24] We mention briefly the role of citizen monitoring in the concluding section.

The Landmines Convention suggests the interesting lesson that an arms control agreement may actually be more rigorous, fair, and have greater legitimacy if the great powers are not included in the negotiations. The success of the campaign that led to the convention seems to have established a norm that may in time envelop the great powers. Kenneth Rutherford offers a detailed analysis of the role of NGOs in creating and sustaining the momentum that led to the Ottawa Convention.[25] The NGO community, he argues, was able to place the issue on the international agenda, and to coalesce support for a landmine ban, because it succeeded in shifting the terms of debate from a discussion of the military utility of landmines to their humanitarian impact. By focusing on their indiscriminate nature, and their use against civilian populations as a weapon of economics, for example, to deny access to fertile farm land in civil wars, the NGO community set the pace for negotiations and diplomats followed. Rutherford suggests that NGOs can replicate their success with other weapons or practices that, like landmines, are contrary to fundamental humanitarian principles.

Multilateral Treaties on Weapons of Mass Destruction (WMD)

Let us now focus attention on the NPT, CTBT, CWC, and the BWC—the four critical multilateral treaties addressing weapons of mass destruction. The first three of these possess explicit verification and enforcement provisions, and share the key feature that aside from the removal of certain privileges, any direct enforcement measures must be authorized by the U.N. Security Council. The Biological and Toxin Weapons Convention does not have compliance or verification provisions.

Under Article I of the NPT, the nuclear weapons states undertake not to transfer nuclear weapons or other nuclear explosive devices to other states, and not to help nonnuclear weapons states acquire nuclear weapons. Under Article

VI, they also undertake to "pursue negotiations in good faith" on measures directed to the cessation of the nuclear arms race at an early date, and to nuclear disarmament. There is no explicit mechanism referred to in the treaty for establishing compliance with these obligations. For their part, nonnuclear weapon states, in Article II, agree not to acquire nuclear weapons and, in Article III, agree to conclude safeguards agreements with the International Atomic Energy Agency (IAEA) covering all fissionable materials within eighteen months of accession to the treaty. While this safeguards article commits all nonnuclear-weapon-state parties to accept international safeguards on their civilian nuclear power programs, it contains no similar restriction for the nuclear weapon states.

IAEA inspections are the primary vehicle for establishing compliance with safeguards obligations. Article XII.C of the IAEA Statute states that inspectors are to report any noncompliance to the Board of Governors via the director-general, and the board "shall report the non-compliance to all members and to the Security Council and General Assembly of the United Nations."[26] According to Article VI, the thirty-five members of the Board of Governors must include the ten states which are the "most advanced in the technology of atomic energy including the production of source materials," effectively ensuring that the nuclear weapons states are members.

If the board judges that corrective action has not been taken in a reasonable time, it may move to curtail agency assistance or suspend that member from the "exercise of the privileges and rights of membership." Disputes related to the application of safeguards can also be referred to the International Court of Justice (ICJ) under Article XVII.A., although this depends on the court agreeing to adjudicate such a dispute.

The IAEA has referred two cases to the U.N. Security Council: the failure of North Korea (DPRK) to permit inspection of suspect facilities under its safeguard's agreement and Iraq's noncompliance with IAEA inspections carried out under Security Council Resolution 687. The United States has recently asked that the IAEA also consider the case of Iran, though the matter has not yet been referred to the Security Council. These cases and their aftermaths are discussed in more detail below.

The Comprehensive Test Ban Treaty prohibits any nuclear explosion, whether for weapons or peaceful purposes. It establishes a far-reaching international verification regime based on national technical means, seismic monitoring, radionuclide, hydroacoustic and infrasound monitoring, on-site inspections, and confidence building measures. The use of national technical means in verification is explicitly permitted. As with other treaties, the CTBT provides for withdrawal for supreme national interests. Although all the nuclear weapon states have signed the treaty, the U.S. Senate refused to give its consent to ratification and the treaty has not yet entered into force.

Article V of the CTBT, "Measures to Redress a Situation and to Ensure Compliance, Including Sanctions," states that the conference, consisting of all states parties, may recommend to states parties collective measures which are in conformity with international law to ensure compliance. This article also notes that the conference, or alternatively, if the case is urgent, the executive council (consisting of fifty-one member states elected by the conference), may bring compliance issues to the attention of the United Nations. The conference does not have the power to impose sanctions; it may only recommend them. The Article does not specify the U.N. body to which acts of noncompliance may be referred. However, the drafters understood that concerns about noncompliance with Article I (the fundamental undertaking on testing) would be brought to the attention of the U.N. Security Council.

A few days before the Senate vote on the Comprehensive Nuclear Test Ban, Senator Richard Lugar (R-IN), explaining why he planned to vote against ratification, asserted that, "the Treaty simply has no teeth." He questioned the deterrent value of sanctions on a state determined to pursue a nuclear program, and expressed no confidence in the U.N. Security Council to address a serious case of noncompliance without resort to the veto by one of the five permanent members. He stated that *"the enforcement mechanisms of the CTBT provide little reason for countries to forgo nuclear testing"*[27] [emphasis added]. A short time after the Senate's rejection of the treaty, former Secretary of State Henry Kissinger, in applauding the Senate's action, said that arms control agreements, "especially of the toothless variety, may have come to the end of the road." He called for tougher sanctions against states acquiring weapons of mass destruction and the nations that supply them.[28]

Although Lugar and Kissinger directed their statements at the CTBT, their underlying concerns extended to the nonproliferation regime more generally, and especially to the NPT. If a state pledged not to acquire nuclear weapons or other weapons of mass destruction (and here Lugar and Kissinger are clearly thinking not of the declared nuclear weapon states, but of countries such as Iraq, North Korea, and Iran), goes forward to obtain these weapons regardless, will other countries and the Security Council be willing to act to stop it? They are skeptical. However, it is not so clear what they believe is required to "put teeth" into the multilateral agreements. We discuss a couple of possibilities in the concluding section.

The Bush administration, while generally supportive of the NPT, clearly shares this skepticism concerning the treaty's enforcement provisions. In a statement read in Geneva at the second meeting of the Preparatory Committee for the 2005 Review Conference of the NPT, at the end of April 2003, Secretary of State Colin Powell put forward this challenge to the NPT parties:

> In recent months, one state [North Korea] declared its withdrawal from the Treaty. Another party [Iran] admitted to construction of secret nuclear facilities. Others are procuring technologies that would enable them to produce clandestinely the fissile material needed for a nuclear weapon. NPT parties—weapon states and non-weapon states alike—must take strong action to deal with cases of non-compliance and to strengthen the Treaty's nonproliferation undertakings. We cannot allow the few who fail to meet their obligations to undermine

the important work of the NPT. . . . The NPT can only be as strong as our will to enforce it, in spirit and in deed.[29]

The NPT is widely perceived to be under siege with the defection of North Korea and the feared defection of Iran, discussed further below. In addition, a thirteen-point program agreed at the 2000 NPT Review Conference, which included commitments by the five declared nuclear powers to take steps toward nuclear disarmament, is widely perceived to have been abandoned. "That agreement is now gathering dust on some filing cabinet somewhere. . . . For the first time since the 1950s there isn't a global framework . . . to get rid of nuclear weapons."[30]

In the next section, we address the cases of Iraq, North Korea, and Iran, and initiatives that are being considered by the Bush administration and others to strengthen compliance.

The Chemical Weapons Convention bans the production, acquisition, stockpiling, transfer, and use of chemical weapons, and requires the destruction of existing chemical weapon stockpiles and production facilities. The Organization for the Prohibition of Chemical Weapons (OPCW), established by the CWC for implementation and verification of the treaty, has developed an elaborate regime for inspections, declarations, and other means to verify compliance. Like the CTBT, it details specific measures that could be taken once noncompliance has been established, including the restriction or suspension of the party's rights under the convention, sanctions, and, in cases of "particular gravity," referral to the U.N. Security Council. Of incalculable importance, the CWC also provides powerful economic incentives for countries to join, and comply with, the convention. The convention calls for signatories to limit trade in chemicals with nonsignatories, a potentially devastating consequence for at least some of the nonsignatories.

So far, most countries have signed and ratified the treaty. Nevertheless, some of those that have done so are widely considered to be pursuing chemical weapons capabilities. A few countries have not signed, including Egypt and Syria, arguing that they will not do so until Israel gives up its nuclear arsenal. Israel, in turn, has signed the convention but has not yet ratified it.

Last in this category is the Biological and Toxin Weapons Convention, which entered into force in 1975 and currently has 143 parties. The convention prohibits all use of disease as a weapon of war, but fatally it has no provisions for verifying or monitoring compliance. Not surprisingly, there have been some grievous instances of noncompliance. Leaders of Russia have acknowledged that the Soviet Union continued an offensive biological weapons program until at least 1992. The United Nations Special Commission on Iraq (UNSCOM) revealed that a significant biological weapons effort was underway in Iraq before the Gulf War. And John Holum, then director of the U.S. Arms Control and Disarmament Agency, claimed at the fourth BWC review conference in 1996 that twice as many states had or were seeking biological weapons as in 1975.[31]

Clearly, in order to be effective, the BWC must have elaborated verification procedures. In the past several years, an ad hoc group established by the states party to the convention did develop a draft protocol to provide measures of verification and enforcement similar in many respects to those of the CWC. The proposed protocol sought to "build confidence through transparency" and create a "web of deterrence" supported by an increased flow of information.[32]

The composite text contained three basic pillars for the verification regime, adapted from the CWC:[33]

1. Mandatory declarations of all biological weapons and dual-use facilities;
2. Routine "managed access" clarification visits to declared, "relevant" facilities, conducted by an international body of inspectors; and
3. Short-notice challenge inspections at sites suspected of noncompliance by another signatory.

However, in July 2001, the Bush administration rejected the draft. According to U.S. negotiators, the draft did not result in an effectively verifiable BWC. Donald Mahley, the U.S. ambassador to the ad hoc group, declared:

> The draft Protocol will not improve our ability to verify BWC compliance. It will not enhance our confidence in compliance and will do little to deter those countries seeking to develop biological weapons. In our assessment, the draft Protocol would put national security and confidential business information at risk.[34]

Mahley cited three major costs imposed by the composite text: (1) a false sense of security from an inconsequential inspection mechanism; (2) infringement on biodefense efforts and proprietary business information; and (3) weakening of multilateral export control regimes.

At the Fifth Review Conference of State Parties in November 2001, the United States introduced a new package of nine ideas as an alternative to the draft protocol. The major proposals would:

1. Require states to enact domestic legislation criminalizing treaty-prohibited activities, similar to United States Biological Weapons Antiterrorism Act of 1989. Though mandated by the BWC, only 46 percent of signatories have such laws;
2. Permit the UN secretary-general to investigate compliance concerns;
3. Create voluntary exchanges of information and visits to questionable sites;
4. Adopt a code of ethics for scientists, implement biosafety procedures, and restrict access to particularly dangerous microorganisms; and
5. Support World Health Organization efforts to identify and respond rapidly to disease outbreak.[35]

Some of these initiatives have been incorporated in the new agenda for the BWC review conferences. However, all of these actions would be politically—not legally—binding and would be implemented individually on a domestic basis. The investigative power assigned the secretary-general does not offer any significant advantages over the status quo. Though the Bush Administration had cited the weakness of the protocol as one reason for its dismissal, it offered a less comprehensive and entirely unenforceable set of alternatives. At the very least, these steps should be made legally binding.

While other nations viewed the suggestions as nominally constructive, the United States destroyed the tenuous consensus by unexpectedly suggesting, on the last day of the conference, that the ad hoc group and its verification mandate be disbanded. This was not supported by other countries, and at present an international dialogue on verification of the BWC continues, but just barely.

In sum, with regard to the four fundamental multilateral treaties on weapons of mass destruction, it is fair to say that there is widespread compliance with the NPT, but without any real consensus yet among the parties on how to secure compliance if one, two, or more countries decide to obtain nuclear weapons. There is imperfect compliance with the CWC, though it is perhaps too early to make any categorical judgments. The BWC, in the striking absence of any verification or enforcement mechanisms, has unquestionably been widely violated. The CTBT has not yet entered into force, but so far signatories have refrained from testing.

In looking to the future, we call attention to the fact that, quite apart from specific treaties and agreements, there exist international norms that even in the absence of a treaty can be understood as binding prohibitions applying to all states. For example, George Bunn has argued that even though the CTBT has not entered into force, the resumption of testing by the nuclear weapon states would be seen by most of the rest of the world as unacceptable. It would constitute a political (rather than narrowly legal) violation of their NPT commitments to pursue disarmament.[36] Certainly, the nuclear testing by China in 1995 and by France in 1996, and more recently in 1998 by India and Pakistan, were considered by much of the international community and global public opinion as trespassing international sensibilities and thus deserving of some sort of censure, including in the case of India and Pakistan economic sanctions (though these have since been relaxed).

Indeed, it is in the shadow world between explicit treaty commitments and implicit norms of international behavior that some of the most significant questions of compliance are likely to arise in the future. This potential is perhaps most striking with respect to withdrawal from a treaty, although such withdrawal, if done with due notice, may not contravene any formal obligation. It is not difficult to imagine some country that had scrupulously adhered to the NPT, for instance, announcing at some point its intention to withdraw, possibly making all the weapons-usable material that had been under international safeguards henceforth available for weapons. In such an instance, despite the fact that withdrawal was a right under the treaty, the international community might well consider the withdrawal to be "illegitimate" and deserving of actions to force continued adherence with the treaty. This certainly is a future compliance problem of great moment and one that has not, to our knowledge, been adequately explored.

Some Compliance Dramas

With this background, we now examine and contrast the responses by the international community to the pursuit and acquisition of nuclear weapons by Iraq, North Korea, and Iran. The United States has taken the lead in all cases, at times supported by and at other times resisted by other Security Council members and the larger international community.

Compelling Compliance: The Case of Iraq

The saga of Iraqi compliance with international treaties and Security Council resolutions played out in three acts. In the first act, the decade or so before the first Gulf War, Iraq blithely trampled on its commitments under the NPT, of which it was a party, undertaking a clandestine program of nuclear weapons development while ostensibly adhering to IAEA safeguards at declared sites. Inspections after the war also revealed substantial biological and chemical weapons programs in Iraq—the bioweapons work in clear violation of Iraq's commitments under the BWC. Iraq had not ratified the CWC.

The second act was the decade after the first Gulf War during which time the U.N. imposed and carried out a rigorous inspection and sanctions regime on Iraq. And the third act, and possibly the most revealing about compliance, covers the events in 2002-2003 leading to the second Gulf War.

Act I: Violating the NPT

Iraq's elaborate and clandestine nuclear and biological weapons programs, which were revealed after the first Gulf War, highlighted the need for two critical components of compliance—verification and enforcement. Clearly without verification there cannot be effective compliance. This understanding has had a salutary effect, prompting the IAEA to establish an enhanced system of safeguards known as the Additional Protocol, INFCIRC 540. The additional protocol is intended to provide the IAEA with greater access and inspection authority in search of clandestine nuclear activities. While the new protocol has been broadly adopted (at this writing seventy-eight countries have signed onto such protocols), it has not yet been adopted by several countries of critical concern, including Iran.

Without a verification system that could have revealed Iraq's weapons programs in violation of international treaties, there was no real occasion to observe how enforcement could have been carried out. Let us suppose, however, that the programs were discovered before the war. In this case, the nominal sequence of actions would have been for the IAEA to report the violations to the Security Council, and for the Security Council then to take steps to stop the programs. Would the council have done anything effective? Given the actions of the council during the second two acts, this appears uncertain. But to understand this better, we consider in more detail the happenings during the last two acts.

Act II: The First Gulf War and Aftermath
    In the aftermath of the Gulf War, which coincided with a period of remarkable unanimity among the Security Council's Permanent Five, the United Nations moved to compel Iraq to destroy all of its weapons of mass destruction. The U.N. Security Council established UNSCOM and instructed it to oversee and certify the "destruction, removal, or rendering harmless, under international supervision, of all Iraqi chemical and biological weapons, stocks of agents, related subsystems . . . and facilities, and all ballistic missiles with a range greater than 150 kilometers, related major parts, repair and production facilities."[37] The IAEA was similarly empowered to assist in the elimination of Iraq's nuclear weapons program.

UNITED NATIONS SPECIAL COMMISSION
    UNSCOM was an initiative unprecedented in the history of the United Nations.[38] Its executive chairman reported directly to the Security Council, not to the secretary-general. It was funded initially through voluntary contributions and later through Iraqi oil revenues paid into a U.N.-managed escrow account. It was staffed primarily not by U.N. civil servants, but by experts on loan from governments. UNSCOM was also supported by an unprecedented level of intelligence sharing and cooperation, which came primarily from the United States, the United Kingdom, and France. This support, which was critically important to UNSCOM's success, included a dedicated U-2 aircraft, special monitoring equipment, and weapons experts for inspection teams. Such cooperation became a matter of controversy in 1999 when it was revealed that the United States had used certain UNSCOM inspection teams in a collection effort involving signal intercepts, and for purposes not directly related to the expressed goals of UNSCOM.[39] The damage to UNSCOM's credibility was immediate, and though the episode was not solely responsible for UNSCOM's demise, it played a significant part.
    Still, during its term, UNSCOM achieved a great deal. The scope of Iraq's weapons programs was revealed and the programs then largely dismantled under UNSCOM's tenure. Between 1992 and 1994, UNSCOM's chemical destruction teams destroyed over 690 tons of chemical agent, including tabun, sarin, and mustard, both in bulk and weaponized form, and thousands of munitions, filled and unfilled. Later, in 1998, chemical weapons inspectors developed evidence that Iraq had weaponized VX, the most deadly agent known. Until 1995, Iraq denied ever weaponizing biological agents. On the basis of its own investigation

of exports of growth media to Iraqi hospitals and institutions and of information obtained following the 1995 defection of Lt. Gen. Hussein Kamel Hassan and subsequent excavation of a trove of documents, UNSCOM learned that Iraq had deployed both anthrax and botulinum toxin on aerial bombs and Scud warheads.[40] Eventually UNSCOM supervised the destruction of al-Hakam, Iraq's primary biological production facility, along with related production equipment and materials. In the missile area, UNSCOM destroyed forty-eight Scud missiles, a number of fixed and mobile launch pads, thirty chemical missile warheads, Iraq's "super gun" and a variety of support equipment and materials.[41]

Aside from the strong political consensus behind UNSCOM's creation and the terms of the cease-fire agreement, UNSCOM's efforts to achieve compliance by Iraq were backed by the threat or use of force. The Security Council also gave, and repeatedly affirmed, UNSCOM's right to "immediate, unconditional and unrestricted access to any and all areas, facilities, equipment, records and means of transportation which they wish to inspect."[42]

In December 1998, following a report to the Security Council by the UNSCOM executive chairman detailing Iraq's continuing refusal to cooperate with its inspection teams, even under new conditions established for the inspection of so-called sensitive sites by the U.N. secretary-general, the United States and the United Kingdom launched four days of air strikes.[43] Iraq responded by stating that its cooperation with UNSCOM was at an end and vowed never again to host U.N. weapons inspectors. This, coupled with the growing outcry over sanctions and deep divisions in the Security Council over how to address the situation, led to a one-year effort to develop a follow-on inspection regime. International support for the use of force under these conditions was limited and no other coalition member joined the United States and United Kingdom in bombing missions.

UNITED NATIONS MONITORING, VERIFICATION, AND
INSPECTION COMMISSION (UNMOVIC)

In December 1999, the Security Council adopted resolution 1284, establishing UNMOVIC. Unlike the unanimous or near unanimous resolutions that established UNSCOM and granted it broad authorities, resolution 1284 was adopted with four abstentions, three from permanent members—France, Russia, and China. Those abstentions signaled the indifference with which some members would treat the new regime, and Iraq's swift dismissal of it confirmed that the council's ambivalent message was well received in Baghdad. UNMOVIC differed from UNSCOM in important ways. Its chairman would report to the secretary-general and his/her staff would be "regarded as international civil servants subject to Article 100 of the U.N. Charter."[44] Long-time UNSCOM experts saw such language as a not-so-subtle broadside against their integrity. The resolution also implied that UNMOVIC should concern itself primarily with monitoring and verifying Iraq's compliance with its disarmament obligations and not, as UNSCOM was, with actively seeking to uncover evidence of noncompliance.[45]

It would be almost four years before UNMOVIC inspectors entered Iraq, in late November 2002.

IRAQ SANCTIONS AND THE OIL-FOR-FOOD PROGRAM

By far the most controversial element of the compliance mechanisms deployed against Iraq were the wide-ranging sanctions imposed at the outset of the Gulf War. By any measure, the sanctions were extraordinarily severe. U.S. estimates are that by 1998 the sanctions had cost Iraq more than $120 billion.[46] Most strikingly, a United Nations Children's Fund (UNICEF) survey of child mortality in Iraq estimated that during the same eight-year period, 1991-1998, there had been an additional half million deaths of children under five in the country as a whole.[47]

The Oil-for-Food program was established in 1996 by U.N. Security Council resolution 986, which allowed Iraq to export $2 billion in oil, in six-month increments, the proceeds of which were placed in a U.N.-managed escrow account. The ceiling on oil sales was eased in 1998 and lifted entirely in 1999. From these funds, Iraq has been allowed to purchase food, medicine, and certain consumer goods items. Under the program, which at this writing is in the process of being phased out, Iraq entered into contracts with suppliers, which must then be submitted to the United Nations for approval. According to the U.N., as of May 2003, approximately $28 billion in humanitarian supplies and equipment had been delivered to Iraq.[48]

The issue of whether Iraq or the international community, in particular the United States and the United Kingdom, which were the staunchest supporters of tough sanctions, is to blame for the suffering of Iraqi civilians under sanctions has been the subject of highly politicized debate. Throughout the 1990s, there was a growing consensus among human rights observers, diplomats, and policymakers that the sanctions on Iraq were unacceptable. Human Rights Watch argued that, "in deploying instruments of coercion, including non-military instruments such as an embargo, the U.N. Security Council must be governed by the core humanitarian principle of minimizing threats to life and bodily harm of innocent people who bear no responsibility for the government policies being sanctioned."[49] This perspective was shared by those charged with dealing with their consequences. U.N. Assistant Secretary-General Denis Halliday, the first U.N. humanitarian coordinator in Iraq, resigned in October 1998 to protest what he called the "genocidal impact" of economic sanctions, while his successor, Hans von Sponeck, resigned a year later voicing similar concerns.[50]

While the sanctions clearly played a large role in crippling Iraq's economy and plunging a once prosperous nation with a strong middle class into poverty, it is also true that Iraq's leadership exploited the severity of sanctions to its own ends.[51] Regardless of who is to blame for the suffering of Iraq's citizens, the efforts of the U.N. Security Council to maintain a tough sanctions policy, while allowing for the importation of food and humanitarian relief, met with limited success over time. The will of the international community to uphold and enforce sanctions eroded sharply as Iraq's poverty deepened. Outright violations of the sanctions grew widespread and the insistent calls of nongovernmental organizations to remedy Iraq's humanitarian crisis could not be ignored. The lesson drawn by the international community is that broad-brush sanctions, even when coupled with a mechanism to oversee the purchase and distribution of humanitarian relief, do not work and are not sustainable over the long term. (This is reflected in subsequent sanctions regimes, in particular for the former Yugoslavia, that sought, with mixed results, to impose targeted financial sanctions aimed at regime leadership.)

The great weakness in compliance strategy exposed by UNSCOM's tenure now appears to be its overreliance on sanctions. As international support for a punitive sanctions regime eroded, so did the will to support an aggressive inspection and disarmament regime. Furthermore, the explicit linkage of sanctions to UNSCOM's very existence placed the organization in an increasingly untenable position.

Act III: The Second Gulf War and Its Antecedents

By early 2002 the Bush administration's public statements regarding Iraq's leadership and alleged links to terrorism and retention of weapons of mass destruction made it clear that the United States was willing to use force if necessary to secure Iraqi compliance with earlier U.N. resolutions.

Under strong pressure from the United States, on November 8, 2002, the U.N. Security Council adopted unanimously resolution 1441, declaring Iraq in "material breach" of its U.N. obligations and offering it a "final opportunity to comply." The resolution gave UNMOVIC broad inspection authority and the right of immediate, unrestricted access throughout Iraq.[52] While the Security Council was unanimous in demanding Iraq's full compliance, several members remained skeptical of United States and United Kingdom claims that Iraq retained weapons of mass destruction and that such weapons remained a threat. In an effort to allay those concerns and bolster the case for war against Iraq, Secretary of State Colin Powell presented a detailed intelligence briefing to the Security Council on February 5, 2003, drawing in signals intercepts, satellite imagery, and defector intelligence.[53]

UNMOVIC inspections resumed on November 27, 2002, and continued through March 18, 2003, the eve of the second Gulf War's start. The story of Iraq's compliance with UNMOVIC during that period is mixed. UNMOVIC chairman Hans Blix submitted a detailed document to the Security Council in early March highlighting areas of noncompliance and outlining actions Iraq would have to take in order to account for its prohibited weapons.[54] The Security Council, however, was divided on whether or not to give Iraq more time to comply and the inspectors more time to seek weapons of mass destruction.

The United States, the United Kingdom, and several other countries in a "coalition of the willing" ultimately undertook military action to depose the Saddam Hussein regime without a resolution explicitly authorizing the use of force, arguing (after failing to win agreement to a follow-on resolution) that resolution 1441 contained all the necessary legal authority. The British government, echoing U.S. arguments, set forth a legal basis for use of force on grounds that (a) U.N. Security Council resolution 1441 was adopted under Chapter VII of the U.N. Charter authorizing the use of force; (b) according to 1441 Iraq remains in material breach of its Security Council obligations, including resolutions 678, which explicitly authorized use of force to restore peace and security to the region, and 687, the ceasefire resolution; and (c) that Iraq's failure to comply with 1441 represented a "further material breach" reviving the authority to use force under 678.[55] Compliance was achieved in this instance by force, though we suppose it may be argued that given at the time of this writing, no weapons of mass destruction being found, that compliance had been earlier achieved.

The second Gulf War reflects in many ways the culmination of a unilateralist approach to compelling compliance. By mid-2002, the limited objective of compelling Iraq to comply with its Security Council obligations became inextricably linked with the Bush administration's goal of removing Saddam Hussein from power. The conflation of these very separate issues into a single rationale for war has created confusion over the war's true objectives, and led to an aggravation of U.S. relations abroad. The failure of United States and British forces to find yet significant elements of Iraq's weapons programs further undermines the rationale for use of force, in particular its legal underpinnings, which relied heavily on Iraq's noncompliance on weapons issues.

Another consequence of the war with respect to compliance is that the authority for finding and dismantling Iraq's weapons of mass destruction now appears to have been permanently removed from the United Nations. UNMOVIC has not been granted permission by the United States and United Kingdom, the two primary coalition partners, to resume inspection activity in Iraq, though the IAEA was permitted to undertake a limited mission aimed at accounting for looted stores of nuclear material at one site. While this situation could change (UNMOVIC's funding has not been cut by the Security Council, indicating that it may yet have a life), it is a disappointing coda to what began as an ambitious, even idealistic, undertaking in multilateral arms control.

Negotiating Compliance: Bargaining with North Korea

Iraqi compliance was secured at end by force, and to an extent by Security Council mandated inspections backed by the threat of force. In North Korea, the approach to compliance has focused on negotiation—and here the efforts at compliance can best be divided into two acts rather than three: Act I (from March 1993 to the Fall of 2002) and Act II (from October 2002 to the present).

Act I: 1993-2002

The first North Korea crisis erupted in March 1993 when North Korea announced its intention to withdraw from the NPT. North Korea joined the NPT in 1985 but did not sign a safeguards agreement with the IAEA until January 30,

1992. North Korea began operating a small research reactor in 1986; and, in 1989, shut down the reactor for approximately 100 days, enough time to unload the core, allowing for the possibility of reprocessing the spent fuel to recover the contained plutonium. Experts believe that possibly 7 to 14 kilograms of plutonium could have been separated—enough for one to two nuclear warheads.

In 1992 and 1993, inspections conducted by the IAEA uncovered numerous discrepancies in North Korea's declaration of the amount of nuclear material in its possession. "North Korea's refusal to resolve the discrepancies, its termination of IAEA's inspections, and its subsequent announcement that it intended to withdraw from the NPT" led the director-general of the IAEA to bring the matter to the Security Council in 1993. The council, in turn, authorized the United States to pursue negotiations with North Korea to resolve the issue.[56]

It appears that the United States did not initially rule out the use of military force. In his confirmation hearings in February 1994, the secretary of defense-designate, William Perry, said that the United States should use "aggressive diplomacy" against North Korea, and noted that while he had no objection to carrots, "there are sticks downstream also."[57] Whatever Perry actually wished to convey, the media interpreted his statements to include a threat to use military force if necessary. Nevertheless, the United States emphasized diplomatic over military initiatives in its negotiations with North Korea.[58]

In October 1994, these talks resulted in an arrangement known as the Agreed Framework. Under the framework, North Korea agreed to freeze its nuclear program. This included stopping operation of its research reactor, halting any further reprocessing at Yongbyon, placing all the spent fuel from the research reactor under IAEA inspections, and stopping construction of two graphite reactors that was then underway. The containment of the spent fuel was particularly important, in that the plutonium in the fuel was enough for four to five nuclear warheads.[59] In exchange, the United States pledged to lead an international coalition to provide two light-water reactors (LWRs) and 500,000 tons of heavy fuel per year until the first reactor came on line. The United States, Japan, and South Korea created a multilateral agency, the Korean Economic Development Organization (KEDO), to carry out these reciprocal obligations. The cost of the LWRs, estimated at $5 billion, was to be borne largely by South Korea and Japan.

The final, and key, paragraph specifies that "when a significant portion of the LWR project is completed, but before delivery of key nuclear components, the DPRK will come into full compliance with all its safeguards agreements with the IAEA, including taking all steps that may be deemed necessary by the IAEA . . . with regard to verifying the accuracy and completeness . . . on all nuclear material in the DPRK."[60] In a sense, the Agreed Framework was a holding operation—freezing, but not dismantling the North Korean nuclear program—until some future stage.

The deal, though periodically endangered, doggedly went forward until the fall of 2002. It represented a compliance strategy that appeared to have worked. From Pyongyang's point of view, it could be argued that North Korea successfully induced the United States to begin a dialogue and relax its political and economic sanctions. From the point of view of the international community, the agreement succeeded (at least for a time) in halting North Korea's nuclear weapons program, and more recently possibly also in suspending its missile programs. In addition, a larger process of reconciliation between North and South Korea and between the United States and North Korea was initiated.[61]

Act II: 2002 to the Present

The Agreed Framework began to fall apart in the Fall of 2002 with North Korea's public admission that it was pursuing a heretofore clandestine uranium enrichment program. In October 2002, the United States confronted North Korea with intelligence of the activity. In response, North Korea reportedly suggested that the program was indeed designed to produce weapons grade uranium.

This sparked an escalating spiral of actions by the United States and North Korea that unraveled the Agreed Framework. In December 2002, KEDO cut off delivery of the fuel oil shipments; and in the first three months of 2003, North Korea announced its withdrawal from the NPT, restarted its nuclear research reactor, ended IAEA inspections, removed seals on the spent fuel rods, and possibly also began to reprocess some of this spent fuel. North Korea asserted that its withdrawal (with no further notice) was justified by virtue of its previous notification of intent to withdraw in 1993.[62]

While North Korea's uranium enrichment program began long before the Bush administration took power, the atmosphere of tension between the two was heightened by the inclusion in President Bush's January 2002 State of the Union Address of North Korea as one of the "Axis of Evil" states.[63] Indeed, shortly after the onset of the second Gulf War, the North Korean Foreign Minister stated that "the U.S. is seriously mistaken if it thinks that the DPRK will accept the demand for disarming while watching one of the three countries the U.S. listed as part of an "axis of evil" already subject to the barbarous military attack."[64]

Although the international community has appeared united in its desire to bring North Korea back into the NPT fold, all of the other members of the Security Council and neighbors of North Korea, including Japan, Russia, and China, have been largely content to allow the United States alone to try to achieve this desired outcome. The United States, for its part, has tried to involve other countries in the negotiations, while North Korea has wanted to deal with the United States alone. At the end of April 2003, reportedly under some pressure from China, North Korea did agree to a meeting in Beijing with representatives from the United States and China.

The question remains, however, what could negotiations achieve? No compliance strategy appears attractive. The use of force by the United States, with or without Security Council approval, would be uncertain of success, and risky. Precision attacks against the nuclear facilities might destroy the North Korean reprocessing plant and research reactor, but they would likely not be able to destroy the spent fuel, or certainly any already-separated plutonium. And such attacks would risk severe retaliation by North Korea against Seoul by its formidable artillery arrayed just north of the DMZ. A large-scale preemptive attack on North Korea, including on the DMZ artillery, could possibly succeed, but again at great risk of substantial U.S. and South Korean casualties.[65] On the other hand, simply standing by as North Korea obtains nuclear weapons also appears risky, especially given North Korea's willingness in the past to sell advanced ballistic missiles to other countries. William Perry, secretary of defense during the first crisis in 1994, has recently noted:

> There are overwhelmingly strong reasons for not wanting a war with North Korea. . . . The million-man army they have lined up, the thousands of artillery pieces they have targeted at Seoul, all of those guarantee that even in the absence of nuclear weapons, a war would be a catastrophe. . . . In spite of that, we risked a war in 1994 to stop that nuclear program and I think we would do it again.[66]

The United States at present seems to favor a stick-and-carrots diplomatic approach, backed by the threat of severe economic sanctions, which could most effectively be applied by China and Japan. But these countries are reluctant to push North Korea against the wall, and do not want to suffer the economic consequences of the regime's collapse. With respect to carrots, the United States appears ready to offer significant economic incentives to North Korea, but insists that first it must renounce its nuclear weapons program. The United States is especially wary of rewarding North Korea for threatening to obtain nuclear weapons. This overall U.S. position (as of May 2003) was summarized clearly in a statement at the second session of the preparatory committee for the 2005 review conference of the NPT by U.S. Assistant Secretary of State for Nonproliferation, John Wolf:

> If NPT withdrawal and threats to acquire nuclear weapons become the currency of international bargaining, our world will be in chaos. . . . While all out options remain available, we are determined to end North Korea's threat through peaceful, diplomatic means. . . . It is important for every country represented here to send the same message to the DPRK: abandon your nuclear weapons ambitions and return to compliance with the NPT. . . . There must be serious consequences for those who violate their NPT commitments.[67]

Anticipating Noncompliance: The Case of Iran

Iran represents a different kind of challenge to compliance than that posed by Iraq and North Korea. These latter countries were evading commitments under the NPT clandestinely—they were clearly in noncompliance with formal undertakings. This may or may not be so with Iran. But so far it is Iran's declared nuclear programs, all under, or soon to be under, international safeguards, which have caused concern. It is less ongoing clandestine activities (though there have been some) than it is Iran's ultimate motives that most worry observers.

Iran's intention to complete construction of the Bushehr reactor was the first alarm. This large light water reactor is one of two such reactors begun initially at a site near Bushehr under the Shah and then damaged during the Iraq-Iran war. With Russian assistance, the reactor is now nearing completion. The United States has persistently pressured Russia to pull out of its agreement with Iran. But, with Iran accepting full IAEA safeguards on the reactor, Russia has so far seen no reason to end its assistance.

Even more than the Bushehr reactor, however, it is other recent revelations that have set off alarm bells among nonproliferation experts. Thus, in a speech in February 2003, President Mohammad Khatami acknowledged the existence of a uranium enrichment facility at Natanz (confirmed two weeks later in a visit to the site by Director-General Mohamed El-Baradei of the IAEA), and the operation or construction of uranium mines and uranium conversion facilities. He also noted that Iran wishes the capability to reuse fuel from power reactors, which may imply an intention to separate plutonium from reactor-spent fuel. The day following President Khatami's comments, Gholamreza Agahazadeh, the head of the Iranian Atomic Energy Commission elaborated—among other matters noting the existence of a heavy water plant and plans to produce uranium metal. Since heavy water is not needed in the light water reactor under construction at Bushehr but could be used in a production reactor to produce plutonium, and uranium metal has few civilian uses but is vital to nuclear weapons, the existence of these program do support contentions that Iran may have underway, or at least is considering, a nuclear weapons program.[68]

In the speech by John Wolf noted above, he asserted that, in light of the revealed programs, Iran poses "the most fundamental challenge ever faced by the NPT."[69] At the urging of the United States, the IAEA issued a report to a June 2003 meeting of the Board of Governors raising serious concerns about Iran's nuclear intentions, but stopping short of asserting that Iran's actions were a violation of the NPT. The board did not refer the matter to the U.N. Security Council, preferring instead to urge Iran to sign the IAEA's Additional Protocol and to allow more intrusive inspections.[70]

The compliance strategy of the United States and other countries might now be called anticipatory. It is to make the costs to Iran of embarking on an explicit nuclear weapons program as high as possible. The hope is that by drawing Iran into a strengthened safeguards regime, it would make it harder for Iran to develop weapons capabilities clandestinely and, therefore, allow the international community a greater range of options should the regime ultimately abandon safeguards. Above all, the case of Iran spotlights the issue discussed earlier—whether the norm of nonproliferation can be made powerful enough to dissuade a country from withdrawing from the NPT and by so doing withdraw also from safeguards obligations.

Approaches to Strengthening Compliance

Norms and the Behavior of Nuclear Weapons States

Collective actions against the proliferation of weapons of mass destruction, and especially of nuclear weapons, will be more achievable if backed by a strong international consensus on the legitimacy and universality of the norms to be defended. In our view, this requires commitments by the nuclear weapon states to support such norms, even if this requires some limitations on their own freedom of action.

Norms can be seen as principles of behavior that countries hope will be widely adopted by other states. Eventually, these principles may be codified through negotiations into treaties, and national laws. But what are the norms to be adopted? In the view of the nuclear weapon states, of course, the principal norm affecting nuclear weapons is their nonproliferation to countries that do not now possess them or to terrorist groups. The more fundamental norm to much of the rest of the world is, by contrast, the nonpossession of nuclear weapons.[71]

Indeed, the overwhelming majority of nations have repeatedly expressed the belief that there should be no nuclear weapons in the arsenal of any state. This view has been expressed in many ways, including through numerous General Assembly documents, that include the record of the very first plenary meeting on January 10, 1946.[72] The accession to the NPT by 187 states (182 of which are nonnuclear), the treaty's preamble and its articles, all establish a norm against possession. Article VI commits nuclear weapons states "to pursue negotiations in good faith on effective measures relating to cessation of the nuclear arms race at an early date and to nuclear disarmament." More recently, this nonnuclear norm and obligation was buttressed by the 1995 indefinite extension of the NPT, a 1996 World Court judgment, and the April 2000 "unequivocal commitment" by the nuclear weapons states to eliminate their weapons.

There certainly are nonfrivolous technical and political reasons for the nuclear weapon states not to pursue complete nuclear disarmament. We do not argue this point in this paper. We do wish to emphasize however, that the norm of nonproliferation will never be as compelling and strong as the nuclear weapon states wish it to be until they grapple with more determination than they yet have with the rest of the world's desire for nuclear disarmament. While complete nuclear disarmament may not soon be achievable, it certainly is within the capabilities of the nuclear weapon states to act in ways to make nuclear weapons appear less important politically. Recent U.S. statements and actions indicating a desire by the United States to develop new nuclear weapons, and particularly new weapons that could be used first in a conflict, go exactly in the wrong direction. For example, the administration's policy paper on proliferation of December 2002, stated an apparent willingness by the United States to use nuclear weapons first to confront the proliferation of weapons of mass destruction.

A strong declaratory policy and effective military forces are essential elements of our contemporary deterrent posture, along with the full range of political tools to persuade potential adversaries not to seek or use WMD. The United States will continue to make clear that it reserves the right to respond with overwhelming force—including through resort to all of our options—to the use of WMD.[73]

In the spring of 2003, Congress agreed to soften a 1994 amendment that prevented research and development of low-yield nuclear weapons, with the new stipulation being that research is permitted, though still not development. The Defense Authorization Act of 2003 approved funding to the weapons labs to study bunker-busting nuclear weapons. Also, the Defense Authorization Act of 2004 charges the weapons labs to shorten the time to prepare for underground nuclear testing from the current three years to eighteen months. Thus, at present the U.S. position, therefore, appears to be that: there are situations in which it is permissible for the United States to use or threaten to use nuclear weapons; to deploy nuclear weapons anywhere; to not give up the option eventually to test nuclear weapons; and to explore the development of new nuclear weapons.

Proponents of these policies believe, of course, that they are prudent. Should not the United States be ready to use nuclear weapons to destroy chemical and biological weapons in deep underground bunkers—the scenario that is most driving interest in new nuclear weapons? But this view is, we believe, shortsighted. First of all, analyses published this year by Robert Nelson of Princeton University and the Council on Foreign Relations have shown that the notion of building a nuclear weapon that could destroy underground bunkers without causing massive damage above ground is illusory.[74]

Similar (and related) to its views on no first use, the administration's views toward the Comprehensive Test Ban Treaty appear ambiguous at best. The declared rationale for the CTBT is that "the cessation of all nuclear weapon test explosions and all other nuclear explosions, by constraining the development and qualitative improvement of nuclear weapons and ending the development of advanced new types of nuclear weapons, constitutes an effective measure of nuclear disarmament and nonproliferation in all its aspects."[75] This treaty has almost universal support, the U.N. General Assembly in 1996 voting 158-3 to endorse the treaty prohibiting all nuclear test explosions in all environments for all time. It now has 160 signatories.

However, according to the United States, the CTBT relates only to actual explosive nuclear tests, and does not otherwise constrain "the development and qualitative improvement of nuclear weapons." The U.S. ambassador to the CTBT negotiations noted a significant difference in expectation and intention between the five nuclear weapons states and the majority of nonnuclear weapon states. The latter, he explained, expect that banning all nuclear tests will bring about the deterioration and decay of all existing nuclear weapons stockpiles, while the five nuclear weapons states believe that even without testing they can maintain for the foreseeable future the viability, safety, and reliability of their nuclear stockpiles.[76]

Indeed, as part of a domestic agreement between the U.S. president and the nuclear weapons laboratories, a long list of conditions was attached when the treaty was submitted to the U.S. Senate for ratification. These conditions were intended to permit the maintenance and modernization of the U.S. nuclear arsenal for the indefinite future.[77] They included: (1) a science-based stockpile stewardship program to ensure a high level of confidence in the safety and reliability of nuclear weapons in the active stockpile, including the conduct of a broad range of effective and continuing experimental programs; (2) the maintenance of modern laboratory facilities and programs in nuclear technology that will attract, retain, and ensure the continued application of human scientific resources to programs on which continued progress in nuclear technology depends; (3) the maintenance of the basic capability to resume nuclear test activities prohibited by the CTBT; and (4) the understanding that if the president could no longer certify a high level of confidence in the safety or reliability of a nuclear weapon stockpile, the United States would be prepared to withdraw from the CTBT under the standard "supreme national interests" clause in order to conduct whatever testing might be required.

Experts at the Natural Resources Defense Council (NRDC) have argued reasonably that these conditions make clear that "the U.S. government clearly intends to maintain under the CTBT, and indeed significantly enhance, its scientific and technical capabilities for undertaking the development of advanced new types of nuclear weapons."[78] Of particular concern are U.S. Department of Energy plans for "all" the nuclear weapons in the U.S. stockpile to be replaced with either "modified versions or with entirely new weapons."[79]

Despite the stockpile stewardship program and the conditions attached to the ratification, which include keeping open and at an advanced stage of readiness the nuclear weapons tests site, the CTBT was not approved by the U.S. Senate and so cannot enter into force. It is possible that further conditions increasing U.S. latitude for new weapons design, the addition of more intrusive and early verification, and greater powers of enforcement of compliance may be among the provisions that could be added to any future effort at ratification, if any. Of course, we realize that many of the conditions were attached by the U.S. administration in order to secure Senate consent to ratification. Nevertheless, to much of the world outside the orbit of the nuclear weapon states, the conditions appear as an implicit and creeping unilateral renegotiation of the CTBT. It will be all the harder for the United States and other nuclear weapon states to compel compliance with the letter of the CTBT if they seek, or appear to seek, the development of new nuclear weapons counter to the spirit of the test ban.

The incessant hedging of the United States no first use commitment and attitudes toward the CTBT unfortunately work against norms opposing nuclear weapons use. With the United States preeminent in conventional capabilities, it is foolish and dangerous for it to stress the utility of nuclear weapons. To the extent possible, the United States and other countries should work toward making nuclear use unthinkable and to move away from thinking of nuclear devices as weapons. This is not the time, when terrorist use of nuclear weapons has emerged as a potential nightmare, India and Pakistan trade believable nuclear threats, and North Korea threatens to develop nuclear weapons, for the United States to undermine the fifty-plus year nuclear taboo. Certainly, nothing would make the use of nuclear weapons by terrorists or states more likely than the prior use of nuclear weapons by the United States (or any other country). In addition, the use of nuclear weapons by the United States or another nuclear weapon state could shatter the Non-Proliferation Treaty and lead to the rapid spread of nuclear weapons to several more countries.

The 1993 Chemical Weapons Convention provides another cautionary tale. Here, the "implementing legislation" passed by Congress contains a number of conditions considered by some arms control analysts to "violate the letter and intent of the convention."[80]

Among the conditions the United States imposed on its ratification of the convention is the right of a presidential veto on any challenge inspection on national security grounds. According to John Gee, deputy director-general of the OPCW, which is responsible for the treaty's implementation, "the convention is quite clear on challenge inspection: there is no right of refusal. So that condition would appear to me at least prima facie, to be contrary to the provisions of the convention."[81] Another U.S. condition is that no chemical sample collected by OPCW inspectors in the United States could be taken out of the country for analysis. Gee observes that, "it was always understood during the work of the Preparatory Commission here that off-site meant, in effect, out of country." No other state has placed unilateral conditions on its legislation covering implementation. It seems plausible that other states may follow the U.S. lead and introduce similar conditions.

Overall, the United States appears to assert a kind of "exceptionalism" in which it claims a freedom of action denied to everyone else. This view undermines the normative force of international treaties affecting the proliferation of weapons of mass destruction.

Counterproliferation

Nowhere is this assertion of exceptionalism more vivid than in the U.S. doctrine of counterproliferation. The doctrine did not originate with the Bush administration. At the start of the Clinton administration, Secretary of Defense Les Aspin made clear that the United States should be prepared to use military force to counter proliferation.[82] But the doctrine has been given new emphasis in a Bush administration convinced that the United States should consider more systematically and seriously than it had hitherto a range of unilateral actions to enforce treaties and norms. In the previously referenced policy paper of December 2002, "Strategies to Combat the Proliferation of Weapons of Mass Destruction," the administration explained the critical characteristics of counterproliferation,[83] and arguably, in April 2003 in the invasion of Iraq, justified in part by the threat of proliferation of weapons of mass destruction, converted the doctrine to action.

According to the December document, U.S. nonproliferation policy rests on three "pillars." These are support for multilateral and bilateral nonproliferation and arms control regimes; consequence management—essentially homeland security to defend against the use by others of weapons of mass destruction; and counterproliferation. By counterproliferation, the United States asserts the right and intention to interdict the movement of WMD materials, technology, and expertise to hostile states and terrorist organizations, and to develop military capabilities accordingly to allow this.

Part of the controversy over the newly emphasized doctrine is the implied determination of the United States to use force, unilaterally if necessary, to prevent or to react to the proliferation of weapons of mass destruction. In the case of Iraq, the issue of unilateral action was somewhat fuzzed in that the United States claimed to be acting on authorization provided by previous Security Council resolutions and, in fact, to be taking action to enforce them.

The claim underlying counterproliferation is to a right of anticipatory self-defense, and it relies heavily on the right to armed reprisal (except that the "reprisal" is to occur before any actual attack has taken place). However, there is a norm, derived both from the practice of the United Nations and its member states and from the opinions of the World Court, that armed reprisal is generally contradictory to the U.N. Charter, and many legal scholars argue that the charter forbids anticipatory self-defense.[84] Israel's bombing of Iraq's Osirak reactor in June 1981 is a classic example of counterproliferation, though it was subsequently chastised by the U.N. Security Council.[85]

Only a state that could ensure that it could not be held accountable by the international community would feel confident in pursuing a policy of counterproliferation. It would also need to feel that it would be safe from the likely larger consequences of possibly undermining the structure of international norms that could follow from acting above the law, or rather taking the law into its own hands. For the United States, the end of the Cold War has seemed to create such conditions, or so at least is argued by proponents of counterproliferation.[86] A study on U.S. policy in the post-Cold War period argues that over the past decade, "unencumbered by Cold War fears of sparking confrontation with the powerful Soviet Union, American policy makers turned frequently to threats and the use of force."[87] It is against this background that counterproliferation needs to be read.[88]

Of course, such a unilateral policy offers no internationally shared basis for ensuring compliance and certainly cannot address noncompliance by another nuclear weapon state, or indeed any large country. The dangers of a unilateral approach have been put exceptionally well by Harald Müller.[89] Müller points out that the actions of a superpower under the illusion that it can remedy compliance problems unilaterally, or supported by "alliances of the willing" ultimately erode and undermine the treaty it seeks to enforce. With that erosion, Müller states "the ability of the superpower to enforce agreements unilaterally will decline. It will become apparent just how much previous compliance policy, even if it was executed unilaterally and criticized by many, relied upon the acquiescence or silent support of treaty communities that supported the norms and rules that were to be enforced." What follows is "pure power politics based on perceived (likely short-term and narrowly defined) national interests."

Aside from the assertion of a right to unilateral action, the December policy description of counterproliferation also discusses the potential use by the United States of nuclear weapons to confront proliferation, as discussed in the preceding section. We simply reiterate here the conclusion from that section that this sort of exceptionalism—in this case, the right to use nuclear weapons first—undermines the still-powerful existing norm against any use of nuclear weapons.

The trouble with counterproliferation is that it demeans international norms. This has been put well by Randy Rydell, a senior political affairs officer in the U.N. Department for Disarmament Affairs:

> In recent years, "counter-proliferation" has received increased attention, and not just in the United States, as a means to cope with the threats posed by these materials. This policy or doctrine, as the case may be, is in essence a regulatory scheme, one that simply draws more on military responses to the problem—it reserves its prohibitory language for specific cases and avoids universal norms. It tacitly assumes the eternal availability of the relevant bomb materials and offers nothing by way of global prohibitory norms relating to the production or use of such materials. Yet the adequacy or effectiveness of such an approach is open to serious question, particularly when the central security problem is defined as global in scope and inescapability tied to the realities of threats posed by weapons-usable nuclear materials, wherever they may be.[90]

Strengthened Safeguards and the Role of Special U.N.-Mandated Inspections

Iraq's clandestine nuclear program before the first Gulf War led to the development by the IAEA of strengthened safeguards procedures, allowing the IAEA to look for undeclared nuclear activities. The establishment and experiences of UNSCOM and UNMOVIC showed the possibilities of united Security Council actions to seek out and, if necessary, to destroy, weapons of mass destruction. The abrupt decision of North Korea to withdraw from the NPT illustrates the fragility of the current nonproliferation regime. The construction by Iran of several facilities which do not appear to be needed for civilian nuclear power, but which could be highly relevant to a nuclear weapons program, suggests the value of ensuring to the extent practical that countries cannot simply end all safeguards by withdrawing from the NPT. All of these experiences suggest the value of a strengthened safeguards system along the following lines.

The Adoption Universally of the IAEA Additional Protocol, INFCIRC 540

As noted, in the wake of the discovery that Iraq before the first Gulf War, while a seemingly a compliant party to the NPT, had underway a very substantial clandestine nuclear weapons program, the IAEA developed an additional safeguards protocol allowing the agency to look for undeclared nuclear activities in a country as well as inspecting declared facilities. This strengthened safeguards system, INFCIRC 540, has now been accepted by several important countries, but others remain outside the system. In the latter category is Iran. The United States, along with other countries, has called for a strong effort to make adherence to the additional protocol universal. Were this done, it would be much more difficult for countries to prepare a nuclear weapons program in secret, setting the stage for an eventual withdrawal from the NPT.

Declaration of New Facilities Prior to Construction

In 1992, the IAEA called on all countries to notify the Agency at the initial stages of planning and constructing new nuclear facilities. Under the then-existing safeguards agreement, a country was not obliged to do this until six months before it was planning to introduce nuclear material into the facility. And Iran had not accepted the IAEA call before its centrifuge work at Nantanz was made public by others. Thus, this work and the secrecy surrounding it did not violate any existing agreement. Again, it will be critical to make the notification called for universal.

Backup Safeguards

Under the NPT, all nuclear facilities and nuclear material in nonnuclear weapon states must be put under IAEA safeguards. But there is a question of what happens to the safeguards once a country withdraws from the treaty. In some cases, where the facilities and material have been supplied through exports by other countries, these countries may have residual bilateral safeguards rights. For example, the United States apparently has such rights on reactors and other technologies it has exported. In cases such as these, a country could not simply shake off safeguards by an NPT withdrawal. Of course, it could seek to end the bilateral safeguards also, but this would require another, and perhaps more politically costly, action. For example, there would be a stronger barrier to proliferation by Iran if Russian aid in completing the Bushehr reactor carried also bilateral safeguards as well as Iran's acceptance of IAEA safeguards under its NPT obligations. Indigenous nuclear programs in Iran—which its centrifuge and heavy-water programs may be—would not lend themselves to residual safeguards in the same way as imported facilities and materials; but possibly there could be ways to persuade Iran to accept such backup safeguards, which would come into play if Iran withdrew from the NPT.

Enforcing Compliance

Strengthening safeguards, making nuclear weapons programs more difficult to conceal, and increasing the political costs of a country proliferating are important goals. But what if a country is willing to incur the political costs?

As noted earlier, several arms control treaties call in extremis for parties to seek compliance through action by the Security Council, which could authorize the use of force or the application of sanctions. However, as the United Nations Association of the USA (UNA-USA) points out, while "several nonproliferation treaties and agreements provide that violations can or must be referred to the Security Council, not one of them specifies what action the Council should take."[91]

One possible course might be to institutionalize and make permanent a group such as UNMOVIC. The idea would be to have this group ready to enter a country where proliferation suspicions have been raised (as was the case in Iraq in 2003) to look for all weapons of mass destruction, with the activation of the group to be authorized by a Security Council resolution. If a country denies such access or otherwise does not cooperate with the inspections, the council could then authorize sanctions, and in extremis, force.

To make such council action credible, the veto powers of the permanent members of the Security Council might have to be altered in some way. In a book detailing his efforts to oversee the dismantling and monitoring of Iraq's weapons programs, Richard Butler argues that there are few issues facing the international community grave enough to warrant an exceptional level of action and agreement among the five permanent members of the Security Council. Chief among these is the need to control and ultimately eliminate weapons of mass destruction. Butler calls on the Permanent Five to act in concert to enforce nonproliferation treaties by, among other things, not threatening use of the veto in a way that would preclude any useful collective action to remedy serious cases of noncompliance.[92]

We realize the difficulties of modifying Security Council veto procedures— a host of unintended consequences are not hard to conjure up. But we believe that the Butler idea should be further explored.

Smart Sanctions

During the Cold War, with the threat of Security Council vetoes by the United States and Soviet Union, multilateral sanctions were rarely imposed. Before 1990, the U.N. Security Council imposed them twice—against Rhodesia in 1966 and South Africa in 1977.[93] Since 1990, the council has acted on numerous occasions, imposing sanctions against Iraq, the former Yugoslavia, Libya, Liberia, Somalia, Cambodia, Haiti, Angola, Rwanda, Sudan, Sierra Leone, and Afghanistan. At the same time, economic sanctions have become increasingly important to U.S. policy: more than thirty-five countries were targeted by American sanctions from 1993 to 1996.[94] A report by the U.S. International Trade Commission identified some sixteen separate laws mandating sanctions for various actions related to missile, nuclear, biological, or chemical weapons proliferation.[95] If terrorism-related sanctions are added, the list doubles.

The economic costs and foreign policy efficacy of traditional sanctions are now under increasing attack. The seminal study, conducted by Gary Hufbauer, Jeffrey Schott, and Kimberly Ann Elliott, concluded that in 115 cases of sanctions, both bilateral and multilateral (but predominantly bilateral), imposed between 1914 and 1990, forty cases performed well enough to be judged a credible alternative to military force.[96] This conclusion has been questioned most forcefully by Robert Pape, who has argued that virtually none of the forty so-called successes stand up to the scrutiny of hindsight. More generally, he asserts that a state's determination to pursue its own policy objectives will usually stand independent of threats of economic punishment.[97] Furthermore, the humanitarian suffering caused by economic sanctions become a rallying point for besieged nations and can incite less rather than more compliance.[98]

The efficacy and economic costs of unilateral sanctions are also under increasing attack in the United States. The executive branch resents Congress' attempts to legislate foreign policy with the blunt instrument of sanctions, and questions their effectiveness in achieving foreign policy goals.[99] U.S. industry points to their economic cost.[100]

Calls for making sanctions "smarter," that is, targeted more directly on the states, policies, and individuals claimed to be in noncompliance, are increasingly voiced in U.S. debates. Targeted or "smart" sanctions may take the form of sanctions on financial transactions, arms embargoes, or travel restrictions. For instance, there are efforts to link access to U.S. capital markets as a sanction, specifically against China.[101] The Interlaken process, sponsored by Switzerland, has focused primarily on using the technology and tactics of anti-money laundering forces to locate sanctioned financial assets, monitor their movement and identify their true owners.[102] The Bonn-Berlin process, an initiative of the German Foreign Office, has sought to improve the efficacy of arms embargoes and travel or aviation-related sanctions, which are most often cited as targeted or "smart" sanctions.[103]

Several scholars have noted that smart sanctions have produced mixed results. Richard Haass somewhat sardonically has called them "not so smart sanctions."[104] The problem is that money is fungible and it can be extraordinarily difficult to limit access in a globalized economy. Cortright and Lopez point out that targeted financial sanctions, applied to Iraq, various former-Yugoslav entities, and UNITA in Angola, had little impact, except possibly in the case of Serbia, where nearly $3 billion in assets were frozen.[105] In a detailed analysis of smart sanctions in practice, Beate Bull and Arne Tostensen conclude that, while well intentioned, smart sanction regimes are too often unenforceable and beset by operational and institutional weaknesses.[106] They point out that there are significant limitations to the ability of the United Nations and NGOs, for example, to adequately monitor the humanitarian impact of sanctions, and that some of features of smart sanctions, for example, limiting the duration of sanctions a priori, may make it more difficult to compel compliance. Importantly, the authors also note that, though one of the most persuasive arguments in favor of sanctions is that they are a "soft tool of persuasion" in lieu of military force, in practice the use of sanctions has often escalated to military action.

Regardless of the form sanctions may take, the fact remains that the capacity to use, or withstand, sanctions reflects a state's economic and political strength. Studies of sanctions suggest that successful economic (or more accurately humanitarian) and thus political coercion depends on the extent of the asymmetries between the sanctioner(s) and the sanctioned, most notably the weakness of the target state's economy, its lack of alternative supply and markets, and its incapacity to produce appropriate substitutes.[107] Thus, states with large, globalized economies are able to both impose and withstand sanctions with little social or economic pain. States with smaller and less globalized economies are both inherently less capable of using sanctions and more vulnerable to them. International action against noncompliance through this mechanism becomes heavily dependent on a single state or group of states, particularly those that are relatively invulnerable to reciprocal action.

Citizen Compliance

As we noted earlier, an intriguing aspect of the Landmine Convention is its use of citizen monitoring. Compliance is to be achieved through exposing noncompliance to the scrutiny of national and international public opinion by nongovernmental organizations, in the words of Laurie Weisberg, "the eyes and ears of the human rights machinery."[108] The NGOs would focus not only on how states parties fulfill the narrowly defined legal terms of the treaty, but also on the actions of those corporations, individuals, nonstate actors, and nonsignatory countries involved in landmine manufacture, use, and export.

Criminalization and Individual Responsibility

Matthew Meselson and Julian Robinson have examined the issue of individual responsibility, proposing in 2001 a draft convention that would make it a crime for individuals to "develop, produce, acquire, retain, transfer or use" biological and chemical weapons under international law. Specifically, they have called for a new treaty that would define "specific acts involving biological or chemical weapons as international crimes, like piracy or aircraft hijacking."[109] Any person committing such acts would "face prosecution or extradition" should that person be found in the territory of a state party to the convention. Meselson and Robinson make clear that the act must be committed "knowingly" to be considered criminal. An admissible defense might be if the accused "reasonably believed" that the conduct in question was not prohibited; acting on orders from a superior would not constitute an acceptable defense.

The issue of a reasonable defense is not an insignificant one in totalitarian states like North Korea or Iraq, where scientists faced severe penalties for refusing work in weapons research and development. Even in the absence of a convention proposed by Meselson and Robinson, the issue of individual responsibility hangs over the current occupation of Iraq, where United States and United Kingdom authorities are encountering reluctance among former weapons scientists to be forthcoming with information about prohibited weapons for fear of prosecution. One obvious remedy, not yet widely promoted by occupying forces, would be to offer immunity in exchange for relevant information.

Another possibility for enforcing compliance has been offered by Ashton Carter and William Perry. They propose targeting individuals and groups within a state rather than the country itself. They call for making prohibited weapon development a universal individual crime for which individual offenders could be subjected to prosecution and extradition wherever they may be found. The idea uses the power of national criminal law against individual criminals, rather than the power of international law against governments. It builds on analogous developments in the law of piracy and treaties declaring the criminality of airplane hijacking, crimes of maritime navigation, theft of nuclear materials, and crimes against diplomats.[110]

Developing this idea, Michael Scharf argues that the international community should apply international criminal law to prosecute and punish offending leaders before an international tribunal or domestic courts. Unlike sanctions or the use of force, "criminalization avoids collective punishment by directly targeting those responsible for the international violations . . . and can strengthen international political will to maintain sanctions and take more aggressive actions if necessary."[111]

Barry Kellman and David Gualtieri consider analogous responses to nuclear smuggling and similar activities that presumably would not have state sanction. They call for international criminal enforcement of laws to "investigate, apprehend, and prosecute those who engage in illicit weapons activities." Their goal is an integrated legal regime in which "arms control and criminal law enforcement—two previously-unrelated branches of international law—can be implemented explicitly for maximum efficacy."[112] Kellman takes this a step further in subsequent writings, likening the use of biological agents to slavery or torture and meriting designation as a *"jus cogens* crime against humanity." He highlights significant gaps in existing laws, in particular the absence of laws prohibiting possession of biological agents, which undermine law enforcement.[113] He proposes a dual system of national penal legislation to criminalize "preparation, assistance and construction of relevant facilities to produce biological weapons" and international regulatory standards under which each state would "accept the obligation to extradite or prosecute suspected perpetrators."[114]

These suggestions pose the obvious question about what should be classed as "prohibited" or "illicit" activities, and how that would be determined. The

United States and other nuclear weapons states may well accept that biological and chemical weapons work should be prohibited, but not accept that work on nuclear weapons falls into the same category, despite the prevailing treaty obligations and norms against possession of nuclear weapons.

The criminalization approach can be effected in a way more consonant with international norms, through an international convention along the lines of the "Harvard-Sussex Draft" cited above.[115] The use of criminal law to hold individuals responsible to an international convention already exists in the form of the International Criminal Court (ICC), which was created to investigate and prosecute genocide, crimes against humanity, and war crimes.[116] The convention for the establishment of the court was agreed to on July 17, 1998, and has so far been signed by 144 states (the United States, China, Israel, India, and Pakistan are all nonsignatories). The United States, in particular, objects to a court that could indict U.S. citizens without its consent and continues to withhold support for the ICC.[117]

Societal and individual responsibility may be developed more positively than these suggestions of criminal liability. Joseph Rotblat, Nobel Laureate and one of the founders of the Pugwash movement, has argued persuasively that exposing malfeasance should become part of the scientist's duty and overall ethos.[118] More generally, active civil society organizations and citizens could become the ultimate guarantors of compliance by states.

Conclusion

While the above ideas, and others, are worthy of further study, we recall Müller's observation that "findings about institutional weaknesses should not be construed as relieving the actors, especially the leading ones, of their basic duty to play by the rules and to integrate themselves into the multilateral frameworks that need to be saved, maintained, and improved if states are to enjoy the security benefits that multilateral arms control can provide."[119]

Such willingness to play by the rules appears especially critical where compliance must depend on a powerful response by a united Security Council, supported by a largely united international community when confronted with a country's defection from an international norm. This is all the more the case in instances where the norm in question is not embedded in an explicit treaty commitment. At the top of the list of such instances, we would place the prospect that some country will seek to withdraw from one of the multilateral treaties on weapons of mass destruction upon due notice of intent to withdraw as required by the letter of the treaty. This eventuality, in our view, presents one of the most serious "compliance gaps" now existing, and the one requiring today the most urgent attention and a clear international consensus on how to proceed.

Notes

1. Initially, the two authors, along with Zia Mian, set out to do two chapters, one reflecting an essentially "northern" point of view and one a more "southern," that is one representing the perspectives of the nonnuclear weapon states outside of the political orbits of the great powers. We then decided that we could better represent the conflicting viewpoints in a single chapter, while not disguising differences where they arise. As we worked together to this end we came around to the first goal of producing two chapters. This chapter, however, includes much material that we worked on together; and the authors wish to acknowledge significant contributions by Zia Mian.

2. Abram Chayes and Antonia Handler Chayes, *The New Sovereignty: Compliance with International Regulatory Agreements* (Cambridge, MA: Harvard University Press, 1995), 22.

3. Chayes and Chayes, *The New Sovereignty*, 22.

4. See Article XV of the ABM Treaty; Article XV of the INF; and Article XVII of START.

5. For an examination of the ABM Treaty and the issue over the Soviet Union's Krasnoyarsk radar facility, see Harald Müller, "The Internalization of Principles, Norms, and Rules by Governments: The Case of Security Regimes," in Volker Rittberger and Peter Mayer, eds., *Regime Theory and International Relations* (Oxford: Clarendon Press, 1993), 361-88.

6. James Dao, "Democrats Are Warned on Missile Stance," *Washington Post*, July 17, 2001.

7. "Preservation of and Compliance with the Anti-Ballistic Missile Treaty," 54th Session, Disarmament and International Security Committee (First Committee), A/C.1/54/L.1, 12 October 1999.

8. Philipp C. Bleek, "Russia Ratifies START II, Extension Protocol; ABM-Related Agreements Also Approved," *Arms Control Today*, 30, no. 4 (May 2000): 39-42. See also David E. Sanger, "Bush Offers Arms Talks to China as U.S. Pulls Out of ABM Treaty," *New York Times*, December 14, 2001.

9. Camille Grand, "Missile Defense: The View from the Other Side of the Atlantic," *Arms Control Today*, 30, no. 7 (September 2000): 12-18.

10. *Rationale and Requirements for U.S. Nuclear Forces and Arms Control* (Fairfax, VA: National Institute for Public Policy, January 2001), 105.

11. Current MTCR members are Argentina, Australia, Austria, Belgium, Brazil, Canada, Czech Republic, Denmark, Finland, France, Germany, Greece, Hungary, Iceland, Ireland, Italy, Japan, Luxembourg, The Netherlands, New Zealand, Norway, Poland, Portugal, Russia, South Africa, Spain, Sweden, Switzerland, Turkey, Ukraine, United Kingdom, United States.

12. Norman Kempster and Rone Tempest, "U.S. Imposes Sanctions on China, Pakistan Over Missile Deal; Arms Technology: Export of Satellite Gear to Beijing Is Banned. Both Asian Nations Deny Violating Controls," *Los Angeles Times*, August 26 1993.

13. Sanctions were imposed June 25, 1991, and waived April 7, 1992 (*Federal Register* 57, 11768). On August 24, 1993 sanctions were imposed and waived on November 1, 1994 (*Federal Register* 59, 55522).

14. Jane Perlez, "China to Stop Selling A-Arms Delivery Systems," *New York Times*, November 22, 2000.

15. Andrew J. Pierre, ed., *Cascade of Arms: Managing Conventional Weapons Proliferation* (Washington, D.C.: Brookings Institution Press, 1997).

16. CFE: Conventional Armed Forces in Europe Treaty, www.acq.osd.mil/acic/treaties/cfe/cfe_es.htm.

17. Jeffrey D. McCausland, "NATO and Russian Approaches to 'Adapting' the CFE Treaty," *Arms Control Today*, 27, no. 5 (August 1997): 12-18.

18. The Wassenaar agreement website is http://www.wassenaar.org/; its members are Argentina, Australia, Austria, Belgium, Bulgaria, Canada, Czech Republic, Denmark, Finland, France, Germany, Greece, Hungary, Ireland, Italy, Japan, Luxembourg, Netherlands, New Zealand, Norway, Poland, Portugal, Republic of Korea, Romania, Russian Federation, Slovak Republic, Spain, Sweden, Switzerland, Turkey, Ukraine, United Kingdom, and the United States.

19. In 1993, data on exports and imports agreed on what was bought and sold only 22 percent of the time, www.dfait-maeci.gc.ca/arms/convweap2-e.asp.

20. National reports on implementation of the Program of Action (PoA) can be found at http://disarmament.un.org/cab/salw-nationalreports.html.

21. The website for the Convention on the Prohibition of the Use, Stockpiling, Production and Transfer of Anti-personnel Landmines and on Their Destruction, Ottawa, 1997 is at www.icbl.org.

22. Article VIII.

23. "Alliant and Textron Team for New Anti-Personnel Landmine Alternative," *Defense Daily*, June 28, 2000.

24. Laurie Weisberg, "The Role of Civil Organizations in Monitoring the Convention on the Prohibition of the Use, Stockpiling, Production, and Transfer of Anti-personnel Mines and on Their Destruction: A Proposal for a Cooperative Compliance Mechanism," in Peter Gizewski, ed., *Non-Proliferation, Arms Control and Disarmament: Enhancing Existing Regimes and Exploring New Dimensions* (Toronto: Centre for International and Security Studies, 1998).

25. Kenneth R. Rutherford, "The Evolving Arms Control Agenda: Implications of the Role of NGOs in Banning Antipersonnel Landmines," *World Politics* 53, no. 1 (October 2000): 74.

26. See IAEA statutes, www.iaea.org/worldatom/Documents/statute.html.

27. Richard Lugar, statement, released October 7, 1999. Much of the statement is reprinted in *The Bulletin of the Atomic Scientists* (January/February 2000): 44-46.

28. Henry A. Kissinger, "Arms Control to Suit a New World," *Los Angeles Times*, November 21, 1999.

29. Statement delivered by Assistant Secretary of State John S. Wolf, Second Meeting of the 2005 NPT Review Conference, Geneva, April 28, 2003. Text at www.state.gov/t/np/rls/rm/20034.htm

30. Dan Plesch, senior researcher at the Royal United Services Institute, as quoted by Peter Popham, "Nuclear War Risk Grows as States Race to Acquire Bomb; Geneva Fears Grow of Further Defections from Non-Proliferation Treaty," *The Guardian* (London), April 29, 2003.

31. Graham S. Pearson, "The Protocol to the Biological Weapons Convention Is within Reach," *Arms Control Today*, 30, no. 5 (June 2000): 15-20.

32. Michael Moodie "The BCW Protocol: A Critique." Special Report No. 1, (Washington: DC: Chemical and Biological Arms Control Institute (CBACI), 2001): 12-13.

33. Robert Mulcare, "A Critical Analysis of the Chemical Weapons Convention and the Biological and Toxin Weapons Convention," May 2003, Princeton University. This paper was done for a Woodrow Wilson School Policy Task Force, "The Proliferation of Weapons of Mass Destruction," Spring 2003, under the direction of Harold A. Feiveson.

34. Donald Mahley, "Statement by the United States to the Ad Hoc Group of Biological Weapons Convention States Parties," Geneva, July 25, 2001, www.state.gov/t/ac/rls/rm/2001/5497.htm.

35. Statement by President George W. Bush. "Strengthening the International Regime against Biological Weapons," November 2001, www.state.gov/t/ac/rls/rm/2001/7907.htm.

36. George Bunn, "The Status of Norms against Nuclear Testing," *The Nonproliferation Review* 6, no. 2 (Winter 1999): 20-32.

37. U.N. Security Council resolution 687, April 3, 1991, Section C, para 8. Subsequently, numerous crises between Iraq and U.N./IAEA inspectors resulted in Security Council pleas to cooperate and tacit warnings of further actions if compliance was not forthcoming. Furthermore, this and subsequent Iraq resolutions were adopted under Chapter VII of the U.N. charter, permitting the use of force in situations that threaten international peace and security.

38. For details, see the UNSCOM website at www.un.org/Depts/unscom/unscom.htm.

39. Seymour Hersh, "Saddam's Best Friend," *The New Yorker*, April 5, 1999.

40. UNSCOM also found documentary evidence that Iraq had weaponized a biological agent with a "time to effect of greater than one week." This is not consistent with either anthrax or botulinum toxin but could be *Clostridium perfringens* spores of which Iraq admitted producing 340 liters but denied weaponizing.

41. Information retrieved from www.un.org/Depts/unscom/Achievements/achievements.html.

42. U.N. Security Council resolution 707, August 15, 1991, para. 3(ii).

43. "Letter dated 15 December 1998 from the Executive Chairman of the Special Commission . . . pursuant to paragraph 9 (b) (i) of Security Council resolution 687 (1991) to the Secretary-General," www.un.org/Depts/unscom/s98-1172.htm.

44. Article 100 of the U.N. Charter states that: "1. In the performance of their duties the Secretary-General and the staff shall not seek or receive instructions from any government or from any other authority external to the Organization. They shall refrain from any action which might reflect on their position as international officials responsible only to the Organization. 2. Each Member of the United Nations undertakes to respect the exclusively international character of the responsibilities of the Secretary-General and the staff and not to seek to influence them in the discharge of their responsibilities."

45. Preambular paragraph two of U.N. Security Council resolution 1284 states (emphasis added): ". . . that UNMOVIC will undertake the responsibilities mandated to the Special Commission by the Council with regard to the verification of compliance by Iraq with its obligations under paragraphs 8, 9 and 10 of resolution 687 (1991) and other related resolutions, that UNMOVIC will establish and operate, as was recommended by the panel on disarmament and current and future ongoing monitoring and verification issues, a reinforced system of ongoing monitoring and verification, which will implement the plan approved by the Council in resolution 715 (1991) and address unresolved disarmament issues, and that UNMOVIC will identify, as necessary in accordance with its mandate, additional sites in Iraq to be covered by the reinforced system of ongoing monitoring and verification."

46. Remarks of the president on Iraq, December 19, 1998, www.whitehouse.gov/WH/New/html/19981219-2655.html.

47. Results of the 1999 Iraq Child and Maternal Mortality Surveys, UNICEF, 1999, www.unicef.org/reseval/iraqr.htm.

242   *Harold A. Feiveson and Jacqueline W. Shire*

48. U.N. Office of the Iraq Programme, Fact Sheet, www.un.org/Depts/oip/latest/basfact_000610.html.

49. Human Rights Watch letter to the U.N. Security Council, January 4, 2000, www.hrw.org/hrw/press/2000/01/iraq-ltr.htm.

50. Phyllis Bennis, "And They Called It Peace: U.S. Policy on Iraq," *Middle East Report* 215 (Summer 2000).

51. Some Iraqi physicians ordered by the Ba'ath leadership to blame sanctions for the deaths of infants and children have since come forward to admit that so-called baby parades were staged events for the international media and that Iraq had the financial resources to import the medicines it required even under sanctions. Matthew McAllister, "Blood of Innocents: Doctors Say Hussein, Not UN Sanctions, Caused Children's Deaths," *Newsday*, May 23, 2003.

52. Text of the resolution is available at www.un.org/Depts/unmovic/.

53. Colin L. Powell, "Remarks to the Security Council.," February 5, 2003, www.state.gov/secretary/rm/2003/17300.htm.

54. See "Cluster Document" at www.un.org/Depts/unmovic/.

55. "Legal Basis for Use of Force against Iraq," www.number-10.gov.uk/output/Page3287.asp.

56. U.N. Security Council resolution 825, May 11, 1993.

57. Gilbert A. Lewthwaite, "Perry warns of North Korea 'Nightmare'," *Baltimore Sun*, February 3, 1994.

58. Lee Sigal, *Disarming Strangers: Nuclear Diplomacy with North Korea* (Princeton, NJ: Princeton University Press, 1998), 75 and 244.

59. James T. Laney and Jason T. Shaplen, "How to Deal with North Korea," *Foreign Affairs* 82, no. 2 (March/April 2003): 16.

60. Agreed Framework between the United States of America and the Democratic People's Republic of Korea, Geneva, October 21, 1994, www.kedo.org/pdfs/AgreedFramework.pdf.

61. "U.S. Exploring N. Korean's Remark about Scrapping Missile Program," *Washington Post*, September 1, 2000.

62. Colin Robinson and Stephen Baker, "Stand-off with North Korea: War Scenarios and Consequences" (Washington, D.C.: Center for Defense Information, 2003).

63. In the president's words, "States like these [Iraq, Iran, and North Korea], and their terrorist allies, constitute an axis of evil, arming to threaten the peace of the world. By seeking weapons of mass destruction, these regimes pose a grave and growing danger. They could provide these arms to terrorists, giving them the means to match their hatred. They could attack our allies or attempt to blackmail the United States. In any of these cases, the price of indifference would be catastrophic." President George W. Bush, State of the Union Address, January 29, 2002, www.whitehouse.gov/news/releases/2002/01/20020129-11.html.

64. "Statement of Foreign Ministry Spokesman Blasts UNSC's Discussion of Korean Nuclear Issue," Korean Central News Agency (KCNA), April 6, 2003, www.acronym.org.uk/docs/0304/doc01.htm.

65. Barbara Demick, "Seoul's Vulnerability Is Key to War Scenarios; Any U.S. Strike on the North May Provoke a Catastrophic Retaliation against South's Capital," *Los Angeles Times,* May 27, 2003.

66. Remarks spoken at the Brookings Institution as reported by Barbara Demick, "Seoul's Vulnerability Is Key to War Scenarios."

67. John Wolf, Statement to the Second Session of the Preparatory Committee for the 2005 Review Conference of the Parties to the Treaty on the Non-proliferation of Nuclear Weapons, April 28, 2003, Geneva, http://usinfo.state.gov.

68. David Albright and Corey Hinderstein, "Furor over Fuel," *Bulletin of the Atomic Scientists* 59, no. 3 (May/June 2003): 12-15.

69. Wolf statement.

70. Mark Landler, "U.S. and UN Press Iran on Nuclear Program," *New York Times*, June 18, 2003, 3.

71. Steven Lee, "Nuclear Proliferation and Nuclear Entitlement," *Ethics and International Affairs*, 9 (1995): 101-31.

72. Verbatim record of the First Plenary Meeting, London, January 10, 1946, www.un.org/Depts/dhl/landmark/amajor.htm#Digitization%20Programme.

73. The White House, *National Strategy to Combat the Proliferation of Weapons of Mass Destruction*, December 2002, www.whitehouse.gov/news/releases/2002/12/WMDStrategy.pdf.

74. Robert Nelson, "Low-Yield Earth Penetrating Nuclear Weapons," *Science & Global Security* 10, no. 3 (2002): 1-20.

75. For treaty text, see Preparatory Commission for the Comprehensive Nuclear-Test-Ban Treaty Organization at www.ctbto.org/ctbto/treaty.html.

76. Andrew Lichterman and Jacqueline Cabasso, *A Faustian Bargain: Why Stockpile Stewardship is Incompatible With the Process of Nuclear Disarmament* (Oakland, CA: Western States Legal Foundation, March 1998).

77. President Clinton's letter of transmittal of treaty to U.S. Senate, September 22, 1997, www.clw.org/ef/ctbtbook/clinton.html.

78. Christopher E. Paine and Matthew G. McKinzie, "End Run: The U.S. Government's Plan for Designing Nuclear Weapons and Simulating Nuclear Explosions under the Comprehensive Test Ban Treaty" (Washington, D.C.: National Resource Defense Council, August 1997), 23.

79. Greg Mello, "That Old Designing Fever," *Bulletin of the Atomic Scientists* 56, no. 1 (January/February 2000): 51-7.

80. Erik J. Leklem, "CWC Implementing Legislation Passed by Senate; Future Uncertain," *Arms Control Today* 28, no. 4 (May 1998): 30.

81. "The CWC at the Two-Year Mark: An Interview with Dr. John Gee," *Arms Control Today* 29, no. 3 (April/May 1999): 3-9.

82. Hans Kristensen and Joshua Handler, "The USA and Counterproliferation: A New and Dubious Role for U.S. Nuclear Weapons," *Security Dialogue* 27, no. 4 (December 1996): 387-99.

83. The White House, *National Strategy to Combat the Proliferation of Weapons of Mass Destruction*.

84. See the discussion in Michael P. Scharf, "Clear and Present Danger: Enforcing the International Ban on Biological and Chemical Weapons through Sanctions, Use of Force, and Criminalization," *Michigan Journal of International Law* 20, no. 3 (Spring 1999): 477-523.

85. U.N. Security Council resolution 487, June 18, 1981. "Strongly condemns the military attack by Israel in clear violation of the Charter of the United Nations and the norms of international conduct. . . . Calls upon Israel to refrain in the future from any such acts or threats thereof . . . considers that the said attack constitutes a serious threat to the entire IAEA safeguards regime. . . . Calls upon Israel urgently to place its nuclear facilities under IAEA safeguards. . . . Considers that Iraq is entitled to appropriate redress for the destruction it has suffered."

86. Michael Klare, *Rogue States and Nuclear Outlaws: America's Search for a New Foreign Policy* (New York: Hill and Wang, 1995), 213.

87. Barry M. Blechman and Tamara Cofma Wittes, *Defining Moment: The Threat and Use of Force in American Foreign Policy since 1989* (Washington, D.C.: Henry L. Stimson Center, Occasional Paper no. 6, May 1998).

88. See also Harald Müller and Mitchell Reiss, "Counterproliferation: Putting New Wine in Old Bottles," *Washington Quarterly* 18. no. 2 (Spring 1995): 143-54. Of course, the United States also was willing to consider armed intervention during the Cold War. See Barry M. Blechman and Stephen S. Kaplan, *Force without War, US Armed Forces as a Political Instrument* (Washington, D.C.: The Brookings Institution, 1978), 547-53.

89. Harald Müller, "Compliance Politics: A Critical Analysis of Multilateral Arms Control Treaty Enforcement," *The Nonproliferation Review* 7, no. 2 (Summer 2000): 77-90, esp. 87.

90. Randy J. Rydell, "Fissile Nuclear Materials and the Future of Nuclear Disarmament and Non-Proliferation," Conference on Nuclear Non-Proliferation, hosted by the Center of Analysis and Planning, Greek Ministry of Foreign Affairs, Athens, Greece, May 30-31, 2003, 2.

91. Report of the UNA-USA Project on the Security Council and Nonproliferation, *Confronting the Proliferation Danger: The Role of the U.N. Security Council* (New York: United Nations Association of the USA, 1995), p. 6.

92. Richard Butler, *The Greatest Threat: Iraq, Weapons of Mass Destruction and the Crisis of Global Security* (New York: Public Affairs, 2000), 233.

93. David Cortright and George Lopez, *The Sanctions Decade Assessing UN Strategies in the 1990s* (Boulder, CO: Lynne Rienner, 2000), 1.

94 Richard N. Haass, ed., *Economic Sanctions and American Diplomacy* (New York: Council on Foreign Relations, 1998), 1.

95. *Overview and Analysis of Current U.S. Unilateral Economic Sanctions* (Washington, D.C.: U.S. International Trade Commission, August 1998).

96. Gary Hufbauer, Jeffrey Schott, and Kimberly Ann Elliott, *Economic Sanctions Reconsidered: History and Current Policy* (Washington, D.C.: Institute for International Economics, 1985, and 2nd ed., 1990). A third edition analyzing 170 cases of economic sanctions was published in June 2001.

97. Robert Pape, "Why Economic Sanctions Do Not Work," *International Security* 22, no. 2 (Fall 1997): 90-136.

98. Margaret P. Doxey, *International Sanctions in Contemporary Perspective* (Houndmills, United Kingdom: Macmillan Press, 2nd ed., 1996).

99. Doxey, *International Sanctions in Contemporary Perspective*.

100. Another study by the Institute for International Economic found that, in 1995 alone, sanctions reduced U.S. exports by between $15 and 19 billion. Gary Clyde Hufbauer, Kimberly Ann Elliott, Tess Cyrus, and Elizabeth Winston, "U.S. Economic Sanctions: Their Impact on Trade, Jobs and Wages," Working Paper Special (Washington, D.C. Institute for International Economics, 1997).

101. Thomas Catan, Joshua Chaffin, and Stephen Fidler, "U.S. Markets Could Be Foreign Policy Tool," *Financial Times*, May 24, 2000.

102. Second Interlaken Seminar on Targeting United Nations Financial Sanctions, March 29-31, 1999, www.smartsanctions.ch/int2_papers.htm.

103. See research papers from the expert seminars of the Bonn International Center for Conversion (BICC) on *Smart Sanctions: The Next Step—Arms Embargoes and Travel Sanctions*, www.bicc.de/info/.

104. Richard N. Haass, "Sanctioning Madness," *Foreign Affairs* 76, no. 6 (November/December 1997): 74-85.

105. Cortright and Lopez, *The Sanctions Decade*, 210.

106. Beate Bull and Arne Tostensen, "Are Smart Sanctions Feasible?" *World Politics* 54, no. 3 (April 2002): 373-403.

107. Doxey, *International Sanctions in Contemporary Perspective.*

108. Laurie Weisberg, "The Role of Civil Organizations in Monitoring the Convention on the Prohibition of the Use, Stockpiling, Production, and Transfer of Antipersonnel Mines."

109. Matthew Meselson and Julian Robinson, "A Draft Convention to Prohibit Biological and Chemical Weapons under International Criminal Law," Harvard Sussex Program on CBW Armament and Arms Limitation, November 1, 2001, www.fas.harvard.edu/~hsp/crim01.pdf.

110. Ashton Carter and William Perry, *Preventive Defense: A New Security Strategy for America* (Washington, D.C.: Brookings Institution, Washington, 1999).

111. Michael P. Scharf, "Clear and Present Danger."

112. Barry Kellman and David Gualtieri, "Barricading the Nuclear Window—a Legal Regime to Curtail Nuclear Smuggling," *University of Illinois Law Review* 96, no. 3 (1996): 667-741.

113. Barry Kellman, "Responses to the September 11 Attacks: An International Criminal Law Approach to Bioterrorism," *Harvard Journal of Law and Public Policy* 25 (Spring 2002): 721-42.

114. Kellman, "Responses to the September 11 Attacks." See also, Barry Kellman, "Biological Terrorism: Legal Measures for Preventing Catastrophe," *Harvard Journal of Law and Public Policy* 24 (Spring 2001), 417-61.

115. "A Draft Convention to Prohibit Biological and Chemical Weapons under International Criminal Law," *The CBW Conventions Bulletin* 42 (December 1998), www.fas.harvard.edu/~hsp/pdf.html.

116. See Human Rights Watch, www.hrw.org/campaigns/icc/icc-main.htm.

117. Coalition for an International Criminal Court, www.igc.org/icc/index.html.

118. See Joseph Rotblat, The Nobel Lecture, 1995, www.pgs.ca/pages/mem/rotblnpa.html.

119. Müller, "Compliance Politics," 89.

9

The American Problem:
The United States and Noncompliance in the
World of Arms Control and Nonproliferation

Zia Mian

Noam Chomsky tells a story that he attributes to St. Augustine: A captured pirate was brought before the emperor Alexander the Great; "How dare you molest the sea?" asked Alexander. "How dare you molest the whole world," replied the pirate, who continued, "Because I do it with a little ship only, I am called a thief; you, doing it with a great navy, are called an emperor."[1]

In a number of ways, as Chomsky notes, the story of the pirate and emperor can serve as a powerful analogy for many contests over international power, legality, and justice in the modern world. The story is used here as a useful lens for an assessment of compliance with international nuclear arms control, nonproliferation, and disarmament treaties and with the larger set of expectations of how states should behave on these issues. It serves to link very directly the questions of identifying and dealing with noncompliance with a particular arms control agreement (or any other agreement for that matter) with the questions of who decides, and how, about what are the treaty obligations or expectations to be complied with, and what constitutes noncompliance.

The significance of such an approach becomes apparent if one asks, for instance, why the United States with its many thousands of nuclear weapons claimed a right to attack and occupy Iraq, and threatens North Korea and Iran, for having tried to acquire such weapons. Or, more generally, why is proliferation of nuclear weapons now presented as a more significant threat to global security than continued possession of these weapons? Or, why is there no international convention banning nuclear weapons despite the United Nations having called for the elimination of nuclear weapons and of all other weapons of mass destruction in the very first General Assembly resolution, on January 24, 1946?

This chapter focuses on the United States and its compliance with nuclear arms control and nonproliferation agreements. There are broad reasons for this focus. Firstly, with a view to formulating a normative perspective on compliance, it seems reasonable to insist that existing and proposed mechanisms for establishing compliance with international agreements and expectations ought to be judged by how well they can work when applied to the most powerful state in the system. The United States has had a dominant position in international relations for many decades. This position has become even more powerful with the end of the Cold War. The United States dominates the global economy; it has a military capability far greater than that of any other state; it has an almost overwhelming presence in international financial and political institutions; it has a pervasive cultural presence. These sources of power enable the United States to strongly shape the context and the conduct of government policy in other states. This includes determining the nature of international negotiations, the resulting agreements, and the interpretation of commitments therein. This is particularly important at a time when the United States' leadership believes that it should enter into treaties only "when they carve American interests in stone."[2] There are obvious implications and challenges for the international community and for democratically minded American citizens concerned that their nation should not seek to set itself above or apart from the rest of the world.

Secondly, as the dominant state in the international system the United States has been particularly concerned about noncompliance with nuclear agreements. For many years U.S. military planners, strategic analysts, associated academics, and arms control activists have sought to find means to identify and deal with noncompliance, especially in regions the United States sees as economically or politically important.[3] By and large, this search has been through the lens of U.S. national interests.[4] Not surprisingly, less scrutiny has been given to the U.S. record of noncompliance.

Thirdly, the United States is directly implicated in many of the major problems over the past decade involving compliance with both long-standing and recent nuclear arms control agreements. The United States has already withdrawn from the 1972 Anti-Ballistic Missile (ABM) Treaty, the Cold War era bilateral superpower pact banning defenses against ballistic missiles; it is the first withdrawal by any state from any arms control treaty. The future of the 1996 Comprehensive Test Ban Treaty (CTBT), which bans all nuclear weapons tests, is in doubt as the United States starts research and development of new low yield nuclear weapons. Of particular importance are concerns about its compliance, and its handling of noncompliance by others, with the 1968 Nuclear Non-Proliferation Treaty (NPT), the multilateral agreement to restrict the further spread of nuclear weapons and to eliminate existing ones. It is worth noting that, because of U.S. policy, agreements on other types of weapons of mass destruction are also in jeopardy. The United States has imposed conditions on its ratification of the 1993 Chemical Weapons Convention, including the right to refuse inspections of U.S. facilities, that are seen as violating the treaty.[5] It has also rejected the draft protocol on verification of the Biological Weapons Conventions.[6]

A similar focus has been suggested by Harald Müller, who argues that the "most powerful state in the world has slowly but visibly moved away from embracing multilateralism, international law, and international organization as central components of national policy." He argues, therefore, that rather than international organizations or the treaties dealing with arms control and disarmament, "today's problems lie in the actors" and thus any remedy must address "the actor problem."[7] Put bluntly, for the majority of the international community the "actor problem" is the *American problem*.

It may seem presumptuous to make the United States the focus of an assessment of compliance. The United States, by and large, prides itself on the seriousness with which it takes its international commitments and the efforts it makes to protect and enhance freedom and security for all. These claims are strongly held across domestic political boundaries. President Clinton's 1999 report, *A National Security Strategy for a New Century*, announces that, "at this moment in history, the United States is called upon to lead—to marshal the forces of freedom and progress; to channel the energies of the global economy into lasting prosperity; to reinforce our democratic ideals and values; to enhance American security and global peace."[8] President Bush's 2002 National Security Strategy declared,

> Today, the United States enjoys a position of unparalleled military strength and great economic and political influence. In keeping with our heritage and principles, we do not use our strength to press for unilateral advantage. We seek instead to create a balance of power that favors human freedom. . . . By making the world safer, we allow the people of the world to make their own lives better."[9]

But others have made similar claims in the past. As the story of the pirate and the emperor reveals, emperors claim legitimacy for their exercise of power by justifying it as being for the "common good," in this case protection of the law-abiding against pirates. The fact that emperors have to seek some kind of larger legitimacy indirectly registers the presence of the invisible majority, who are neither pirates nor emperors and may feel beset by both pirates and emperors. While the pirate may not care, the emperor faces more prevalent, enduring, and demanding needs to justify the empire and seek consent for imperial authority or keep facing challenges, any of which may in time become a problem.

Before proceeding further, the implicit question of whether the United States is an imperial power needs to be made explicit. Michael W. Doyle has argued that "empire" is not about territoriality as much as it is a relationship where one state uses force, or other forms of power, to control the exercise of sovereignty by another state, and offered as a definition:

> Empire . . . is a relationship, formal or informal, in which one state controls the effective political sovereignty of another political society. It can be achieved by force, by political collaboration, by economic, social or cultural dependence. Imperialism is simply the process or policy of establishing or maintaining empire.[10]

The evidence of United States imperialism is painfully clear and all too familiar to many states and people in the global South. The United States has a long history, going back to its founding, of intervening, often violently and with appalling effect, in other countries.[11] A major study of the use and threat of use of force by the United States between 1946 and 1975 lists 215 incidents in which U.S. armed forces were used "as part of a deliberate attempt by the national authorities to influence, or to be prepared to influence, specific behavior of individuals in another nation without engaging in a continuing contest of violence."[12] The list excludes actual wars. The familiar examples of U.S. intervention include the overthrow of the governments of Guatemala and Iran, its efforts to overthrow the government of Cuba, the war against Vietnam, the bombing of Cambodia and Laos, and the destabilization of Nicaragua.[13] The end of the Cold War brought little change. A follow-up study looking at the use and threat of use of force between 1989 and 1998 observed that "unencumbered by Cold War fears of sparking confrontation with the powerful Soviet Union, American policy makers turned frequently to threats and the use of force."[14] The U.S. invasion, conquest, and occupation of Afghanistan in 2001 and of Iraq in 2003, and the subsequent threats of use of force against North Korea, Syria, and Iran need to be seen as recent expressions of a more enduring pattern.

Matching the history of U.S. imperial attitudes and practices is an equally long tradition of claims to noble intent and denial of its imperial practice; the claims made by Presidents Clinton and Bush marked no new ground. William Appleman Williams has noted that for U.S. policymakers and the larger elite, "transforming the realities of expansion, conquest, and intervention into pious rhetoric about virtue, wealth, and democracy reached its culmination during the decades after World War II."[15] If anything the "pious rhetoric" has become more desperate, with growing calls to embrace the American empire as an instrument for the common good of humanity.[16] It is worth recalling Noam Chomsky's cautionary note from the time of the Vietnam War, as the United States unleashed the largest aerial bombardment in history:

> It is an article of faith that American motives are pure, and not subject to analysis. . . . Although it is nothing new in American intellectual history—or, for that matter, in the general history of imperialist apologia. . . . The long tradition of naiveté and self-righteousness that disfigures our intellectual history, however,

must serve as a warning to the Third World, if such a warning is needed, as to how our protestations of sincerity and benign intent are to be interpreted.[17]

With these considerations in mind, this essay begins with a discussion of legitimacy, fairness, and justice, introducing briefly the criteria for legitimacy and fairness in international law and institutions offered by Thomas M. Franck and the idea of justice as a process advanced by John Rawls. These ideas underlie the presumptions of community that make possible consensual international agreements—the alternative being the imposition of an arrangement, with compliance becoming a synonym for obedience. They also serve to establish a context for judging the institutions, processes, and outcomes associated with the origin, nature, and enforcement of arms control and nonproliferation agreements.

The following section looks at the origins and development of nuclear arms control and its place in the policies of the superpowers, especially the United States, in the Cold War. It focuses on how the ideas, values, agreements, and practices of arms control were linked to changing perceptions and circumstances of power and of the role of those bureaucratic institutions most responsible for the conduct of the Cold War.

The end of the Cold War and absence of any clear countervailing capacity, international or domestic, able to contain an imperial United States has thrown the arms control process into possibly terminal crisis. To get a sense of the dynamics of the crisis, the chapter looks at the example of the ABM Treaty, once seen as a corner stone of superpower arms control and then dismissed by leading U.S. policymakers as a Cold War relic. In particular, it considers the repeated efforts by the United States to reinterpret the treaty to allow it deploy a national missile defense and its eventual withdrawal from the treaty in late 2001.

Turning to multilateral arms control agreements, the chapter looks at the CTBT. It is an example of the pursuit of advantage by a great power and how a treaty was first resisted, then subverted, and finally denied and undermined by the U.S. nuclear weapons laboratories, military planners, and policymakers committed to the use of force.

The United States has become ever more concerned about noncompliance—its own noncompliance notwithstanding—with the nuclear nonproliferation regime, in particular the NPT. It has cited noncompliance as justification for its threats and waging of war. The chapter therefore looks in detail at the NPT, its origins, and the pattern of its enforcement, especially over the past decade. As cases, the chapter addresses how the weapons states have avoided complying with their commitments, despite efforts by the international community, and how they have dealt with noncompliance by Israel, Iraq, North Korea, India, and Pakistan. The recent U.S. campaign against Iran's covert efforts to develop nuclear weapons is not addressed here.[18] These cases show that what matters for the United States in determining and responding to noncompliance with the NPT is not the nature or degree of noncompliance but the particular U.S. interest in these states and their respective regions. It is suggested that rather than a "double standard," it is an American standard that is applied.

The overall argument of the chapter is that even elementary criteria of legitimacy, justice, and fairness are hard to find in either the origins, content, or enforcement of international arms control and nonproliferation agreements. It is argued that the degree of noncompliance by the emperor is so systemic as to dwarf anything a pirate could possibly conceive. But this structural noncompliance is not the real issue. Compliance is not the ultimate goal that the international community (states and people) seeks, it is merely an effect. The goal is peace and justice, and for that much stronger transnational institutions for participatory democracy and a disposition for justice are required. As many have long recognized, an America dominated by powerful, increasingly global economic interests, an entrenched scientific-military-industrial complex, and driven by an imperial ideal is the most important obstacle to this goal.[19]

A Prelude on Legitimacy, Fairness, and Justice

Arms control agreements do not spring fully formed into a waiting world. They are the result of struggles, sometimes intense and long fought, which have pitched states against each other, and have involved bitter, drawn out battles within and between national bureaucracies, politicians, and publics. They carry the marks of these struggles in their timing, text, and operation. It is important, therefore, to attend to the politics, diplomacy, and context of treaties as much as their actual text.

This is important because agreements able to elicit consent rather than requiring compulsion to be sustained are constrained by the need to command some degree of support, and to conform with certain presumptions about how they are to be properly arrived at and what they should look like. That is, they must appear to be "lawful" to be seen as legitimate. The recourse to law is significant. While the economic and military resources of the great powers may be expressed through problematic international law, it is important to note that law, like other social institutions, has its own characteristics, history, and logic. It requires a certain autonomy if it is to function. In particular, law inherently must orient itself towards standards of universality and equity. As the historian E. P. Thompson noted, "If the law is evidently partial and unjust, then it will mask nothing, legitimize nothing, contribute nothing to . . . hegemony."[20] It will instead require unending enforcement, perhaps of ever-greater severity.

There are long standing differences over the legitimacy, fairness, and justice of international law, institutions, and conduct. The sense that current international processes are marked by injustice and unfairness runs deep among many in the global South and among the less self-interested in the North. One need look no further than judgments about the processes and agreements that are supposedly focused on organizing collective international action to preserve the future well-being of humanity and the planet. For instance, writing about the 1992 United Nations Conference on Environment and Development (UNCED), otherwise known as the Earth Summit, Tariq Banuri argues that, "whereas Northerners see UNCED as a welcome unfolding of collective action to save humanity, many Southerners, government functionaries as well as non-governmental organization (NGO) activists, albeit for different reasons, fear in it the emergence of a new imperialism, of new conditionalities, and of new obstacles to the alleviation of poverty and oppression."[21]

Considerable scholarly attention has been devoted to clarifying questions of justice and fairness in international negotiations and institutions. It is worth reviewing some of this briefly and using it as a guide to the subsequent discussion of arms control, nonproliferation, and noncompliance. In a very influential interpretation, Thomas Franck argues that the two discourses that now dominate international relations are those of legitimacy and justice. Franck suggests that crucial to legitimacy is "right process," that is, that a particular law or institution come into being through a mechanism that is in accord with generally accepted notions of what is the right way to create such things.[22] The characteristics of a legitimate agreement, once it is arrived at, Franck suggests, are determinacy, validation, coherence, and adherence. Determinacy refers to the extent to which the particular law is seen as clear about what is permitted and what is not. Validation refers to the ways and means by which the international community indicates its satisfaction or otherwise with the method by which the agreement was arrived at. The requirement for coherence is simply that the rule should be applied systematically to the situations where it is meant to apply, that is, it treats like cases alike. Lastly, adherence is the larger contextual requirement that an agreement fits properly within the broader principles and expectations shared by a community rather than being simply an ad hoc response to a particular situation.

While Franck has identified some key principles that can be used to judge international conduct and agreements, there are some important qualifiers. Four observations can be made about Franck's argument. First, it is unhistorical, leaving open the possibility that the most powerful states permit no alternatives to the processes that they dominate and so, by default, existing practice becomes in time "due process." Second, it is statist, treating legitimacy as a matter only for states and formal policy judgments by government officials. This omits both the crucial role of bureaucracies and institutions, which is where contests over legitimacy often take place, and the role of publics and civil society, which is where judgments over legitimacy are also made, even though they may not immediately prevail. Third, judgments over legitimacy, no matter where and by whom they are made, are structured by both persuasion and coercion. Moreover, these instruments of communicative, economic, and military power are profoundly unequally disposed. Fourth, Franck's description of legitimacy seems to presume that justice is not in itself a key requirement for legitimacy, and it leaves open the possibility of the practice of legitimacy hindering the pursuit of justice.

However, justice has received attention in its own right. A notable and widely regarded example is John Rawls' theory of justice, which presents the idea of 'justice as fairness.' Briefly, Rawls suggests that judgment, to be just, should be made from "the original position of equality," that is a situation where "no one knows his place in society, his class position or social status, nor does any one know his fortune in the distribution of natural assets and abilities, his intelligence, strength, and the like;" Rawls describes this as judgment behind a "veil of ignorance."[23] In effect, justice as fairness requires that those who participate in the judgment should propose or acknowledge only that which they would accept if they were in the same situation as any other members of the community and had to make a binding commitment. There are obvious implications for the conduct of states in international affairs and in particular their dealings in collective institutions and in negotiations intended to provide mutual security and well-being.[24]

This brief discussion of legitimacy and justice can be combined and applied to an example concerning the United Nations, an institution now widely regarded as the legitimate site for the international community to deliberate and arrive at collective decisions on agreements, as well as for it to judge and respond to noncompliance by individual states. The example deals with the veto power of some members of the U.N. Security Council and has direct relevance for our concern here about compliance and noncompliance with arms control agreements. The origins of the veto usefully illuminate some of the structural issues that need to be considered when looking at compliance by the great powers, and in particular "the American problem." It is particularly apt given the failed U.S. efforts in early 2003 to seek a Security Council resolution authorizing its use of force against Iraq.

The U.N. Charter gives the Security Council "primary responsibility for the maintenance of international peace and security." The Security Council is empowered to use sanctions and military force to this end. The United States, Russia, Britain, France, and China, as well as being the major nuclear weapons states, are the only permanent members of the Security Council and are alone in having the power of veto over council decisions. At the founding conference of the United Nations in San Francisco in 1945, fifty nations met to draw up the charter. A history of the veto notes that: "Major disagreements arose between Great Britain, the Soviet Union, and the United States on the one hand, and the other smaller and less powerful nations on the other."[25] The major powers insisted that the charter give them power to veto actions by the Security Council, and the less powerful states resisted. The history records that, "At one point during the conference, . . . several delegations of smaller nations became somewhat unruly in their opposition to the veto," whereupon one of the U.S. delegates, Senator Tom Connally (D-TX), "told them that they could go home from San Francisco if they wished and report that they had defeated the veto but they could also report that they had torn up the Charter." In short, no veto, no United Nations. The United States and the other victors of World War II prevailed.

This situation rightfully raises questions about the legitimacy and justice of such a process and outcome. The U.S. Secretary of State, Edward R. Stettinius, Jr., in a radio address in May 1945 noted that the veto "has been criticized both here and elsewhere as giving a privileged position to the large nations," but justified it by claiming that the veto was "not a question of privileges, but of using the present distribution of military and industrial power in the world for the maintenance of peace."[26] The onset of the Cold War quickly left such justifications behind. There was little peace to be found as the United States and Soviet Union intervened in other states and clashed in proxy wars around the world. The Soviet Union and the United States liberally used the veto.

The efficacy of the veto during the Cold War stemmed in large part from the fact that the superpowers were willing to respect each other's "military and industrial power." The use of the veto was simply a diplomatic marker indicating the degree of willingness to use this power over the issue in question. With the end of the Cold War, the United States was no longer contained by possible Soviet reaction and started, in Phyllis Bennis' apt phrase, "calling the shots" at the United Nations, with Secretary of State Madeleine Albright claiming in 1995 that "the UN is a tool of American foreign policy."[27]

As the case of the U.S. war on Iraq has subsequently shown, when the United Nations shows signs of refusing to act as a "tool" the United States is willing to damn it to irrelevance. Finding it hard to get U.N. support for the use of force against Iraq, in a clear threat President Bush declared to the U.N. General Assembly in September 2002: "All the world now faces a test, and the United Nations a difficult and defining moment. Are Security Council resolutions to be honored and enforced, or cast aside without consequence? Will the United Nations serve the purpose of its founding, or will it be irrelevant?"[28]

Nonetheless, despite U.S. bullying and bribes, the overwhelming majority of Security Council members refused to support a proposed U.S. resolution authorizing a U.S. attack on Iraq, with France and Russia making clear they would use their veto.[29] The U.S. withdrew its resolution and in March 2003 invaded Iraq, regardless. This outcome has important implications for the legitimacy, fairness, and justice of any institutional arrangements for compliance that are reliant on U.S. and Security Council participation.

The Career of Nuclear Arms Control

The question of international control over atomic weapons was raised as soon as they were created at the end of World War II.[30] For the United States, as one of the earliest studies argued, the fear was that not only might "regular rivals on the same level" acquire these "absolute weapons" but that "possibly some of the nations lower down in the power scale might get hold of atomic weapons and change the whole relationship of great and small states."[31] These twin challenges have marked U.S. policy ever since.

The United Nations took up the issue in its first resolution, as noted earlier. Having built and used the atomic bomb, the U.S. adopted a policy of monopoly and exclusion, to keep what was called its "winning weapon." U.S. efforts to think about some form of control through the United Nations sought to preserve this monopoly until the final stage of a lengthy plan, while ensuring no other state would or could build them. The Baruch plan, presented by the United States to the U.N. in 1946, has rightly been described as an arrangement that "did not differ in substance from an ultimatum the United States might have given Russia to forswear nuclear weapons or be destroyed."[32] The Soviet Union refused to support it and within a few years had tested its own nuclear weapons. The U.S. goal of maintaining a nuclear capability while seeking to deny it to others was eventually shared by the Soviet Union and in time by the other nuclear weapons states and underlies the NPT.

The second effort at nuclear arms control can be traced to the mid-1950s and to the Soviet offer of a plan for nuclear disarmament, reductions in conventional forces, and a system of inspections. Matthew Evangelista's study of these talks argues that, even though it had earlier supported these principles, the United States eventually rejected the Soviet plan because of opposition from the U.S. military and the U.S. Atomic Energy Commission, which "exercised effective veto power over US disarmament policy."[33] The U.S. preference for continuing the arms race was not, however, confined to these institutions. McGeorge Bundy claims that, "what [U.S. Secretary of State] Dulles feared about proposals for disarmament in 1955 was simply that they might lead to agreement."[34] The reasons are instructive. Bundy suggests that Dulles "did not fear the nuclear arms race, because he had confidence the Russians could not keep up."[35]

Within a few years, however, it became apparent the Soviet Union could keep up and arms control emerged out of the recognition that open conflict between the U.S. and Soviet Union would be mutually ruinous and that something needed to be done.[36] As Thomas Schelling observed in a 1961 essay laying out some of the earliest thinking on arms control: "our present military policies and prospects . . . cannot promise security from a major thermonuclear war; and even modest improvements achieved through cooperation with the Soviets would be welcome."[37] Schelling was also very blunt about what such "cooperation" was intended for. Arms control was, he argued, "designed to preserve a nuclear striking power," and it was "an open question whether we ought to be negotiating with our enemies for more arms, less arms, different kinds of arms, or arrangements superimposed on existing armaments."[38] Disarmament had now become "an open question."

From this arms control perspective, the United States and Soviet Union should agree to manage their conflict and to find ways to stabilize and regulate the relationship of mutual assured destruction that the vast nuclear arsenals of the superpowers had created. As Schelling put it, the need was to "tranquilize relations . . . while hating and distrusting."[39] Thirty years later, he stood by those earlier perceptions arguing that, "the purpose of arms control was to make deterrence work."[40] Marcus Raskin has drawn out this darker aspect of arms control, arguing that arms control talks by their nature "eschew essential moral, legal and criminal questions" and that "there is a necrophiliac quality to the technical expertise which calculates one missile against another, as diplomats become brokers in charred bodies." Inevitably, Raskin suggests, "when such negotiations are divorced from the fundamentally criminal nature of the weaponry or strategies under discussion, arms control talks are reduced to narrow quibbles between state representatives on the character and size of mutually genocidal forces."[41]

The first two decades of the arms control era brought a series of agreements.[42] The first of these was the 1959 Antarctic Treaty, which recognized the emergence of possible territorial disputes (the United States and Soviet Union did not recognize the claims of other governments) and prohibited military activity there. It codified the status quo. Given public fears and mobilization against nuclear weapons and testing, compounded during the 1962 Cuban missile crisis with the fear of nuclear war, it was no great surprise that the first substantial superpower agreements came soon thereafter, in 1963, with the "Hotline" agreement establishing direct emergency communications between leaders in Washington and Moscow, and the Limited Test Ban Treaty, which prohibited atmospheric nuclear testing. These were followed by the 1967 Outer Space Treaty, which banned nuclear weapons from space, and then the NPT (this is discussed at length later in this essay). Nineteen seventy-one saw the Seabed Arms Control Treaty, prohibiting nuclear weapons from the seafloor, the Agreement on Measures to Reduce the Risk of Outbreak of Nuclear War, and the "Hotline" modernization agreement. The following year saw both the Biological Weapons Convention, outlawing biological weapons, and the Incidents at Sea Treaty. But the most significant agreements that year were the Anti-Ballistic Missile Treaty, and the Interim Agreement (SALT I), which for the first time limited offensive nuclear arms. The culmination of the process can be said to be the 1973 Prevention of Nuclear War agreement, in which the superpowers committed themselves to "make every effort" to avoid nuclear war.

The changing fortunes of arms control, when looked at in detail, show the impact of domestic political circumstances, especially the political and bureaucratic dynamics of national security policy making and the role of the institutions set up to wage the Cold War.[43] The superpowers brought distinct perspectives to these management efforts. Robin Ranger argues that it is possible to distinguish U.S. from Soviet arms control thought and practice, where "the Western, especially the American view . . . has stressed the idea of arms control as a means of securing apolitical, technical solutions to the threats to strategic stability," which he labels "technical arms control." The Soviet Union, on the other hand, "sought to provide political counters to threats to strategic stability," and so preferred "political arms control."[44] The two perspectives have important consequences. The emphasis on science and technology rather than politics serves to privilege the United States even among the nuclear weapon states, and more particularly those institutions within it which command the appropriate expertise.

The influence of the U.S. military and the weapons complex underlies a key problem with arms control, identified by Allan Krass as the fact that "it is assumed that the competition continues unabated in all areas not covered by the agreement. Anything not forbidden is permitted."[45] In this situation, verification is a crutch for arms control agreements in that it is supposed to detect and warn of potential violations of an agreement, deter such violations, and build public confidence in the viability of the agreement.[46] But verification also serves to institutionalize distrust; Krass calls this "the self-fulfilling nature of distrust."[47] It is not surprising then to read the damning indictment of arms control in January 2000 offered by General Lee Butler, who retired in 1994 as commander-in-chief of the U.S. Strategic Command: "The traditional arms control process . . . is not just stalled but dysfunctional. It is freighted with psychology, language, assumptions, and protocols that perpetuate distrust, constrain imagination, limit expectations, and prolong outcomes."[48]

The urge "to tranquilize relations . . . while hating and distrusting" that underlies arms control, to use Schelling's description, proved itself vulnerable to political forces that sought to embrace their hate and distrust rather than manage it. In his history of U.S.-U.S.S.R. negotiations in the 1980s, Strobe Talbott has identified how, under President Reagan, "the arms control enterprise came into the hands of a group of people who were extremely critical of the results of that enterprise as it had been conducted by the three previous administrations. These people differed . . . from their predecessors—in their world outlook, their view of America's adversaries in Moscow, their own conception of their own opportunities and obligations."[49] According to Talbott, "the president and his men had been determined as much as possible to wipe out the vestiges of the old regime. This meant altering if not scrapping the diplomacy that had held sway since the 1950s, discrediting if not discarding the agreements that earlier administrations had signed."[50] This impulse toward the untrammeled exercise of U.S. power was also evident in increasingly aggressive interventions and invasions in the Third World, for example, in Nicaragua, El Salvador, Angola, Libya, and Grenada.

Over the past decade, U.S. policymakers have seen Soviet disintegration followed by Russia's economic and political collapse and now find themselves spending hundreds of millions of dollars each year to secure Russian nuclear weapons and fissile materials as part of an effort to stop its nuclear weapons complex from hemorrhaging.[51] So even though Russia retains thousands of nuclear weapons, it is no longer perceived as a state at par with the United States. As the perception of parity has eroded, so arms control seems to have fallen deeper into crisis.

There is certainly a sharpening sense of gloom among advocates of nuclear arms control. Jonathan Schell, the author of the classic warning about the dangers of nuclear weapons, *The Fate of the Earth*, observed that, "ten years after the collapse of the Soviet Union, the startling fact is that nuclear arms control is faring worse in the first days of the twenty-first century than it did in the last days of the Cold War."[52] He is by no means alone in his judgment. A 1997 study of the United States and its arms control policies suggested that "the rate of progress in virtually all areas of arms control and nonproliferation has slowed noticeably since 1993 . . . its continued progress is by no means guaranteed."[53] A grimmer picture still was painted in *The Nuclear Turning Point*, a collaborative volume by leading independent academic experts and proponents of nuclear arms control. It argued that, "nuclear arms control is at a crossroads" and warned that, "the present arms control regime could unravel."[54]

There are certainly some, such as former U.S. Secretary of State Henry Kissinger, who have welcomed the possible end of arms control and supported the rethinking of U.S. policy. Arms control has served its purpose, argues Kissinger, because "the end of the Cold War has transformed global strategic conditions."[55] Echoing Kissinger's argument that the collapse of the Soviet Union demands rethinking U.S. policy, David Gompert, vice president of the Rand Corporation, has suggested that, "now predominant and unthreatened, the United States is no longer a status quo power."[56] In short, the end of the Cold War is seen as having released the United States from needing to constrain or regulate its military capabilities, or limit its political and economic ambitions.

The United States is now in a position to remake the shape of the world.[57] But it has not been easy. Condoleeza Rice, national security adviser to President Bush, observed in early 2000 that, "the United States has found it exceedingly difficult to define its national interest in the absence of Soviet power."[58] She has argued that the United States finds itself in a position akin to the time soon after the end of World War II, "when American officials thought up the Marshall Plan and helped create NATO and the United Nations and the International Monetary Fund, and undertook the Cold War."[59] But the world has not been totally transformed. It remains overshadowed by the institutions, technologies, ideas, values, and agreements created during the Cold War. Where these have become an obstacle to now unfettered U.S. ambitions, they are being pushed aside.

The Anti-Ballistic Missile (ABM) Treaty

On December 13, 2001, President Bush announced formal withdrawal of the United States from the 1972 U.S.-Soviet Anti-Ballistic Missile Treaty.[60] The ABM Treaty banning missile defenses was widely regarded as the foundation of superpower arms control—a decade earlier it was offered by Thomas Schelling, one of the founders of arms control, as proof of "the doctrinal victory of arms control in this country."[61] The victory was clearly short-lived. The story of the rise and fall of the ABM Treaty offers vivid evidence of the dynamics of U.S. policy on arms control and its approach to compliance.

As noted earlier, the U.S.-Soviet/Russian arms control treaties were the result of an arms race, strategic parity, massive overkill, and public fears. It was recognized, for instance, in 1970 by General Bruce K. Holloway, commander-in-chief of the Strategic Air Command, that "the central fact of our time . . . is the present relative equality of the US and Soviet strategic military power . . . this power is the foundation of all diplomacy as well as war."[62] The recognition of this balance of terror and the need for some kind of discipline on the part of both superpowers (at least with regard to each other) also entailed that coercion and other means to enforce compliance would have been fruitless and even counterproductive. Not surprisingly, superpower treaties contain no provisions for enforcing compliance, whether through sanctions or other means. Instead, the task of ensuring compliance with these arms control agreements has been predominantly one of negotiation and "regime management."[63]

The ABM Treaty was the example par excellence of this approach to arms control and compliance. It was widely welcomed and there was an "extraordinary level of Senate support for the ABM Treaty" when it was signed by the United States.[64] The treaty was put to a severe test as part of a larger assault on arms control by the Reagan administration when it launched in March 1983 its Star Wars program to develop space-based missile defenses. For U.S. military planners at that time, Janne Nolan has reported, "it was no longer technically challenging or strategically advantageous to keep adding more warheads to nuclear arsenals."[65] Space beckoned as a new arena for the pursuit of military advantage. To legitimize its research, development, and testing of new antiballistic missile systems, the Reagan administration presented a new interpretation of the ABM Treaty. The prospect that the United States was on course to violate the treaty elicited criticism from the public, the arms control community, Congress, and U.S. allies.[66] Under pressure, the Star Wars program eventually was restricted to research.

It was the collapse of the Soviet Union that offered the real measure of U.S. commitment to its ABM Treaty obligations. In 1995, the U.S. Congress mandated the deployment of a national missile defense system by 2003, and a year later the Clinton administration announced that it would develop over the next three years and then prepare to deploy a National Missile Defense (NMD) system within a further three years. In early 1999, the U.S. Senate voted 97-3 for a bill calling for the "United States to deploy as soon as is technologically possible an effective National Missile Defense system."[67] The program was pursued even though it was clear that the deployment of an antiballistic missile system would violate the ABM Treaty, which forbids such systems. Former Secretary of State Henry Kissinger, who was national security adviser to President Nixon when the treaty was signed, supported scrapping the ABM Treaty, arguing that the situation had changed since the treaty was negotiated.[68] Put simply, the United States should now do what it wanted because it could do so.

However, under domestic and international pressure, especially from its traditional allies, the United States again sought to unilaterally reinterpret the treaty and its protocols. In June 2000, U.S. government lawyers determined that limited work could begin on building the radars associated with the NMD system, work previously seen as violating the treaty—U.S. officials explained that this new interpretation was the result of "better lawyers."[69] U.S. allies in Europe and other key leaders decried the effort to evade the treaty's obligations.[70] The final decision to begin work was again delayed. The failure of some of the tests of the NMD system may have contributed to this decision in the last days of the Clinton administration.

President Bush, who is more enthusiastic about missile defense, declared in July 2001 that the United States would proceed with its NMD plans no matter what.[71] It was only a matter of time until the conflict between this U.S. policy and the ABM Treaty would become too great to avoid. The Pentagon's Compliance Review Group determined that U.S. NMD plans would violate the ABM Treaty in 2002.[72] Soon afterwards, the United States announced its intent to withdraw.

The Comprehensive Test Ban Treaty (CTBT)

The history and present crisis over the Comprehensive Test Ban Treaty offer an important insight into the fairness and justice of international arms control negotiations. They show how the United States has tried and to some measure succeeded in delaying and shaping key arms control treaties so that it can sustain its own capacity to maintain and develop its nuclear weapons. To recall the formulation used by John Rawls, the United States has steadfastly refused "the original position of equality."

In 1954, the radioactive fallout from the United States' "Bravo" thermonuclear explosion affected hundreds of inhabitants of the Marshall Islands and the Japanese fishermen in the Lucky Dragon, causing the death of at least one. This led Indian Prime Minister Jawaharlal Nehru to propose a nuclear test ban in 1954.[73] It also triggered public protests against the health and environmental effects of radioactivity from U.S. and Soviet atmospheric testing of nuclear weapons.[74] By creating domestic pressure to end nuclear testing, the protests spurred efforts to reach the first significant superpower arms control treaty, the 1963 Limited Test Ban Treaty, forbidding nuclear explosive testing in the atmosphere, space, and underwater.

The United States' nuclear weapons laboratories were a major obstacle to this treaty. But there were other opponents as well; Paul Nitze records that "the Joint Chiefs of Staff, when they realized that President Kennedy was indeed serious about concluding a test ban treaty with the Soviet Union, raised a storm of protest, as did the AEC laboratories."[75] Herbert York has noted that in order to get support for ratification of the Limited Test Ban Treaty, President Kennedy agreed to a "vigorous" nuclear weapons development program, supported by underground nuclear testing.[76] The development and testing of nuclear weapons continued apace.

The public pressure for a ban on all nuclear testing faded but did not disappear. By the late 1970s, President Carter decided that a Comprehensive Test Ban was both possible and necessary, could be verified, and was in the United States' national interest. Herbert York, who was the chief U.S. negotiator at the subsequent CTBT talks in 1979-1980, recalled that the talks came within six months of a final treaty. The talks failed, according to York, because "most of the military, including the Joint Chiefs of Staff and, essentially, the entire permanent civilian nuclear staff, opposed it openly and strongly."[77]

The opposition to the CTBT among U.S. officials hardened in the early 1980s under the Reagan administration. While doubts were often couched in terms of verification of any possible treaty, a senior U.S. official admitted in 1986 that: "even if we could verify compliance with a comprehensive test ban at this time, it would not be in our interest or the interest of the world to undertake such a ban."[78] Thus, when the U.N. General Assembly voted 143-2 for a test ban in December 1987, there were eight abstentions, and the United States and France opposed the resolution. Another resolution, calling for a halt to all nuclear explosions, was supported 137-3, with the United States, France, and United Kingdom (UK) opposed. A year later, in December 1988, the vote was 146-2.[79]

In the 1990s, however, with the end of the Cold War and growing concerns about the proliferation of nuclear weapons, the United States began to change its position on the CTBT. In 1992, the United States Congress voted for a moratorium on nuclear testing and called for a test ban by 1996. The treaty was negotiated at the Conference on Disarmament in a relatively brief period between 1993 and 1996. This treaty had almost universal support, with the General Assembly in 1996 voting 158-3 to approve the treaty prohibiting all nuclear test explosions in all environments for all time. The United States was the first state to sign, and the other nuclear weapon states followed suit. The treaty now has 167 signatories, and over 100 states have ratified it.[80] Among the nuclear weapon states, only France, Russia, and the United Kingdom have ratified.

The official U.S. perception of the CTBT while it was being negotiated and later considered for ratification was very different from that of most other states. The U.S. ambassador to the CTBT negotiations explained:

> It is important to recognize that the motivation of the thirty-eight countries that joined together in this negotiation is not the same. The majority believes, as I understand it, that the banning forever of all nuclear tests in all environments will bring about, and bring about rapidly, the deterioration and decay of all existing nuclear weapons stockpiles. As I understand it, all five nuclear weapons states believe that without testing we can nevertheless maintain for the foreseeable future the viability, the safety and the reliability of our nuclear stockpiles.[81]

This was a far cry from the intention and expectation of the majority of states involved in negotiating the treaty.

Secretary of State Madeleine Albright went further and argued that the treaty would in fact strengthen the United States:

> Under the CTBT, America would gain the security benefits of outlawing nuclear tests by others, while locking in a technological status quo that is highly favorable to us. We have conducted more than 1,000 nuclear tests—hundreds more than anyone else. We do not need more tests to protect our security. Would-be proliferators or modernizers, however, must test if they are to develop the kind of advanced, compact nuclear weapons that are most threatening.[82]

But it seems even this was not enough.

The declared rationale of the CTBT is that "the cessation of all nuclear weapon test explosions and all other nuclear explosions, by constraining the development and qualitative improvement of nuclear weapons and ending the development of advanced new types of nuclear weapons, constitutes an effective measure of nuclear disarmament and nonproliferation in all its aspects."[83] However, according to the official U.S. interpretation of the CTBT, this "does not imply that the Treaty prohibits the development of new types of nuclear weapons, or the improvement of existing weapons."[84]

The United States feels able to evade a basic goal of the CTBT, banning the development of new nuclear weapons, because of a long list of conditions that were attached to the treaty when it was submitted to the U.S. Senate for consent to ratification. These conditions were explicitly intended to permit the maintenance and modernization of the U.S. nuclear arsenal for the indefinite future, and the retention of nuclear weapons laboratory facilities and programs as well as the capability to resume nuclear testing.[85] In addition, under the 1994 Nuclear Posture Review and the 1997 Quadrennial Defense Review, there is a requirement from the Department of Defense to the Department of Energy, which has responsibility for managing the nuclear weapons complex, that it "maintain the capability to design, fabricate, and certify new warheads."[86] Knowledgeable U.S. analysts argue that these conditions and the multibillion dollar new experimental and computational facilities being developed in the weapons laboratories show that "the US government clearly intends to maintain under the CTBT, and indeed significantly enhance, its scientific and technical capabilities for undertaking the development of advanced new types of nuclear weapons."[87]

Despite this, on October 13, 1999, the U.S. Senate refused to give its consent to the ratification of the test ban.[88] Arguing against ratification, Henry Kissinger noted that "six former secretaries of defense, four former national-security advisors and four former CIA directors opposed ratification, while four former secretaries of state, myself included, refused to endorse it."[89] The non-ratification added to pressures already at work to interpret the terms of the CTBT as permitting the development of new kinds of nuclear weapons. The U.S. Department of Energy plans for "all" the nuclear weapons in the U.S.

stockpile to be replaced with either "modified versions or with entirely new weapons."[90]

An early sign of support for these efforts towards new weapons, despite the test ban, was the 2001 U.S. Defense Authorization Bill, which included a provision for a study and "limited research and development" on the "defeat of hardened and deeply buried targets." The sponsors of this provision in the U.S. Senate have argued that it is meant to make possible research and development on low-yield nuclear weapons, circumventing a 1994 ban.[91] In 2002, the ban was lifted and funding approved for steps to reduce the time required to resume nuclear testing from three years to eighteen months.[92]

As the United States pursues new nuclear weapons, there is little that the CTBT can do to deal with this noncompliance. It is generally understood, though not specified, that under the CTBT, as with other treaties, the concerns about noncompliance could be brought to the attention of the U.N. Security Council if questions of international peace and security are involved. This arrangement by its very nature leaves the nuclear weapons states outside any restrictions, given their veto. This makes it all the more ironic that concerns about the CTBT's lack of compliance enforcement measures, what was called a lack of teeth, figured significantly in the U.S. Senate ratification debate.[93] The concern now is that the United States seeks the end of the test ban regime. The U.S. boycott of a November 2001 U.N. conference to support ratification of the Treaty was apparently because "the Pentagon hoped that a US boycott would contribute to hastening the death of the nuclear pact."[94]

The driving forces against the Comprehensive Test Ban and for nuclear weapons testing are not hard to see. Nuclear weapons designers and military planners are pushing for new designs using arguments couched in strategic terms relevant for the new world. Paul Robinson, the director of Sandia National Laboratory and chairman of the Policy Subcommittee of the Strategic Advisory Group for the Commanders-in-Chief of the U.S. Strategic Command has proposed developing a special low-yield "To Whom It May Concern" nuclear arsenal, directly at Third World countries.[95] Stephen Younger, director of the Defense Threat Reduction Agency and former associate laboratory director for nuclear weapons at Los Alamos National Laboratory, has argued that in the post-Cold War world, the United States needs new kinds of low-yield nuclear weapons because it faces "new threats" and the continued U.S. "reliance on high-yield strategic [nuclear] weapons could lead to self-deterrence, a limitation of strategic options."[96] This is by no means the first time such suggestions have come from U.S. weapons laboratories. In 1970, Harold Agnew, director of Los Alamos National Laboratory, suggested that, "if people would prepare the right spectrum of tactical weapons, we might be able to knock off this sort of foolishness we now have in Vietnam and the Middle East or anyplace else."[97]

The United States is renewing its embrace of a nuclear arsenal in the post-Cold War world, knowing that this more deeply embeds nuclear weapons in national and international structures of political and military thinking and action.

It could be argued, following Jonathan Schell, that the perversity of this policy shows that the United States pursues these weapons not out of a profound fear of attack but for "deep seated, unarticulated reasons growing out of its own, freely chosen conceptions of national security."[98] The reasons are, however, not hard to find. The search is for nuclear weapons that U.S. policymakers would be more able to use against targets in the Third World, and whose use Americans might more readily accept.

The Nuclear Nonproliferation Treaty (NPT)

The period since the end of the Cold War has seen a massively nuclear-armed, imperial U.S. seeking to deal with small, Third World states in pursuit of nuclear weapons. These dramatic struggles over compliance with the international system of controls over nuclear weapons have concerned the NPT and the attendant norms against nuclear proliferation. To understand these conflicts requires looking at the origin and content of the NPT, its requirements for compliance, and provisions for dealing with noncompliance and enforcement. The question to ask is whether the nuclear weapons states have acted justly and legitimately in their approach to the issue of proliferation.

Following the first U.N. General Assembly resolution of January 24, 1946, calling for "the elimination from national armaments of atomic weapons and of all other major weapons adaptable to mass destruction" the United States and the Soviet Union offered competing plans for controlling the spread of nuclear weapons. In 1947, the Soviet Union proposed a disarmament agreement at the U.N. Atomic Energy Commission (UNAEC). Bertrand Goldschmidt, the former head of the French Atomic Energy Commission and a participant in those talks, has argued that "if the UNAEC—in 1948 . . . at a time when there was still only a single nuclear weapon state possessing a small stock of bombs—had agreed [to the proposed treaty] . . . the nuclear arms race and its tragic acceleration probably could have been slowed down considerably or even avoided."[99] The United States and its allies rejected the Soviet plan. Goldschmidt argues that "if the . . . arguments, which we then put forward, had been applied 20 years later to the NPT they would indubitably have led to the rejection of this treaty which is now the main pillar of our nonproliferation regime."[100]

The history of the NPT can be traced to an Irish resolution introduced in 1958 to the U.N.'s First Committee, which called on nuclear weapon states not to transfer control of nuclear weapons to nonnuclear weapon states, and on non-nuclear weapons states not to produce such weapons.[101] The United States opposed it. In 1964, China tested nuclear weapons for the first time. A year later, the superpowers had become sufficiently concerned about the need to restrict the possible spread of nuclear weapons that they presented separate draft treaties on nuclear nonproliferation to the Eighteen Nation Disarmament Conference (the forerunner of the Conference on Disarmament). The treaty drafts envisioned not a universal set of prohibitions, but rather a two-tier system in which the five states that had tested nuclear weapons would retain them and not share them, while other countries would agree not to acquire nuclear weapons. The drafts made no mention of arms control and disarmament except in the preambular paragraphs.[102]

Peter Clausen, a historian of the NPT, has noted that for the United States the timing of this initiative was linked to its pursuit of its interventionist policies and global interests: "it was no accident that the period of the treaty negotiations corresponded to the high water mark of America's postwar global activism . . . the spread of nuclear weapons in a region of vital interest to the United States could increase the risks of containment and threaten American access to the region."[103] The Soviet interest in nonproliferation stemmed from concerns about possible U.S. sharing of nuclear weapons with its North Atlantic Treaty Organization (NATO) allies, in particular West Germany, the emergence of a nuclear China and (as with the United States) the need to limit possible threats in regions where it may choose to intervene. These concerns were well founded. During the late 1960s, the United States had deployed thousands of nuclear weapons and their components to other countries, including Canada, Cuba, Greenland, Iceland, Japan, Morocco, Philippines, Puerto Rico, South Korea, Spain, Taiwan, Belgium, Greece, Italy, Netherlands, Turkey, United Kingdom, and West Germany.[104] At that time, the United States had a stockpile of over 32,000 nuclear warheads, and the Soviet Union over 6,000.

In 1967, the United States and Soviet Union submitted identical treaty drafts. The draft contained no treaty article dealing specifically with disarmament. Instead, the superpowers proclaimed their good intentions in a nonbinding preambular paragraph. They were:

> Desiring to further the easing of international tension and the strengthening of trust between States in order to facilitate the cessation of the manufacture of nuclear weapons, the liquidation of all their existing stockpiles, and the elimination from national arsenals of nuclear weapons and the means of their delivery pursuant to a treaty on general and complete disarmament under strict and effective international control.[105]

It was eventually Mexico that proposed including an article on disarmament in the treaty, which eventually became Article VI, and commits all parties "to pursue negotiations in good faith on effective measures relating to cessation of the nuclear arms race at an early date and to nuclear disarmament."

It was clear early on that even this limited obligation was not welcomed by the nuclear weapons states and would not be readily met. "Under the pressure of the non-aligned states as well as from some of their own allies," Mohammed Shaker notes in his history of the NPT, "the two superpowers merely accepted in the NPT to undertake to pursue negotiations in good faith, but not, as pointed out by one American negotiator, 'to achieve any disarmament agreement, since it is obviously impossible to predict the exact nature and results of such negotiations.'"[106] Even this evidence of the intention to not take the treaty seriously suggests some limited good faith that was not there. Bill Epstein, a veteran U.N. official in the area of arms control and disarmament, records that "one of the American negotiators conceded privately that the NPT was 'one of the greatest con games of modern times.'"[107]

The scale of the "con" has become starkly apparent. The nuclear weapons states were able to ensure that there were no compliance provisions applicable to them. They were bound only by "good faith." If they chose not to exercise it, who could make them do otherwise? Thus, thirty years after the NPT was opened for signature, there remain five declared nuclear weapon states which among them possess tens of thousands of nuclear weapons.

For their part, the nonnuclear weapons states have sought to hold the weapons states to their Article VI obligations to disarm. Their efforts have been treated as little more than attempts to plead and to cajole. The fact that many nonnuclear states were dependent on, and often simply clients of, the major powers has meant that other political and economic interests mute the demands they are willing or able to make. The only feature of the NPT that could serve as leverage on the nuclear weapons states is for individual states to withdraw from the treaty, or to agree collectively to either amend or to bring about the end of Treaty.[108] The NPT came with a twenty-five-year lifetime and a requirement for a conference of the signatories at that time to determine whether to extend it and for how long. In principle, the nonnuclear weapon states could have demanded that the nuclear weapons states either comply with their Article VI obligation to disarm or face the end of the NPT bargain by allowing the treaty to lapse. But, despite their frustration, the nonnuclear weapons states have not been interested in bringing down the NPT, either individually or collectively—no state, as of this writing, has ever withdrawn from the treaty (although North Korea has given notice of its intention to do so, there has been no formal determination of its status with regard to the treaty).[109]

The opportunity for the nonnuclear weapons states to bring the treaty to an end came at the 1995 NPT Review and Extension Conference. But, as the president of the conference, Jayantha Dhanapala, observed: "It was clear from the very beginning that all delegations did want to extend the Treaty." The real issue at the conference was that among a large number of delegations "there was a desire for an indefinite extension plus"; the plus being "further commitments towards nuclear disarmament in terms of concrete action."[110] In short, the demand was for the nuclear weapons states to take seriously and fulfill their treaty commitments. It was not to be.

The United States, the other nuclear powers, and some U.S. allies worked for and got an indefinite extension without conditions or commitments on disarmament. Miguel Marin Bosch, Mexico's Ambassador to the conference, explained that the final decision indefinitely extending the NPT "was what the five permanent members of the Security Council wanted and secured in order to continue being the nuclear haves in a world of overwhelmingly nuclear have-nots."[111] Bosch went on to apportion responsibility among the nuclear weapons states, observing that "it is a unipolar 1946 world—there is only one super-power."[112]

While the links between the outcome of the NPT Review and Extension Conference and the interests it served are important, it is also necessary to attend to the way the decision was arrived at. The evidence suggests the "diplomacy" was far from meeting even elementary criteria for fairness and justice. According to Indonesia's ambassador, the 1995 decision was arrived at "simply by the use of pressure tactics against smaller countries . . . many countries complained to us about pressure with conditionalities and other types of pressure."[113] Other representatives of states from the South expressed similar concerns about the coercive private diplomacy. The Venezuelan ambassador, when asked why his state had supported indefinite extension, explained that, "there had been too much pressure . . . applied in all directions," adding that "most of the developing countries are going through difficult times, including my own."[114] More directly, the Venezuelan ambassador complained that, "this decision has been extracted by force."[115] Iran's ambassador made the connection between the means used to arrive at the indefinite extension decision and the implications for its legitimacy. He noted that "a lot of pressures . . . promises and sometimes threats were put on non-aligned countries . . . by certain nuclear weapons states, in particular the United States, as well as certain Western countries . . . this might call into question the method by which the indefinite extension was reached."[116]

It was noted earlier that validation (the signals of support or dissatisfaction with an agreement) and adherence (how an agreement fits into the larger set of shared principles and institutions) are important contributors to an agreement's legitimacy. The judgment of key nonnuclear weapons states makes clear that the 1995 conference added significantly to the growing crisis of legitimacy of the NPT. The crisis became even more acute when, in a 1996 ruling on a case brought before it by the U.N. General Assembly, the International Court of Justice (ICJ) gave its unanimous advisory opinion that under the NPT nuclear weapon states have "an obligation to pursue in good faith and bring to a conclusion negotiations leading to nuclear disarmament in all its aspects"[117] [emphasis added]. The U.S. ambassador to the U.N. Conference on Disarmament, Robert Grey, was dismissive: "Our own view is very clear: we don't think it helpful or useful to discuss nuclear disarmament or negotiate nuclear disarmament in a multilateral context."[118]

In the light of the court's judgment, the continued refusal by the nuclear weapon states to even permit negotiations on the elimination of nuclear weapons may be read as noncompliance with the NPT. The ICJ judgment and the lack of subsequent progress have given rise to recurring resolutions at the General Assembly demanding action. In December 1999, a paragraph recalling the court's ruling was put to the vote and adopted by 156 to 3—the United States, Russia, and France voted against, while the United Kingdom, Israel, and Bulgaria abstained.[119] This demand from an overwhelming majority of the international community was simply ignored by the nuclear weapons states. They did not open negotiations on how to comply with the court's judgment.

The nonnuclear weapons states have persisted in their efforts to seek full compliance with the NPT by the nuclear weapons states. Building on the World Court and General Assembly resolutions, the nuclear weapon states were placed under pressure by demands for nuclear disarmament from the "New Agenda Coalition" states (Brazil, Egypt, Ireland, Mexico, New Zealand, South Africa, and Sweden). At the April 2000 Review Conference of the NPT, the weapons states responded by including in the final document an "unequivocal undertaking . . . to accomplish the total elimination of their nuclear arsenals."[120] The seriousness of this "undertaking" became evident soon thereafter. While international newspaper reports declared "5 Atom Powers Agree to Scrap Arsenals" (*International Herald Tribune*), Ambassador Grey suggested that there were "different evaluations of what has been achieved" and other U.S. officials explained that the agreement "did not represent a significant shift in United States policy."[121] Ambassador Grey was a little more blunt later, saying the declaration "will have no more impact than its had in the past. It's more of the same."[122]

At the 2000 review of the NPT, the states parties agreed to thirteen practical steps as part of the effort to implement Article VI of the treaty.[123] The first of these was a commitment to urgent signature and ratification of the CTBT to achieve its early entry into force. With the Bush administration having made it clear that it will not consider ratification of the test ban, there is no prospect of entry into force. Another step was preserving and strengthening the ABM Treaty. The United States has since withdrawn from this treaty. There has been no significant progress on the other steps. A veteran observer of the NPT was moved to observe that in 2003 the NPT "faces some very serious challenges—even threats—that could result in its rather early demise unless great care is taken to address its limitations."[124]

Enforcing the NPT

While the most powerful states have limited their compliance with the NPT to the narrowest interpretation of certain specific obligations and refused compliance with other parts of the treaty, they have insisted that others comply with all the rules. Part of the problem lies in the structure of the treaty itself, the way in which it plays to power, and in particular the role given to the International Atomic Energy Agency (IAEA) and its Board of Governors, whose membership is determined in such a way that the nuclear weapons states are permanent members.[125] The board is supposed to report noncompliance to the Security Council and General Assembly of the United Nations.

It is worth looking briefly at how the IAEA, its board, and its general conference work in practice. One particularly illuminating example was provided by the events following the 1981 Israeli attack on Iraq's Osirak nuclear reactor.[126]

The Director-General and Board of Governors of the IAEA strongly condemned Israel's action and asked the General Conference of the IAEA to consider suspending Israel from the exercise of its rights and privileges. The General Conference stopped short and voted only to suspend all technical assistance to Israel. The following year, the General Conference considered a resolution to refuse Israel's participation in the meeting. When the vote went against Israel, the United States demanded an appeal, and when this was lost the official history of the IAEA records that "the delegations of the United Kingdom and the USA walked out of the conference hall, followed closely by most other Western delegations. Before withdrawing from the General Conference, the US delegate announced his government would reassess its policies regarding United States support for and participation in the IAEA and its activities."[127] In short, the United States would pull out of the IAEA or at least severely undermine its functioning. The history also notes that the United States has been and remains the largest contributor to the IAEA budget and its technical assistance programs. It came as no surprise when, a few months later, the IAEA Director-General and its board declared that Israel remained a full member of the IAEA, and the United States resumed its relationship with the agency.

Given this background, it is worth comparing the responses of the NPT machinery, the United States, the Security Council, and the larger international community to the pursuit of nuclear weapons by Israel, Iraq, North Korea, India, and Pakistan. In each case, the United States took the lead, at times supported by and at other times resisted by other Security Council powers and the larger international community. Given the international role played by the United States and the importance the United States has attached to nonproliferation, it is important to frame this discussion by recalling how the United States officially describes its interests in each case.

Proliferation: Threat and Response, an annual report from the Office of the U.S. Secretary of Defense, proclaims (as it has done for the past five years with hardly any change in wording) that for the Middle East, U.S. goals and interests include "maintaining a steadfast commitment to Israel's security and well-being" and "building and maintaining security arrangements that assure the stability of the Gulf region and unimpeded commercial access to its petroleum reserves."[128] In the case of North East Asia, the report declares U.S. interests are "to seek a stable and economically prosperous region." For South Asia, the interests are more security oriented, namely, "preventing another Indo-Pakistan war, enhancing regional stability, and stemming the proliferation of weapons of mass destruction." It will become clear that, for the United States, nuclear nonproliferation is, in fact, subordinate to its other specific national economic and military interests.

Colluding with Israel

Israel has the biggest and most successful nuclear weapons program outside of the five major nuclear weapons states.[129] It has not signed the NPT and is believed to maintain a stockpile of at least 100 and perhaps several hundred nuclear weapons and to possess ballistic missiles with a range up to 4,000 kilometers (Jericho-2), as well as aircraft capable of delivering nuclear weapons and submarine launched nuclear cruise missiles.[130] The reporting, analysis, and concern about Israel's nuclear weapons capabilities and of the role played by the United States have not been proportionate. This reflects the privileged position Israel holds not just in U.S. policy but also in much of the U.S. arms control and nonproliferation community.

United States support for Israel, especially among the policymaking community, has been unaffected by actions which, if taken by any other state, would have been seen as completely unacceptable. These actions include Israel's being prepared to use nuclear weapons in its 1973 war,[131] its 1982 invasion of Lebanon, in which almost 20,000 people were killed and many more injured,[132] its subsequent occupation of South Lebanon until early 2000, its policy of assassinations and bombings directed against Palestinian leaders in third countries, most notably in 1985 in Tunisia,[133] to say nothing of its widespread violation of international law as part of its illegal occupation of the Palestinian West Bank and Gaza. It takes far less for any other state to be dubbed a "rogue state" and subject to censure and punishment by the United States and its allies.

The United States has never tried to restrain Israel's nuclear weapons program. This has been despite occasional Israeli fears that the program might become an issue. According to Avner Cohen, when President John F. Kennedy met with Israeli Prime Minister David Ben Gurion in May 1961, they discussed Israel's nuclear weapons ambitions and capability for perhaps fifteen minutes and "Kennedy did not try to extract a promise that Israel would not develop a nuclear weapons capability in the future [and] exerted no new pressure and Ben Gurion had no need to use all the arguments he had prepared."[134] Cohen reports that Ben Gurion "felt relieved." By 1968, as the NPT was being negotiated, President Lyndon Johnson was content simply to tell Israel that, while its accession to the NPT was important to the United States, the United States would provide military assistance to Israel nonetheless.

Military support for Israel deepened even further under President Richard Nixon, who pledged "to keep Israel strong."[135] Subsequently, the United States and Israel have developed increasingly close military cooperation, concluding in 1970 an agreement known as the Master Defense Development Data Exchange, which gave Israel access to information on a range of military technologies.[136] The degree and quality of cooperation between the United States and Israel have grown markedly over time and now extend far beyond the supply of military technology. In 1987, the director of Defense Research and Development for Israel's armed forces noted that the two countries had a "dynamic array of joint R and D projects, weapons evaluations, exchange of lessons learned in war, and sharing of test results for weapons systems . . . [which] has transformed the concept of cooperation into a fantastic process benefiting both nations."[137] Israel may even have had access to U.S. and French nuclear weapons design and test expertise.[138] The United States has underpinned its cooperation through the provision of $70-80 billion of military and economic aid to Israel over the past two decades, and it presently provides well in excess of $3 billion a year. It has been noted that, "as stunning as these amounts are, they substantially underestimate the magnitude of [U.S.] assistance . . . they do not reflect the numerous special privileges being accorded to Israel."[139] In 1997, an amendment to the U.S. Defense Authorization Act barred U.S. companies from taking or selling high-resolution satellite pictures of Israel.[140] It is the only state with this protection.

There have been repeated demands from the international community that Israel should give up its nuclear weapons and accede to the NPT. It is the only state in the Middle East that is not a party to the treaty, making it impossible for the Middle East region to become a nuclear weapon free zone. Demands for such a zone have repeatedly been made by states within the region and by the larger international community through U.N. General Assembly resolutions, as well as in review conferences of the NPT parties. The 1995 NPT agreement on "Principles and Objectives for Nuclear Non-Proliferation and Disarmament" specifically encouraged all NPT states parties to exert "every effort" to universalize membership of the treaty. In December 1998, the U.N. General Assembly voted 158-2 in support of a resolution that "calls upon the only state in the region that is not a party to the NPT to accede without further delay and not to develop, produce, test or otherwise acquire nuclear weapons."[141] Only Israel and the United States voted against the resolution. The United States chose to support Israel rather than comply with its obligations under the NPT and respect the clearly stated wishes of the overwhelming majority of the international community.

Since then, the strategic interdependence between the United States and Israel has shown every sign of becoming even tighter. In 1998, the United States signed a Memorandum of Agreement with Israel committing it to "enhancing Israel's defense and deterrent capabilities" and "upgrading the framework of the US-Israel strategic and military relationship, as well as the technological cooperation between them."[142] The agreement included a U.S. commitment to providing "ways and means of assuring and increasing Israel's deterrent power by supplies of modern technology and weapons systems."[143] It is hard to read this as anything other than a promise of active U.S. support for Israel having and keeping nuclear weapons.[144]

The United States is not alone in heaping nuclear favors on Israel. France provided the Dimona facility to Israel for making weapons grade plutonium and a reprocessing plant for recovering it, as well as helping with the Jericho missile program. Germany has agreed to pay most of the $900 million cost of the three Dolphin submarines it is building for Israel, which are capable of firing long-range nuclear-capable cruise missiles.[145] Israel is reported to have tested such missiles to a range of almost 1,500 kilometers.[146]

The United States and Israel seem increasingly willing to make explicit the violation of the NPT. In February 2000, an agreement was signed giving Israeli scientists access to "limited nuclear information" from the U.S. nuclear weapons laboratories—such access had previously been restricted because of Israel's refusal to sign the NPT.[147] In making the announcement, U.S. Secretary of Energy Bill Richardson pointed out that Israel "is not treated in a similar fashion as others on our list of sensitive countries." The "sensitive countries" list is the familiar gallery, including India, Pakistan, Iran, Iraq, and North Korea.[148]

The Harrowing of Iraq

In sharp contrast to sustained U.S. military, economic, and political support for Israel has been its ruthless and unprecedented use of sanctions and force against Iraq to compel compliance with arms control agreements and U.N. resolutions, culminating in the 2003 invasion and occupation. This case reveals the complex interplay of U.S. politics, interests, and power, with the international community, international institutions, and public opinion over the question of compliance.

The 2003 war against Iraq has been described as the first "disarmament war."[149] But this takes U.S. claims at face value and ignores both context and precedent. A proper place to start to understand the 2003 war is the enduring U.S. interest in the Middle East region. The U.S. Department of Defense report, *Proliferation: Threat and Response*, describes the U.S. interest there, apart from protecting Israel, as "building and maintaining security arrangements that assure the stability of the Gulf region and unimpeded commercial access to its petroleum reserves."[150] The report explains that, "the proliferation of NBC [nuclear, biological, chemical] weapons and the means of delivering them poses a significant challenge to the ability of the United States to achieve these goals."[151]

The need for political stability and access to oil, more properly continued U.S. control, in the region, explains why while Iraq's invasion of Kuwait in 1990 led to a massive United States military intervention and the first U.S.-Iraq war, Iraq's 1980 invasion of Iran merited no comparable U.S. effort to defend Iran. Rather, in the Iran-Iraq war, the United States actively sided with Iraq. As a former U.S. ambassador to Iraq argued, "we were concerned that Iraq should not lose the war with Iran, because that would have threatened Saudi Arabia and the Gulf." The Iran-Iraq war came soon after the Iranian revolution freed the country from the U.S.-backed regime of the shah, with radical Islamists seizing power afterwards.[152] Iraq threatened U.S. interests in attacking Kuwait, a U.S. client, but not when it attacked postrevolutionary Iran.

The justification given for the first U.S.-Iraq war was that it was a response to Iraq's invasion of Kuwait. Iraq's aggression against Kuwait was subsequently used to justify the efforts to disarm Iraq of its weapons of mass destruction, including through the use of sanctions and eventually as a basis for the second U.S.-Iraq war.[153] But it is worth keeping in mind that, barely a year before Iraq attacked Kuwait, the United States had invaded Panama. The U.N. General Assembly denounced the U.S. assault as a "flagrant violation of international law."[154] A similar resolution brought before the U.N. Security Council had the support of all members except for the United States and its traditional nuclear-armed allies (and former colonial powers) Britain and France, and one other member, Canada (Finland abstained).[155]

Iraq's use of chemical weapons against Iran in the Iran-Iraq war, and against the Kurds in the late 1980s, was another key argument used to explain for U.S. policy toward Iraq at the time of and after Iraq's attack on Kuwait. It was referred to repeatedly by President George W. Bush and other U.S. policy makers in the run-up to the second U.S.-Iraq war. But this conveniently overlooks the U.S.-Iraq relationship leading up to and at the time these weapons were actually being used. A *Washington Post* investigation revealed that, during the 1980s "the administrations of Ronald Reagan and George H. W. Bush authorized the sale to Iraq of numerous items that had both military and civilian applications, including poisonous chemicals and deadly biological viruses, such as anthrax and bubonic plague."[156]

Even though it was known that Iraq had been making "almost daily use" of chemical weapons against Iran, the United States, according to a National Security Council official, "actively supported the Iraqi war effort," with billions of dollars and "by providing military intelligence and advice to the Iraqis."[157] The *New York Times* reported "American military officers said President Reagan, Vice President George Bush and senior national security aides never withdrew their support for the highly classified program in which more than 60 officers of the Defense Intelligence Agency were secretly providing detailed information on Iranian deployments, tactical planning for battles, plans for air strikes and bomb-damage assessments for Iraq," while at the same time "the C.I.A. provided Iraq with satellite photography of the war front."[158] Similarly, Iraq's use of chemical weapons against the Kurds, most notoriously in 1988 against the town of Halabjah, was met with increased U.S. military assistance.

In 1991, as part of the cease-fire ending the first U.S.-Iraq war, the U.N. Security Council created the United Nations Special Commission (UNSCOM) and mandated it to discover and destroy Iraq's chemical and biological weapons, ballistic missiles, and related production infrastructure.[159] The IAEA was separately charged with uncovering and destroying Iraq's nuclear weapons complex. These weapons programs were a clear breach of Iraq's international treaty commitments, including the NPT. Considering the failure of the Security Council to act in the case of Israel, it is almost perverse that the U.N. resolution justified action against Iraq in part by "recalling the objective of the establishment of a nuclear-weapons-free zone in the region of the Middle East . . . and the need to work towards the establishment in the Middle East of a zone free of such weapons."

UNSCOM was a new initiative in the history of both the U.N. and arms control.[160] Its executive chairman reported directly to the Security Council, not to the U.N. secretary-general. In addition to its chairman, the commission consisted of twenty members: the United States, the Russian Federation, the United Kingdom, France, China, Germany, Japan, Canada, the Netherlands, Australia, Austria, Belgium, the Czech Republic, Finland, Italy, Norway, Poland, Venezuela, Nigeria, and Indonesia—in other words, the permanent members of the Security Council, twelve states that could be classed as U.S. allies, along with one state each from Latin America, Africa, and Asia. No Arab country was a member.

UNSCOM was staffed not by U.N. civil servants, but by experts provided by and for the most part paid by their respective governments. The United States had a significant presence. UNSCOM was also supported by unprecedented intelligence sharing and cooperation by the United States, including a dedicated U-2 spy plane, equipment, and weapons experts for inspection teams. It was later revealed that U.S. intelligence agencies were using agents disguised as UNSCOM inspectors to monitor Iraqi military activity and collect information used for planning U.S. air attacks.[161] The UNSCOM inspectors were withdrawn from Iraq by the United Nations in late 1998 as the United States threatened and prepared to attack Iraq.[162] Iraq was bombed by U.S. and British planes in a 70-hour bombing campaign across the country in December 1998. Many of the targets attacked were sites that had been visited by the UNSCOM inspectors, leading Iraq to refuse to allow the inspectors to return.[163]

There was no authorization for the attacks from the Security Council and no state was willing to join the United States and United Kingdom in these bombing missions. This may be because they appeared to have a larger purpose, with U.S. officials seeing the bombing as a tool to "contain and degrade the Iraqi military, humiliate Saddam Hussein, and perhaps generate opposition to his rule."[164] This larger plan was made clear in a 1998 U.S. law authorizing $97 million in aid and equipment for armed insurgents in Iraq attempting to topple the government.[165]

Accompanying the inspections and the use of military force was a set of wide-ranging, severe, and destructive sanctions imposed on Iraq at the outset of the Gulf War in 1990. Official U.S. estimates are that by 1998, when the sanctions were replaced by a U.N. managed oil-for-food program, the sanctions had cost Iraq more than $120 billion.[166] There was an accompanying humanitarian tragedy. A UNICEF survey of child mortality in Iraq estimated that during the same eight year period, 1991-1998, there had been an additional half million deaths of children under five in the country as a whole.[167]

The humanitarian impact of the sanctions regime has raised great disquiet among many, including those charged with dealing with their terrible consequences. U.N. Assistant Secretary-General Denis Halliday, the first U.N. humanitarian coordinator in Iraq, resigned in October 1998 to protest what he called the "genocidal impact" of economic sanctions, while his successor, Hans von Sponeck, resigned a year later voicing similar concerns.[168] Senior U.S. officials saw differently. Secretary of State Madeleine Albright was asked in a television interview, "we have heard that over half a million children have died. I mean, that's more than died in Hiroshima. And, you know, is the price worth it?" To which she replied, "I think this is a very hard choice. But the price—we think the price is worth it."[169] It is a breathtaking judgment.

The original Security Council resolution on Iraq stated explicitly that sanctions "shall have no further force or effect" once Iraq complied with the weapons inspection regime contained in the resolution. In 1998, on the basis of IAEA reports, Russia, France, and China urged the Security Council to recognize the completion of Iraq's nuclear disarmament, but the move was opposed by the United States.[170] Following the U.N. withdrawal of UNSCOM, in 1999 the Security Council created a new inspection body, the United Nations Monitoring, Verification and Inspection Commission (UNMOVIC). But Iraq again refused to allow inspectors to enter the country.

The coming to power in 2001 of a hard-line conservative Republican government under President George W. Bush, with strong ties to the oil industry, marked the start of a yet more aggressive U.S. policy toward Iraq. Many senior members of the Bush administration were veterans of his father's administration that had waged the first U.S.-Iraq war, and had subsequently been arguing and organizing for further use of force against Iraq, and other states. It included the authors of a 1992 Pentagon Defense Planning Guidance that was notable for being "conspicuously devoid of references to collective action through the United Nations" and proposed that, "the United States be postured to act independently when collective action cannot be orchestrated."[171] Also, it included signatories to a 1998 letter to President Clinton, organized by a group calling itself the Project for a New American Century, urging "a strategy for removing Saddam's regime from power . . . [using] a full complement of diplomatic, political and military efforts."[172]

The attacks on September 11, 2001, against New York and Washington and the widespread support for war against the Taliban regime in Afghanistan opened a window of opportunity for the United States to move on Iraq. In late 2001, the United States decided to go to war against Iraq, with President Bush's speechwriters being asked to make a case for war against Iraq for the forthcoming 2002 State of the Union Address.[173] In the speech, Bush declared that the United States confronted an "axis of evil," naming North Korea, Iran, and Iraq, but focused his charge on Iraq and its pursuit of weapons of mass destruction and ties to Al-Qaeda.[174] After the war, it became clear that there was little if any evidence to substantiate these claims.[175]

In choosing war, and in keeping with the perspective of leading officials in the Bush administration, the United States initially dismissed demands that any military action against Iraq should be authorized by the United Nations. The U.S. Congress passed a resolution authorizing the use of force against Iraq without U.N. authority.[176] The United States, in fact, initiated in mid-2002 a sustained and increasingly intense series of air attacks against Iraq to lay the foundations for a subsequent invasion.[177]

In an effort to head off a U.S. attack on Iraq, in November 2002 the Security Council unanimously passed resolution 1441, establishing an unprecedented inspections regime, including the right of UNMOVIC inspectors to "immediate, unimpeded, unconditional and unrestricted access to any and all, including underground, areas, facilities, buildings, equipment, records and means of transport which they wish to inspect, as well as immediate, unimpeded, unrestricted, and private access to all officials and other persons."[178] While U.S. officials, supported by the United Kingdom, declared that any delay or sign of resistance by Iraq in its compliance with the resolution opened the door for the use of force, the other permanent members of the Security Council emphasized that it was for the United Nations weapons inspectors to determine and report any violations to the Security Council, and for the council to "take a position."[179]

U.S. plans for war also met determined resistance from public opinion. People took to the streets in a massive popular mobilization in the United States and around the world, arguably the largest mass movement in the twenty years since the antinuclear movements of the early 1980s, leading the *New York Times* to talk of the struggle between "two superpowers on the planet: the United States and world public opinion."[180]

Despite this, on February 24, 2003, the United States and United Kingdom proposed a Security Council resolution, with support from Spain, declaring that Iraq had failed to comply with resolution 1441, opening the way to the use of force.[181] Russia, France, and Germany countered with a memorandum calling for at least four more months of inspections, asserting that "the conditions for using force against Iraq are not fulfilled . . . no evidence has been given that Iraq still possesses weapons of mass destruction or capabilities in this field."[182] A revised U.S.-UK resolution that was tabled on March 7 gave Iraq a deadline of March 17, by which time the Security Council had to be satisfied that Iraq was in unconditional and active cooperation with UNMOVIC and had handed over all weapons of mass destruction, delivery systems, and information on its programs.[183] This was rejected by France, Russia, and China, the other permanent members of the council, with France and Russia announcing that they would veto the resolution should it be brought to a vote.[184] The United States sought and failed even to get support from a majority of members of the Security Council, despite what was characterized as "courtships, arm-twisting, compromises and back-room deal-making."[185]

As war seemed inevitable, U.N. Secretary-General Kofi Annan made clear that, "if the US and others were to go outside the Council and take military action, it would not be in conformity with the Charter."[186] The United States and United Kingdom withdrew their resolution on March 17, and two days later launched a war on Iraq.

Bargaining with North Korea

On January 10, 2003, North Korea announced its intention to withdraw from the NPT. It had made a similar announcement a decade earlier, in March 1993. It is the only state to have declared its withdrawal from the NPT. The crises that led up to these announcements and its subsequent resolution offers another instance of noncompliance and a set of reactions very different from those evident in the cases of Israel and Iraq.[187] The example of North Korea shows how far the United States is willing to go to negotiate over noncompliance when it chooses to do so.

North Korea initiated a nuclear research and development program with Soviet support in the late 1950s, receiving training for nuclear scientists and engineers and, in 1965, a research reactor.[188] This was in keeping with similar efforts underway around the world. In 1953, President Eisenhower had launched the Atoms for Peace Program in part as an effort to cultivate influence among developing countries. This provoked a competition with the Soviet Union to supply nuclear know-how. Over the next few decades, North Korea began to build an infrastructure that could support a nuclear weapons program (as did South Korea, a U.S. ally, for that matter). However, in December 1985, under Soviet pressure, North Korea joined the NPT, as South Korea had done a decade earlier.

For a number of reasons, the deadline for North Korea to sign the obligatory safeguards agreement with the IAEA only came in 1988, and it was missed by North Korea in part because it sought some larger benefit from its signature.[189] It demanded, in particular, the removal of U.S. nuclear weapons from South Korea and an assurance that the United States would not use nuclear weapons against it.[190] In 1991, the United States announced the removal of its nuclear weapons from South Korea, albeit as part of a larger set of unilateral measures coordinated with the Soviet Union to withdraw all tactical nuclear weapons from overseas (the goal was to ensure that the collapse of the Soviet Union would not leave any of its tactical nuclear weapons in any of the successor states except Russia). In December 1991, North and South Korea agreed, in a joint declaration on a Non-Nuclear Korean Peninsula, that they would "not test, manufacture, produce, introduce, possess, store, deploy, or use nuclear weapons" and would "not possess facilities for nuclear reprocessing and uranium enrichment."[191] In January 1992, North Korea signed the IAEA safeguards agreement.

Matters soon took a turn for the worse. The IAEA and North Korea began to negotiate the inspections that underpin safeguards. The U.S. government, a dominant player in the IAEA, "was urging the IAEA to tighten up its monitoring procedures" and at the same time "pressing South Korea to insist on elaborate and intrusive inspections of its own."[192] U.S. policy regarding North Korea at this time has been described as one of "using the IAEA to pry open access to North Korea's nuclear facilities, in an effort to constrain its nuclear program without offering anything in return."[193] The IAEA, still flinching from its failure to detect Iraq's clandestine nuclear weapon program, began to become more assertive, seeking special inspections at nuclear sites in North Korea.

North Korea resisted the inspections demand and, in March 1993, announced that, as allowed under the NPT, it would withdraw after ninety days. Matters came to a head in April 1993, when the IAEA's Board of Governors voted to refer the matter to the U.N. Security Council. A week later, the Security Council passed a resolution urging "all member states to encourage the DPRK to respond positively to this resolution and encourages them to facilitate a solution."[194] The United States, for its part, began to consider military action, including possibly attacking North Korea's nuclear facilities.[195] The U.S. did, however, open high level talks with North Korea, and North Korea suspended its withdrawal from the NPT.

Despite the negotiations, the United States was prepared to use coercion. For example, in early 1994, U.S. Secretary of Defense William Perry announced that he had ordered military preparations and warned that the United States was looking at "grim alternatives."[196] These preparations included the U.S. Joint Chiefs of Staff putting together a plan to attack North Korea.[197] President Clinton has explained that "We actually drew up plans to attack North Korea and to destroy their reactors and we told them we would attack unless they ended their nuclear programmes."[198] As Lee Sigal notes, North Korea needed little reminder of the history of U.S. nuclear threats (most notably during the Korean War) or the massive U.S. military presence in South Korea, and now "bristled at every threat."[199]

Eventually, in October 1994, the United States and North Korea arrived at a deal, dubbed the Agreed Framework. Its elements were very similar to what North Korea had proposed and the United States rejected a year earlier, and included North Korea freezing and dismantling its nuclear weapons program, based on plutonium production reactors and reprocessing plants, in exchange for two new light-water nuclear reactors for electricity generation and a supply of heavy fuel oil until these were completed.[200]

The prospect for improved U.S.-North Korean relations suffered a setback with the victory of the Republicans in the United States. Congressional elections in 1994, who rejected the Agreed Framework and sought to overturn it by ending funding for it.[201] There were persistent problems with the implementation of the agreement, including a United States failure to meet its commitment to deliver heavy fuel oil.[202] The promise to lift sanctions and improve relations fared a little better. In 1997, North Korea threatened to break the agreement and to resume its nuclear activities. This may have been when North Korea sought and acquired uranium enrichment technology from Pakistan, opening a second route to nuclear weapons material.[203] It also tested a new long-range missile, the first since before the Agreed Framework, in the fall of 1998.[204]

Following a trip by Defense Secretary Perry to North Korea, there was agreement to end missile tests in exchange for a lifting of U.S. sanctions and improved relations. By late 2000, the United States and North Korea formally announced that "neither government would have hostile intent toward the other," that they would make "every effort in the future to build a new relationship free from past enmity."[205]

The Bush administration took a much harder line with North Korea after coming to power in 2001. Most dramatically, it sought to discourage South Korea from continuing to pursue efforts to improve its relations with the North.[206] A year later, President Bush listed North Korea as one of three states making up an "axis of evil," which were a threat to the United States and international peace. As it became clear that the United States was intent on attacking Iraq, North Korea, fearing it might be next, demanded a formal guarantee that it would not be attacked. The United States refused.

The crisis came to a head in October 2002, when the United States confronted North Korea over its uranium enrichment program and North Korea announced an end to its compliance with the Agreed Framework.[207] The United States followed suit, suspending the heavy fuel oil shipments. The IAEA responded to North Korea's uranium enrichment program by unanimously adopting a resolution declaring that any such program would be a violation of the NPT.[208] North Korea, in turn, demanded that the IAEA remove the seals and cameras that were safeguarding North Korean nuclear facilities, and, when that was refused, removed them unilaterally and ordered IAEA monitors to leave.[209] The U.S. response was to propose a policy of "tailored containment" through the Security Council, involving political and economic pressure to force North Korea to give up its nuclear program.[210] Seeking to assure U.S. allies, and North Korea, U.S. Secretary of State Powell insisted that, "we have no intention of attacking North Korea."[211] But, at odds with the U.S. demands to cut off all aid (except food aid), South Korea, Russia, China, and Japan wanted to continue economic assistance to North Korea and sustain the Agreed Framework while pursuing talks.[212]

The U.S. effort to find a bargain with North Korea continued even though North Korea had announced its withdrawal from the NPT, the director-general of the IAEA had cited "chronic noncompliance" by North Korea, calling it "a country in defiance of its international obligations," and the IAEA Board of Governors had unanimously demanded North Korea return to compliance with the NPT.[213] According to Secretary of State Colin Powell, North Korea had "thumbed its nose at the international community," while the White House promised more "steady, steely diplomacy."[214] Chinese and Russian leaders also insisted that the way forward lay in dialogue.[215]

Through early 2002, U.S. leaders repeatedly affirmed that they sought a diplomatic settlement and would not invade North Korea, although they would not rule out attacks directed against North Korea nuclear facilities.[216] North Korea demanded from the United States a "legally-binding non-aggression treaty" and a halt to efforts to impose economic pressure. In exchange, it offered "to clear the U.S. of its security concerns," a proposal widely interpreted as abandoning its nuclear program. With the United States refusing to consider such a treaty, North Korea restarted its reprocessing of spent nuclear fuel to recover plutonium for nuclear weapons.[217] The U.S. response was to switch its attention to organizing allies in an effort to prevent North Korea from selling either nuclear material or long-range missiles, including through the interception of ships at sea.[218] The key U.S. ally in the region, South Korea, and the major powers bordering the region, Russia and China, are, however, not involved.

When North Korea formally announced, for the first time, in June 2003 that it was seeking nuclear weapons, the United States, in what was described as a "deliberately measured" response, insisted that, "there is an opportunity for a diplomatic solution, a political solution."[219] As the *New York Times* noted, regarding North Korea the United States has adopted "a strategy that appears to be the opposite of the administration approach to Iraq: for each new North Korean declaration, Mr. Bush has responded with the equivalent of a shrug."[220]

Containing India and Pakistan

A final example of efforts to bring about compliance with the international norms and agreements on nuclear arms control deals with the acquisition and testing of nuclear weapons by India and Pakistan. While the former three cases were all areas of prime U.S. interest, South Asia is a case of noncompliance in a region that is seen to have little limited economic significance or strategic importance over much of the past half-century. It also illustrates the use of sanctions as a way to prevent proliferation and for seeking compliance, and how tightly such sanctions are tied to other U.S. interests.

India began laying the base for its nuclear energy and nuclear weapons program soon after its independence in 1947.[221] Its early progress was facilitated by the U.S. Atoms for Peace Program, which permitted India to train over 1,300 nuclear scientists and engineers in the United States between 1955 and 1977.[222] India's first major research reactor was acquired from Canada in a 1955 deal, and both Canada and the United States supplied power reactors. India early on adopted a strategy for keeping its nuclear weapons option. U.S. ambivalence to India acquiring nuclear weapons at that time is evident in a 1961 memo to then Secretary of State Dean Rusk that suggested the United States help India acquire a nuclear weapon and conduct a test, so that a "friendly Asian power beat Communist China to the punch."[223] The idea was not taken up and China tested first, in 1964. India's first nuclear test came in 1974, using plutonium from a Canadian supplied research reactor.

Pakistan, a close Cold War ally of the United States in Asia, mostly watched as India developed its nuclear infrastructure but tried to stay in the game. Like India, it acquired a Canadian power reactor and refused to sign the NPT. Pakistan launched a serious effort to build nuclear weapons starting in 1972, assigning greater urgency to the program after India's 1974 test. While India had built its own plutonium reprocessing plant, Pakistan, recognizing its more limited capabilities, sought to purchase one from France.

Following India's 1974 nuclear test and with evidence of Pakistan's efforts to follow suit, the United States proposed the formation of a Nuclear Suppliers Group (NSG). The initiative sought to limit proliferation by managing the international trade in key nuclear technologies. It also provided a means of involving France, which was not a party to the NPT and thus was not bound by the treaty's provisions requiring full-scope safeguards on nuclear sales. The NSG has gradually tightened its restrictions on nuclear and dual-use trade.

The United States also resorted to direct sanctions, but only against Pakistan. These were applied to Pakistan in 1977 to dissuade it from working on a plutonium reprocessing capability, and again in 1979 because of its efforts to procure uranium enrichment technology.[224] In 1981, following the Soviet invasion of Afghanistan and Pakistan's willingness to support the United States against the Soviet Union, the sanctions were systematically waived each year for six years. Instead, the United States delivered several billion dollars of economic and military aid to Pakistan and chose not to make an issue of its nuclear weapons program. Similarly, in 1985 the U.S. Congress passed the Pressler Amendment, which requires the president to certify each year that Pakistan does not possess a nuclear device before any economic or military aid can be given. For several years, such certification was given even though there was mounting evidence that Pakistan had acquired a nuclear weapons capability.[225] It took the end of the Afghan war and the collapse of the Soviet Union before the sanctions were finally imposed on Pakistan.[226] By then, Pakistan, with help from China, had acquired nuclear weapons.

In May 1998, first India and then Pakistan tested nuclear weapons. In a unanimous June 1998 resolution condemning the tests, the Security Council called on both states "immediately to stop their nuclear weapon development programs, to refrain from weaponization or from the deployment of nuclear weapons, to cease development of ballistic missiles capable of delivering nuclear weapons and any further production of fissile material for nuclear weapons, to confirm their policies not to export equipment, materials or technology that could contribute to weapons of mass destruction or missiles capable of delivering them and to undertake appropriate commitments in that regard."[227] It also urged "India and Pakistan, and all other States that have not yet done so, to become Parties to the Treaty on the Non-Proliferation of Nuclear Weapons and to the Comprehensive Nuclear Test Ban Treaty without delay and without conditions." The resolution made it clear that "in accordance with the Treaty on the Non-Proliferation of Nuclear Weapons, India or Pakistan cannot have the status of a nuclear-weapon State." In effect, the council determined that India and Pakistan should disarm and join the NPT as nonnuclear weapons states. No action was taken; the United States applied sanctions to both states, but these were quickly relaxed for domestic political and economic reasons.[228] These sanctions were imposed only because legislation required them to be, and U.S. policymakers went through the motions.[229]

Neither India nor Pakistan has signed the CTBT or NPT. Indeed, the only conditions that seem to have been met to date are for no further nuclear tests, no deployment of weapons, and commitments not to export nuclear weapon related technologies. This appearance of compliance may be short-lived. The Security Council had also urged "India and Pakistan to exercise maximum restraint and to avoid threatening military movements, cross-border violations, or other provocations in order to prevent an aggravation of the situation," yet the two soon fought an eleven-week war in Kargil, Kashmir, in the spring of 1999. The Security Council took no action.

A different set of imperatives came into view when, in spring 2000, President Clinton made the first visit to South Asia by a U.S. president since 1978. Earlier differences on nuclear weapons were set aside. He made it clear that the United States was willing to engage with India on new terms. A joint statement declared that, "India and the United States will be partners in peace, with a common interest in and complementary responsibility for ensuring regional and international security."[230] India in effect agreed to "complement" the exercise of U.S. interests in return for the United States making a place for India in the international arena. One early expression of this was India's unprecedented support for President Bush's plan to deploy a National Missile Defense.[231] The United States has lifted its remaining sanctions on India, which have stood in the way of a burgeoning military cooperation. The lifting of the sanctions was intended to permit greater joint military planning, joint military operations, and U.S. supply of weapons and military technology to India.[232] This has included stronger links with Israel, the key U.S. ally in the Middle East. In 2001, India signed a $2 billion deal for Israeli military hardware.[233] The two states have been officially discussing what are described as "similar strategic concerns," including "nuclear nonproliferation, stability in West Asia and the Persian Gulf as well as the spread of extremism and terrorism."[234]

Since September 11, when India offered to support the United States in its war in Afghanistan, New Delhi has developed even closer military ties to the United States. The unprecedented level of military cooperation has involved joint naval patrols, exercises, training, and the largest sale of U.S. arms to India to date, involving $140 million worth of radar equipment.[235] India's rapidly growing military budget, and plans to spend as much as $100 billion in the next decade, has attracted interest from other international arms manufacturers, especially Russia, France, and the United Kingdom.[236]

U.S. relations with Pakistan have seen a similar transformation. Following a military coup in October 1999 by General Pervez Musharraf, the chief of the army, the United States demanded a return of democracy. This demand, like that for progress on meeting the terms of the Security Council resolution, was muted by concern over Pakistan's growing economic and political crisis, which is marked by a spiraling debt burden, a growing balance of payments problem, and increasingly militant Islamist groups. Some in Washington feared that putting pressure on Pakistan could hasten its collapse. As General Anthony C. Zinni, commander-in-chief of U.S. Central Command (which encompasses Pakistan) cautioned, "If Pakistan fails we have major problems . . . hardliners could take over, or fundamentalists or chaos."[237] The implicit concern was that victory for radical Islam or chaos in Pakistan could lead to the transfer of nuclear weapons to groups inimical to U.S. interests in the oil rich regions of the Middle East, or elsewhere. The goal has become to prevent this danger by saving Pakistan from collapse.

These concerns grew after the September 11 attacks. The United States needed Pakistan's support to wage war against the Taliban and Al-Qaeda in Afghanistan. Soon after September 11, the United States rescheduled $396 million of Pakistan's debt, approved a $300 million credit line for private investors, over $100 million help patrol borders and fight drug trafficking, followed by $600 million in foreign aid.[238] In June 2003, coinciding with an official visit by President Pervez Musharraf, the United States rewarded Pakistan's support in the "war against terrorism," with a further $3 billion aid package, of which half was military support.[239] Washington has been willing to overlook Pakistan's continued development of nuclear weapons and testing of ballistic missiles, its relationship with North Korea, to say nothing of the problems with the Pakistani national elections of 2001.

There remain two areas of active U.S. concern. The first is possible ties between Pakistani nuclear scientists and radical Islamic groups. In the wake of September 11, it was discovered that three scientists in Pakistan's nuclear weapons program had met with Taliban and Al-Qaeda leaders.[240] There was a possibility that several others may have had similar ties.[241] The second issue of concern has been the physical security of Pakistan's nuclear facilities, nuclear weapons, and fissile materials.[242] The United States has offered and Pakistan has been willing to accept help in this area.[243] It has also been claimed that the United States has made plans to try to seize Pakistan's nuclear weapons should the Musharraf regime collapse and radical Islamic groups come to power.[244] More dramatically, the Bush administration's December 2001 *Nuclear Posture Review* proposed that "in setting requirements for nuclear strike capabilities," it was necessary to consider "unexpected contingencies" which involved "sudden and unpredicted security challenges," citing as an example "a sudden regime change by which an existing nuclear arsenal comes into the hands of a new, hostile leadership group."[245]

The United States and the larger international community have found ways to "cope" with noncompliance by India and Pakistan. This is despite the widespread belief that there is a real possibility of nuclear war in South Asia.[246]

States and Peoples

Despite its great power, systemic noncompliance, involvement in many acts of noncompliance by chosen states, and its success in confronting challenges to its interests over the past several decades, there is anxiety among policymakers in the United States about a crisis of compliance. This has led to a search for ways to hone mechanisms that it can use to more effectively discipline other, less powerful, states and so to compel greater obedience. These include the unilateral use of force, expanded U.N. enforcement, sharper sanctions, and directly barring individuals from work on weapons of mass destruction.[247] These approaches presume there is no need to ensure that treaties and norms of international behavior are derived by a process seen universally as fair, legitimate, and equitable. The issue is simply one of finding sufficiently sharp "teeth" that can ensure compliance by others with the agreements that already exist. These teeth are most obviously sanctions and direct military action (counterproliferation), instruments that are particularly suited to U.S. strengths and that could not be used against it. Naturally, from this perspective, there is no question of finding ways to bring about compliance by the United States.

For the international community, recent experience with U.S. policy on the ABM, CTBT, NPT, and Chemical and Biological Weapons Conventions has raised what Harald Müller politely called "the actor problem," and in this chapter has been put more directly as "the American problem." How is the world to deal with noncompliance by the United States given that the United States is the most powerful state in the international system and has a long history of imperial thought, practice, and apologetics?

There are two options. The first is to use collective international action through international institutions. One variant calls for an enhanced role for the United Nations. Since the issue is one of compliance with agreements dealing with international peace and security, enforcement would in the final analysis depend on the use of sanctions or military force and it would be the Security Council that would become the final arbiter of compliance. The past behavior of the Security Council offers little basis for hope.

The crisis over the legitimacy and justice of the rules and structures of the United Nations and its Security Council is only part of a much larger and enduring failure of the U.N. system in dealing with issues of disarmament and peace. Setting aside the complete failure to meet its founding principle, namely, "to save succeeding generations from the scourge of war," the U.N. system and in particular the Security Council have ignored other important responsibilities. Article 26 of the U.N. Charter declares that: "in order to promote the establishment and maintenance of international peace and security with the least diversion for armaments of the world's human and economic resources, the Security Council shall be responsible for formulating . . . plans to be submitted to the Members of the United Nations for the establishment of a system for the regulation of armaments."

There has only been one plan in nearly sixty years that came close to meeting any reasonable criteria for regulating armaments and thus for meeting the obligations of Article 26. Issued by the United States and the Soviet Union on September 20, 1961, this was "The Joint Statement of Agreed Principles for Disarmament Negotiations."[248] These principles, known as the McCloy-Zorin agreement after its U.S. and Soviet authors, were subsequently adopted unanimously by the U.N. General Assembly on December 20, 1961. The goal of disarmament negotiations, the joint statement declared, was general and complete disarmament, which "shall ensure that States have at their disposal only such non-nuclear armaments, forces, facilities, and establishments as are agreed to be necessary to maintain internal order and protect the personal security of citizens." The road map was explicit: the disarmament program should be implemented in an agreed sequence, in stages, until it is completed, with each measure and stage carried out within specified time limits. The goals were:

(a) disbanding of armed forces, the dismantling of military establishments, including bases, the cessation of the production of armaments, as well as their liquidation or conversion to peaceful uses;
(b) the elimination of all stockpiles of nuclear, chemical, bacteriological, and other weapons of mass destruction, and the cessation of the production of such weapons;
(c) the elimination of all means of delivery of weapons of mass destruction;
(d) the abolition of organizations and institutions designed to organize the military effort of states, the cessation of military training, and the closing of all military training institutions; and
(e) the discontinuance of military expenditures.

The McCloy-Zorin principles for disarmament are now almost completely forgotten, even in the arms control community.[249] The scale of the failure is stark, and the United States is not the only culprit. In 2002, there were over 30,000 nuclear weapons in the world; with the United States having some 7,600 deployed warheads (with another 3,000 as spares and reserves, and over 10,600 intact warheads and 5,000 plutonium cores in storage) and Russia about 20,000 warheads (over 8,000 are deployed), while China has about 400 weapons, France has 450, and the United Kingdom, 185 weapons deployed.[250] World military spending in the aftermath of the Cold War; for the period 1992 to 2001, amounted to $7,625 billion (in 1998 dollars).[251] By far the largest share of this spending was by the United States (36 percent of all military expenditure in 2001) with the other permanent members of the Security Council taking up four out of the next five places. The effort to sustain the distribution of military power in the world is evident; the peace that was promised is hard to see.

The conspicuous absence of significant international agreements on military spending and conventional weapons can be traced in large measure to the military production industries and the governments in the United States and Western Europe. The combined arms sales of the largest 100 arms manufacturers in the Organization for Economic Cooperation and Development (OECD) countries and developing countries in 2000 amounted to $157 billion, with the United States having a 60 percent share, and its Western European allies responsible for another 30 percent (i.e., a total of 90 percent of arms sales); these sales reflect the fact that 43 out of these top 100 arms producers, and 7 out of the top 10, are U.S. corporations, while another 38 of the top 100 companies are Western European.[252] Further, as John Harvey has noted: "international trade in military aircraft between industrialized and developing countries nations is well established, pervasive and lucrative . . . it is no wonder then that the western nations have achieved some success in establishing the Missile Technology Control Regime, but have not attempted even to seek, much less reach, agreement on the desirability of discouraging sales of advanced strike aircraft."[253]

The role of the Security Council has long been an issue within the United Nations. James A. Paul, in a summary of the debate within the U.N. about the role of the Security Council, noted that, "UN members are especially concerned that the Council operates inconsistently, that it often does not enforce its own resolutions and that it sometimes ignores or even violates international law."[254] Developing a mechanism to bypass the Security Council and empower the General Assembly would certainly introduce greater equity and fairness into decision-making on questions of compliance and permit appropriate international responses to noncompliance by the United States.

There is an existing procedure that could serve as the basis for collective action by the larger international community. The "Uniting for Peace" resolution, adopted by the General Assembly in November 1950, allows the assembly to take action if the Security Council, because of a lack of unanimity of its permanent members, fails to act in a case where there appears to be a threat to the peace, breach of the peace, or act of aggression. The assembly is empowered to make recommendations which can include, in the case of a breach of the peace or act of aggression, the use of armed force to maintain or restore international peace and security. An alternative path to empowering the General Assembly would involve amending the U.N. Charter.

Any proposed mechanism must deal with the fact that the members of the General Assembly and the Security Council, as well as the United Nations as an institution, are subject to pressure by those able to exercise it. Under the present circumstances, this is largely American power. Although, as the Security Council's refusal to authorize a United States attack on Iraq suggests, this power need not prevail. But the fact that the United States went ahead regardless illustrates that the underlying reality is, as U.S. Secretary of State George Marshall pointed out in 1948, that if there is "a complete lack of power equilibrium in the world, the United Nation's cannot function successfully."[255]

If international institutions are too easily prone to imperial influence, and too easily ignored when they do not consent, then what is left? In an earlier study of compliance with arms control regimes, Harald Müller concluded that "the more regime compliance issues become a matter of domestic discourse, the better the chances of compliance with regime rules."[256] This is an important observation in that it emphasizes the role of citizens and domestic political institutions in shaping state policy and government attitudes toward international treaties and obligations. This is what is missing from the story of the pirate and the emperor. The analogy, for all its power, personalizes the confrontation. It fails to make explicit that the sources and conduct of policies and the interests underlying them are located in the politics of the empire. It is there where pressure must be brought to bear.

Transforming U.S. politics when it comes to international issues is no easy matter. Experience has shown that the U.S. government and its policy elites are often able to powerfully shape public sensibilities about particular issues, creating in effect a common sense that supports official positions which are inclined to be coercive and imperial.[257] This is by no means a radical observation. In the case of the United States, the baleful influence of the infamous "military-industrial-scientific complex" has been well known at least since President Eisenhower's famous 1961 warning of the "conjunction of an immense military establishment and a large arms industry . . . [whose] total influence—economic, political, even spiritual—is felt in every city, every State house, every office of the Federal government." He went on to argue that, "in the councils of government, we must guard against the acquisition of unwarranted influence, whether sought or unsought, by the military industrial complex."[258] To this can be added the other economic interests that rely on this military complex to protect markets and ensure a ready and cheap supply of raw materials. The struggle for compliance must confront the very basis of the economic, social, and political system of the United States.

There is a long history of efforts by the international antinuclear peace movement to incite action by citizens for nuclear disarmament. The movement has had significant successes, even if it remains on the margins of much conventional academic discussion of the history of arms control. Mass mobilization by peace movements against the threat of nuclear war and the dangers of radioactive fallout from atmospheric nuclear testing in the 1950s led to the first ban on nuclear testing. In the 1960s, it helped lay the basis for the ABM Treaty; in the early 1980s, Western Europe saw the largest political mobilization by citizens in decades, with hundreds of thousands of people demanding nuclear disarmament by the United States and U.S.S.R. Similarly, in June 1982, almost a million people joined a protest in New York City for an end to the nuclear arms race. These demonstrations led to the Intermediate Nuclear Forces Treaty.[259] The effectiveness of such public action is recognized in Joseph Nye's observation that among the "crucial political roles" of arms control, "the first is to reassure the publics."[260]

Civil society initiatives have been able to be effective in the post-Cold War period.[261] A notable example was a six-year campaign by Parliamentarians for Global Action (a New York-based nongovernmental organization with over 1,000 members who are legislators in eighty countries), to call a conference of the signatories of the 1963 Partial Test Ban Treaty to consider an amendment to the treaty that would serve to turn it into a comprehensive ban on all nuclear tests. The campaign succeeded and the conference was called in 1991 in New York, with almost 100 of the 119 signatories present. But, just before the conference began, the United States announced that if the amendment were voted on, it would exercise its right of veto as one of the three depository states (the others are the United Kingdom and Russia) and so prevent it coming into force. The United Kingdom supported the United States, while Russia was willing to accept the amendment and an end to nuclear testing. During the conference itself NGOs played a major role, and an assessment of the process and the outcome has suggested that a combination of NGOs and smaller states was able to confront and expose the United States on the issue of nuclear testing.[262] The initiative, and the possibility that it would be repeated, is credited with helping create the pressure which led the Conference on Disarmament to agree on a negotiating mandate for the CTBT two years later.

A more recent example is the campaign for a Nuclear Weapons Convention, a treaty to eliminate nuclear weapons. This emerged from a 1995 study by the International Network of Engineers and Scientists Against Proliferation (INESAP), "Beyond The NPT: Toward A Nuclear Weapon Free World," and from the founding of Abolition 2000, a global network to eliminate nuclear weapons. The latter now has over 2,000 member organizations in more than ninety countries.[263] These initiatives led to a project by the International Physicians for the Prevention of Nuclear War, the International Association of Lawyers Against Nuclear Arms, and INESAP to produce a Model Nuclear Weapons Convention.[264] In 1997, Costa Rica submitted the Model Convention as an official U.N. document, describing it as "a work in progress setting forth the legal, technical and political issues that should be considered to obtain an actual nuclear weapons convention."[265] These efforts have garnered support from governments of nonnuclear weapons states, which have used U.N. General Assembly resolutions to call for such a convention annually for the past several years, and there have been efforts to discuss it in various parliaments.[266]

The determined efforts of civil society and the nonnuclear weapons states to achieve nuclear disarmament and to seek compliance by the weapons states with their NPT obligations can be read as an instance of what has been called "rightful resistance," that is, a popular contestation promoted by the relatively powerless, through an innovative use of laws, policies, and other officially promoted values, working within and at the boundaries of existing official institutions, with the powerful presented as "disloyal" to their own norms.[267] Recent scholarship and experience shows strongly that transnational coalitions of civil society groups, which share an identity and operate across state boundaries, can serve as "teachers of norms" within and between states.[268]

There is clearly a need for new kinds of international institutions, where civil society can more effectively organize and represent the aspirations of people outside the context and confines of nation states and become a more significant force in the international system. Richard Falk and Andrew Strauss have proposed a Global People's Assembly as a way to meet this need.[269] In particular, they have stressed that it would serve as a forum where "the ability to opt out of collective efforts to protect the environment, control or eliminate weapons, safeguard human rights, or otherwise protect the global community could be challenged."[270]

The challenge of compliance becomes how to build civil society and more specifically peace movements that can impose compliance on states from within and without. This may be the only hope to achieve compliance by the most powerful. This task may be made more or less difficult depending on the way the goal and the path are understood. For much of the past fifty or so years, the peace movement has been focused on the bomb. It has relied on the devastating destructive power of nuclear weapons, the risk of nuclear war by design or by accident, the high economic costs of nuclear weapons, and the profound environmental consequences associated with the production of nuclear weapons to mobilize public concern. The soaring nuclear arsenals and bitter, crisis-ridden confrontation of the Cold War provided fuel for such efforts. But the dwindling of public fears in the United States after the end of the Cold War has served to emphasize Mahatma Gandhi's observation after the destruction of Hiroshima that it would be a mistake to believe that the bomb's destructive power would so disgust the world as to make it forswear nuclear weapons. The answer to the bomb has to be found elsewhere.

In the final analysis, the need for state compliance with arms control and disarmament agreements and for public participation in an alert and active anti-nuclear peace movement, while important, are not the real issues. The struggle is for peace and justice and that requires transforming the institutions, economies, cultures, and ways of thinking that are the social and economic engines of competition, exploitation, hostility, and conflict, and putting in place institutions that are oriented toward participatory democracy and that cultivate a disposition for justice.

Notes

1. Noam Chomsky, *Pirates and Emperors: International Terrorism in the Real World* (Montreal: Black Rose Books, 1987), 9.
2. Thom Shanker, "White House Says the U.S. Is Not a Loner, Just Choosy," *New York Times*, July 31, 2001.
3. The literature and institutional effort that has been generated is enormous.
4. Noam Chomsky, *American Power and the New Mandarins* (New York: Vintage Books, 1969).
5. John Gee, the deputy director-general of the Organization for the Prohibition of Chemical Weapons, the body charged with implementing the treaty, observed that the U.S. conditions on its ratification appear "prima facie to be contrary to the provisions of the convention." "The CWC at the Two-Year Mark: An Interview with Dr. John Gee," *Arms Control Today* (April/May 1999): 8.
6. Vernon Loeb, "U.S. Won't Back Plan to Enforce Germ Pact," *Washington Post*, July 21, 2001.
7. Harald Müller, "Compliance Politics: A Critical Analysis of Multilateral Arms Control Treaty Enforcement," *The Nonproliferation Review* (Summer 2000): 88-9.
8. The White House, *A National Security Strategy for a New Century*, December 1999, www.globalsecurity.org/military/library/policy/national/nss9912.htm.

9. The White House, The National Security Strategy of the United States of America, September 20, 2002, www.globalsecurity.org/military/library/policy/national/nss-020920.pdf.

10. Michael W. Doyle, *Empires* (Ithaca, NY: Cornell University Press, 1986), 45.

11. For a list of U.S. interventions, excluding declared wars, from 1787 to 1941, see William Appleman Williams, *Empire as a Way of Life: An Essay on the Causes and Character of America's Present Predicament along with a Few Thoughts about an Alternative* (Oxford: Oxford University Press, 1980).

12. Barry M. Blechman and Stephen S. Kaplan, *Force without War: U.S. Armed Forces as a Political Instrument* (Washington D.C.: The Brookings Institution, 1978), 547-53.

13. Noam Chomsky, *Deterring Democracy* (London: Verso, 1991).

14. Barry M. Blechman and Tamara Cofma Wittes, *Defining Moment: The Threat and Use of Force in American Foreign Policy Since 1989*, Occasional Paper No. 6 (Washington, D.C.: Henry L. Stimson Center, May 1998).

15. Williams, *Empire as a Way of Life*, ix.

16. See, for example, Michael Ignatieff, "The American Empire—Get Used to It," *New York Times Magazine*, January 5, 2003, 22-7; and Max Boot, "American Imperialism? No Need to Run from the Label," *USA Today*, May 6, 2003.

17. Noam Chomsky, *American Power and the New Mandarins*, 330-1.

18. For a discussion, see chapter 8 by Harold A. Feiveson and Jacqueline W. Shire in this volume.

19. Williams, *Empire as a Way of Life*.

20. E. P.Thompson, *Whigs and Hunters* (London: Penguin, 1975), 263.

21. Tariq Banuri, "The Landscape of Diplomatic Conflicts," in Wolfgang Sachs, ed., *Global Ecology: A New Arena of Political Conflict* (London: Zed Books, 1993), 49.

22. Thomas M. Franck, *Fairness in International Law and Institutions* (Oxford: Clarendon Press, 1995), 25-46, 477, 481.

23. John Rawls, *A Theory of Justice* (Cambridge, MA: Harvard University Press, 1971 and rev. ed. (Cambridge, MA: Belknap Press, 1999), 11.

24. For a critical perspective on the application of Rawls' ideas to international affairs, see Fernando R. Teson, "The Rawlsian Theory of International Law," *Ethics and International Affairs* 9 (1995): 79-99. For a discussion specifically about nuclear proliferation, see Steven Lee, "Nuclear Proliferation and Nuclear Entitlement," *Ethics and International Affairs* 9 (1995): 101-31.

25. Anjali V. Patil, *The UN Veto in World Affairs 1946-1990: A Complete Record and Case Histories of the Security Council's Veto* (London: Mansell, 1992), 5, 15.

26. Radio Report to the American People on the San Francisco Conference by U.S. Secretary of State Edward R. Stettinius, Jr. (Washington, D.C.: U.S. Department of State Bulletin, May 28, 1945).

27. Phyllis Bennis, *Calling the Shots: How Washington Dominates Today's UN* (New York: Olive Branch Press, 2000), 245.

28. Patrick E. Tyler, "A Deepening Fissure," *New York Times*, September 13, 2002.

29. Steven R. Weisman, "A Long, Winding Road to a Diplomatic Dead End," *New York Times*, March 17, 2003.

30. Gregg Herken, *The Winning Weapon: The Atomic Bomb in the Cold War 1945-1950* (Princeton, NJ: Princeton University Press, 1982).

31. Frederick S. Dunn, Bernard Brodie, Arnold Wolfers, Percy E. Corbett, and William T. R. Fox, *The Absolute Weapon: Atomic Power and World Order* (New York: Harcourt, Brace and Company, 1956), 5.

32. Herken, *The Winning Weapon*, 171.

33. Matthew Evangelista, "Cooperation Theory and Disarmament Negotiations in the 1950s," *World Politics* 42, no. 4 (July 1990): 502-28.

34. McGeorge Bundy, *Danger and Survival: Choices about the Bomb in the First Fifty Years* (New York: Random House, 1988), 301.

35. Bundy, *Danger and Survival*.

36. See, for instance, Bernhard G. Bechhoefer, *Postwar Negotiations for Arms Control* (Washington, D.C.: The Brookings Institution, 1961).

37. Thomas C. Schelling, "Reciprocal Measures for Arms Stabilization," *Daedalus: Proceedings of the American Academy of Arts and Sciences* 89, no. 4 (Fall 1960): 894.

38. Schelling, "Reciprocal Measures," 893.

39. Schelling, "Reciprocal Measures," 895.

40. Thomas C. Schelling, "The Thirtieth Year," *Daedalus:Proceedings of the American Academy of Arts and Sciences* 120, no. 1 (Winter 1991): 21-31.

41. Marcus Raskin, "Nuclear Extermination and the National Security State," in *New Left Review*, ed., *Exterminism and Cold War* (London: Verso, 1982), 205-6.

42. See Arms Control and Disarmament Agreements (Washington, D.C.: U.S. Arms Control and Disarmament Agency, 6th ed., 1996).

43. On the domestic politics of U.S. nuclear weapons policy during and after the Cold War, see McGeorge Bundy, *Danger and Survival*; Janne E. Nolan, *Guardians of the Arsenal: The Politics of Nuclear Strategy* (New York: Basic Books, 1989); and Janne E. Nolan, *An Elusive Consensus: Nuclear Weapons and American Security after the Cold War* (Washington, D.C.: Brookings Institution Press, 1999).

44. Robin Ranger, *Arms and Politics 1958-1978: Arms Control in a Changing World* (Toronto: MacMillan, 1979), vii.

45. Allan S. Krass, *Verification: How Much Is Enough?* (Philadelphia: Taylor and Francis, 1985), 162.

46. William F. Rowell, *Arms Control Verification: A Guide to Policy Issues for the 1980s* (Cambridge, MA: Ballinger, 1986), 148.

47. Allan S. Krass, *Verification*, 165.

48. Lee Butler, "Zero Tolerance," *Bulletin of the Atomic Scientists* (January/February 2000): 20-22, 72-5.

49. Strobe Talbott, *Deadly Gambits: The Reagan Administration and the Stalemate in Nuclear Arms Control* (New York: Knopf, 1984), xii.

50. Talbott, *Deadly Gambits*, 343.

51. See Matthew Bunn, Oleg Bukharin, Jill Cetina, Kenneth Luongo, and Frank von Hippel, "Retooling Russia's Nuclear Cities," *Bulletin of the Atomic Scientists* (October 1998): 44-50.

52. Jonathan Schell, "The Folly of Arms Control," *Foreign Affairs* 79, no. 5 (September/October 2000): 27.

53. Allan S. Krass, *Verification*, 1-2.

54. Harold A. Feiveson, ed., *The Nuclear Turning Point* (Washington, D.C.: Brookings Institution Press, 1999), 6.

55. Henry Kissinger, "Arms Control to Suit a New World," *Los Angeles Times*, November 20, 1999.

56. David C. Gompert, "Sharpen the Fear," *Bulletin of the Atomic Scientists* 56, no. 1 (January/February 2000): 22-3, 76-7.

57. The economic and political interests that are being pursued are the theme of much of the recent literature on globalization, see, for instance, Richard Falk, *Predatory Globalization* (New York: Polity Press, 1999).

58. Condoleeza Rice, "Promoting the National Interest," *Foreign Affairs* 79, no. 1 (January/February 2000): 45.

59. Nicholas Lehman, "Without a Doubt," *New Yorker*, October 14, 2001.

60. David E. Sanger, "Bush Offers Arms Talks to China as U.S. Pulls Out of ABM Treaty," *New York Times*, December 14, 2001.

61. Schelling, "The Thirtieth Year," 21-31.

62. Bruce K. Holloway cited in H. P. Metzger, *The Atomic Establishment* (New York: Simon and Schuster, 1972), 45.

63. For details of the compliance management provisions in the various superpower treaties, see chapter 8 in this volume by Feiveson and Shire. A model of compliance as a management problem has been advanced by Abram Chayes and Antonia Handler Chayes, who claim it is not "willful disobedience but the lack of capability or clarity or priority" that is the primary source of noncompliance. Chayes and Chayes, *The New Sovereignty: Compliance with International Regulatory Agreements* (Cambridge, MA: Harvard University Press, 1995), 22. Subsequent events have revealed how limited was this explanation.

64. Michael Krepon and Dan Caldwell, eds., *The Politics of Arms Control Treaty Ratification* (New York: St. Martin's Press, 1991), 463.

65. Nolan, *Guardians of the Arsenal*, 154.

66. For an analysis, see Harald Müller, "The Internalization of Principles, Norms, and Rules by Governments: The Case of Security Regimes," in Volker Rittberger and Peter Mayer, eds., *Regime Theory and International Relations* (New York: Clarendon Press, 1993), 361-88.

67. Craig Cerniello, "Senate, House Approve Bills Calling for NMD Deployment," *Arms Control Today* (March 1999). President Clinton signed the bill the following day.

68. Henry Kissinger, "The Next President's First Obligation," *Washington Post*, February 9, 2000.

69. Steve Schmitt and Steven Lee Myers, "Clinton Lawyers Give a Go-Ahead to Missile Shield: Loophole Seen in Treaty," *New York Times*, June 15, 2000.

70. Marc Lacey, "Putin Bends Clinton's Ear Hoping to Halt Missile Shield," *New York Times*, July 22, 2000.

71. David E. Sanger, "Bush's Travels: Antimissile Diplomacy," *New York Times*, July 24, 2001.

72. James Dao, "Defense Panel Sees ABM Violations as Arising Soon," *New York Times*, August 1, 2001.

73. See George Perkovich, *India's Nuclear Bomb* (Berkeley: University of California Press, 1999) and George Bunn, "The Status of Norms against Nuclear Testing," *The Nonproliferation Review* (Winter 1999): 20-32.

74. Lawrence S. Wittner, *The Struggle against the Bomb, Volume Two, Resisting the Bomb—a History of the World Nuclear Disarmament Movement 1954-1970* (Stanford, CA: Stanford University Press, 1997).

75. Paul H. Nitze, *From Hiroshima to Glasnost* (New York: Grove Weidenfeld, 1989), 191.

76. Herbert York, *Making Weapons Talking Peace: A Physicist's Odyssey from Hiroshima to Geneva* (New York: Basic Books, 1987), 283.

77. York, *Making Weapons Talking Peace*, 288

78. Richard Perle, Testimony to the US Senate in 1986, cited in Philip G. Schrag, *Global Action: Nuclear Test Ban Diplomacy and the End of the Cold War* (Boulder, CO: Westview Press, 1992), 40.

79. In 1987, A/RES/42/27, urgent need for a comprehensive test ban treaty, and, in 1988, A/RES/43/64; see Schrag, *Global Action*, 42, fn. 176.

80. As of July 2003.

81. Andrew Lichterman and Jacqueline Cabasso, *A Faustian Bargain: Why Stockpile Stewardship Is Incompatible with the Process of Nuclear Disarmament* (Oakland, CA: Western States Legal Foundation, March 1998).

82 Madeleine Albright, "A Call for American Consensus," *Time*, November 22, 1999.

83. For treaty text, see Preparatory Commission for the Comprehensive Nuclear-Test-Ban Treaty Organization, www.ctbto.org/ctbto/treaty.shtml.

84. U.S. Department of State, Article by Article Analysis of the CTBT, a report accompanying President Clinton's letter of transmittal of treaty to the U.S. Senate, September 22, 1997, see Federation of American Scientists, www.fas.org/nuke/control/ctbt/text/index.html.

85. Letter of transmittal to the U.S. Senate.

86. *Stockpile Stewardship Plan FY 2000* (Washington, D.C.: Office of Defense Programs, U.S. Department of Energy, March 15, 1999).

87. Christopher E. Paine and Matthew G. Mckinzie, *End Run: The U.S. Government's Plan for Designing Nuclear Weapons and Simulating Nuclear Explosions under the Comprehensive Test Ban Treaty* (Washington, D.C.: National Resources Defense Council, August 1997), 23.

88. Craig Cerniello, "Senate Rejects Comprehensive Test Ban Treaty; Clinton Vows to Continue Moratorium," *Arms Control Today* (September/October 1999).

89. Henry Kissinger, "Arms Control to Suit a New World."

90. Greg Mello, "That Old Designing Fever," *Bulletin of the Atomic Scientists* (January/February 2000): 51-7.

91. Ian Hoffman, "Low-Yield Nuke Bombs Endorsed," *Albuquerque Journal*, August 15, 2000, and Philip Bleek, "Defense Bill Bars Unilateral Nuclear Reductions, Orders Posture Review," *Arms Control Today* (November 2000): 26.

92. Carl Hulse and James Dao, "Cold War Long Over, Bush Administration Examines Steps to a Revamped Arsenal," *New York Times*, May 29, 2003.

93. This perspective came out clearly during the U.S. Senate's refusal to ratify the Comprehensive Test Ban Treaty. See Henry A. Kissinger, "Arms Control to Suit a New World" and Senator Richard Lugar, statement released October 7, 1999. Much of the statement is reprinted in the *Bulletin of the Atomic Scientists* (January/February 2000): 44-6. For a further discussion, see chapter 8 by Feiveson and Shire in this volume.

94. Colum Lynch, "U.S. Boycotts Nuclear Test Ban Meeting," *Washington Post*, November 12, 2001.

95. C. Paul Robinson, *A White Paper: Pursuing a Nuclear Weapons Policy for the 21st Century* (Livermore, CA: Sandia National Laboratories, March 22, 2001), www.sandia.gov/media/whitepaper/2001-04-Robinson.htm.

96. Stephen M. Younger, *Nuclear Weapons in the Twenty-First Century* (Los Alamos, New Mexico: Los Alamos National Laboratory, June 27, 2000, #LAUR-00-2850).

97. Cited in Peter Metzger, *The Atomic Establishment* (New York: Simon and Schuster, 1972), 54. For U.S. planning for use of nuclear weapons against Vietnam, see Peter Hayes and Nina Tannenwald, "Nixing Nukes in Vietnam," *Bulletin of Atomic Sci-*

entists (May/June 2003): 52-5. For the declassified documents on U.S. military planning for the use of nuclear weapons, see the website of the Public Education Center, www.publicedcenter.org/stories/vietnam-nukes/.

98. Jonathan Schell, *The Unfinished Twentieth Century* (London: Verso, 2001), 47.

99. Bertrand Goldschmidt, "A Forerunner of the NPT? The Soviet Proposals of 1947," *IAEA Bulletin* (Spring 1986): 58-64.

100. Goldschmidt, "A Forerunner of the NPT?" 63.

101. For a detailed history of the NPT, see Mohammad I. Shaker, *The Non-Proliferation Treaty: Origin and Implementation 1959-1979*, 3 vols. (New York: Oceana Publications, 1980).

102. For the American and Soviet drafts, see Shaker, *The Non-Proliferation Treaty*, vol. 3, 937 and 940, respectively.

103. Peter A. Clausen, *Nonproliferation and the National Interest: America's Response to the Spread of Nuclear Weapons* (New York: Harper Collins, 1993), 93-4.

104. Robert S. Norris, W. M. Arkin, W. Burr, "Where They Were," *Bulletin of the Atomic Scientists* (November/December 1999): 26-35, 66-7.

105. Shaker, *The Non-Proliferation Treaty*.

106. Shaker, *The Non-Proliferation Treaty*, 567. The U.S. negotiator was Gerard Smith.

107. William Epstein, *The Last Chance: Nuclear Proliferation and Arms Control* (New York: Free Press, 1976), 118.

108. Using the amendment provision in the NPT to transform the treaty into one abolishing nuclear weapons has been proposed; see Zia Mian "NGO Remarks to NPT Delegates," NPT Review Conference Prepcom 2000, New York, 1997; and Zia Mian and M. V. Ramana, "Diplomatic Judo: Using the NPT to Make the Nuclear Weapons States Negotiate the Abolition of Nuclear Weapons," *Disarmament Diplomacy* (April 1999): 7-10.

109. Christine Kucia, "North Korea's Nuclear Nonproliferation Treaty Status," *Arms Control Today* (July/August 2003): 24.

110. Susan B. Walsh, "Delegate Perspectives on the 1995 NPT Review and Extension Conference," *The Nonproliferation Review* (Spring-Summer 1995): 1.

111. Miguel Marin-Bosch, "Nuclear Disarmament on the Eve of the Twenty-First Century: Is This as Good as It Gets?" *Disarmament Diplomacy* (April 1999): 5-6.

112. Walsh, "Delegate Perspectives," 7.

113. Walsh, 6.

114. Walsh, 9.

115. Walsh, 9.

116. Walsh, 13.

117. John Burroughs, *The (Il)legality of Threat or Use of Nuclear Weapons*, International Association of Lawyers against Nuclear Arms (Münster, Germany: Lit Verlag, 1997).

118. "U.S. Interest and Priorities at the CD: Interview with US Ambassador Robert T. Grey, Jr.," *Arms Control Today* (October 1998): 3-8.

119. *Disarmament Times*, XXII, no. 5 (December 1999).

120. Rebecca Johnson, "The 2000 NPT Review Conference: A Delicate, Hard-Won Compromise," *Disarmament Diplomacy* (May 2000): 21.

121. Johnson, "The 2000 NPT Review Conference," 15.

122. John Burroughs, "More Promises to Keep: 2000 NPT Review Conference," *Bombs Away: Newsletter of the Lawyers Committee on Nuclear Policy* 13, no. 1 (Fall 2000, rev.): 4.

123. Report of the Main Committee I, NPT/CONF.2000/MC.I/1, *Final Document of the 2000 NPT Review Conference*, vol. II, part III (New York: United Nations, 2000), 420-1.

124. Rebecca Johnson, "Incentives, Obligations and Enforcement: Does the NPT Meet Its States Parties' Needs?" *Disarmament Diplomacy* (April/May 2003): 3.

125. For the details of the NPT's formal mechanisms for establishing and respond-ing to noncompliance, see chapter 8 by Feiveson and Shire in this volume.

126. A history of the IAEA's response to this incident is given in David Fischer, *History of the International Atomic Energy Agency: The First Forty Years* (Vienna: In-ternational Atomic Energy Agency, 1997), 103-8.

127. Fischer, *History the International Atomic Energy Agency*, 107.

128. *Proliferation: Threat and Response* (Washington, D.C.: U.S. Government Printing Office, January 2001).

129. For a history, see Avner Cohen, "Most Favored Nation," *Bulletin of the Atomic Scientists* (January/February 1995) and Avner Cohen, *Israel and the Bomb* (New York: Columbia University Press, 1998).

130. *Israel Special Weapons Guide*, Federation of American Scientists, www.fas.org/nuke/guide/israel/index.html.

131. See Seymour M. Hersh, *The Samson Option: Israel's Nuclear Arsenal and American Foreign Policy* (New York: Random House, 1991).

132. Jay Ross, "War Casualties Put at 48,000 in Lebanon," *Washington Post*, Sep-tember 3, 1982.

133. On October 1, 1985, Israel attacked the headquarters of the Palestine Liberation Organization in Tunis, with U.S.-supplied jets, killing over seventy people. Frank J. Prial, "Israeli Planes Attack P.L.O. in Tunis," *New York Times*, October 2, 1985. The United States supported the attack, but eventually abstained in the 14-0 U.N. Security Council vote condemning Israel. Elaine Sciolino, "UN Body Assails Israeli Air Strike," *New York Times*, October 5, 1985.

134. Cohen, *Israel and the Bomb*, 111, 156.

135. Cohen, *Israel and the Bomb*, 316, 326.

136. For a history of U.S.-Israel military cooperation, see Stephen Green, *Living by the Sword: America and Israel in the Middle East 1968-1987* (Boston: Faber and Faber, 1988).

137. Green, *Living by the Sword*, 222.

138. Eric Arnett, "Implications of the Comprehensive Test Ban for Nuclear Weap-ons Programmes and Decision Making," in Eric Arnett, ed., *Nuclear Weapons after the Comprehensive Test Ban: Implications for Modernisation and Proliferation* (Oxford: Oxford University Press, 1996), 15.

139. Duncan L. Clarke, Daniel B. O'Connor, and Jason D. Ellis, *Send Guns and Money: Security Assistance and U.S. Foreign Policy* (Westport, CT: Praeger, 1997), 169.

140. Ben Iannotta, "Setting the Rules for Remote Sensing," *Aerospace America*, (April 1999).

141. A/RES/53/80, Risk of Nuclear Proliferation in the Middle East.

142. U.S.-Israel Memorandum of Agreement, October 31, 1998; see the website of the Center for Nonproliferation Studies, http: cns.miis.edu/research/wmdme/isrl_moa.htm.

143. Howard Diamond, "New U.S.-Israeli Strategic Dialogue Announced; Israel Acquires New Submarine," *Arms Control Today* (July/August 1999).

144. The cooperation extends to missile defenses also. There are plans to link Israel's Arrow-2 antiballistic missile system to U.S. radar systems. "Arrow-2 to be Linked to U.S. Radar Detection," *Israel Line*, February 12, 1999.

145. Howard Diamond, "New U.S.-Israeli Strategic Dialogue Announced."

146. Uzi Mahnaimi and Peter Conradi, "Fears of New Arms Race as Israel Tests Cruise Missiles," *Sunday Times* (London), June 18, 2000.

147. "Israel/U.S. Agreement on Limited Nuclear Technology," *Israel Wire*, February 23, 2000.

148. "Israel Granted Access to DoE Nuclear Projects," *Jane's Defence Weekly*, March 1, 2000.

149. Peter Slevin and Colum Lynch, "Focus at U.N. Turns to Iraq's Recovery; Germany, France Stress Organization's Role," *Washington Post*, March 20, 2003.

150. *Proliferation: Threat and Response*, 33.

151. *Proliferation: Threat and Response*, 33.

152. The shah had been put in power by the 1953 CIA-sponsored coup that overthrew the elected government of Prime Minister Mohammad Mossadegh. For a history of the coup, see Stephen Kinzer, *All the Shah's Men: An American Coup and the Roots of Middle East Terror* (New York: John Wiley and Sons, 2003).

153. Michael Dobbs, "U.S. Had Key Role in Iraq Build-Up," *Washington Post*, December 30, 2002.

154. Paul Lewis, "Deal Is Reached at U.N. on Panama Seat as Invasion Is Condemned," *New York Times*, December 30, 1989.

155. Paul Lewis, "Fighting in Panama: United Nations; Security Council Condemnation of Invasion Vetoed," *New York Times*, December 24, 1989.

156. Dobbs, "U.S. Had Key Role."

157. Dobbs, "U.S. Had Key Role."

158. Patrick E. Tyler, "Officer Say U.S. Aided Iraq in War Despite Use of Gas," *New York Times*, August 18, 2002.

159. U.N. Security Council resolution 687, April 3, 1991.

160. For details, see the UNSCOM website, www.un.org/Depts/unscom/unscom.htm.

161. Seymour Hersh, "Saddam's Best Friend," *New Yorker*, April 5, 1999.

162. Bradley Graham and John M. Goshko, "More Forces Sent to Gulf as Clinton Warns Iraq; U.N. Arms Inspectors Pulled from Baghdad," *Washington Post*, November 12, 1998.

163. Howard Schneider, "Defiant Iraq Will Not Allow New U.N. Arms Inspectors to Enter," *Washington Post*, August 24, 2000.

164. Edward Cody, "Under Iraqi Skies, a Canvas of Death," *Washington Post*, June 16, 2000.

165. Carl Hulse, "U.S. Said to Approve Anti-Hussein Funding," *New York Times*, February 2, 2001.

166. Remarks of the president on Iraq, December 19, 1998, www.whitehouse.gov/WH/New/html/19981219-2655.html.

167. Results of the 1999 Iraq Child and Maternal Mortality Surveys (New York: United Nations Children's, 1999), www.unicef.org/reseval/iraqr.htm.

168. Phyllis Bennis, "And They Called It Peace: U.S. Policy on Iraq," *Middle East Report* 215 (Summer 2000).

169. CBS News, *60 Minutes*, May 12, 1996.

170. Howard Diamond, "UN Maintains Sanctions on Iraq as Security Council Split Grows," *Arms Control Today* (April 1998).

171. Patrick E. Tyler, "U.S. Strategy Plan Calls for Insuring No Rivals Develop," *New York Times*, March 8, 1992.

172. Steven R. Weisman, "Pre-emption: Idea with a Lineage Whose Time Has Come," *New York Times*, March 23, 2003.

173. Julian Borger, "How I Created the Axis of Evil," *The Guardian* (London), January 28, 2003.

174. David E. Sanger, "The State of the Union: The Overview; Bush, Focusing on Terrorism, Says Secure U.S. Is Top Priority," *New York Times*, January 30, 2002.

175. James Risen, David E. Sanger, and Thom Shanker, "In Sketchy Data, Trying to Gauge Iraq Threat," *New York Times*, July 20, 2003. On the absence of ties between Iraq and Al-Qaeda, see James Risen, "C.I.A.; Captives Deny Qaeda Worked with Baghdad," *New York Times*, June 9, 2003; and Walter Pincus, "Report Cast Doubt on Iraq-Al Qaeda Connection," *Washington Post*, June 22, 2003.

176. "Resolution that Congress Approved on the Right to Use Force in Iraq" *New York Times*, October 12, 2002.

177. Michael R. Gordon, "U.S. Air Raids in '02 Prepared for War in Iraq," *New York Times*, July 20, 2003.

178. "Where the Draft Resolution Stands: A Final Opportunity to Comply," *New York Times*, November 7, 2002.

179. Julia Preston, "Security Council Votes, 15-0, for Tough Iraq Resolution; Bush Calls It a 'Final Test,'" *New York Times*, November 9, 2002.

180. Patrick E. Tyler, "A New Power in the Streets," *New York Times*, February 17, 2003.

181. "U.S.-British Draft Resolution Stating Position on Iraq," *New York Times*, February 25, 2003.

182. Elaine Sciolino, "France and Germany Call for Long Inspections," *New York Times*, February 25, 2003.

183. Felicity Barringer, "U.N. Split Widens as Allies Dismiss Deadline on Iraq," *New York Times*, March 8, 2003.

184. Elaine Sciolino, "France to Veto Resolution on Iraq War, Chirac Says," *New York Times*, March 11, 2003; Elizabeth Neuffer and John Donnelly, "US Support Lags; Vote Put Off Vetoes Vowed; Compromise on Iraq Eyed," *Boston Globe*, March 11, 2003.

185. Tom Zeller, "How to Win Friends and Influence Small Countries," *New York Times*, March 16, 2003; Paul Blustein, "Bush May Use Trade Pacts for Iraq Leverage," *Washington Post*, March 15, 2003.

186. Patrick E. Tyler and Felicity Barringer, "Annan Says U.S. Will Violate Charter If It Acts without Approval," *New York Times*, March 11, 2003.

187. For a history, see Lee Sigal, *Disarming Strangers: Nuclear Diplomacy with North Korea* (Princeton, NJ: Princeton University Press, 1998).

188. Alexandre Y. Mansourov, "The Origins, Evolution, and Current Politics of the North Korean Nuclear Program," *The Nonproliferation Review* (Spring/Summer 1995): 25-38.

189. Sigal, Disarming Strangers.

190. Mitchell Reiss, *Bridled Ambitions: Why Countries Constrain Their Nuclear Capabilities* (Washington, D.C.: Woodrow Wilson Center Press, 1995), 236.

191. Riess, *Bridled Ambitions*, 239.

192. Riess, 42.

193. Riess, 48.

194. S/RES/825 (1993).

195. Sigal, Disarming Strangers, 60-1.

196. R. Jeffrey Smith, "Perry Sharply Warns North Korea," *Washington Post*, March 31, 1994.

197. William J. Perry, "Its Either Nukes or Negotiation," *Washington Post*, July 23, 2003.

198. Elaine Monaghan, "Clinton Planned Attack on Korean Nuclear Reactors," *The Times* (London), December 16, 2002.

199. Sigal, *Disarming Strangers*, 229. The U.S. nuclear threats against Korea during the Korean war are described in Bundy, *Danger and Survival*, 238-45.

200. Alan Riding, "U.S. and North Korea Sign Pact to End Nuclear Dispute," *New York Times*, October 22, 1994.

201. Steven Greenhouse, "Republicans Oppose Deal with Koreans," *New York Times*, November 27, 1994.

202. "North Korea Says U.S. Is Hampering Oil Supply," *New York Times*, July 2, 1996.

203. David E. Sanger and James Dao, "U.S. Says Pakistan Gave Technology to North Korea," *New York Times*, October 18, 2002.

204. Sheryl Wu Dunn, "North Korea Fires Missile over Japanese Territory," *New York Times*, September 1, 1998.

205. Steven Mufson, "Clinton Might Visit N. Korea Next Month," *Washington Post*, October 13, 2000.

206. Howard French, "Seoul Fears U.S. Is Chilly about Detente with North," *New York Times*, March 25, 2001.

207. David E. Sanger, "North Korea Says It Has a Program on Nuclear Arms," *New York Times*, October 17, 2002.

208. Serge Schmemann, "U.N. Agency Demands North Korea End Atomic Program," *New York Times*, November 30, 2002.

209. *Disarmament Diplomacy* (February/March 2003): 40.

210. Michael R. Gordon, "U.S. Readies Plan to Raise Pressure on North Koreans," *New York Times*, December 29, 2002.

211. David Pilling and Peter Spiegel, "US and Japan Agree Stance on North Korea's Nuclear Arms," *Financial Times*, December 17, 2002.

212. Steven R. Weisman, "Japan Says Nuclear Effort in Korea Merits Hard Line," *New York Times*, December 17, 2002.

213. *Disarmament Diplomacy*: 41

214. David E. Sanger and Julia Preston, "U.S. Assails Move by North Koreans to Reject Treaty," *New York Times*, January 11, 2003.

215. *Disarmament Diplomacy*: 44.

216. Guy Dinmore and Andrew Ward, "Pyongyang Warns of 'Total War' if US Attacks Nuclear Facilities: US 'Retains Options'," *Financial Times*, February 7, 2003.

217. "North Korea Restarts Reactor; IAEA Sends Resolution to UN," *Arms Control Today* (March 2003): 16-17.

218. David E. Sanger, "Bush Shifts Focus to Nuclear Sales by North Korea," *New York Times*, May 5, 2003. The states involved in this Proliferation Security Initiative are the United States, Australia, France, Germany, Italy, Japan, the Netherlands, Poland, Portugal, Spain, and the United Kingdom.

219. David E. Sanger, "North Korea Says It Seeks to Develop Nuclear Arms," *New York Times*, June 10, 2003.

220. David E. Sanger, "President Takes a Softer Stance on North Korea," *New York Times*, July 22, 2003.

221. For histories of India's nuclear program, see Itty Abraham, *The Making of the Indian Atomic Bomb* (London: Zed Press, 1998) and George Perkovich, *India's Nuclear Bomb*.

222. Report by the comptroller-general of the United States, *Difficulties in Determining if Nuclear Training of Foreigners Contributes to Weapons Proliferation* (Washington, D.C.: U.S. General Accounting Office, April 23, 1979).

223. Perkovich, *India's Nuclear Bomb*, 52.

224. For details, see Leonard S. Spector, *Nuclear Proliferation Today* (New York: Vintage Books, 1984), 70-110.

225. Leonard Spector, *Nuclear Ambitions: The Spread of Nuclear Weapons, 1989-1990* (Boulder, CO: Westview Press, 1990), 89-117.

226. Dennis Kux, "Pakistan," in Richard Haass, ed., *Economic Sanctions and American Diplomacy* (New York: Council on Foreign Relations, 1998), 157-76.

227. U.N. Security Council resolution 1172.

228. Dinshaw Mistry, "Diplomacy, Sanctions, and the U.S. Nonproliferation Dialogue," *Swords and Plowshares* XII, no. 1 (Spring 2000): 3-5.

229. Randy Rydell, "Giving Nonproliferation Norms Teeth: Sanctions and the NPPA," *The Nonproliferation Review* (Winter 1999): 1-18.

230. *US-India Relations: A Vision for the 21st Century*, www.pub.whitehouse.gov/urires/I2R?urn:pdi://oma.eop.gov.us/2000/3/21/25.text.1

231. "India to Hear Out Armitage on NMD," *The Hindu*, May 11, 2001.

232. Alan Sipress, "U.S. Seeks to Lift Sanctions on India: Aim Is to Bolster Military Relations," *Washington Post*, August 12, 2001.

233. Kesav Menon, "Defense Deal with Israel," *The Hindu*, July 18, 2001.

234. Atul Aneja, "India, Israel to Hold Security Dialogue," *The Hindu*, May 16, 2001.

235. Celia W. Dugger, "Wider Military Ties with India Offer U.S. Diplomatic Leverage," *New York Times*, June 10, 2002.

236. Saritha Rai, "Arms Makers See Great Potential in India Market," *New York Times*, February 12, 2003.

237. Dana Priest, "An Engagement in 10 Time Zones," *Washington Post*, September 29, 2000.

238. Michael Wines, "Leasing, If Not Building, an Anti-Taliban Coalition," *New York Times*, November 18, 2001.

239. David E. Sanger, "Bush Offers Pakistan Aid, but No F-16's," *New York Times*, June 25, 2003.

240. John F. Burns, "Pakistan Atom Experts Held Amid Fear of Leaked Secrets," *New York Times*, November 1, 2001.

241. Douglas Frantz, James Risen, and David E. Sanger, "Nuclear Experts in Pakistan May Have Links to Al Qaeda," *New York Times*, December 9, 2001.

242. Douglas Frantz, "U.S. and Pakistan Discuss Nuclear Security," *New York Times*, October 1, 2001.

243. Alex Wagner, "U.S. Offers Nuclear Security Assurance to Pakistan," *Arms Control Today* (December 2001): 24.

244. Seymour Hersh, "Watching the Warheads," *New Yorker*, November 5, 2001.

245. For excerpts from the 2001 *Nuclear Posture Review*, see the website of Global Security, www.globalsecurity.org/wmd/library/policy/dod/npr.htm.

246. M. V. Ramana and Zia Mian, "The Nuclear Confrontation in South Asia," *SIPRI Yearbook 2003: Armaments, Disarmament and International Security* (Oxford: Oxford University Press, 2003), 195-212.

247. For a discussion of these, see chapter 8 by Feiveson and Shire.

248. "Joint Statement of Agreed Principles for Disarmament Negotiations," of the Soviet Union and the United States (The McCloy-Zorin Agreement) in Richard Falk and Saul H. Mendlovitz, *The Strategy of World Order, vol. 4, Disarmament and Economic Development* (New York: World Law Fund, 1966), 281-2.

249. The McCloy-Zorin Agreement is not even mentioned in recent work, for example, Allan S. Krass, *The United States and Arms Control: The Challenge of Leadership* (Westport, CT: Praeger, 1997).

250. Hans M. Kristensen and Joshua Handler, "World Nuclear Forces," *SIPRI Year Book 2002: Armaments, Disarmament and International Security* (Oxford: Oxford University Press, 2002), appendix 10A, 525-67.

251. Elisabeth Skons, Evamaria Loose-Weintrab, Wuyi Omitoogun, Petter Stalenheim, "Military Expenditure," *SIPRI Year Book 2002*, 231-96.

252. Reinhilde Weidacher and the SIPRI Arms Industry Network, "Arms Industry Data," *SIPRI Year Book 2002*, Appendix 7A, 354-63.

253. John R. Harvey, "Regional Ballistic Missiles and Advanced Strike Aircraft: Comparing Military Effectiveness," *International Security* 17, no. 2 (Fall 1992): 79.

254. James A. Paul, "Security Council Reform: Arguments about the Future of the United Nations System," www.globalpolicy.org/security/pubs/secref.htm#veto.

255. James Traub, "Who Needs the U.N. Security Council?" *New York Times Magazine*, November 17, 2002.

256. Harald Müller, "The Internalization of Principles, Norms, and Rules by Governments: The Case of Security Regimes," in Volker Rittberger and Peter Mayer, eds., *Regime Theory and International Relations* (New York: Clarendon Press, 1993), 388.

257. The classic studies of this process in U.S. foreign policy include Noam Chomsky, *American Power and the New Mandarins*; Noam Chomsky, *For Reasons of State* (New York: Pantheon Books, 1973); Noam Chomsky and Edward Herman, *Manufacturing Consent: The Political Economy of the Mass Media* (New York: Pantheon Books, 1988).

258. This well-known speech informs some arms control literature, for example, Steven E. Miller, "Politics over Promise: Domestic Impediments to Arms Control," *International Security* 8, no. 4 (Spring 1984): 67-90.

259. See Lawrence S. Wittner, *The Struggle against the Bomb, Vols. I and II, One World or None—a History of the World Nuclear Disarmament Movement through 1953* (Stanford, CA: Stanford University Press, 1993); and also David Cortright, *Peace Works: The Citizen's Role in Ending the Cold War* (Boulder, CO: Westview Press, 1993).

260. Joseph S. Nye, Jr., "Arms Control and International Politics," 161.

261. The success of civil society in creating the 1999 Landmines Convention is discussed by Feiveson and Shire in this volume.

262. John Burroughs and Jacqueline Cabasso, "Confronting the Nuclear Armed States in International Negotiating Forums: Lessons for NGOs," *International Negotiation* 4 (1999): 457-80.

263. For INESAP, see www2.hrz.tu-darmstadt.de/ze/ianus/inesap/inesap.html and for Abolition 2000, see www.abolition2000.org.

264. *Security and Survival: The Case for a Nuclear Weapons Convention* (Cambridge, MA: International Physicians for the Prevention of Nuclear War, the International

Association of Lawyers Against Nuclear Arms and the International Network of Engineers and Scientists Against Proliferation, 1999).

265. A/C.1/52/7, November 17, 1997.

266. *Nuclear Weapons Convention Monitor*, Issue 1 (Cambridge, MA: International Physicians for the Prevention of Nuclear War, April 2000).

267. Kevin J. O'Brien, "Rightful Resistance," *World Politics* 49 (October 1996): 31-55. This analysis builds on an important literature on resistance that is legitimized by an appeal to norms put in place by those with power within a community. See especially James C. Scott, *Domination and the Arts of Resistance* (New Haven, CT: Yale University Press, 1990).

268. Matthew Evangelista, *Unarmed Forces: The Transnational Movement to End the Cold War* (Ithaca, NY: Cornell University Press, 1999). The larger roles and practice of transnational groups are addressed in Margaret E. Keck and Kathryn Sikkink, *Activists Beyond Borders: Advocacy Networks in International Politics* (Ithaca, NY: Cornell University Press, 1998).

269. Richard Falk and Andrew Strauss, "Toward Global Parliament," *Foreign Affairs* 80, no. 1 (January/February 2001): 212-8.

270. Falk and Strauss, "Toward Global Parliament," 216.

Conclusion

Gaps, Commitments, and the Compliance Challenge

Edward C. Luck

The Compliance and Commitment Gaps

This volume has sought to disaggregate four sets of questions by sector and by geography: (1) Are there persistent compliance gaps and do they matter in terms of public policy? (2) Where do they occur and why? (3) What lessons should be gleaned from past experience with compliance mechanisms? and (4) Are there systematic biases in the kinds of norms that are enforced vigorously or whose compliance is allowed to lapse? Such a differentiated study was compelled by the striking disjuncture between the existing scholarly literature and the media headlines of the day. By and large, students of compliance, largely legal scholars, have given a relatively sanguine account in which the deliberate disregard for a state's obligations under international law is the exception, not the rule. Fair enough, yet the most acute and threatening challenges to international order—whether terrorism, possible weapons of mass destruction (WMD) in Iraq, Iran, and North Korea, humanitarian crises in Africa, Asia, and the Balkans, or Washington's refusal to hop aboard the multilateral bandwagon—revolve around questions of compliance. Clearly, where you stand or whether such challenges constitute a compliance crisis depends a lot on where you sit.

Indeed, as the eight case studies confirm, the compliance phenomenon looks like a very different animal when viewed from distinct issue clusters or parts of the world. Yet two trends are evident in each of the areas studied. One, awareness of compliance issues and concerns about their policy implications are growing in each of these sectors, in some cases to disconcerting proportions. Two, in each subject the demands of international law are getting more far-reaching, more demanding, and more intrusive over time, as new standards are codified and new public expectations and constituencies are engaged. Each such step has racheted up the demands for compliance, as well as the standards for implementation. A more aroused public, a more attentive media, and the revolution in communications technologies—the very stuff of globalization—have made it more difficult, at the same time, to keep either one's noncompliance or a regime's compliance shortcomings a secret. The very growth in research on compliance, documented in the Downs and Trento chapter, testifies to a growing awareness that implementation problems are, more than ever, the soft underbelly of attempts to build international law and order.[1] But, as they also note, this volume represents one of only a handful of attempts to draw out the policy implications of these developments.

At this early stage in the development of this field, there is no consensus on the impact of noncompliance on the achievement of important policy objectives, in part because the depth and breadth of its effects vary so much from issue to issue. In their overall assessment, Downs and Trento note that "most states continue to comply with most multilateral agreements most of the time, if only because a high percentage of multilateral agreements are either coordination agreements from which states have little incentive to defect or very modest regulatory agreements that require relatively few departures from what states are currently doing." They warn against exaggerated claims of a general trend toward noncompliance. Their caution is well taken. As they acknowledge, however, more serious compliance gaps have appeared in various human rights and humanitarian regimes and in the implementation of some environmental and arms control agreements.

When viewed from a political perspective, moreover, there is little reason to be sanguine about compliance issues. While noncontroversial coordination or regulatory agreements may far outnumber those that are likely to generate compliance disputes, it is the latter—in places like Iraq and North Korea—that inevitably spur much greater media, public, and official attention. Their breach may also have the most far-reaching consequences for public policy, a realm in which a few noisy failures can often matter more than multiple quiet successes. In political terms, it may matter less whether states and nonstate actors are technically in compliance with international agreements than whether publics and other states parties perceive them to be fulfilling the intent and spirit of such conventions, for this goes to the heart of the credibility of international law. Clearly the task of implementing legal agreements among sovereign nation states is far more daunting and uncertain than that facing domestic legal systems, yet publics and commentators alike may well judge international compliance by the more familiar standards of the latter. For instance, citing "the success of domestic law" as reason for hope for more effective legal regimes among nations, Arthur M. Schlesinger, Jr. has declared that "law is not law if, in the last resort, it is not enforced."[2]

In that regard, the two chapters on arms restraint—by Feiveson and Shire and by Mian—see little prospect of weaker states finding the means of enforcing arms control provisions when major powers ignore them. In part, they argue, this is bound to be the case when the big powers control the process of shaping treaty provisions in the first place. Both chapters find uneven compliance rates for the various conventions seeking to curb weapons of mass destruction. In their view, moreover, it is the United States and other major powers, not developing countries as Downs, Trento, and other compliance theorists assert, that are primarily responsible for undermining compliance with and confidence in multilateral arms control agreements. Yet, at the same time, as Feiveson and Shire acknowledge, American critics of such regimes have forsaken them in large part because of doubts about their effectiveness, thus feeding a downward spiral.

All of the authors in this volume find compliance lapses, to one degree or another, in their sectors. The chapters by Herbst and by Katalikawe, Onoria, and Wairama are particularly outspoken about the virtual bankruptcy of human rights and humanitarian regimes in much of Africa. They find little connection between the normative regimes and actions on the ground, due both to a lack of will to enforce the former and to the critical roles played by nonstate actors that are not parties to the conventions. In an analysis stressing domestic factors, Moon presents a remarkably mixed and culturally nuanced picture of South Korea's uneven response to trade and financial standards. While McNamara believes that, despite highly publicized disputes, "compliance with the international laws and norms that govern economic life is relatively high," she warns of worrisome complications even for the well-established and highly institutionalized trade regime down the road. Sands and Linehan, on the other hand, point to a growing awareness of compliance challenges for multilateral environmental agreements, but conclude both that the major shortcomings so far have been limited to biodiversity and fisheries conservation and that, as Downs, Trento, and earlier studies have asserted, developing countries have faced the greatest implementation problems, largely because of weak capacity.

These are dynamic times both for norm setting and for the development of compliance mechanisms. The global norm-building process accelerated markedly in each of these areas with the end of the Cold War, leaving the fabric of international norms and institutions far more densely woven today than ten or fifteen years ago. What is less clear is whether compliance is getting worse over time, or whether the bar has simply been raised by all these new agreements, along with our cognizance of the implementation challenges they pose. As Sands and Linehan note, early multilateral environmental accords lacked compliance provisions altogether and there has only been about a decade of experience with environmental compliance—hardly enough time to gauge long-term trends. In trade, McNamara sees the advent of the World Trade Organization (WTO), the contentions over globalization, and the emergence of "trade-and" issues as ushering in a new and uncertain era. In assessing the role of the tribunals for Rwanda and the Balkans, Côté addresses a pathbreaking and potentially risky phenomenon: the extension of the rules of law to civil conflicts; the ending of impunity for individual violators; and the invocation of the binding authority of the Security Council in such cases. The reactions of the United States and, to a lesser extent, other major powers to the subsequent International Criminal Court (ICC) have served to underscore just how controversial and fragile this path may prove to be in the years ahead.

None of the chapters, however, call for perfect or complete compliance. Some degree of noncompliance not only is expected in each subject area, at times it may be widely accepted or even desirable, as Downs and Trento have pointed out. As conditions change over time, as generic rules are applied to specific circumstances, or as tougher standards are accepted, some flexibility may well be in order, especially when the norm is widely understood to be a goal or standard to which states parties should aspire over time. Often noncompliance stems more from a lack of capacity than of will. Yet, in each sector, there are times when some state or nonstate actors deliberately choose to violate, circumvent, or reinterpret the rules. At those points, not only is their commitment to the normative regime tested, but so too is the commitment of other parties to maintaining the integrity of the regime. In these cases, the compliance gap is perpetuated by an equally persistent commitment gap.

Another way of drawing distinctions among the hundreds of existing normative regimes, therefore, is by the depth of commitment states and other actors demonstrate to ensuring a regime's implementation, whether through monitoring, reporting, incentives, or sanctions. As Downs and Trento point out in their discussion of the phenomenon of incentive compatibility, this side of the compliance equation has received relatively little study or analysis. Yet it is obvious that different norms invoke qualitatively different levels of response not only within states but also among them. This can be seen in the way states draft the relevant agreements, as well as in the risks and costs they are willing to bear to help implement full compliance, at home and abroad. For example, how specific are the conventions? Do they require states parties or other actors to undertake particular courses of action? Are monitoring and reporting provisions included to assess compliance over time? Are there penalties to be paid for noncompliance and/or incentives for good behavior? And does the regime specify compliance mechanisms and ways of distributing their costs, particularly when the political stakes are high?

Setting aside those coordination agreements that do not risk significant defections, it is possible to envision a spectrum of norms, placed according to the degree to which parties appear to be committed to ensuring compliance and norm implementation. Rather than asking whether actors would have a motivation to defect, as most studies have, such a categorization would look to the other side of the equation, that is, to assess the strength of the regime on the basis of the costs other states parties appear to be willing to pay to buttress compliance and to discourage defection even when some actors might be tempted to do so. Feiveson and Shire, for example, comment on how ill-prepared other capitals have been to react to North Korea's threatened defection from the Nuclear Non-Proliferation Treaty (NPT) regime, even though they have been very concerned about the implications of such a step. McNamara, moreover, asks whether the large number of trade disputes "indicates the fragility of the trade system or the health of its laws and norms." Noting that many of these differences have been resolved through the WTO's dispute settlement system, she concludes that "if violators are ignored international law is probably weak, but if violators are at least subject to public scrutiny and/or criticism, that may be good news for the system." In this case, decisions of the WTO can be enforced by compensatory unilateral action on the part of the damaged party, offering true incentive compatibility through a process of bilateral reciprocity under multilateral rules and procedures.

All international law is not equal, at least when viewed through political eyes and practical experience. When a state becomes a party to an international convention, it undertakes certain legal obligations and, in some fashion, can be held accountable for upholding its provisions. The degree of its commitment to ensuring that the larger purposes of the convention are fulfilled in specific cases and in operational terms, however, is necessarily a political matter. There is no automaticity here, particularly given the paucity of compliance or enforcement provisions in most international conventions.[3] The degree of commitment, moreover, will depend on to whom the legal obligations are seen to be undertaken: to people, to the world, or to the nation. In this regard, the policy issues of concern to this study could be bunched into three broad and, at points, overlapping clusters: those that focus on the individual human condition; those that address transnational problems whose resolution would benefit many countries; and those that speak to the core interests of individual nation-states.

Human Interests. The degree of national commitment to compliance in the first cluster—to those regimes seeking to bolster human rights, human security, and humanitarian standards—is usually relatively modest and tends to be episodic and ad hoc. By definition, these norms are often designed to protect individuals and groups from abuse, neglect, or incompetence on the part of governments or armed groups. Their natural advocates and allies come from civil society or from states that are either far away or interested, in part, because of geopolitical, economic, or ideological factors. Those asserting the primacy of individuals over states should not be surprised by the fact that the latter usually limit their support to public diplomacy, capacity building, and/or humanitarian assistance. The conventions in this cluster are generally longer on high principles than on specific compliance mechanisms or on commitments to undertake either incentives or sanctions. As one would expect, civil society actors play a major part not only in monitoring and reporting, but also in the provision of material support for these regimes.

Transnational Interests. Over the past three decades, dating at least from the landmark 1972 Stockholm conference on the environment and spurred by transnational epistemic communities, global issues have defined one of the most active sectors for norm codification and international institutional development. Even when East-West tensions on geopolitical and security issues soured bilateral relations, it was widely recognized that both sides, as well as the South, had shared interests in tackling an array of global environmental, resource, health, and commons problems. However, the existence of shared interests among many states does not in itself provide assurance that a workable arrangement for the sharing of burdens and commitments will necessarily follow. Some free riding and finger pointing may be inevitable, as perceptions differ concerning which countries have a greater stake in preserving the norm or greater capacity for implementation and enforcement. States certainly have an interest in encouraging compliance with these transnational norms, but these interests may be perceived as more important over the long term than over the life of a particular national administration or parliamentary term. As several of the case studies suggest, compliance issues in this cluster tend to become much more problematic and controversial as they begin to demand more in the way of domestic policy trade-offs, as has been the case with the Kyoto protocol.

Core National Interests. It is to the third cluster—to those norms affecting in a direct way a country's physical security and economic prosperity—that states respond to compliance challenges most energetically, forcefully, and assuredly. It is here, in the words of Downs and Trento, where a state's reputation for reliability will matter the most. Where national leaders may empathize with the moral content of humanitarian norms and may appreciate the long-term importance of transnational issues, it is on more traditional concerns of national security and economic welfare that they are most likely to feel compelled to act. Multilateral cooperation is often essential to achieving national goals in this cluster, but states, particularly powerful ones, will seek to maintain maximum flexibility in choosing among and mixing unilateral and multilateral responses, whether through incentives, sanctions, or a combination of the two. Reciprocity, and, therefore, deterrence, is usually a key pillar of compliance schemes in this cluster.

Because the normative regimes on this end of the spectrum are so closely related to national interests and because their compliance mechanisms depend so heavily on national action, critics have frequently charged, as Mian, Feiveson, and Shire do in this volume, that they are manipulated for narrow national purposes by one or more major power. Regimes on the human interest end of the spectrum, on the other hand, sometimes seem so divorced from national interests that their violation often elicits only a weak or general response from most national leaders. In this context, it is understandable that most nonbinding normative regimes, sometimes called soft law, address either human interests or transnational interests.[4] It appears, moreover, that when they are applied to matters involving the core national interests of major powers it is usually because more exacting arrangements could not be negotiated for one reason or another.[5]

Table C.1. The Commitment Spectrum: Degree of State Commitment to Ensuring Compliance

Low Human Interests	Moderate Transnational Interests	High Core National Interests
Examples		
human rights	environment	physical security • weapons of mass destruction
humanitarian concerns	global commons (law of the sea, outer space, etc.)	• large-scale aggression • terrorism
democratic practices	global issues (health, (narcotics, crime, etc.) local conflict (peacekeeping, landmines, small arms trade)	economic prosperity • trade • finance
Compliance Mechanisms		
ad hoc responses	heavily dependent on cooperative multilateral mechanisms, backed by national legislation	heavily dependent on reciprocity and national action
monitoring, fact-finding and reporting (naming) and shaming)	monitoring, fact finding, and reporting	multilateral role supportive not central, includes monitoring, reporting, and legitimization
provision or denial of incentives, including capacity building	provision or denial of incentives	lesser role for incentives
larger role for private organizations and civil society	some role for private organizations, experts, and civil society	punishment, deterrence, and use of threats
public diplomacy	capacity building judicial processes, arbitration	

(Continued)

(Table C.1—*Continued*)

Low	Moderate	High
Human Interests	Transnational Interests	Core National Interests

Domestic Constituencies

broad but thin support, vague policy options	divisive if domestic costs and trade-offs appear high	generally broad national consensus
advocacy NGOs, some opinion leaders, and some parliamentarians	advocacy NGOs, expert transnational (epistemic) communities	usually bipartisan appeal, parliaments ready to budget high costs
skeptics too, divisions on policy responses, tends to be episodic	parliamentarians often split over specific policy responses as are opinion leaders	dissenters may pay, or fear they will pay, a domestic political price

Table C.1 takes a first cut at picturing such a commitment spectrum, offering some sample international regimes that might fall within each of the three clusters, along with descriptions of the kinds of compliance mechanisms and domestic constituencies that might be associated with each cluster. Paradoxically, of the three clusters, in a number of cases it has been in the middle category, in regimes addressing global issues that affect the long-term interests of many countries, that the most elaborate multilateral compliance mechanisms have been negotiated in recent years. Some of the more complex and subtle compliance provisions, for instance, can be found in multilateral environmental agreements (MEAs). According to Sands and Linehan, states have been reluctant to agree to include provision in MEAs for unilateral recourse to binding dispute resolution (the 1982 U.N. Convention on the Law of the Sea is a notable exception) and there is a general perception that, with their global nature, the commitments in most MEAs are not suited to bilateral and confrontational dispute resolution. Formal dispute resolution is seen as a last resort.

As Feiveson and Shire point out, some multilateral arms control agreements, such as those on antipersonnel landmines and on weapons that have indiscriminate effects, have resulted from the success of public and nongovernmental organization (NGO) efforts to portray these primarily as humanitarian rather than as national security issues. The effect has been to move them away from the high end of the commitment spectrum and into the moderate commitment/transnational interest category, where a number of the agreements have detailed compliance provisions but few, if any, on enforcement. As Mian points out, however, most of the Soviet-American arms control agreements depended on unilateral monitoring and regime management rather than on complex compliance or robust enforcement mechanisms. They tended to embody the core national interest model in which elaborate compliance mechanisms were neither needed nor appropriate.

On the human interest end of the spectrum, on the other hand, states presumably do not negotiate precise and demanding compliance provisions because they do not want to be held legally and politically accountable for strong and costly action against defectors. Perceptions also tend to vary, even among states parties, about the limits of state action allowed under the norms. Nonstate actors, however, play a larger unofficial role in monitoring and reporting in this sphere, helping to compensate for uneven and modest state involvement.

On the national interest end of the spectrum, in contrast, compliance matters so much to powerful states that they would prefer to keep the option of coercive unilateral responses open to be supplemented as needed by multilateral ones and to be legitimated by global conventions and resolutions. This combination, and the flexibility of response it permits, is also perceived as providing the most persuasive deterrent to serious defections, whether under the WTO or treaties on terrorism or nuclear weapons. When core national interests are threatened, larger states look first to their own capacities to respond and then to allies, ad hoc coalitions, and more formal multilateral processes. As in the case of the September 2001 terrorist attacks on the United States, that response is strongest when all of these levels work in unison.

The concerns at this end of the spectrum tend to unite, rather than divide, otherwise disparate constituencies in the body politic. Here, broad support across party lines is likely for even costly compliance or enforcement measures. For example, though the Republican Party in the United States is known for its skepticism about the utility, or at least the centrality, of multilateral institutions, it has strongly supported those global institutions it views as contributing to freer trade, to curbing terrorism, or to slowing the proliferation of nuclear weapons. On such central issues, it is those who call for a weak response to norm violations that are put on the defensive in domestic debates, while at the other end of the commitment spectrum it is those calling for strong national action to buttress global norms and institutions who have to first prove their case. The contrast between the U.S. responses to North Korea, Iraq, or Osama bin Laden and those to Rwanda, Liberia, or Sierra Leone testifies, once again, to the fact that not all international norms are equal in the face of domestic and geopolitics.

The fact that states parties have a greater commitment to ensuring compliance with some norms than with others, however, does not mean that the latter are not of value. But it does suggest that there are qualitative differences in the nature of the norms, in the functional purposes they serve, and, therefore, in the compliance expectations they engender. Many of the regimes on the high end of the commitment spectrum reflect economic and security obligations that states undertake to each other. In essence, they are seen as mutual assurances, albeit of a multilateral character, to respect each other's interests and to play by the rules in terms of interstate relations. They are to be observed with some consistency and rigor. Defection is possible, but the consequences could be quite substantial and broad ranging, including both bilateral counteractions and multilateral damage to one's reputation for reliability. A state that harbors terrorists, invades its neighbors, or cheats repeatedly on trade or arms control norms will soon lose its good standing in the community of states.

In signing human rights or humanitarian conventions, on the other hand, states essentially undertake obligations to their citizens to live up to international standards. If they fail to do so, they can be held accountable in the court of world opinion and, more importantly, by domestic political processes.[6] At times democratic governments will take some account of another state's human rights or humanitarian record in the course of bilateral relations. But international sanctions are rarely invoked even in cases of severe violations and other governments generally do not treat such a defection as a failure to live up to a specific obligation to them. As Downs and Trento point out, it would be ludicrous to threaten to take reciprocal action by treating one's own citizens just as badly. Indeed, the whole point of such conventions is to set standards to which all societies should aspire and by which all should be judged.

To be of value, human rights and humanitarian standards—unlike trade or arms control norms—should be set higher than normal practice, as an aspiration and goal, so that some initial compliance gap is to be expected. Over time, of course, the gap should begin to narrow as practice comes to mirror the standard. As Downs and Trento put it, the goal is "to establish a set of universally accepted human rights standards that will gradually be incorporated into state constitutions and diffuse into the agendas of political parties within states." On the intergovernmental front, however, there has been little agreement on what specific countermeasures other countries could effectively or legitimately take to convince violators to change their ways. Within democratic societies, there is little dissent about the desirability of persuading other governments to respect human rights. There is little clarity and certainly no consensus, however, on how this should be done or on how these goals stack up against other priorities, such as fighting terrorism or promoting trade.

Nevertheless, over the past half century the compliance gap in the human rights realm has indeed narrowed quite dramatically in some regions, particularly since the end of the Cold War. By lobbying for the expansion of international norms and by then drawing public attention around the world to the extent to which various states are living up to those standards, human rights advocacy groups have worked hard to close what has been the largest compliance gap in a sector with relatively modest intergovernmental compliance mechanisms.[7] And this has been accomplished despite only sporadic efforts by individual states or regional groups to reward good behavior or to penalize poor performance. Here, more than in any of the case studies presented in this volume, the long-term power of universal ideals, of naming and shaming techniques, and of persistent nongovernmental advocacy has been evident. Here, as well, can be seen the primary importance of domestic forces, backed by the international community and legitimated by global norms.

Yet progress toward meeting humanitarian standards has been much more uneven, slipping backwards in some places. Like its human rights cousins, humanitarian law seeks to impose rules on how governments, subnational groups, and individual citizens interact. Unlike human rights, however, humanitarian law seeks to ensure that such codes of conduct are respected during times of armed conflict, when they are likely to be under the greatest strain and are hardest to enforce. Though largely developed with interstate conflict in mind, these norms—like the conflict resolution mechanisms of the United Nations—are increasingly being asked to cope with the intrastate and transnational conflicts that are the dominant mode of warfare in our time. In most of these crises, weak governments are being challenged by rebel groups that, as Katalikawe, Onoria, and Wairama point out, are not recognized by most governments, are not parties to humanitarian conventions, and are often not allowed to participate in regional peace processes. Not only are both rebel and government forces prone to violate humanitarian norms in Central Africa, they observe, but so are "quasi-state actors," which "are created by the State or an offshoot of its security agencies but that have no official or legal relationship with the State itself." Under such circumstances, Herbst ruefully concludes, "having all the states of the world come together to adopt international humanitarian law towards domestic conflict is like recruiting criminals to write gun control laws."

In terms of compliance, should nonstate actors be seen as a problem or a solution? On the one hand, the case studies cited numerous examples of the important, sometimes decisive, role played by various nonstate actors in shaping the codification of international norms, in determining how fully they are then carried out, and/or in monitoring and reporting on how well the implementation process is proceeding. On matters such as trade, finance, environmental protection, labor standards, and the trade in small arms, the adherence of private firms to global conventions is essential for proper implementation. Unlike rebel groups, in most societies the private sector will have a significant voice both in shaping the national stance in multilateral negotiations and, afterwards, in the crafting of national implementing legislation.

On the other hand, the place of nonstate actors as either a subject or an object of international law remains largely in limbo. As Herbst pointedly laments, in Africa one set of nonstate or quasi-state actors is heavily engaged in violating the most basic humanitarian principles while another set is fully occupied with reporting on the other's bad behavior. In many parts of the world, national and international security is threatened by terrorists, arms and narcotics smugglers, and criminal syndicates—what Secretary-General Annan calls "uncivil society"—operating across state lines. Governments are understandably hesitant to grant nonstate actors either a formal place at the negotiating table or status as a party to interstate agreements, yet they somehow hope to persuade them to follow the rules anyway.

In field after field, advocacy NGOs were in the vanguard of the movement to develop international norms and standards over the past decade. Yet, as several of the case studies illustrate, their track record on the compliance side has been somewhat more uneven. Feiveson and Shire see room for such groups to play a larger role in monitoring compliance with several types of arms control agreements in the future. Yet, for all of their resourcefulness in spurring governments to action, NGOs are not equipped, and generally do not attempt, to substitute for states in the compliance process. Katalikawe, Onoria, and Wairama, for instance, point out that both prominent NGOs, such as Amnesty International and Human Rights Watch, and U.N. Special Rapporteurs have chronicled serious abuses in Angola, Sudan, and the Congo. "The end-result," however, "seems to have been the production of reports on the humanitarian situations in those States without subsequent processes or mechanisms for accountability or enforcement."

Compliance gaps are also likely to emerge in normative regimes in which NGOs are more successful in spurring multilateral norm-building processes than in persuading key nation states to join the new regimes or to abide by their provisions once they do. Examples of the former would include the landmines convention and the International Criminal Court. In both cases, coalitions of transnational NGOs joined with like-minded governments to achieve wide agreement on potentially important new accords, but they failed to convince the United States, the most pivotal country, to become a party. The Kyoto Protocol has faced a similar hurdle. The basic premise shared by many advocacy NGOs—that national priorities need to be subordinated to transnational ones—puts them in a poor position to argue in national fora and legislatures about the trade-offs that would be required among national values, resources, and capacities. The situation in regard to human rights and humanitarian conventions has been different, but also somewhat troubling. Public groups have helped to persuade large numbers of states to sign onto these accords through a combination of moral suasion and peer pressure, but the resulting politics of appearances have not always been sufficient to ensure full implementation as well. As Moon cautions, moreover, initial compliance does not necessarily ensure sustained enforcement and implementation efforts over time.

Given these factors, there appears to be a growing disjunction between the course of norm building within global fora and the distribution of power outside of them. This chasm was vividly displayed in the divisive Security Council debates prior to the intervention in Iraq in the spring of 2003. Unless there is greater convergence between these two processes—whether through a change of heart in Washington and some other capitals or through a shift in NGO efforts from short-term global to long-term national lobbying, or both—the compliance and commitment gaps are likely to grow. As a result, despite Downs' and Trento's reassuring words about the marginal impact of reputation, over time public confidence in international law and institutions could well ebb, compounding the tendency to seek unilateral answers to global problems.[8]

Implications for Policy

Though legal obligations may sound absolute, policymaking is all about trade-offs and choices, about matching limited resources to open-ended and disparate commitments. Unlike single-issue advocates or distant theorists, policymakers have no choice but to be interdisciplinary, to recognize the effects that decisions to act or not to act in one issue cluster will have on others. The war on terrorism, for example, has provided a number of governments with an excuse to suspend or weaken human rights guarantees, though individual liberties and international security are both well-established global norms. Even powerful countries like the United States have limited resources to apply to encouraging others, whether through inducements or sanctions, to live up to their international commitments. Legislative or even executive action to encourage compliance with accords in one area, say the environment, may well set a precedent for parallel action in other areas, such as human rights, health, or development. Prospects for reciprocal action by the affected state or group must also be taken into account, especially when enforcement steps are being considered. These tit-for-tat equations can be seen most graphically in trade issues and the whole structure of the WTO regime, but they can also be observed in questions as diverse as human rights or the environment. As they say, those in glass houses are reluctant to throw the first stone.

In a world of some 200 nation-states, moreover, there is never a shortage of situations in which one state party or another is falling a bit short on its obligations. Choices need to be made about where pressures or incentives can most productively be applied, as well as about how acting in one case will affect others. As priorities are set and such choices are made, critics may well see patterns of favoritism and inequity, as Mian does, but neither national nor international policymakers have the luxury of not choosing. Inaction also has consequences. Advocates for a particular set of norms naturally are inclined to feel that that is where attention and resources are most needed, while officials need to address a wider range of constituencies and causes. Likewise, the paucity of research on compliance models that cut across issue and geographic areas has allowed an overly narrow understanding of the dimensions and dynamics of the compliance challenge, as well as of why states are far more cautious about acting in the defense of some norms than others.

As Downs and Trento trenchantly observe, there has been remarkably little analysis, or even recognition, of the problem of incentive compatibility. Advocacy groups, in particular, have tended to propose compliance packages that are simply too ambitious, risky, and costly from the perspective of those states and institutions that would have to invoke them. It is no easy matter, of course, to design operational steps and strategic approaches that would be both sufficiently persuasive to would-be violators to get the job done and sufficiently economic in terms of the political, financial, and military resources to be expended that the costs will be considered reasonable and proportionate in the eyes of the potential enforcers. This is particularly true because violators often have a bigger stake in violating the rules than others have in defending them, at least in the short run. As the Herbst and Katalikawe, Onoria, and Wairama chapters underline, this tends to be the case most pointedly and tragically on the human interest side of the commitment spectrum. It is not by coincidence that rarely is automaticity built into the compliance provisions—if there are any—of multilateral conventions or that the enforcement mechanisms of international organizations are either weak or nonexistent. None of the enforcement machinery mandated under Chapter VII of the U.N. Charter, for example, has been fully developed or implemented.

Nevertheless, step by step, norm by norm, a wide range of less dramatic compliance practices has been developed and employed with at least limited success over the past decade. The case studies identify a dozen such practices that offer some promise for the future.

Reporting. The most progress has been in the realm of transparency, monitoring, and reporting. Once thought of as the softest and weakest of the compliance tools potentially available, reporting has gained greater respectability in recent years across the range of issue areas addressed in this volume. As recognized by the democratic process school, three larger social and political trends—(a) the movement toward more democratic institutions and practices within countries; (b) the global communications revolution; and (c) the globalization of finance, trade, and culture—have created a momentum toward openness that has proven irresistible in all but a handful of leftover authoritarian or totalitarian states. These trends, plus the growing assertiveness of nongovernmental groups of various stripes, have enhanced the immediate, and more importantly the longer-term, impact of monitoring and reporting tools. The simple technique of naming and shaming, used so persistently by human rights advocates through the years, is now employed extensively and with considerable sophistication in every issue area addressed in this volume.

Linking reporting and penalties. Reporting violations is most potent, of course, when there is a reasonable chance that it will trigger tougher enforcement steps, such as financial or trade sanctions or even military action. So the linkage of such reporting tools, long the mainstay of compliance efforts on the low-commitment end of the spectrum, to core national interest concerns, such as terrorism and weapons of mass destruction, has imparted a renewed appreciation of their potential. Saddam Hussein, for instance, preferred to have his country endure a decade of damaging sanctions than to permit the U.N. weapons inspectors to complete their work. Throughout most of the world, however, inspections by international teams from multilateral organizations, such as the International Atomic Energy Agency (IAEA) and the Organization for the Prohibition of Chemical Weapons (OPCW), have come to be seen as an essential component of both national and international security. Fearing both direct sanctions and probable spillover and regroups alike are eager to stay off the lists that the U.S. government and others are compiling of those who aid or abet terrorists. In its landmark resolution 1373 of September 28, 2001, the Security Council, acting under Chapter VII, called on member states to exchange information and take a series of measures against terrorists, created a Counter-Terrorism Committee (CTC) of the whole, and called on member states to report to the CTC on what actions they were taking to implement the resolution within 90 days and subsequently as required by the CTC.

Self-reporting. Self-reporting, as the United Nations has called for on a variety of arms, human rights, and economic matters over the years, obviously invites an array of omissions, miscountings, and distortions, as well as selective participation. The requirement that states report to international institutions, however, offers several advantages even if the information produced is incomplete or inaccurate: it underlines that such data are of legitimate international concern and reinforces the legal and political position of nongovernmental groups seeking to monitor and report on related developments; it compels national officials to ponder how their country's compliance record would look to wider international audiences and how such information should be organized and presented; the very refusal of a government to be straightforward in responding to such a request for information may give those concerned with compliance issues a better sense of its sensitivities and intentions; and the reporting process offers independent groups, international monitors, local officials, and other governments a platform and opportunity for undertaking parallel research and reporting efforts. In some fora, such as the U.N. Commission on Human Rights, some environmental regimes, and the International Labor Organization, states are compelled to defend both their compliance record and the way they have reported on it.

Rapporteurs and inspection panels. Sands and Linehan cite several multilateral environmental agreements that incorporate inspection panels or secretariat reviews as ways of regularizing the process of screening for possible compliance shortcomings. Likewise, the U.N.'s long-standing practice of appointing individual rapporteurs to investigate and report on particular human rights cases has been echoed by the Security Council's increasing use of individuals, small panels, or even its own visits to report on how well parties to various conflicts—or those who profit from the related trade in arms, jewels, timber, or other valuable resources—are following its edicts. Recent reports have been quite specific, even naming names.

As Feiveson and Shire note, in 1995 an international and independent blue-ribbon commission, under the leadership of McGeorge Bundy, urged the Security Council to create the position of Special Rapporteur to report to it annually, or more frequently if needed, on the status of the proliferation of weapons of mass destruction.[9] The report would address not only whether states parties were living up to their obligations under the various nonproliferation conventions, but also, just as centrally, whether any developments related to the spread of weapons of mass destruction—including their acquisition by nonstate actors or by states that are not parties—threatened the council's broader mandate for the maintenance of international peace and security. In this sense, the council can act to further the intent of an arms treaty, something that could be as easily threatened by nonparties as by parties.

At that time, the idea of creating such a rapporteur's post stirred substantial interest, but was not adopted. Now, given the debates about WMD in Iraq and continuing worries about developments in Iran and North Korea, as well as about those terrorist groups that have repudiated the very notion of interstate conventions and that have vowed to acquire biological, chemical, or nuclear capabilities, it would make good sense to revisit this and other proposals for giving the Security Council or its counterterrorism committee their own means of evaluating dangerous developments both inside and outside of the formal nonproliferation regimes. In an age when nonstate actors of all stripes have come to play more influential roles on the world scene in all of the sectors addressed in this volume, including security, the question of compliance has taken on a more urgent dimension, going well beyond the fine points of legal analysis.

Common law. In this regard, it is worth recalling the distinction made by Feiveson and Shire between "explicit treaty commitments and implicit norms of international behavior." As they pointed out, a number of noncodified norms have evolved and developed over the years that help to govern the behavior of states toward weapons of mass destruction, even though they have never been formally negotiated or ratified. Surely such a common law approach would be apt in the case of those who would in any way assist terrorists in the acquisition of such weapons or related materials, whether or not explicitly covered by the 1979 convention on nuclear materials or the accords on biological and chemical weapons. As Dinah Shelton has noted, it is commonly believed that nonbinding norms, or soft law, have been "more frequently utilized in the subject areas of environment and human rights than in trade and arms control."[10] But it could be productive to explore how nonbinding norms could be used more fully to supplement, rather than to replace, hard law in the latter sectors.

Leadership and Individual Responsibility. As these case studies illustrate, leadership in achieving compliance can come at very different levels and from inside and outside governments or, in democratic societies, most powerfully from a combination of both. Moon stresses the critical role played by presidential leadership in spurring and guiding trade and financial reform, while Feiveson and Shire focus on the "citizen-based model" of monitoring and reporting. In undertaking such parallel efforts, NGOs and research institutions not only can help keep governments honest, they can also develop significant independent centers of expertise, analysis, and ideas. While national officials may sometimes take a more relaxed view of what constitutes adequate compliance, NGOs and advocacy groups are likely to assert a adequate compliance, NGOs and advocacy groups are likely to assert a more rigorous and literal interpretation of treaty provisions and to treat them as a floor rather than as a ceiling in terms of fulfilling the larger purposes of the normative regime.

Public groups, in that sense, may be less concerned about whether a state—or a nonstate actor—is in legal compliance than about whether it is complying with the spirit of the agreements, as they see it. Their larger objective may have less to do with compliance per se, in fact, than with feeding into domestic social and political processes—as Moon, Mian, Feiveson, and Shire recommend—in the expectation of changing national priorities and conceptions of what constitutes core national interests. Embarrassing a particular government or administration for a poor compliance record vis-à-vis widely accepted international norms may be one place to start. Another is to target sanctions not just against countries, but also against individuals, firms, or armed groups that flout international law, as the Security Council has increasingly done in recent years.

Themes of criminalization and individual responsibility emerge in several of the case studies, most prominently in those by Côte, by Katalikawe, Onoria, and Wairama, and by Feiveson and Shire. In essence, if the state proves unresponsive to its international obligations, it may be up to private citizens or individual officials to refuse to take part in or to expose actions contrary to the provisions of international law, whether they take the form of genocide, the development and production of weapons of mass destruction, environmental destruction, or sanctions busting. The regional tribunals for Rwanda and the Balkans, in Côté's view, are helping to overcome the "state inertia" that has for too long defined "the traditional limitations of international humanitarian law." The end result could be greater accountability and fuller compliance, as the architects of the ICC expect, or it could be a determination by national officials that it is safer to discourage or even to roll back the development of norms and compliance mechanisms that pose potential conflicts with deep-seeded national interests, traditions, and policies. The Bush administration apparently has chosen the latter tack vis-à-vis the ICC. Publics, as well, may be forced to make newly difficult choices between national interests and international standards or between domestic and international legal processes, as has been the case in Chile, Croatia, and Serbia. The question of where and how to prosecute transnational terrorists and their supporters who operate in oblique, hidden, and stateless ways poses these issues starkly.

National Infrastructure and Capacity Building. As Moon, Downs, and Trento emphasize, initial compliance rates sometimes prove unsustainable over time, as conditions change within countries. Since full and consistent implementation is unlikely if a state party fails to put in place parallel national legislation and executive institutions, most of the case studies call for efforts to build local capacity for implementation. In the environmental field, note Sands and Linehan, it has long been recognized that poorer and weaker

tional institutions and wealthier parties to develop the capacity to ensure full implementation. Such provisions have been added to Kyoto and other MEAs, as well as to Security Council resolutions concerning the enforcement of humanitarian norms, trade sanctions, arms embargoes, and, most recently and pointedly, counterterrorism. The heart of U.N. efforts to assist the struggle against terrorism, embodied in resolution 1373 and the creation of the Security Council's Counter-Terrorism Committee, has been to help member states identify weaknesses in their relevant national legislation and administrative structures and to match them with potential sources of assistance in patching these gaps. Of course, as Moon's South Korean case study illustrates, a legislative and administrative facade will mean little if the national will to enforce international standards is lacking.

Interactive Processes. The case studies underline the value of dialogue, technical exchanges, and consultations between international agencies and national policymakers—often aided by nongovernmental experts, convenors, and facilitators—as adjuncts to the compliance process. According to the managerial school, such interactions, usually at a technical rather than political level, may help to avoid misunderstandings and an adversarial tone, while permitting local conditions and culture to be taken into account. On finance issues, according to Moon, the frequent interactions between the International Monetary Fund (IMF) and South Korean officials, as well as their joint participation in the larger epistemic community of experts in international finance, eased the acceptance of some quite far-reaching IMF conditions. McNamara and Sands and Linehan found similar processes of communication and dialogue underway in their fields. The Kyoto accords, in fact, were to rely quite extensively on the work of expert review teams, national accounting and tracking mechanisms, and technical input from nongovernmental experts as part of an implementation process that would depend more on facilitation than enforcement.

Dispute Resolution Mechanisms. On trade issues, often treated as matters of national priority, McNamara reports a growing sense of judicialization, as dispute settlement processes become more formalized and more commonly invoked. Feiveson and Shire point to the central place accorded to dispute settlement mechanisms in the series of arms control agreements reached bilaterally between the United States and Soviet Union during the Cold War. In multilateral environmental accords, according to Sands and Linehan, the preference for noncontentious and consultative means of resolving disputes over judicial or adversarial ones has long been pronounced.

Power versus Institutionalization. The contrasting Korean experience in dealing with the IMF and the more formal General Agreement on Tariffs and Trade (GATT)/WTO regime suggests to Moon that machinery may matter more than the degree of institutionalization of the legal regimes, as the more centralized and hands-on enforcement capacity of the IMF proved a good deal more persuasive in the Korean case. McNamara, as well, found little overall correlation, at least in trade and finance, between the formality of a regime's correlation, at least in trade and finance, between the formality of a regime's institutional structure and its effectiveness in gaining compliance. In humanitarian affairs, Herbst and Katalikawe, Onoria, and Wairama concluded that the utter lack of compliance machinery reflected the paucity of will to enforce international norms in the first place. In such cases, even a few steps toward modest institutional engineering would be welcomed. For arms issues, moreover, as Mian and Feiveson and Shire attest, power tends to determine both the content of the norms and the shape of related machinery. Because the institutional engineering on such core issues reflects global strategic and power relationships, it cannot be expected to overcome or compensate for them. These cases suggest that (1) on the low end of the commitment spectrum machinery can make a difference if it helps to remind publics and governments of their responsibilities; (2) on the high end of the commitment spectrum institutions, such as the WTO and IMF, that are linked to national will and power matter precisely because of that linkage; and (3) tinkering with institutional engineering without reference to larger questions of power and will is not an especially useful enterprise.

Sanctions and Inducements. While the chapters on humanitarian issues lament the unwillingness of the Security Council or powerful member states to apply timely and tough sanctions on major violators, Mian decries that the U.N. sanctions regime on Iraq led to widespread public suffering without achieving the desired policy outcomes. Clearly, ways need to be found to make sanctions a more effective instrument for boosting compliance with important international norms. Several of the authors have underlined the potential utility of better targeted sanctions, which would increase the pressure on decision-making elites while decreasing the chances of large-scale collateral harm to civilian populations.[11] A related theme, which emerges in several of the case studies, is the utility of compliance strategies that employ both targeted sanctions and selective inducements. The latter, it appears, are most apt in issue areas that fall in the lower to moderate range of the commitment spectrum, such as humanitarian and environmental questions. The combination of threats and inducements, however, has been used effectively on issues of trade and finance as well. According to Moon, the possibility of multilateral sanctions was taken seriously in Seoul in part because they were backed up by parallel bilateral warnings from the United States. Indeed, it makes little sense to try to assess the impact of multilateral sanctions and inducements without taking bilateral and regional relationships into account.

Flexible and Mixed Strategies. It seems, from the results of the case studies, that the most successful compliance regimes have been those that employ a range of tools that can be applied as needed (and as available). Sands and Linehan contend, for example, that it helps not only to have a range of institutional means on tap, but also to look to international organizations, NGOs, and the private sector, as well as governments, as potentially important allies in these efforts. Moon, Mian, and Feiveson and Shire likewise emphasize the value of mobilizing public constituencies, whether to monitor their country's own compliance behavior or to persuade it to act against noncompliance by others. Even at the high end of the commitment spectrum, flexibility in the choice of policy tools to persuade others to comply with agreed norms can be very helpful, because they may have just as great a commitment to defecting from the regime or at least to appearing not to be compelled to back away from doing so. To keep risks manageable in high-end cases, an incremental and varied strategy may be advisable, as has been employed so far in dealing with North Korea's nuclear ambitions. On the low end of the spectrum, on the other hand, the only choice may be to employ a modest and incremental approach.

Implications for Theory and Research

In their chapter on conceptual issues, Downs and Trento identify seven schools of thought about compliance matters.[12] These derive from three quite distinct approaches to understanding compliance: transformationalism, managerialism, and realism. While hardly exclusive, each approach describes a particular policy orientation and ordering of factors that might move states parties and other relevant actors. When viewed from the perspectives offered by the eight case studies and the proposed commitment spectrum, it appears that each school is based on an understanding of a different part of the elephant. The transformationalist school, for instance, can draw some encouragement from the catalytic role played by nonstate actors and the dynamic nature of the compliance process. These factors highlight the possibility that NGOs and epistemic communities, working within societies and on a transnational basis, can over time begin to transform national values, perspectives, and priorities. With few sticks or carrots to employ, the human rights movement has made important strides in many parts of the world, if viewed from a decidedly long-term and evolutionary perspective. Certainly it took a geopolitical shift of historic proportions, the end of the Cold War, to create the conditions for more rapid movement. Yet it can also be conjectured that persistent human rights advocacy by the West and by courageous domestic critics over four decades, institutionalized in the Helsinki process, helped to bring about the change in geopolitical conditions in the first place. In less dramatic fashion, the environmental story reflects a similar process. At the same time, it should not be forgotten that nonstate actors of a different ilk have been among the worst violators of these same rights.

If the transformationalist school seems to fit best with the human interest issues in the first column of the commitment spectrum, the managerial school is most descriptive of the transnational issues in the moderate commitment, or middle, column. As noted earlier, here the compliance mechanisms tend to be relatively well developed, to involve significant work by international secretariats, and to have a decidedly multilateral character. Capacity building is considered to be of some importance, especially for those developing countries with greater will than institutional or financial resources. As described by Sands and Linehan, in the environmental realm considerable reliance is placed on consultations among parties, on expert panels, and on communication mechanisms.

The realist school, on the other hand, can gain some nourishment by looking at the compliance problems faced on topics, such as terrorism, trade, and weapons of mass destruction, found in the third column under core national interests. Moon offers compelling testimony in his emphasis on the role of bilateral U.S. pressures in convincing Korea to implement the economic and financial reforms called for by the IMF. Here, among the questions traditionally labeled as high politics, the soft approaches favored in the managerial school generally seem out of place,[13] while only a decided optimist could conclude that transformationalist processes have decidedly reshaped the dynamics of these issues over the past half century. Yet various advocacy groups continue to try to bridge columns by attaching transnationalist causes to core national interests. Examples include the U.N.'s emphasis on human security and the emergence of the "trade-and" issues noted by McNamara. As she points out, mixing these two sets of issues raises complex political and compliance dilemmas.

Each of the main schools, in other words, has its place in the overall scheme. Each describes some piece of the whole; but none comes close to capturing the breadth and diversity of the compliance challenge. When one moves from theory to practice, the case studies illustrate that mixed strategies, borrowing as needed from the tools favored by each of the schools, usually work best. Flexibility and adaptability, not faithfulness to a pet theory, are the keys to operationalizing an effective compliance strategy.

Traditional writings on compliance, largely the products of legal scholars, have given insufficient attention to a number of under-researched themes and factors that played prominent roles in the eight case studies. Three themes, in particular, stand out: (1) domestic factors often have a substantial role in determining the extent to which states comply with international conventions to which they are a party; (2) strategic shifts in the global geopolitical landscape matter a great deal in defining the opportunities to create and implement international norms; and (3) issues of power and equity are rarely resolved to everyone's satisfaction and may be major barriers to institutionalization, as well as to compliance, in the years ahead. All three factors underline the dynamic nature of the codification, implementation, and compliance process, which looks substantially different than it did a decade ago and could well change in unexpected ways over the next ten years as well.

Domestic Factors. As noted earlier, though states parties to international conventions usually assume similar obligations under their provisions, their will and capacity to carry them out may vary substantially based on domestic circumstances unrelated to their international commitments. The mix of domestic pressures will change over time, sometimes to the detriment of compliance and at other times easing it. Downs and Trento point to civil

conflict as a major cause of poor compliance. Herbst and Katalikawe, Onoria, and Wairama agree, but they would add weak and autocratic government, perennial poverty, and international indifference as elements of the
poor humanitarian record in much of Africa. International tribunals have
been required in Rwanda and the Balkans, as Côté relates, because of insuf-
ficiencies in local judicial capacities and/or continuing political divisions.

Yet, as Moon documents in his chronicle of South Korea's sing-song
record of compliance with IMF and WTO requirements, the pervasiveness
of domestic factors is hardly limited to failed states or situations of conflict.
The policies of developed democracies toward international obligations, in
fact, may be particularly sensitive to cultural proclivities and to shifting
domestic politics, as the history of U.S. dues payments to the U.N. over the
last two decades attests. McNamara, as well, highlights the role of domestic
advocacy groups in the United States and other developed nations in pushing for "trade and" provisions that could well complicate the prospects for
the global trade regime.

In contrast, both smaller countries and most legal writers put considerable stock in international rules and processes as the key to legitimacy. As
the noted legal scholar Thomas Franck phrased it, "legitimacy is a property
of a rule or rule-making institution which itself exerts a pull toward compliance on those addressed normatively because those addressed believe that
the rule or institution has come into being and operates in accordance with
generally accepted principles of right process."[14] But governments must
look to the domestic roots—whether they be cultural, political, or constitutional—of legitimacy as well. For theorists to look through only one end of
this telescope is to see only part of the picture.[15] Legitimacy, therefore, can
take on a subjective cast when domestic and international obligations do not
fully coincide.

Shifting Geopolitical Landscape. The end of the Cold War and the acceleration
of globalization produced a markedly new set of conditions both for the development and codification of international norms and for encouraging
compliance with them. The experience of the past decade, as captured in the
case studies, has been a mixed one in terms of gauging whether progress in
compliance can keep up with the growth in norm setting. To the extent that
the former has lagged, it has been due, in large part, to those same changes
that have produced a more fertile soil for norm creation.

On the positive side of the ledger, the easing of Cold War political ri-
gidities has permitted:

- a more widely held appreciation among government officials and
  opinion leaders in most countries of the value of international
  norms and institutions;
- a consequent willingness to consider the development of new
  norms and the expansion of old ones;

- a growing acceptance, at least in principle, of the legitimacy of efforts to monitor and, if necessary, to enforce compliance with international agreements;
- a somewhat fuller appreciation, in that regard, of the role that civil society can play, both nationally and internationally, in helping to monitor such agreements and publicize non-compliance;
- a willingness to experiment with new forms of international monitoring, reporting, and enforcement; and
- a geographical expansion of the portion of the world that could be subject to on-site international and nongovernmental monitoring and reporting efforts.

In global fora, including the U.N. and the series of world conferences it sponsored during the 1990s, the political metamorphosis of the countries of Eastern Europe and, to a lesser extent, of the Russian Federation usually put them on the side of advocating more law, more monitoring, and greater international enforcement. The promotion of democracy—a term never used in the charter—became a cardinal component of U.N. nation-building and conflict resolution programs following the Cold War. The Security Council, less often paralyzed by the veto, began to pass Chapter VII resolutions authorizing international enforcement action with remarkable regularity. During the 1990s, the council authorized many more Chapter VII military operations and sanctions regimes than it had in its previous forty-five-year history.

These encouraging developments were widely heralded during the heady days of the early 1990s. Yet, ironically, the same bullish conditions that produced these trends had a downside in terms of making it more difficult to put compliance on a firmer footing. For example,

- a declining sense of urgency about world affairs led many developed countries to reduce the spending and attention they devoted to foreign policy and national security, as a portion of national effort;
- some regions, especially Africa, became more tangential to the strategic calculus in major national capitals;
- the sense of which international institutions mattered most began to shift for many countries, with economic questions beginning to supersede military ones, but without a clear strategic vision to order and relate priorities;
- with fewer East-West differences, consensus decision-making rules took hold in many international fora, putting a premium on seeking the appearance of common ground and discouraging the expression of national perspectives, of concerns about potential compliance problems, and of dissenting views;

- as a result, formal agreements on new or expanded norms came more easily, but without sufficient debate, especially on compliance questions, and with little testing of the depth of national commitments or of alternative institutional arrangements;

- fed by a growing involvement of transnational advocacy NGOs, expectations rose rapidly for a more law-based international order, yet states remained cautious about investing heavily in the requisite global infrastructures for reasons of both cost and sovereignty, as noted above;

- the trend toward more global perspectives was matched in several regions by parallel moves toward micronationalism, self-determination, subnational violence, and weakening state structures, compounding the challenges to international regimes and lessening the capacity of some states to implement even well-established norms; and

- these developments, in turn, helped spawn the emergence of terrorism as a global as well as a local scourge, challenging the credibility and sapping the capacities of national, regional, and global institutions.

In this uncertain era, the willingness of states to ensure the implementation of international norms is being tested as never before precisely because the East-West blockages to international action imposed by the logic of the Cold War no longer exist. Now that compliance is expected, as ideological excuses for nonimplementation have faded, its political and material costs to states are being more fully appreciated.

Power and Equity. Questions of equity, emphasized in the chapters by Mian and Herbst, are now raised as pointedly in matters of implementation as they had once been in the codification of those same international norms and standards. In Mian's view, for example, both the nature of multilateral arms control conventions and the way they are implemented are highly inequitable, with the sticks much more visible than the carrots and with power concentrated in the hands of a few interested parties.[16] Yet, while the non-weapon state members have complained vociferously for many years about double standards both in the way the nonproliferation regime was cast and in the way the nuclear powers have interpreted it, only North Korea has chosen to renounce the treaty. The NPT, as a result, arguably remains the most widely vilified and most widely subscribed treaty in history. When it comes to implementation, what is fair may not always be in a state's interests, and vice versa.

The traditional emphasis on equity in legal scholarship about compliance faces a considerable quandary in the emergence of the United States as the world's predominant power. With power relationships now so markedly skewed, Washington officials are understandably reluctant to see American policy options constrained by multilateral rules and procedures, even though at times the invocation of multilateral processes can actually expand the options open to U.S. policymakers. While other capitals are keen to engage the United States in multilateral processes, they also show signs of fearing U.S. dominance of the multilateral system. As this author has argued elsewhere, the result has been that America's longstanding ambivalence about international institutions has been matched by the ambivalence that others feel about American power.[17] Both types of ambivalence were much in evidence during the Security Council's debates about how to handle Iraq in late 2002-early 2003. These dysfunctional dynamics, on top of a persistent North-South divide and growing fissures within the western alliance, have contributed to a declining outlook for international institution building in general and for the multilateral enforcement of global norms in particular, except on especially urgent questions of a transnational character, such as counterterrorism. It has become increasingly difficult to reconcile calls for greater equity within global institutions with the growing asymmetries in power and capacity outside their walls.

In addition to these three major themes, a number of other areas for further research and analysis are suggested by the case studies.

The Action-Reaction Phenomenon. Leaders, parliamentarians, and commentators in many countries have expressed concern about the intrusiveness involved in the monitoring of domestic conditions by international finance, trade, environmental, human rights, and security institutions. In the developing world, much of the consternation has focused on human rights issues, on the emerging doctrine of humanitarian intervention, on IMF conditionality, and on the harshness of sanctions against Iraq. In the United States, and to a lesser extent in other developed countries, both ends of the political spectrum have fretted broadly about the dangers that unaccountable international bureaucracies and one-nation, one-vote fora could pose to national sovereignty and to constitutional processes on a wide range of issues. On the one hand, the frequency of these complaints attests to the strength of globalization and multilateralism, while the political diversity of those voicing them lessens the prospects for the coalescing of a politically potent anti-internationalist political movement. On the other hand, the chorus of worry nevertheless is beginning to act as a drag on efforts to envision the kinds of more interventionist institutions that would be needed in a number of areas to assure anything close to full compliance with existing international norms. Further research and assessment are needed of where these opposing trends will lead and how compliance prospects will be affected.

Spillover and Reputational Effects. Relatively little is known about spillover effects—how the compliance results in one sector might affect the credibility of regimes in other sectors—or about reputational effects—how the way a state or nonstate actor behaves in one sector might affect expectations concerning its performance in another area. Downs and Trento express some doubt about the strength of either effect, though they urge further work on these questions. Tracking studies would be especially helpful. Based on his research, however, Moon believes that South Korea's decisions to comply with trade and finance norms were very much influenced by Japan's positive example. Under what circumstances and to what extent will the compliance decisions of one country be affected by those of another? How important are regional influences in this regard? More fundamentally, what are the effects on a multilateral legal regime if certain powerful states appear to be somewhat selective or inconsistent in their compliance, or if the dominant power, now the United States, seems indifferent to the strengthening of a particular regime? Both arms control chapters raise troubling issues in this regard.

Active and Inactive Parties. While the legal status of all states parties to an international convention may be equivalent, some may view themselves as much more active participants in the regime than others do. The vast majority of the parties to the Non-Proliferation Treaty, for example, have neither the capacity nor the interest to even consider acquiring nuclear weapons. Other than two or three rogue states, those most likely to defect from the larger regime failed to become parties to the accord in the first place. The nuclear suppliers club, on the other hand, was widely criticized for its limited membership, though all of the big powers were either on board or willing to largely cooperate. When is it better to have the numbers and when to have the key parties? Which confers greater legitimacy to the norm? Can compliance regimes be designed in such cases that will be widely seen as both equitable and effective?

Nonstate Actors. One of the most pressing challenges to compliance lies in developing provisions and incentives for involving nonstate actors in the compliance process on the operational level, including through their increasing involvement in the compliance-related activities of international organizations. In this regard, further creative thinking is needed on how to build the nexus between nongovernmental and intergovernmental actors, including importantly through their secretariats, without further alienating member-state governments.

As noted above, flexible and mixed strategies are often the most effective in encouraging parties not to undermine or defect from international agreements. But policymakers could use additional guidance on which combination of tools works best under which circumstances. Further analysis is particularly needed on incentive compatibility and on how to encourage a coordinated international response to threatened defections from core security regimes, such as the NPT.

This volume has not attempted to provide a comprehensive picture of the compliance dilemma. But it has offered an unusually varied set of snapshots of how these questions are being addressed in particular sectors at a given point in time. This comparative approach imparts a sense of the interactive complexity of the whole compliance enterprise, as well as highlighting some best practices to be emulated and some disasters to be avoided. In addition to providing cross-sectoral lessons for policy, the volume testifies to the value of sharing legal and political insights. It has also begun to map priorities for future research: tracking studies to test periodically the kinds of propositions advanced here; in-depth research on additional cases; and broad-based assessments—from both policy and theoretical perspectives—of the overall compliance challenge. Of two things we can be confident: the issue of compliance with international law will remain both vital and dynamic in the years ahead. For, if the 1990s was an era of norm creation and the twenty-first century is opening as an era of implementation, as many believe, then issues of compliance will become increasingly nuanced, as well as increasingly central, in the years ahead.

Notes

1. For two wide-ranging collections of case studies addressing the legal and political dilemmas inherent in managing global legal and administrative regimes, see Dinah Shelton, ed., *Commitment and Compliance: The Role of Non-Binding Norms in the International Legal System* (New York: Oxford University Press, 2000); and P. J. Simmons and Chantal de Jonge Oudraat, eds., *Managing Global Issues: Lessons Learned* (Washington, D.C.: Carnegie Endowment for International Peace, 2001).

2. Arthur M. Schlesinger Jr., "America and the World: Isolationism Resurgent?" Second Louis Nizer Lecture on Public Policy (New York: Carnegie Council on Ethics and International Affairs, December 6, 1995).

3. If, as Peter M. Haas has argued, "compliance is a matter of state choice," then this is even more the case for the commitment to persuade others to comply. Haas, "Choosing to Comply: Theorizing from International Relations and Comparative Politics," in Shelton, *Compliance and Commitment*, 45.

4. The cases included in Shelton, *Commitment and Compliance*, are suggestive in this regard.

5. There is no reason to assume that all major powers necessarily prefer to negotiate binding accords or multilateral legal regimes to deal with core national interests. The U.S. tendency to embrace unilateralist options is a case in point. However, when major capitals choose multilateral regimes to address core national interests, they are not likely to rely on nonbinding or unenforceable provisions.

6. For accounts of the critical part played by nongovernmental groups in the formulation and codification of human rights standards, see Mary Ann Glendon, *A World Made New: Eleanor Roosevelt and the Universal Declaration of Human Rights* (New York: Random House, 2001); and William Korey, *NGOs and the Universal Declaration of Human Rights: A Curious Grapevine* (New York: St. Martin's Press, 1998).

7. See, for example, Kathryn Sikkink, "Human Rights, Principled Issue-Networks, and Sovereignty in Latin America," *International Organization* 17, no. 3 (Summer 1993): 411-41; Margaret E. Keck and Kathryn Sikkink, *Activists beyond Borders: Advocacy Networks in International Politics* (Ithaca, NY: Cornell University Press, 1998); and Susan Burgerman, *Moral Victories: How Activists Provoke Multilateral Action* (Ithaca, NY: Cornell University Press, 2001).

8. Public opinion surveys suggest, for example, that the Security Council's feckless performance prior to the use of force in Iraq badly damaged its reputation both in countries that favored and in those that opposed the war. See, for example, *Views of a Changing World 2003* (Washington, D.C.: The Pew Research Center for the People and the Press, June 3, 2003), 27, http://people-press.org/reports/pdf/185.pdf; and polls by ABC News/*Washington Post*, March 17, 2003 and Gallup/CNN/*USA Today*, March 14, 2003.

9. McGeorge Bundy et al., "Confronting the Proliferation Danger: The Role of the U.N. Security Council" (New York: United Nations Association of the USA, 1995).

10. Shelton, *Commitment and Compliance*, 3.

11. See, for example, the papers and reports from three rounds of conferences on sharpening U.N. sanctions, held between 1998 and 2003, www.smartsanctions.ch/papers.htm.; www.smartsanctions.de; and www.smartsanctions.se. Also see two books by David Cortright and George A. Lopez, *The Sanctions Decade: Assessing UN Strategies in the 1990s* (Boulder, CO: Lynne Rienner, 2000), 221-53; and *Sanctions and the Search for Security: Challenges to UN Action* (Rienner, 2002).

12. Realist, Kantian liberal, democratic process, strategic, managerial, transformationalist, and transnationalism.

13. While managerial theory often cites the provisions of Soviet-American arms control agreements, it should be recalled that such managerial arrangements operated within the larger context of nuclear deterrence and the mutual threat of annihilation.

14. Thomas M. Franck, *The Power of Legitimacy among Nations* (New York: Oxford University Press, 1990), 24.

15. Edward C. Luck, "The United States, International Organizations, and the Quest for Legitimacy," in Stewart Patrick and Shepard Forman, eds., *Multilateralism and U.S. Foreign Policy: Ambivalent Engagement* (Boulder, CO: Lynne Rienner, 2001), 47-74.

16. Presumably the rules of most postwar institutions were shaped by the imbalance of power in a way that serves the interests of the hegemon, the United States, and that works to extend and institutionalize the prevailing asymmetries among states. Such arrangements, however, also serve to give the hegemon an incentive to work to preserve multilateral norms and institutions, providing the less powerful with at least a modicum of assurance against the blatant abuse of power. For the sophisticated development of a similar line of argument, see G. John Ikenberry, *After Victory: Institutions, Strategic Restraint, and Building of Order after Major Wars* (Princeton, NJ: Princeton University Press, 2001), especially chapters 6 and 7.

17. Edward C. Luck, *Mixed Messages: American Politics and International Organization, 1919-1999* (Washington, D.C.: Brookings Institution Press, 1999), esp. 291-94.

Index

Pakistan: Chinese transfer of missile technology to, 209, 210, noncompliance with NPT, 251, 281; nonsignatory of Landmines Convention, 211; nonsignatory of ICC, 238; nuclear testing, 216, 282; nuclear threats towards India, 230; U.S. concern about ties with radial Islamic groups, 284; U.S. economic and military aid, 282; U.S. rescheduling of debt, 284; U.S. sanctions, 282
Pape, Robert, 235
Permanent Court of International Justice (PCIJ), 101
Perry, William, 223, 225, 237,279
Peter, Chris Maina, 170
Pinochet, General Augusto, 170
positive integration, 42, 55
Powell, Secretary of State Colin, 213, 221, 208
Prevention of Nuclear War agreement, 257
Project for a New American Century, 276
Promises Broken (Human Rights Watch Report), 185
Putin, President Vladimir, 208

Quaker U.N. Office, 195

Ranger, Robin, 257
Raskin, Marcus, 257
Rawls, John, 251, 254, 261
Reagan administration, 260, 262
Reagan, President Ronald, 258, 274
realist school, 27, 164, 322
rebel groups: command over territory, 132; exclusion of in peacemaking efforts, 138; incentives to follow international norms, 197; international recognition of, 191, 193, 195, 196, 198; legal status of, 131, 138; list of, in Great Lakes Region, 131; violations of humanitarian law, 138
Refuge Service, The, 195
regimes: defined by Stephen Krasner, 2; defined by John Ruggie, 2;

definition of, 42. *See also* international regimes
regime growth: 2, 3
"regime management," 206, 207, 260
Richardson, Bill, 273
rice. *See* South Korea: agricultural products
Rice, Condoleeza, 259
Risse-Kappen, Thomas, 4
Robinson, Julian, 236, 237
Robinson, Paul, 264
Roh Moo-hyun, President, 67
Rome Convention, 173
Ross, Michael, 35
Rotblat, Joseph, 238
Ruggie, John, G., 2
Rusk, Dean, 281
Russia: abstention from Resolution 1284, 219; bilateral arms control agreements with the United States, 206, 207; biological weapons program, 214; efforts to tighten CFE, 210; nuclear aid to Iran, 226, 233; refusal to sign Landmines Convention, 211; Security Council permanent member, 254; threat to withdraw from START II, 208; use of veto against U.S. resolution authorizing attack against Iraq, 255
Rutherford, Kenneth, 211
Rwanda: Belgian perpetration of "hamatic" superiority complex among the Tutsi over the Hutu, 126; disembowelment of women, 188; French response, 134; *gacaca,* 142, 143; genocide, 123-24, 127, 134, 135, 153, 160; National Reconciliation Commission, 142, 143; Rwandan Patriotic Army, 163; Rwandan Patriotic Front (RPF), 171; Tutsi-Hutu conflict, 123, 126; use of propaganda, 171-72. *See also* International Criminal Tribunal for Rwanda (ICTR)
Rydell, Randy, 232

sanctions: Bonn-Berlin Process, 235; efficacy of, 235, 236;

About the Contributors

Katharina P. Coleman is an assistant professor in international relations at the University of British Columbia in Vancouver, Canada.

Luc Côté spent five years with the Office of the Prosecutor of the International Criminal Tribunal for Rwanda. Afterward, he completed postgrad studies in international law at the Higher Institute for International Studies in Geneva. He is counsel for the Crimes Against Humanity and War Crimes Section of the Department of Justice of the Canadian Government. Currently, he is the chief of prosecutions for the Office of the Prosecutor of the Special Court for Sierra Leone, based in Freetown, Sierra Leone.

George W. Downs is dean of social science and professor in the Department of Politics, New York University. His areas of specialization are international institutions, international cooperation, and research methodology. His current research interests include the enforcement of multilateral regulatory agreements and the determinants of human rights outcomes. Downs is the author of *Bureaucracy, Innovation, and Public Policy*; coauthor of *The Search for Government Efficiency, Tacit Bargaining, Arms Races and Arms Control,* and *Optimal Imperfection: Domestic Uncertainty and Institutions in International Relations*; and editor of *Collective Security beyond the Cold War,* as well as articles in political science, statistics, and law.

Michael W. Doyle is the Harold Brown Professor at Columbia University in the School of International and Public Affairs and Columbia Law School. His publications include *Ways of War and Peace*; *Empires*; and *UN Peacekeeping in Cambodia: UNTAC's Civil Mandate.* He recently served as assistant secretary-general and special adviser to U.N. Secretary-General Kofi Annan.

Harold A. Feiveson is a senior research scientist at Princeton University, and is codirector of Princeton's Program on Science and Global Security of the Woodrow Wilson School of Public and International Affairs. His principal research interests are in the fields of nuclear weapons and nuclear energy policy. He was editor and principal author of the book *The Nuclear Turning Point: A Blueprint for Deep Cuts and De-alerting of Nuclear Weapons.* Before joining Princeton, he was a member of the Science Bureau of the U.S. Arms Control and Disarmament Agency from 1963 to 1967. He is the editor and one of the founders of the international journal, *Science and Global Security.*

Jeffrey Herbst is a professor of politics and international affairs and chair of the Department of Politics at Princeton University. His primary interests are in the politics of political and economic reform and the politics of boundaries. He is the author of *States and Power in Africa: Comparative Lessons in Authority and Control* and several other books and articles. He has also taught at the University of Zimbabwe, the University of Ghana, Legon, the University of Cape Town, and the University of the Western Cape. He is a research associate of the South Africa Institute of International Affairs. He received his Ph.D. from Yale University.

James R. Katalikawe holds LL.B. and Ph.D. degrees from the University of London as well as LL.M. and M.A. degrees from Harvard University and the Fletcher School of Diplomacy, respectively. He has taught at the University of Coventry in the United Kingdom and is currently a senior lecturer with the Department of Public and Comparative Law at the Faculty of Law, Makerere University, Uganda.

Jan Linehan is a visiting scholar at the Melbourne University School of Law. She was formerly the deputy legal adviser and assistant secretary, Environment Branch, at the Department of Foreign Affairs and Trade, Australia.

Edward C. Luck is director of the Center on International Organization and professor of practice in international and public affairs at Columbia University. Since 2001, Dr. Luck has served as a member of the U.N. Secretary-General's Policy Working Group on the United Nations and Terrorism. Previously, he served as one of the architects of the U.N. reform efforts from 1995 to 1997. A past president of the United Nations Association of the USA, he is the author of *Mixed Messages: American Politics and International Organization, 1919-1999* and editor of two other volumes. Dr. Luck has published scores of articles in scholarly and policy journals.

Kathleen R. McNamara is associate professor of government in the Department of Government and School of Foreign Service at Georgetown University in Washington, D.C. She is the author of *The Currency of Ideas: Monetary Poli-*

tics in the European Union and articles on the politics of globalization, central banking, and the Euro.

Zia Mian is a physicist with the Program on Science and Global Security at the Woodrow Wilson School for Public and International Affairs, Princeton University. He researches and writes on nuclear weapons and nuclear power issues in South Asia and global disarmament. Most recently, he coedited *Out of the Nuclear Shadow* with Smitu Kothari. In addition to his research and writing, he works with the peace movement and a number of civil society groups working in the area of nuclear disarmament, including the U.N.'s NGO Committee on Disarmament, Peace and Security, the International Network of Engineers and Scientists Against Proliferation, and Abolition 2000, a network for the elimination of nuclear weapons comprising over 2,000 activist organizations in over ninety countries.

Chung-in Moon is professor of political science at Yonsei University. He is also an adjunct professor of the Asia-Pacific Institute, Duke University. He has published nineteen books and over 180 articles in edited volumes and such scholarly journals as *World Politics, International Studies Quarterly, World Development,* and the *Journal of Asian Studies.* His recent publications include *State, Market and Just Growth, Understanding Korean Politics,* and *Ending the Cold War in Korea.*

Henry M. Onoria holds an LL.B. degree from Makerere University (Uganda) and LL.M. and Ph.D. degrees from the University of Cambridge. Presently, he is a lecturer with the Department of Comparative Law at the Faculty of Law, Makerere University.

Philippe Sands is professor of laws at the University College London and director of its Centre for International Courts and Tribunals. He was a co-founder of the Foundation for International Environmental Law and Development and has written extensively on international and environmental law. His most recent book is *Principles of International Environmental Law.* As a practicing barrister he has acted in cases before leading international courts, including the International Court of Justice, the International Tribunal for the Law of the Sea, and the WTO Dispute Settlement Body.

Jacqueline W. Shire was a foreign affairs officer at the Department of State's Bureau of Political Military Affairs from 1990 to 1998. Her work included tours of duty at the U.N. Special Commission on Iraq, Geneva's Conference on Disarmament, and the United States Mission to the U.N. She is currently a consultant to ABC News in New York.

Andrea W. Trento is a recent graduate of Harvard Law School, where he was coeditor of the *Harvard International Law Journal*. He previously worked at the Carnegie Council on Ethics and International Affairs and received his Bachelor of Arts from Yale College in political science and Italian. Presently, he is a law clerk for a judge on the United States Court of Appeals for the Second Circuit.

Baker G. Wairama holds an LL.B. degree from Makerere University (Uganda) and LL.M. and Ph.D. degrees from Edinburgh University. Presently, he is a lecturer with the Department of Commercial Law at the Faculty of Law, Makerere University.